exploring PRODUCTION

by

R. Thomas Wright
Professor of Industry and Technology
Ball State University
Muncie, Indiana

Richard M. Henak
Professor of Industry and Technology
Ball State University
Muncie, Indiana

South Holland, Illinois
THE GOODHEART-WILLCOX COMPANY, INC.
Publishers

ABOUT THE AUTHORS. . .

R. Thomas Wright is among the leading authorities on technology education in the United States today. Tom is the author of many Goodheart-Willcox technology textbooks. In addition to co-authoring *Exploring Production,* Tom is also the author of *Technology Systems, Manufacturing Systems, Processes of Manufacturing, Exploring Manufacturing,* and the co-author of *Understanding Technology.* Tom has a Bachelor degree from Stout State University, a Master of Science degree from Ball State University, and a Doctoral degree from the University of Maryland. He is currently a professor of Industry and Technology at Ball State University.

In addition to *Exploring Production,* **Richard M. Henak** is also the author of *Exploring Construction.* Dick has a Bachelor of Arts degree from the University of Northern Iowa, a Master of Arts degree from Ball State University, and Doctorate of Education degree from the University of Illinois. Dick is currently a professor of Industry and Technology at Ball State University. Dick is also actively involved in the construction trade and construction education, and is self-employed in the construction field.

Copyright 1993

by

THE GOODHEART-WILLCOX COMPANY, INC.

Previous Edition Copyright 1985

Library of Congress Catalog Card Number 91-39191
International Standard Book Number 0-87006-944-6

2 3 4 5 6 7 8 9 10   93   97 96 95 94 93

Library of Congress Cataloging in Publication Data

Wright, R. Thomas.
    Exploring production / by R. Thomas Wright
and Richard M. Henak.

        p.   cm.
    Includes index.
    ISBN 0-87006-944-6
    1. Industrial management. 2. Production
Management. 3. Manufactures. 4. Construction
industry.
I. Henak, Richard M.   II. Title.
HD31.W72 1993
658.5--dc20   91-39191
                                         CIP

INTRODUCTION

EXPLORING PRODUCTION provides a study of two technological systems—manufacturing and construction. You will be introduced to the efficient use of tools, techniques, resources, and production systems used to produce products and structures. You will also learn about industry as an economic institution to organize and use resources to produce goods, services, and structures.

EXPLORING PRODUCTION also describes materials, their properties, and their applications. You will learn about production processes, including casting and molding, forming, separating, conditioning, assembling, and finishing.

EXPLORING PRODUCTION also explains how companies are organized and managed to produce and sell products. The management aspects included in the book are designing and engineering, developing production systems, manufacturing products, marketing products, and performing financial activities.

EXPLORING PRODUCTION will help you to understand management, tools, techniques, and processes used in the construction system. Information is provided on site preparation, as well as the actual construction process. The various systems installed inside and outside a structure are also explained and illustrated.

You will learn the difference between producing a manufactured project and a constructed product. Owning and managing a manufacturing business is compared with organizing and operating a construction company. In addition, you will have the opportunity to work on model manufacturing and construction activities, which are similar to an actual production process, though on a smaller scale. You will also have the opportunity to study about exciting careers relating to production.

R. Thomas Wright
Richard M. Henak

CONTENTS

ACKNOWLEDGEMENTS

The Authors would like to especially thank the following individuals and companies who provided photographs, drawings, and technical assistance for this book.

A.C. Rochester
AC Spark Plug—GM
Adept Technology, Inc.
Air Products and Chemical Co.
Airco Welding Products
Alcan Aluminum
Allied Molded Products
AMAX Corp.
AMCO Elevators, Inc.
American Association of Blacks in Energy
American Cast Iron Pipe Co.
American Dredging Co.
American Electric Power
American Forest Products Industries
American Galvanizers Association, Inc.
American Institute of Steel Construction
American Iron and Steel Institute
American Metal Stamping Assn.
American Plywood Association
American Woodwork
AMOCO Corp.
AMP Corp.
ARMCO Construction Products
Armstrong World Industries
Armstrong-Blum Mfg. Co.
ARO Corp.
Arvin Industries
Arwood Co.
Asphalt Roofing Manufacturers Assn.
ASPLUNDAH
AT&T
Autodesk, Inc.
Ball Memorial Hospital
Ball State University Photo Service
Barber-Greene Co.
Bethlehem Steel
BIRDAIR, Inc.
Boeing
Boise-Cascade Corp.
Brick Institute of America
Brush Wellman Co.
Buffalo Forge Co.
The Burke Co.
California Department of Water Resources
California Redwood Association
Cambridge Seven Associates, Inc.
Caterpillar, Inc.
Cedar Shake and Shingle Bureau
CertainTeed Corp.
Cincinnati Milacron
CMI
Cold Springs Granite Co.
Combustion Engineering, Inc.
Construction Specifications Institute
Continental Illinois National Bank and Trust Co.
Controlled Energy Corp.
Corps of Engineers, Kansas City District
Courion Industries, Inc.
Cushman Co.
Daimler Benz
Bob Dale
Delta International Machinery Corp.

Des Champs Laboratories
DeVilbiss
DiAcro
DoAll Co.
Domtar Industries, Inc.—Upson Products
Dover Elevators
Dresser Industries, Inc.
Dupont Co.
DYK Prestressed Tanks, Inc.
Electronics Display Systems
Elliott Corp.
EXXON Corp.
Federal Mogul
FMC Corp.
Ford Motor Co.
Forest Products Laboratory
Forging Industry Assn.
Freightliner Corp.
Frigidaire Corp.
Gang-Nail Systems, Inc.
General Electric
General Mills, Inc.
General Motors
George Koch and Sons
Glidden
Goodyear Tire and Rubber Co.
Gray and Ductile Founders' Society
Guy F. Atkinson Co., Ron Chamberlain
Herman Miller, Inc.
Hickson Corp.
HNTB Engineers
Honeywell, Inc.
Idaho Transportation Dept.
INCO
Indiana-American Water Co., Inc.
Ingersoll-Rand Co.
Inland Steel Co.
International Conference of Building Officials
Johns-Mansville Corp.
Jordan Millwork
Kearney and Trecker
Kelly-Creswell Co., Inc.
Kohler Co.
Landis Tool Co.
LeBlond Makino Machine Tool Co.
LeMessurier Consultants
Lennox China
Lennox Industries, Inc.
Leviton Manufacturing Co., Inc.
L.F. Garlinghouse
Libby-Owens-Ford Co.
Lockheed Aircraft Corp.
The L.S. Starrett Co.
MacMillan Bloedel Ltd.
Maine D.O.T.
The Manitowoc Company, Inc.
Manville Building Materials
Martin K. Eby Construction Co., Inc.
Masonite Corp.
McDonnell Douglas Corp.
Metco
Michigan Industrial Co., Scyma Division

Miller Electric Mfg. Co.
Miller Formless, Inc.
Miller-Dunwiddie Architects, Inc.
Minster Machine Co.
Mirro Aluminum Co.
Misener Marine Construction Co.
Mitchell/Giurgola Architects
Monsanto Polymer Products, Inc.
Morgen Manufacturing Co.
Mud Cat Division
Muncie Newspapers, Inc.
Mutual Federal Savings Bank
National Coal Assn.
National Machinery Co.
National Oak Flooring Manufacturers Assn.
National Plastering Industry's Joint
Apprentice-ship Trust Fund
National Steel and Ship Building
Nevada Power Co.
Niles Bolton Associates
Norton
NuTone
Ohio Art Co.
Owens Illinois
Owens-Corning Fiberglas Corp.
Packaging Industries, Inc.
Pease Flooring Co., Inc.
Pella/Rolscreen
Pennsylvania Department of Transportation
Pierce, Goodwin, and Alexander
PPG Industrial
Puckett Bros. Mfg. Co., Inc.
Ransburg Corp.
Raymond International, Inc.
RCA
Republic Building Corp.
Reynolds Metal Co.
Robert Trent Jones II
Mary Robey
Rockwell International Corp.
Rockwell Machine Tool Co.
Rohm & Haas

Frank Samargin
Schlumberger CAD/CAM
SCM Corp.
Sellick Equipment, Ltd.
SENCO Products, Inc.
Rich Seymour
Skidmore, Owings and Merrill
Southern California Edison Co.
Southern Companies Services
Spectra-Physics
Standard Oil Co. of California
Stanley Tools
Stokes
Stran Buildings
Strippit, Inc.
The Stubbins Associates, Inc.
Syracuse China
Taylor Winfield
TEMCOR
Tennessee Valley Authority
Texaco, Inc.
Textron Inc.
Translogic Corp.
UGL
Universal Tank and Iron Works, Inc.
U.S. Department of Agriculture
U.S. Department of Energy
U.S. Department of Transportation, Federal
  Highway Administration
U.S. Elevator
U.S. Steel
Utah Department of Transportation
Vemeer Manufacturing Co.
Venture Ride Manufacturing, Inc.
John Walker
Western Electric
Western Wood Moulding and Millwork Producers
Westinghouse Elevator Co.
Weyerhauser Co.
Whirlpool Corp.
The Wire Assn.

Section I
INTRODUCTION TO PRODUCTION

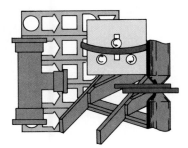

Chapter 1

THE PRODUCTION SYSTEM

After reading this chapter, you will be able to:
☐ Describe what is meant by the word "technology."
☐ Define production technology.
☐ List the major types of production activities.
☐ State purposes for production.
☐ List and describe technologies related to, and supportive of, production.
☐ Explain the three meanings of the term "industry."
☐ Describe technology as a system.
☐ List the major components in a system.
☐ List and define seven main classes of inputs in a production system.
☐ Classify the two production technologies.
☐ Define and list outputs for both construction and manufacturing.
☐ Define the term "goals," and suggest common production goals.

Look around you. You can see two worlds, Fig. 1-1. One is the natural world. It exists separate from human action. It is the ground we walk on, the air we breathe, and the water we drink. It sometimes is cruel as tornadoes destroying homes and floods washing away farms. It is also beautiful, with majestic mountains and beautiful seashores. This world is governed by nature's laws. These are discovered and described by *science*.

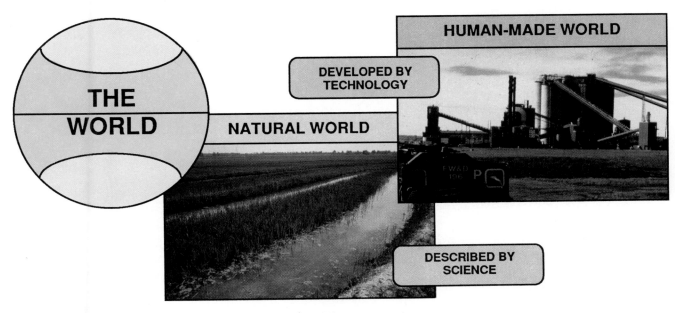

Fig. 1-1. We live in a world made up of natural and human-made elements. (U.S. Department of Agriculture, AMAX Corp.)

The other world is the human-made world. It is the result of people using tools, materials, and systems to build products and structures. We call this action *technology*. It is the things people have made to make life better. Technology means many things to many people. To some it is devices — cars, stereos, computers, robots, etc. To others it is actions or processes — making something. Actually, technology is both. In short, as you can see in Fig. 1-2, technology:

- Is a type of human knowledge.
- Deals with efficient and appropriate actions.
- Involves the use of tools, materials, and systems.
- Produces artifacts — structures, such as buildings, roads, and products.
- Helps people cope with the natural environment.
- Should be used in harmony with the natural environment.

You live in a world shaped by technology. All around you are goods produced by people using technology. You may have come to school in a manufactured bus. It traveled on a constructed road. You opened manufactured doors to enter a constructed building. The room is lit by manufactured lighting fixtures. They receive electricity that travels over constructed power lines. You are reading a manufactured book; it was printed in a constructed factory. Everywhere, you are in contact with or use products created by production technology.

What exactly is production? Simply stated, *technology* is changing the form of materials to

TECHNOLOGY is the knowledge of and practices for using tools, materials, and systems to produce a product or structure.

Fig. 1-2. Technology creates the human-made world.

make them more usable. Value is, thereby, added to materials making them more useful. For example, trees are a common natural resource. They can be harvested and cut into thin sheets of wood called veneer. They veneer can be glued together to form plywood. The plywood can be used as part of a house or for making furniture, Fig. 1-3. At each stage of production, the material is changed and becomes more useful.

Production involves two major types of activities, as shown in Fig. 1-4. Production carried out in a building (factory) is called *manufacturing*.

Fig. 1-3. Production technology changes the form of materials to make them more useful.

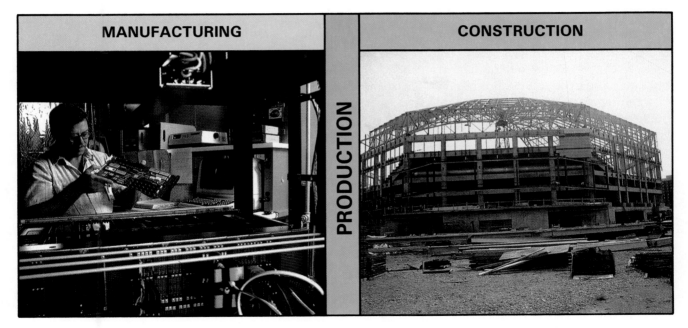

| MANUFACTURING | PRODUCTION | CONSTRUCTION |

Fig. 1-4. Production includes manufacturing technology and construction technology. (AT&T)

Production done on a site where the product is to be used is called *construction*.

IMPORTANCE OF PRODUCTION

Production is important to all of us for many reasons. First, it provides us with products to make life easier and better. We live in greater comfort because of production activities.

Comfort and Production

Some products of production move us from place-to-place, such as cars and airplanes. Others shelter us like schools and homes, yet others keep us informed and entertain us, for example, books and television.

Structures such as towers and roads make it possible for us to use some of our conveniences. Other structures house manufacturing activities. Think of all the manufactured or constructed products you use every day. Then imagine what your life would be like without them.

Employment

Production employs many workers to produce the products and structures we use. This employment is important to a large number of people, Fig. 1-5. It gives them:

- An income.
- A chance to contribute (give something) to society.
- A feeling of belonging to a group.

People need a chance to work. They want to earn their money through honest work. Production pro-

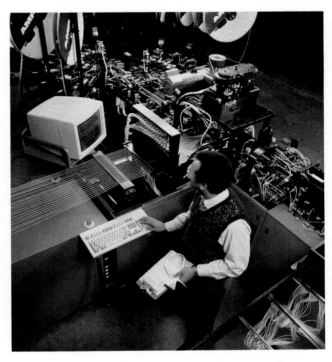

Fig. 1-5. Technology allows people to contribute to society, feel important, and earn a living. (AMP Corp.)

vides work for many people. Of course, not all of them build structures or manufacture products. Many work at other tasks. Some people manage (direct) the work of others. Other people sell buildings and products. Still others service (maintain and repair) the produced goods and structures. Some people transport the products from factories to warehouses. Further, they move the goods to construction sites and stores. Certain people keep personnel (worker) and financial records. Production provides a wide variety of jobs. Many different skills and talents are needed.

Sense of Belonging

Each of us wants to belong to a group. We want to feel needed. Production companies give people a chance to "belong." Individuals are members of a company, a department within the company, and a smaller work group. A person might say "I am a part of the armature assembly group in the motor department of the ABC Company." Others might say, "I am a concrete finisher for XYZ Construction Company." This is belonging.

Contributing To Better Life

Also, we all feel better if we can contribute to society. Production develops and produces products and structures needed by people. Those working for a production company can be proud of helping people live better. They can truly believe that life is a little better because of their work.

Helping The Economy

A third reason production is important relates to us as a nation. The strength of our nation is, in part, dependent on production industries. Our economy is strong partly because of its manufacturing and construction ability. We exchange goods with other countries. Technology (knowledge of doing) developed by production companies is sold to other nations. We erect many structures like roads, dams, and buildings around the world. However, this strength is being constantly tested. Other countries compete with us as they develop their own production technology and abilities.

PRODUCTION AND OTHER TECHNOLOGIES

Production is a technology. It is a way of doing things efficiently. Production (manufacturing and construction) requires a knowledge of efficient and appropriate action. It is one of three basic technologies that people use to produce goods and services.

The other systems are the industrial activities that we normally refer to as *communication* and *transportation.* The three may be described as follows:

- Communication. Changing information into messages. These can be transmitted (moved from the source to a receiver).
- Production. Changing the form of materials to add to their worth either on a site or in a factory. Production includes construction and manufacturing.
- Construction is the process of using manufactured goods and industrial materials to build structures on a site. Manufacturing includes changing materials into usable products in a factory.
- Transportation. Converting energy into power to move people and goods.

Each of these activities is different from the others. Every system has its own way of doing things. However, the three are also highly interrelated, Fig. 1-6. That is, they support each other and are often used together.

Since you are studying production, you need to look at how production activities tie together. At the same time you will see how production relates to, and depends on, the other two technologies. Manufacturing is production completed in a factory. The factory itself was built using construction practices. Manufactured materials and products were used to build the factory. Construction technology was used to erect the plant, complete the roads leading to the plant, pave the parking lots, and bring in the water, electrical, and sewer lines. So, you see, manufacturing and construction depend heavily upon each other, Fig. 1-7.

Support From Transportation

Production also needs support from transportation. Materials arrive at the factory or construction site on transportation vehicles like trucks or railroad cars. Finished products leave factories the same way. Also, workers may use cars and buses to get to work. The resources (inputs) and outputs of production are always being transported.

Support From Communication

Communication is the backbone of any big organization. Information is exchanged between manufacturing plants and construction sites. Drawings and other data are often transmitted over long distances using computer systems. The design center and offices are sometimes miles away from the factory or construction site. Managers at these locations must send and receive information daily. Also, companies communicate to customers through advertisements, announcements, and catalogs.

As you can see by these brief examples, no technology system can stand alone. Each depends on the others for support. All three together are what is called an *economic system*. They are necessary for the success of our efforts to produce and exchange goods and services.

TECHNOLOGY AS A SYSTEM

You have been introduced to production as a technological system. The idea of a system may seem strange to you; it need not be. You already know quite a bit about the systems because you are surrounded by familiar ones. Your home has a heating system. The classroom has a lighting system. Your body has a digestive system. The building you are in was produced using a construction system. The products you use were created by a manufacturing system. All of these systems have five common parts. These, as shown in Fig.1-8, are:

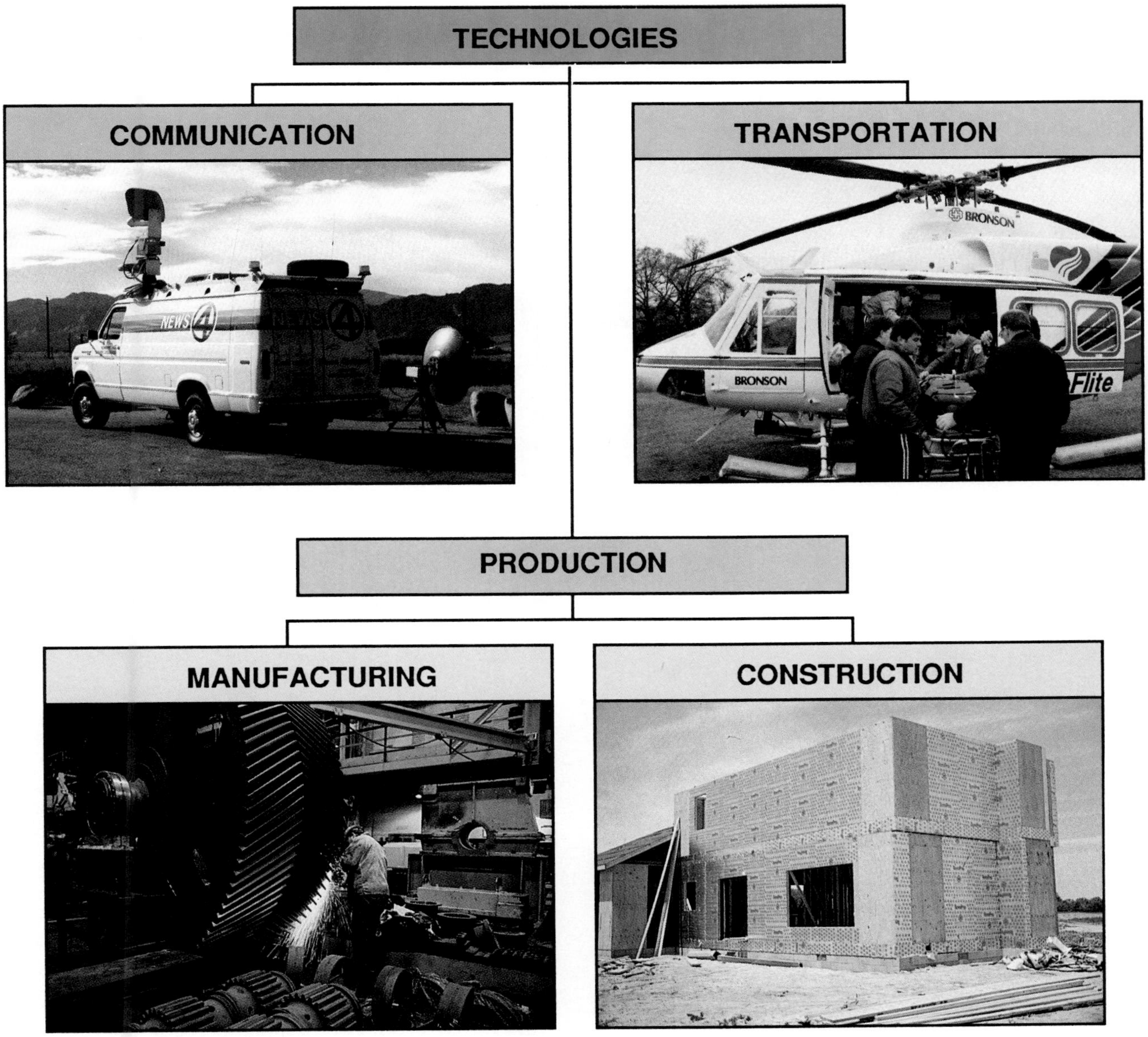

Fig. 1-6. People have developed communication, transportation, and production (manufacturing and construction) technologies. Technology systems are interrelated. (Textron Inc., Inland Steel Co.)

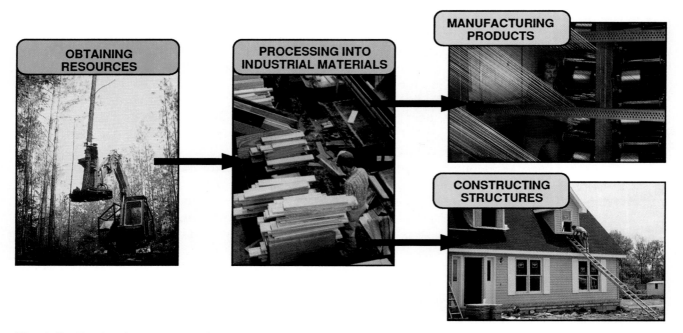

Fig. 1-7. Production systems change raw materials into manufactured products and constructed structures.

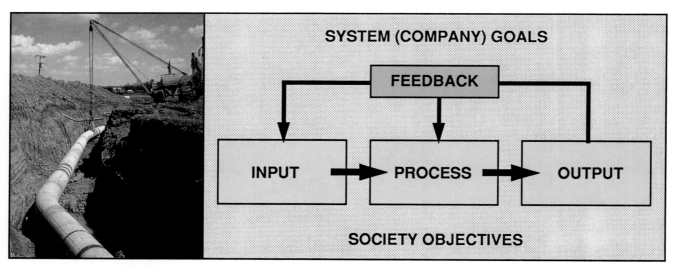

Fig. 1-8. Technology is a system that has inputs, processes, outputs, and feedback.

- Input.
- Process.
- Output.
- Feedback.
- Goal.

A heating system will use fuel and air as its inputs. These inputs are processed (changed) in a furnace. The fuel and air enter into a reaction we call burning. The output is heat energy and exhaust gases, and of course, a warm home is the goal. This temperature is controlled by a thermostat. It measures the temperature of the room and provides feedback (adjusts) the furnace.

Likewise, production systems have the same five parts. Let us look at each of these.

PRODUCTION INPUTS

Products and structures—things like buildings, dams, and roads—are not built out of thin air. A number of inputs or resources are needed. These inputs may be grouped into seven main classes. As you can see in Fig. 1-9, these are:

Fig. 1-9. The inputs to technological systems.

- Natural resources (materials).
- Human resources (labor).
- Capital (plant, machines, and equipment).
- Knowledge (how to do it).
- Energy.
- Finances (money).
- Time.

Natural Resources

Natural resources are the raw materials that are changed into finished items. These resources are the industrial "building blocks" found on earth, Fig. 1-10. Typical natural resources are metal ores, trees, petroleum, water, natural gas, and clay.

Human Resources

Human resources are people. This is a unique (one of a kind) resource. People are individuals. Each person has special abilities and talents that no one else has.

Production needs a wide variety of human talent. Some jobs require great physical skill. Concrete must be placed. Parts must be produced. Other jobs need a person who can organize tasks. Activities must be planned and scheduled. Deadlines must be set. Still other jobs require people skills — the ability to manage and work with people. Employees must be supervised and motivated to do their best work. Some jobs need workers who like to do the same thing over and over. Others need employees who like the challenge of doing different things each day.

Large general contractors hire many people to complete complex projects. They build large buildings, housing developments, dams, roads, and other similar structures. Custom builders use only a few workers to build houses to the owner's design.

Capital

Capital has several definitions. For us, it is the plant and equipment (machines) used to produce

Fig. 1-10. Trees can be used as material inputs to a number of technological systems.

products and build structures. Each enterprise must have some capital investment. Buildings (factories, offices, and warehouses) are needed for company activities. Equipment is needed to move materials, change its form, and process data. Capital is the permanent (lasting) physical resource of a company.

Knowledge

A hidden resource in all companies is *knowledge.* It cannot be directly seen or measured. However, its effect can be. Often the difference between successful and failing companies is knowledge. This knowledge may be in many forms. It could be knowing how to process materials into products or buildings. It could also involve being able to find money to pay for production costs. Understanding how to promote and sell products and buildings is also important. Likewise, management knowledge is essential.

Energy

All technology uses *energy,* Fig. 1-11. This can be physical energy provided by people and animals. However, most of the energy is produced by converting one form of energy into another. For example, falling water is used to turn the generator in a hydroelectric generating plant. This converts mechanical energy into electrical energy. Later the

electrical energy may be converted into mechanical motion by a motor, light by an incandescent bulb, or heat by a resistance heater.

Finances

Another important resource is *finances*. You may have heard the saying, "It takes money to make money." This is very true. A company must have money to purchase the other resources. It costs money to develop and engineer products and structures. Also, a company must buy material, pay for labor, and purchase machines. Finances, or money, are the very foundation of a company. Without it, nothing else can be done.

Time

The final technological resource is *time*. It includes human time needed to produce and sell products and structures. It also includes machine time needed to process materials.

PRODUCTION PROCESSES

Having the proper resources is not enough for success. The company must use them properly. This activity is the "process" part of the production system. It uses two major technologies. These, as pictured in Fig. 1-12, are processing technology and management technology.

Fig. 1-11. Solar collectors may be widely used as energy sources in the future. (U.S. Department of Energy)

PRODUCTION PROCESSES	
PROCESSING TECHNOLOGY	**MANAGEMENT TECHNOLOGY**

Fig. 1-12. Production processes use processing and management technologies.

Processing Technology

As discussed earlier, production changes the form of materials to add to their worth. This form change is called *processing*. It usually involves changing raw materials into industrial materials, such as lumber, sheet steel, and plastic pellets. The industrial materials are then changed into a finished product or structure. Manufacturing may change materials into a stool, garbage can, or styrofoam cup.

A construction company can use materials and manufactured products to produce a building, road, or dam. You will learn more about the types of processing in later chapters.

Processing is a "doing" activity. It involves action and is, therefore, a technology. To understand this technology, people must know about materials and their properties (qualities), as well as the techniques for changing the form of materials.

These two areas of knowledge, as shown in Fig. 1-13, are called *material science* (properties) and *material* (manufacturing and construction) *processing*. These two topics will be covered in the manufacturing and construction technology sections of this book.

Management Technology

It is not enough to be able to process materials. To be successful, a company must do it efficiently. The enterprise must use as little material, labor, capital, energy, time, and money as possible.

This is where *management technology* comes in. Managing is defined as "guiding and directing company activities to ensure efficient operation." Each company activity, from the time a product or structure idea is born until someone buys the output, must be managed. Resources must be wisely used. Processing methods must be efficient. All activities must save as many resources as possible.

Fig. 1-13. Types of knowledge used in production processes.

PRODUCTION OUTPUTS

The output of a production system is a usable *product* or *structure*. This is the reason people developed the system. The number and kinds of products and structures are almost endless. However, for many purposes they are grouped into classes under construction and manufacturing.

Construction Outputs

Construction outputs are the structures that are built on site. They are meant to meet human needs. The outputs of construction can be classified as buildings or heavy engineering (civil) structures, Fig. 1-14.

Buildings

Buildings are structures used to house people and human-based activities. A common type of building is housing. Housing includes the structures built to provide people with shelter. They can be single dwellings, apartments, townhouses, condominiums, or other structures.

Buildings also shelter commercial activities. These include stores, factories, farm buildings, radio and television stations, transportation terminals, and product warehouses.

Heavy engineering structures

A second type of structure is the product of heavy engineering construction activities. These are generally nonbuilding structures. They include sanitary systems, transportation guideways (streets and highways, railroads, canals, and airport runways), communication structures (towers, antenna, etc.), and energy systems (pipelines, electrical transmission lines and towers, and electricity-generating plants).

Fig. 1-14. Construction technology is used to produce buildings and heavy engineering structures.

Manufacturing Outputs

Manufacturing outputs are produced in factories. They are then shipped to the customer. These outputs can be classified as consumer, industrial, or military goods, Fig. 1-15.

Consumer products

Consumer products are manufactured goods that are ready to use. Customers do not need to do any further material processing before they use the

Fig. 1-15. Manufacturing technology provides consumer, industrial, and military products.

product. These products are sold by a typical retail store, dealer, or catalog. Consumer products usually include:

- Durable (hard) goods that are expected to last for a long period of time. Automobiles, kitchen appliances, and furniture are examples of durable goods.
- Nondurable (soft) goods are used up in a short period of time. Food, clothing, and beverages are examples of soft goods.

Industrial goods

Industrial goods are materials and equipment used by industries. Industrial materials need further processing before becoming a useful product. A sheet of plywood is useful only after it is made into a doghouse, desk, or cabinet. The same is true for lumber, sheets of aluminum, and potter's clay. These resources are called *industrial materials.*

Capital goods (equipment) are also industrial goods. They are the machines that process materials. They are used to produce industrial and consumer goods.

Military goods

Military, or *ordnance goods* are the materials of war. They are special products produced for the military forces of a country. Tanks, guns, and bombers are examples.

Other production outputs

So far you have been reading about the desired outputs of production systems. However, these are not the only outputs of production activities. Most industrial activities have undesirable outputs.

Some of these outputs are *scrap* and *waste*. Chips, shavings, and cutoffs are developed during the processing of materials. Some of these can be recycled (used again). Metal scraps can be remelted. Wood chips may become paper, hardboard, or particleboard. Management should always work to reduce and recycle scrap, Fig. 1-16.

In addition, production processes will produce unusable waste. Many manufacturing and construction processes have by-products that are unwanted. Steelmaking produces slag and chemical fumes. Papermaking produces strong-smelling liquids. Many chemical plants produce hazardous (dangerous) wastes. This waste must be disposed of without causing pollution. Construction activities often cause earth to be moved. This can create soil erosion and water pollution.

Management must provide a means of taking care of these undesirable outputs. In many cases,

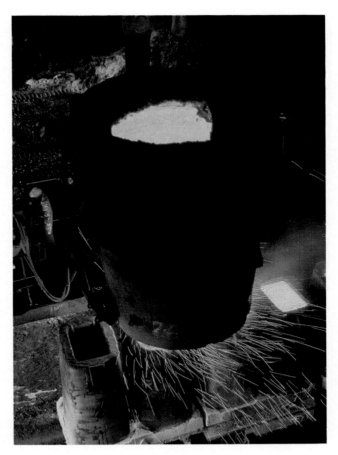

Fig. 1-16. This charge of steel is being produced using scrap. (Inland Steel Co.)

they cannot be easily or cheaply handled. For example, there is always scrap and waste at a construction site. These outputs cannot easily be recycled. They must, however, be carefully dealt with. Often a landfill is used to dispose of these items. A better solution for most scrap and waste is recycling. The materials can become inputs to new production activities.

Likewise, the automobile engine produces carbon monoxide gas and other pollutants as it burns fuel. This deadly poisonous gas is an undesirable by-product. The problem is to reduce it so that the air we breath is safe. Manufacturers must carefully dispose of their waste, too. We need to control technology so that our land, air, and water are safe to use.

Feedback

Production activities should be carefully controlled. They often require adjustments to be made. This is done in terms of feedback. Feedback is the process of using the output to monitor the production process. For example, a quality control department measures the products produced by manufacturing activities. If the products fail to meet required standards, the description of the defects is feedback to the production manager or another person in the same type of position. He or she uses this data to change processing activities. Today, a great deal of the feedback is done automatically. Computer-controlled equipment automatically measures the outputs and adjusts the machines, Fig. 1-17.

PRODUCTION GOALS

Production has two types of goals. One type is the company's goals. The other is the goals society has for the production activity.

Company Goals

A company has a basic goal. The enterprise must have money left after all its expenses (costs) are paid. The "left over" money is called *profit*. This profit allows the company to:

- Reward its owners for investing in the company (pay dividends).
- Become more productive.
- Develop new products and technology.
- Replace equipment.
- Invest in other businesses.

Without profits, companies would go out of business. Workers lose their jobs. With less income, they buy less from merchants in their towns. In general, a whole community feels the negative (bad) effects of a failing company.

Managers have a responsibility (duty) to keep their companies making a profit. This does not mean they should be driven by greed. They should manage well so the workers and the owners receive their fair share. The workers should receive fair wages. The owners should see their company earn a profit.

Society's Goals

Production firms must also react to the goals of society. We want our companies to help their

Fig. 1-17. A plastic injection molder using automatic controls to ensure that good-quality products are produced. (Cincinnati Milacron)

workers have a better life. Each of us wants a higher standard of living. Also, we expect companies to protect the environment (air, water, land). In addition, companies may need to train and retrain workers, give money for community projects, and help with similar activities. Companies are expected to be good "citizens" of the community and nation.

WHY STUDY PRODUCTION?

You now know the meaning of the terms production, industry, and company. Yet, why should anyone want to study production? Stop and think about it, Fig. 1-18. Are you planning to get a job after you finish school? Do you know what jobs are available? Do you have any idea what education is needed for these jobs? Do you know which jobs fit your interests and abilities?

Do you plan on voting for candidates for public office? Will you ever be asked to speak or vote on current issues? Will the candidates and issues affect your life and industries?

Do you buy or use the products of production companies? Can you decide if a product or structure is really worth the selling price? Do you understand how products or structures are made? Do you know how to maintain the simple products and components in a home? Do you know when a product needs servicing?

If you plan on being a worker, employer, voter, consumer, and citizen, you need to understand the world around you. You are living in a complex industrial and technological world. A study of production will help you live in such a world.

SUMMARY

Production is a system that produces products for our use. Production activities can be divided into manufacturing and construction systems.

These systems involve using inputs to create the desired outputs. They change the form of materials using processing and management technologies. The flow within the system is controlled by company and society goals. If successful, production activities will provide products and structures at a fair price without harming the environment. In addition, the owners of the company will earn a profit.

KEY WORDS

All of the following words have been used in this chapter. Do you know their meaning?

Building	Manufacturing
Capital	Material science
Capital goods	Material processing
Construction	Military goods
Consumer product	Natural resources
Economic system	Outputs
Energy	Processes
Feedback	Processing
Finances	Product
Goals	Science
Heavy engineering	Scrap
structure	Structure
Human resources	Technology
Industrial goods	Time
Inputs	Transportation
Knowledge	Waste
Management	
Management	
technology	

TEST YOUR KNOWLEDGE

Write your answers on a separate sheet of paper. Do not write in this book.

1. Write a brief definition of technology.

Fig. 1-18. There are a number of good reasons to study production technology.

2. Producing a product in a factory is called _____.
3. Producing a building from manufactured materials and products is called _____.
4. List the three major types of technologies.
5. Which of the following are parts of a technological system? Inputs, throughputs, outputs, processes, goals, feedback, recycling.
6. List the seven major inputs to all technological systems.
7. Production activities use material processing and management technologies. True or False?
8. List the three types of products of manufacturing systems.
9. Construction produces buildings and heavy engineering structures. True or False?

ACTIVITIES

1. Identify an industry by the product it makes (the steel industry or the residential construction industry for example).

A. View a film on the industry.
B. Find advertisements or pictures from that industry.
C. Prepare a bulletin board or scrapbook from these materials.

2. Complete a simple line production product then discuss it in terms of inputs, processes used, outputs, and goals.

3. With another class member, interview a person employed in a production (manufacturing or construction) enterprise. This person can be a production worker or manager. Find out all you can about the product manufactured or type of structure produced including:

A. Kind of product manufactured (consumer, industrial, or military) or structure built (housing, sanitary systems, roadways, industrial construction, or energy system).
B. What are the inputs, processes, outputs, and goals of the company?
C. Are there problems in controlling waste?
D. Would you like to work in this industry?

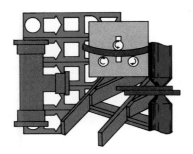

Chapter 2
PRODUCTION MATERIALS

After reading this chapter, you will be able to:
- ☐ Describe types of metals, plastics, ceramics, and composites.
- ☐ List properties of some materials.
- ☐ Define the terms density, hardness, ductility, and opacity.
- ☐ Describe how some material properties are measured.
- ☐ List requirements for selecting materials.
- ☐ List units of measurement for length, volume, and weight.
- ☐ Explain how to select and buy materials.

You have learned that production activities change the form of materials to add to their value. Iron ore, coke, and limestone is processed to produce steel. Silica sand is converted into glass. Wool is changed into yarn that is woven into fabric. As you can see, materials are the foundation for all manufactured products and constructed structures, Fig. 2-1.

TYPES OF MATERIALS

Science groups materials into three types: gases, liquids, and solids, Fig. 2-2. Each type has a use in industry. For example, burning gases produce heat for welding and heat treating. Liquids lubricate surfaces and cool molds. They also are solvents (liquid carriers) for finishes. Solids provide the mass and shape of many products.

Engineering Materials

In many ways, solid materials are the most important type. They are often called *engineering*

materials. These materials have a rigid structure that cannot be changed. They hold their size and shape under normal conditions.

There are over 70,000 different kinds and grades of engineering materials. This number grows

Fig. 2-1. Materials are the foundation for manufacturing and construction activities. (American Iron and Steel Institute)

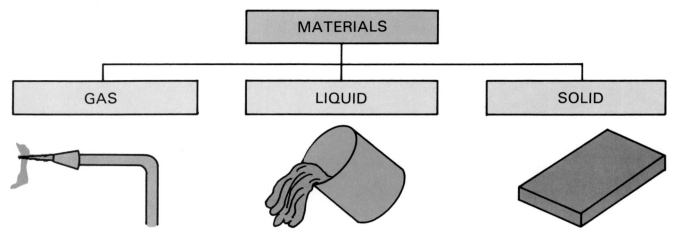

Fig. 2-2. All manufactured and constructed items include one or more of these materials.

almost daily. Scientists and engineers develop new materials as our needs change. For instance, more than a thousand different materials are used to make an average automobile.

Products made from a single material are difficult to find. Even the common lead pencil is made of four different materials. The body is wood, the "lead" is carbon, the eraser is synthetic rubber, and the eraser band is metal.

Engineering materials can be classified as four basic groups. These, as shown in Fig. 2-3, are:
- Metals.
- Polymers (plastics).
- Ceramics.
- Composites.

METALS

Look around you. How many things do you see that are made out of metal? Metals are a very important engineering material!

Metals are crystalline (box-like), inorganic (never were living matter) materials. The crystals are made of atoms arranged in box-like shapes, Fig. 2-4.

These crystals are the basic units of a metal. The grains stick together as molten metal cools, forming a solid material.

Mixing Metals Together

In early history, metals were used in their pure state. Our ancestors used pure copper and iron for many products. Today, however, pure metals are rarely used. Some pure gold is used in making small electronic parts. Also, pure copper is used in special electrical devices. Pure aluminum is used by the chemical and electrical industries.

Most metallic materials are a combination of two or more pure metals. This combination is called an *alloy.* These materials often have better properties than pure metals. They are usually stronger, harder, and resist corrosion (chemical attack) better.

You already know the names of some common alloys used in everyday life. Steel is basically a mixture of iron and carbon. Brass is an alloy of copper and zinc. Solder is a tin-lead alloy. Bronze an alloy of copper and tin. Thousands of alloy are produced by metals industries.

ENGINEERING MATERIALS

METALS   POLYMERS   CERAMICS

COMPOSITES

Fig. 2-3. Types of engineering (solid) materials.

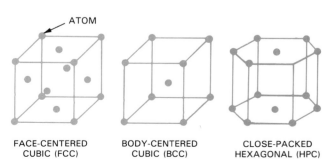

FACE-CENTERED CUBIC (FCC)   BODY-CENTERED CUBIC (BCC)   CLOSE-PACKED HEXAGONAL (HPC)

Fig. 2-4. Three common types of metal crystals that combine to form grains.

Common Metals

There are many common metals in use today. The most widely used are iron-based alloys, aluminum alloys, and copper alloys.

Iron-based alloys

The iron-based alloys are the most widely used of all metals. The industrial revolution was based on them; so is the Western technical culture. The taming of America depended on steel rails and railroad equipment. Steel barbed wire allowed us to farm the plains. Steel was the skeleton of early skyscrapers. Without iron and steel, progress would have been difficult.

Iron-based alloys are inexpensive, strong, and easily worked, Fig. 2-5. They can be divided into two groups:
• Cast iron.
• Steel.

Cast iron. *Cast iron* is any iron-carbon alloy with more than two percent carbon. There are several types of cast iron. They are used to produce complex, heavy shapes. For example, engine blocks are often made of cast iron.

Steel. *Steel* is iron-carbon alloy with less than two percent carbon, Fig. 2-6. Steel can be divided into carbon steels and specialty steels.

Fig. 2-6. This sports arena has a steel roof structure.

As the name suggests, carbon is the main alloy in carbon steel. These steels are divided into three main groups:
• Mild Steel. This is a low carbon, general purpose steel. The most common of all steels, it can be easily forged, bent, or welded.
• Medium Carbon Steel. This steel is stronger than mild steel. It is easy to machine, forge, and cast.

Fig. 2-5. Steel is the most commonly used metal. (Inland Steel Co.)

- High Carbon Steel. Heat treating will harden this steel. It is not easy to machine, weld, or forge.

Specialty steels. Specialty steels are developed for specific use. The most common types are stainless steel and tool steel. Steel may also be coated to protect it from the environment. Two common coated steels are tinplate and galvanized steel. Tinplate is tin-coated steel used for food cans (tin cans) and other similar applications. Galvanized steel has a coating of zinc. It is used for siding, roofing, and automobile body parts.

POLYMERS

Polymers is the scientific name for plastics. Polymers are made from a number of organic (living matter) molecules. These molecules are called mers or monomers (single mers).

Polymers are made by combining monomers to produce a chain-like structure of molecules. The structure is a group of repeating monomers, Fig. 2-7.

Polymers are both natural and synthetic (made by people). Animal and vegetable protein, starch, and cellulose are natural polymers. Most important industrial polymers are synthetic.

Synthetic Polymers

Polymers are formed by chemical action. Basic molecules are united to form the polymer chains. For example, vinyl chloride monomers are united to form polyvinyl chloride. As seen in Fig. 2-8, the result is a chain made up of many (poly) vinyl chloride monomers.

Many different plastics are formed by this same action. The action is called polymerization (joining many molecules). Polymerization is used to

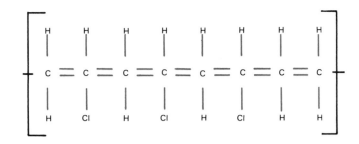

Fig. 2-8. A polyvinyl chloride polymer chain is a number of elements linked together by chemical action. The elements in the chain are carbon (C), hydrogen (H), and chlorine (Cl).

make two classes of plastics — thermoplastics and thermosets.

A *thermoplastic* material has many long polymer chains. These chains are independent. They are not directly connected to each other. They are held in place by weak electrical forces along the chains, Fig. 2-9.

The bonds will weaken if the material is heated. This action allows thermoplastics to be shaped many times. Any time heat is applied, the material becomes soft. If pressure is applied, the material will take a shape. When it cools the weak bonding forces return. The material is held in the new shape.

Thermoset polymers will take a permanent set when heat and pressure are applied. The material has long polymer chains. However, heat causes the material to develop crosslinks between the chains. These bonds form a rigid structure. The individual chains are now connected, Fig. 2-10. They cannot move past each other. Heat and pressure will no longer affect the plastic.

CERAMICS

The term, ceramics, covers a wide range of materials. They can be used to make beautiful, works of art. Abrasives and cement are ceramics.

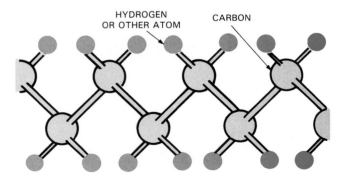

HYDROGEN OR OTHER ATOM   CARBON

Fig. 2-7. A model of a polymer chain showing how the atoms are connected.

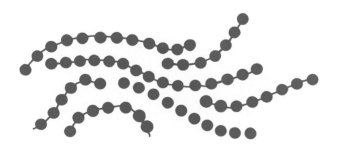

Fig. 2-9. Thermoplastic structure. The chains have weak bonds between them.

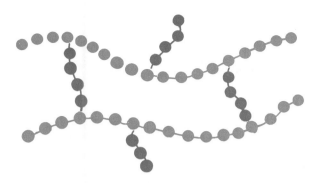

Fig. 2-10. Thermoset structure. The material has strong crosslinks holding the chains together.

Window glass and porcelain enamels on bathroom fixtures are other uses for ceramics. Ceramics are, indeed, the broadest type of engineering material.

Ceramic, is a Greek work for potter's clay. Today, it is used to describe a range of materials which:

- Have a crystalline structure.
- Are inorganic (never living).
- Can be either metallic or nonmetallic.

Ceramic materials, generally, are very stable (not likely to change). They are not greatly affected by heat, weather, or chemicals. They have high melting points. In addition, ceramics are stiff, brittle, and rigid. The ceramics are the hardest of all engineering materials.

The major types of ceramic materials are:

- Clay-based ceramics—These materials have a crystalline body, held in place by a glassy material. This material is the ceramic bonding agent. It holds the clay particles together. Typical clay products include:
- Earthenware—A useful, but weak material used for some dinnerware and drain tile.
- Stoneware—An improved earthenware used for oven and chemical applications.
- China—A translucent (passes light), strong product used for fine dinnerware.
- Porcelain—A hard, dense (heavy) product used for coatings on metal and ceramic maerials.
- Structural clay—A material fired (cured by heat) at low temperatures and used for bricks, decorative tile, and drain tile.
- Refractories—Crystalline materials that do not have a glassy material to bond the grains together. Instead, the crystalline material is fused (bonded) by high temperatures. Refractories are used for firebricks that line furnaces and ovens. They are also used for heat-resistant parts in nuclear power plants, spacecraft, and jet engines.

- Glass—An amorphous ceramic material. (Amorphous means it has no regular internal pattern.) Glass is mostly silica sand with other materials added. The mixture is melted at high temperatures. When it cools, the mixture forms a hard, brittle substance.

COMPOSITES

Metals, ceramics, and plastics are single, uniform materials. Combining two or more of these materials creates a fourth group of materials called *composites.* These base materials are bonded together by adhesion (holding together by physical force; stickiness). For example, fiberglass is a combination of glass fibers and plastic resin. Concrete combines cement, sand, and gravel. Each material keeps its own properties. However, combining them adds special properties to the new material.

A composite has two major parts—a filler and a matrix. The *filler* usually provides the bulk (gives body) for the material. It is the fibers, flakes, sheets, or particles that are the base for the composite. The *matrix* (binding force) is the agent that holds the filler together. It is the bonding agent for the filler.

Composites can be either natural or synthetic. They can either appear in nature or be human-made.

Natural Composites

Nature has produced the most widely used composite. It is wood, Fig. 2-11. Wood is primarily

Fig. 2-11. The most widely used composite is wood.

hollow cellulose fibers (filler) held in place by lignin (matrix). It is like a group of soda straws glued together.

Wood is divided into two major groups—hardwood and softwood, Fig. 2-12.

These categories have nothing to do with the hardness of the material. Hardwoods can be soft and softwoods can be hard. In fact, balsa is classified as a hardwood! The difference between the two is the kind of tree the wood came from. Hardwood trees lose their leaves in the winter. They are called *deciduous* trees. Softwoods are *conifers,* or cone-bearing trees.

Lumber

Lumber is a product of the saw and planing mills. Yard lumber comes in the forms of boards, dimension stock, and timbers. Boards are used for sheathing, siding, flooring, trim, and paneling. Dimension lumber forms parts of a wood frame for a house. Posts and beams are made of timbers.

Manufactured Composites

Synthetic composites are not new. Early settlers mixed straw with mud to make adobe bricks. Later, more important composites were developed. These can be grouped into three categories shown in Fig. 2-13:

• Fibrous
  □ Fibers in a matrix.
  □ The fibers carry the load.
    Examples: glass reinforces plastic to make fiberglass; straw reinforces mud to make adobe brick.

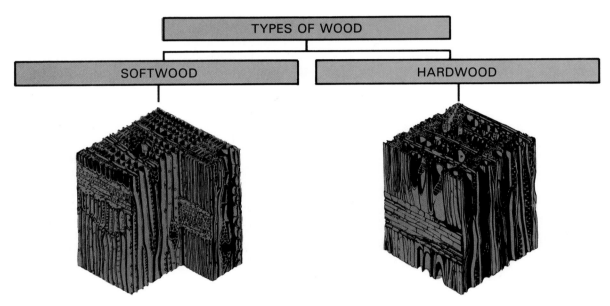

Fig. 2-12. Types of wood and their internal structures. (Forest Products Laboratory, U.S. Forest Service)

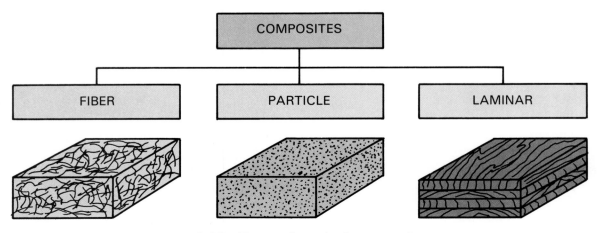

Fig. 2-13. Types of synthetic composites.

- Particulate (or particle)
  - ☐ Particles are held in a matrix.
  - ☐ The load is shared by particles and matrix.
    Examples: flakeboard, particleboard, impregnated metals (metal with pores filled with oil for bearings); concrete (cement-aggregate composite).
- Laminar
  - ☐ Layers (laminates) glued together.
  - ☐ The laminates carry the load.
    Examples: plywood, laminated beams, clad metals (coins, bi-metal thermostat).

Newer uses for composites are being found daily. In many new aircraft the skin and some structural parts are now composites. These materials are lighter and stronger than other materials. Some sports car bodies, fishing poles, and many shower stalls are molded fiberglass.

Concrete

Concrete is one of the most important building materials. It is used in almost every type and size of structure. In buildings it is used for footings, foundations, and walls. It is used for flat structures of all kinds, like roadways and floors.

Ingredients. Concrete is made of two parts: cement paste and aggregate. The cement paste is Portland cement and water. The aggregate consists of fine sand (1/4 inch diameter and less) and stones over 1/4 inch diameter. The cement paste binds the aggregate together and fills the spaces between particles. A chemical reaction between the water and the cement sets (hardens) the concrete.

Admixtures are special chemicals added to concrete. Some chemicals make the concrete set faster. Others will lengthen the setting time.

Concrete with tiny air bubbles in it is called *air-entrained* concrete. An admixture causes the tiny bubbles to form. Air-entrained concrete is easier to work and it resists cracking from freezing and thawing.

Reinforcing rods, called rebar, are used to strengthen concrete. They are made of steel. The surface of each rod is often rough to make the concrete hold better.

Glass, plastic, and wire fibers are sometimes added to concrete. They reduce the number of small cracks that appear in concrete.

Plywood

Plywood is used as support and to decorate the structure. Structural plywood is used as wall sheathing, roof decks, and subfloors. Plywood is made of thin crossbanded layers (with alternate grain at 90° angles). The layers are glued together into panels.

Structural plywood is used where strength is desired. Two basic types are produced. *Interior plywood* is made with glue that is moisture resistant but not waterproof. *Exterior glues* are waterproof. The layers stay bonded even when they are wet and dried many times.

Decorative plywood may have designs cut in it with special machines. Sheets may have a veneer of hardwood or have vinyl coverings or printed patterns.

Other Forms

Wood chips and flakes are bonded with glue. They are formed into panels. The products are called *flakeboard* and *particleboard*.

The grain of chips in a layer can be put in one direction. The result is *oriented strand board,* which has a finish with a minimum of overlapped chips.

A common product is *waferboard*. The chips are laid randomly. *Hardboard* is made of specially processed wood fibers. Chips have been broken down. These panels are usually 4 ft. wide and 8 ft. long.

MATERIAL PROPERTIES

Product designers and engineers have a common problem. They must select a material to fit a need. The material must do a certain job.

The selection of the right material cannot be left to luck. It is a careful, thoughtful act. The designers must "know" materials. They must know the *properties* (characteristics) of may different materials.

A material may need to satisfy several requirements to do the job. For example, it may have to look good and be strong (kitchen chair frame). It might have to be attractive, reflect light, and absorb sound (ceiling tile). The material may have to be strong and transparent (window glass). The examples are endless.

Properties tell the designer how the material will perform or behave under use. Every material has many of its own properties. These can all be grouped into the following categories:
- Mechanical.
- Physical.
- Thermal.
- Chemical.
- Electrical and mechanical.
- Optical.

Mechanical Properties

Mechanical properties are the ability of a material to support (withstand) mechanical force. Typically, these forces, as shown in Fig. 2-14, are:
• Compression.
• Tension.
• Shear.
• Torsion.

Basically, compression squeezes and crushes material. Tension tries to pull it apart. Shear tries to cause two sections of the material to part and slide past each other. Torsion twists the material; it is actually a rotating shear force.

The ability to withstand these forces is measured in several ways. The common mechanical properties, as shown in Fig. 2-15 are:
• Strength.
• Elasticity, stiffness.
• Plasticity, ductility, malleability, brittleness.
• Hardness, wear resistance.
• Toughness.
• Fatigue.

Strength

Strength is the material's ability to bear a mechanical load. There are four strengths: tensile (tension), compressive, shear, and torsion.

Tensile strength is the amount of force needed to pull a material apart. *Compressive strength* is the force that causes a material to rupture (bulge out). *Shear strength* is the force required to cause parts of a material to slide past themselves and separate. *Torsion strength* is the twisting force needed to cause the material to shear and separate.

Elasticity and stiffness

An ability to be flexed or stretched, then return to the original size, is called *elasticity*. The

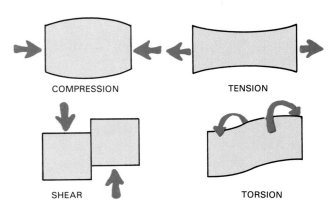

Fig. 2-14. Mechanical properties tell designers how a material will stand up under these stresses.

COMPRESSION TENSION

SHEAR TORSION

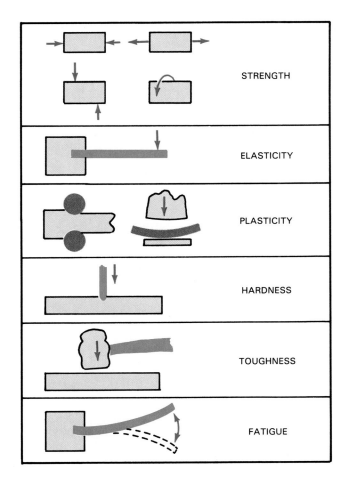

Fig. 2-15. Common mechanical properties that designers and engineers consider in selecting a material.

STRENGTH

ELASTICITY

PLASTICITY

HARDNESS

TOUGHNESS

FATIGUE

resistance to elastic forces is called *stiffness*. Stiffness is the ability to hold a load without flexing. A rubber band is elastic. A piece of glass has high stiffness.

Plasticity

An ability of a solid material to flow into a new shape under pressure is *plasticity*. Two measures of plasticity are:
1. Ductility—Plasticity under tension forces. This is a material's ability to be drawn (pulled) out. Chewing gum is highly ductile.
2. Malleability—Plasticity under compression force. This is a material's ability to be pounded into shape. Modeling clay has high malleability.

Brittleness

Brittleness is the tendency of a material to fracture before material flow (deformation) happens. Brittleness is the opposite of plasticity. Glass has high brittleness. It breaks easily.

Hardness

Hardness is an ability of a material to resist denting. It is directly related to abrasion and wear resistance. Harder material will wear less under use. A diamond is hard.

Toughness

The ability of a material to absorb energy without breaking is known as *toughness.* A hammer head must have high toughness so that it does not shatter when used to strike other materials.

Fatigue

Fatigue is the ability of a material to absorb repeated stress. A material with high fatigue strength can withstand constant flexing or bending. A spring must have high fatigue strength.

Physical Properties

Physical properties describe the size, density, and surface texture of a material, Fig. 2-16. For example, a material can be described by its thickness, width, and length. This overall size is a physical property.

Density indicates the weight of a standard size piece of material. Typically, density is given as pounds per square inch (psi), pounds per square foot, or grams per cubic centimeter.

Different materials can be compared by using their densities. For example, red oak has a density of 43.8 pounds per square foot (lb./sq. ft.). Ponderosa pine's density is 28.6 lb./sq. ft. Using this comparison, you can see that red oak is almost 1 1/2 times more dense than pine. That is to say,

an oak board weighs 150 percent more than the same size of pine board.

Closely related to density is *porosity.* This is the relationship of open space to solid space in the material. A porous material will generally be lighter (less dense) than a nonporous material. Also, a porous material will contain air within it. It will be a better heat insulator. For example, wood is more porous than aluminum. Therefore, wood window frames will insulate a home better than aluminum frames.

The final physical property is *surface texture,* Fig. 2-17. We have all used the terms smooth and rough. These describe surface texture. Some surfaces must be smooth while others need to be rough. A rough surface on a pair of skis would slow down a skier.

Thermal Properties

Thermal means heat. *Thermal properties* relate to a material's reaction to changes in temperature. Three important properties relate to heat:
- Melting and freezing point.
- Thermal conductivity.
- Thermal expansion.

Everyone knows about *melting* and *freezing points.* Both involve thermal (heat) energy. This energy is measured in Btus (British thermal units) or calories. A Btu is the heat energy needed to raise the temperature of one pound of water one degree Fahrenheit. Another measure like the Btu is the calorie. It is the energy needed to heat one gram

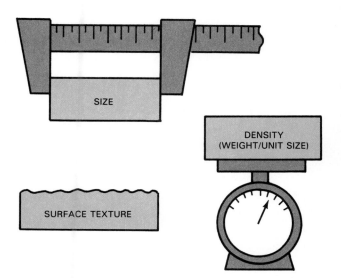

Fig. 2-16. Physical properties refer to size, density, and surface texture.

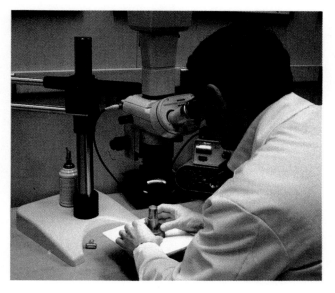

Fig. 2-17. Laboratory technician is checking the physical properties of a steel sample. (Inland Steel Co.)

of water one degree Celsius. It takes thermal energy to melt a solid material. Likewise, a material gives up thermal energy as it freezes.

Thermal conductivity is a material's ability to allow heat to flow in it. Heat energy tends to flow from a hotter area to a colder area. The speed at which this happens in a set period of time is called the coefficient (measure) of thermal conductivity. An insulating material should have a low coefficient of thermal conductivity. It should not allow heat to move from one area to another. However, the liquid in an automobile cooling system must have a high coefficient of thermal conductivity. It should move heat away rapidly.

Thermal expansion is the amount a material changes size with a change in temperature. Solid materials usually expand when heated and shrink when cooled. The increase in length per degree rise in temperature is called the coefficient of thermal expansion.

Chemical Properties

All environments are full of chemicals. The world, in fact, is totally made up of chemicals. The air is a chemical mixture of nitrogen, oxygen, sulphur dioxide (source of acid rain), and many other compounds. Water has many minerals mixed in it. It is said to be "hard" when it contains chemicals that prevent soap from working properly.

A material's chemical properties are the measurement of its ability to resist chemical action. Many chemicals cause engineering materials to corrode. Corrosion is a very complex action. However, we all see the results of it. Steel rusts; glass becomes pitted; plastics become etched or fractured. These are the results of corrosion, Fig. 2-18.

Electrical and Magnetic Properties

Electrical and magnetic properties measure a material's reaction to electrical current and external electromagnetic forces. One measure of these properties is *electrical conductivity.* This is the ability to conduct (transmit) electric current. Materials that carry current are called *conductors.* Those that do not are called *insulators.*

The opposite of electrical conductivity is *electrical resistivity.* It is a measure of a material's resistance to the flow of electric current. Insulators have very high resistivity. They are designed not to conduct electric current. Also, heating coils have high resistivity. They convert electrical energy to heat energy.

Magnetic properties relate to a material's ability to be magnetized by an outside electromagnetic force. This measure is called *permeability.* The

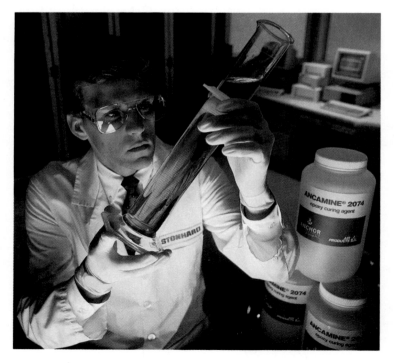

Fig. 2-18. This product manager is testing the chemical properties of a new floor finish. (Air Products and Chemical Co.)

highter the permeability, the easier it is to magnetize a material.

Optical Properties

Optical properties relate to a material's reaction to light waves, Fig. 2-19. Two main optical properties of general importance are:
- Opacity—Ability to stop light waves. Opaque materials block light. Window shades should have high opacity. The opposite is transmittance. Windows should have good transmittance.
- Color—Ability of a material to absorb certain light waves and reflect others. This property determines which light waves are reflected to the human eye.

Acoustical Properties

Acoustical properties relate to a material's reaction to sound waves, Fig. 2-20. Material's will vary in their ability to absorb sound (sound insulator), transmit sound, and reflect sound.

Fig. 2-20. The acoustical properties of a material can be tested in a sound chamber. (Arvin Industries)

SELECTING ENGINEERING MATERIALS

It is not enough just to know about materials. You, also, need to be able to select and buy them. You will have to know how to determine the amount and type of materials you need. This involves two major steps:
- Picking the type and grade of material needed.
- Determining the quantity needed.

Material Grades

Materials come in different grades or compositions. Each material has a system for labeling these conditions. Metals generally use a number system to determine the composition of each alloy. For example, the Aluminum Association has developed a four-digit (number) system to identify aluminum. These four digits are then followed with a code to show the hardness of the aluminum.

A number system is also used for steel alloys. The system uses a four-digit number. The first two digits indicate the alloy. The last two show the carbon content.

Other metals have their system for identifying alloys, too. Each is different and somewhat complex.

Lumber Grades

Careful control can produce a uniform steel, aluminum, or polymer material. However, nature

Fig. 2-19. A laser device uses optical properties to measure the size of a part. (Federal Mogul)

does not hold such tight controls on trees as they grow. Therefore, wood must have a quality grade. The strength and percentage of knots and defects must be identified. There are two separate systems for grading softwood and hardwood lumber.

Softwood grading

There are a number of softwood lumber grades. Three grades of softwood lumber that are commonly used are appearance-grade boards (selects), common boards, and framing lumber.

Hardwood grading

Hardwood lumber is produced to a standard thickness, but it varies in width and length. It is said to be "random width and length." The hardwood grading system has three major grades. These are first and seconds (FAS), selects, and common.

PURCHASING MATERIALS

Engineering materials are purchased by many companies and individuals. These materials are sold in standard sizes or quantities. The typical measurements, as shown in Fig. 2-21, are:
- Units.
- Weight.
- Surface measure.
- Volume.

Some materials are sold by counting *units*. Rolls of plastics are priced by the roll. Screws and bolts are sold by the hundred. Sheets of building materials (plywood, particleboard, hardboard, etc.) are sold individually.

Other materials are sold by their *weight*. Ceramic clay and Portland cement are sold by the pound,

hundred weight, or ton. Plastic pellets are also sold by their weight.

Surface measure is used in measuring many materials. The two typical measures are linear measure and area measure.

Linear measure is simply the length of the material in a unit. Small quantities of metal rod, strips, and angles are sold by the foot. Most indoor trim for houses is also sold by the foot. Since most people cannot figure board feet, many retail yards sell lumber by the foot or piece.

Area measure is a common way to measure partial sheets of building materials. Area is commonly measured in square feet. Plastic laminate (Formica™) is sold by the square foot. Shingles are sold by the square (100 square feet). Area, in square feet, is determined by multiplying the length of the piece (in feet) by its width (in feet).

The last way to measure materials is by **volume.** Two major methods used are cubic yards and board feet. Each of these measures requires you to calculate the mass of the material. You must multiply the thickness, width, and length together. Let us look at ways to determine each of these measures.

Cubic yards is the measure used for concrete. When you buy concrete you must decide the volume of material needed. A cubic yard is the amount of material that would fill a "container" that is one yard high, one yard wide, and one yard long or its equal, Fig. 2-22.

Board feet is the measurement for lumber. Lumber yards purchase lumber from mill by the board feet. A board foot is one inch thick by one foot square, Fig. 2-23. If the lumber is rough (not surfaced to size), you can use the material's actual size. However, for surfaced lumber, you cannot use

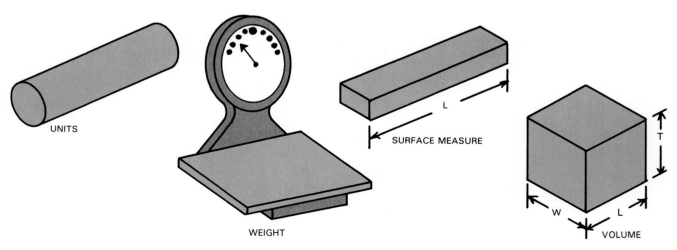

UNITS

WEIGHT

SURFACE MEASURE

L

VOLUME

T

W

L

Fig. 2-21. Methods of measuring the quantities of materials.

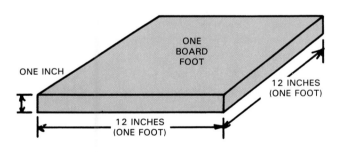

Fig. 2-22. Concrete (top) is sold by the cubic yard.

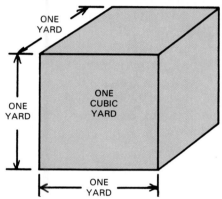

Fig. 2-23. A board foot is calculated by multiplying the width, by the length, by the thickness, and then divided by a constant. It is actually a measure of volume.

the size of the part. Board feet, then, is figured using the nominal (normal or original) size of the material. For example, the nominal thickness for materials less than one inch thick is one inch when figuring board feet. Typical nominal sizes for softwoods are shown in Fig. 2-24.

The number of board feet in a piece of lumber is determined by multiplying the nominal thickness (in inches) by the nominal width (in inches) by the

SOFTWOOD LUMBER SIZES		
	NOMINAL SIZE	**ACTUAL SIZE**
BOARDS	1 × 4 1 × 6 1 × 8 1 × 10 1 × 12	3/4 × 3 1/2 3/4 × 5 1/2 3/4 × 7 1/4 3/4 × 9 1/4 3/4 × 11 1/4
DIMENSIONAL LUMBER	2 × 4 2 × 6 2 × 8 2 × 10 2 × 12	1 1/2 × 3 1/2 1 1/2 × 5 1/2 1 1/2 × 7 1/4 1 1/2 × 9 1/4 1 1/2 × 11 1/4

Fig. 2-24. Nominal sizes of lumber are not the same as their actual size.

length. This answer is then divided by 144. For example, a 1 × 12 board (nominal dimensions) that is 12 inches long would be calculated as follows: 1 × 12 × 12 = 144; 144 ÷ 144 = 1 board foot.

When computing softwood *finish lumber,* use the thickness and width nominal sizes. Even though a 1 × 8 board would actually measure 3/4 inch × 7 1/4 inch, the "1" and the "8" are used in calculating the board measure.

For thicker *construction lumber,* the width nominal sizes are used for both the thickness and the width. For example, a 2 × 4 is really 1 1/2 × 3 1/2. Again, for rough lumber you use the actual sizes. Most hardwoods are sold this way.

SUMMARY

Materials are the foundation of our human-made world. Solid materials make up most of our permanent products. These materials are called engineering materials. They can be divided into metal, polymers, ceramics, and composites.

Each material has a unique set of properties. These properties are what make materials different from one another. A material's properties must be carefully considered as it is chosen for a specific use. Properties are commonly grouped into seven categories: mechanical, physical, thermal, chemical, electrical and magnetic, optical, and acoustical.

Material must be graded and sized for purchase. Commonly, materials are sold by the unit, weight, surface measure, or volume.

KEY WORDS

All the following words have been used in this chapter. Do you know their meaning?

Acoustical properties	Mechanical property
Alloy	Melting point
Brittleness	Metals
Cast iron	Opacity
Ceramic	Optical properties
Chemical properties	Permeability
Composite	Physical properties
Compression	Plasticity
Conifer	Polymer
Corrosion	Porosity
Deciduous	Properties
Density	Shear
Ductility	Steel
Elasticity	Stiffness
Electrical and	Strength
magnetic properties	Surface measure
Electrical conductivity	Tensile strength
Engineering materials	Tension
Fatigue	Thermal conductivity
Filler	Thermal expansion
Freezing point	Thermal properties
Hardness	Thermoplastic
Insulators	Thermoset
Linear measure	Torsion
Malleability	Toughness
Matrix	Volume

TEST YOUR KNOWLEDGE

Write your answers on a separate sheet of paper. Do not write in this book.

1. The three common types of metals are _____, _____, and _____.
2. What is the difference between a thermoplastic and a thermoset material?
3. Which of the following is or are NOT a ceramic material?
   A. Abrasives.   D. Glasses.
   B. Clay.   E. Inorganic cements.
   C. Refractories.   F. Polymers.
4. Ceramics are the hardest of all engineering materials. True or False?
5. _____ is a name given material having grains made up of smaller box-like structures or shapes. These small particles are called crystals.
6. The most common natural composite is _____.

   A. ceramic   C. steel
   B. glass   D. wood

7. What units are used in measuring materials for purchase?
8. _____ is a force that squeezes and crushes a material; _____ attempts to pull it apart.
9. Describe the difference between ductility and malleability.
10. Select the property most important in forming material under pressure:
    A. Ductility.
    B. Plasticity or malleability.
    C. Elasticity.
11. A spring should have the property of brittleness. True or False?
12. Wood floats in water because of the property of _____.
13. What property explains why heating one end of a copper rod will cause the other end to become warm also?
14. Chemical properties measure a material's ability to resist _____.
    A. rust
    B. chemicals (or corrosion)
    C. chemicals
    D. All of the above.
15. _____ is the ability of a material to absorb certain light waves and reflect others.

ACTIVITIES

1. Collect a variety of materials that are used to make cups. (They are often made from steel, aluminum, paper, plastic, and clay [china].)
   A. Arrange these materials according to their hardness, density, thermal conductivity, and strength.
   B. Which material would you use in a cup for the following uses: camping trip, picnic, formal dining, vending machines. Explain the reasons for your selections.
2. You are asked to select a material for a diving board. Which properties would you consider in your selection? Why?
3. Interview a salesperson at a lumber yard. Ask about the methods of measuring various materials for sale.
4. Gather pictures of various materials, then group them by their type (metal, plastic, ceramic, composite). Use the pictures in a scrapbook or bulletin board.
5. With your teacher's help, calculate the linear measure, surface measure, volume (cubic feet and board feet) of several materials.

Materials are the foundation for all products and structures.   (Bethlehem Steel)

Section II
PRODUCTION MANAGEMENT

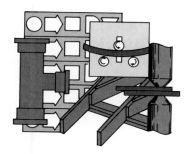

Chapter 3

ORGANIZING A PRODUCTION ENTERPRISE

After reading this chapter, you will be able to:
☐ Describe three methods of ownership.
☐ Discuss advantages and disadvantages of each type of ownership.
☐ Identify steps required by law to form a company.
☐ Identify the roles of managers in companies that manufacture and construct products.
☐ List and explain the tasks of management.
☐ List five kinds of activities carried on by management.
☐ Describe three kinds of company organization.
☐ Describe how a company determines its money needs.
☐ List ways of financing (getting money) for starting a company.
☐ Name two major types of financial records kept by manufacturing companies.
☐ List and describe the major types of budgets.
☐ State the difference between assets and liabilities.

Production enterprises produce the products and structures that make up the human-made world. These enterprises are organized by a person or group of people. These people are often called *entrepreneurs*. They have the ability to see opportunities and capitalize on them.

As the company is organized, decisions are made. The main questions that must be answered are:
• What type of ownership will be used?
• What managerial structure will work best?
• How will finances be raised?
• How will financial records be kept?

Each new company faces the same questions. Let's look at these elements one at a time.

FORMS OF OWNERSHIP

Most companies are publicly owned. In other words, they are owned by one or more individuals. The government does not own them. Also, most companies are formed to make money for the owners. They are said to be *profit-centered.*

There are three forms of public, profit-centered ownership. These are proprietorship, partnership, and corporation. See Fig. 3-1.

Proprietorship

A *proprietorship* is a business enterprise owned by one person—the proprietor. Many small contractors, service stations, antique shops, farms, and retail stores are owned by a single individual.

The proprietorship is easy to form and management structure is simple. The owner directly controls all operations, giving the company flexibility (ability to change easily). It can react quickly to changes in the market. Finally, the owner has the right to all after-tax profits, Fig. 3-2.

However, a proprietorship cannot easily raise money. Thus, its growth is sometimes held back. Also, few individuals have all the talents needed to run a company. Limited management talent can result in serious problems for the enterprise. Finally, the owner is responsible for all debts of the company. If the company fails, the owner must pay the debts with his or her personal wealth.

Partnership

A *partnership* is an association of two or more people who run a legal business. Such businesses usually are easy to start and end. They can offer more management talent. Also, the owners have

Fig. 3-1. Three forms of ownership.

Fig. 3-2. Advantages of a proprietorship.

Corporate owners have a definite advantage. They have limited liability. The corporation, not the owners, is responsibile for all debts. Owners can lose their first investment if a corporation fails. They, however, do not have to furnish money to pay outstanding debts.

Corporations also have some disadvantages. The owners generally have little interest in the daily operations of the company. Their main interest is in dividends. This interest often causes management to work toward big short-term earnings. Long-term growth may not be given proper attention.

Fig. 3-3. A corporation is a "person" in the eyes of the law.

more ways to raise money for the company. The partners must still accept unlimited liability for the company debts. Also, the owner-managers might have arguments. They must share responsibilities as well as profits.

Corporation

Most manufacturing and larger construction companies are corporations. A *corporation* is a legally created business unit. It is an "artificial being" in the eyes of the law, Fig. 3-3. It is created in one state and can operate in all states. Like all beings, corporations can own property. They can sue or be sued and enter into contracts.

FORMING A COMPANY

All enterprises must become a legal company. Most manufacturing and larger construction companies are corporations. Therefore, the rest of this unit is limited to forming a corporation.

As we said before, a corporation is an artificial being. Therefore, it must be born. This birth process must follow steps shown in Fig. 3-4.

Articles of Incorporation

A corporation is controlled by three major things. These are:
- The laws of the state where it is formed.
- The corporate articles of incorporation.
- The corporate bylaws.

Laws of each state vary somewhat. However, all states provide basic rules for ownership and financing of a company. The company must select a state where it wants to incorporate. It prepares an application form. This form is called the *articles of incorporation* or application for a charter. It is filed with the proper state official. The certificate usually requires:
- Name of the company.
- Purpose for forming the company.
- Names and addresses of those people involved in forming it.
- Location of the company office in the state.
- Type and value of the stock to be sold.

Corporate Charter

The state officials review the articles of incorporation. They also determine the filing fee. This fee is generally based on the number and value of the shares of stock to be sold.

When the articles are approved and the fees are paid, a *corporate charter* is issued. This charter authorizes the company to do business in the state. The charter is the corporate "birth certificate."

Corporate Bylaws

The corporate charter is very general. It does not give many directions for running the company. This information is provided in the company *bylaws*, Fig. 3-5. Most bylaws outline:
- Date and location of the annual stockholders' meeting.
- Date and place of periodic board of directors' meetings.
- List of corporate officers with their duties, terms of office, and method of appointment.
- Number, duties, and terms of office of the directors.

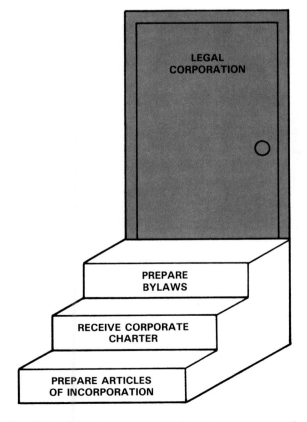

Fig. 3-4. The three steps in forming a corporation.

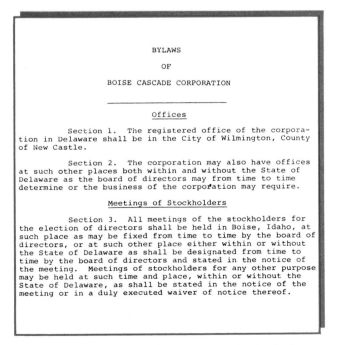

Fig. 3-5. A portion of a corporation's bylaws. (Boise-Cascade Corp.)

- Types of proposals that must have stockholder approval.
- Method to be used to change the bylaws.

The stockholders have the power to develop and change the bylaws. They often delegate this power to the board of directors. In the end, the stockholders have little control over the company. This power rests with the major corporate managers and the board of directors.

PRODUCTION ENTERPRISES

Production enterprises are formed to produce a great variety of products and structures. Each of these companies convert materials into usable products. They employ production and managerial techniques to reach this goal.

Each production system has the same seven components, Fig. 3-6. First, and foremost, every production system must be managed. *Management* coordinates (brings together to do one thing) the basic inputs of *people, machines,* and *materials.* These inputs are paid for with *money.* Materials and machines are purchased. People receive wages or salaries for their time and work. These resources are brought together by *methods.* These are the "ways of doing things." The people use machines to change the form of material. They produce products or construct structures. These outputs are sold in the *market.* People pay to use or own these products.

The money the company gets from sales is called *income.* The income must pay for two things. First, it pays the cost of producing the products. This cost is called *expenses.* The other use for income is *profit.* This is the money left after all expenses (including taxes) are paid.

Profit is used in two ways. Some is kept by the company to reinvest in additional productive capital. It pays for such things as new machines, buildings, or product development. This money is called *retained earnings.* Profit also pays *dividends.* This is a payment to the owners. It rewards them for investing their money in the company. Dividends are usually paid to the owners quarterly (every three months).

MANAGEMENT

Management guides and directs company activities. The goal is efficient use of company resources, Fig. 3-7. An understanding of management can be developed by studying the functions of management (what managers do), levels of management, and managed areas of activity.

Functions of Management

Managers of production activities have four basic functions (tasks). These functions, shown in Fig. 3-8, are described as follows:
- Planning—Setting goals and courses of action (steps) to be followed.

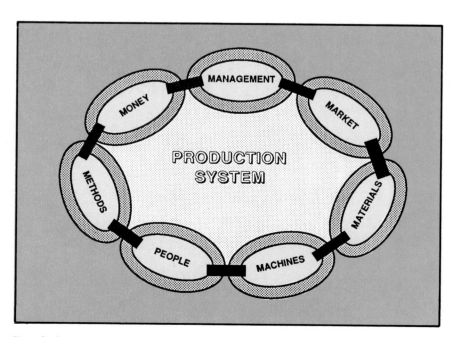

Fig. 3-6. The ingredients for a successful production system.

Fig. 3-7. Managers use many techniques to guide and direct company activities. (American Association of Blacks in Energy)

Fig. 3-8. Managers plan (A), organize (B), direct (C), and control (D) company activities. (Rohm & Haas)

- Organizing — Dividing tasks into jobs and establishing lines of authority (who gives orders to whom).
- Directing — Assigning employees to jobs and encouraging them to complete their work efficiently.
- Controlling — Comparing the results of employees' work with the company plan.

Planning

Planning, Fig. 3-9, is the first step of management. It sets the goals for the company or for one of its activities. Basically, managers' plans begin by gathering information about the task or problem. Once the information is obtained, it is arranged so they have a "picture" of the task or problem. From here, several solutions or courses of action are identified. Finally, the best course of action is decided upon.

Planning is used for all parts of the company. It may be done to establish goals for the entire company. Also, it can be used to set smaller goals, production goals, financial goals, or training goals. These goals can be short term — daily or weekly. They may also be part of long-term goals that cover one or more years.

Organizing

Organizing is assigning resources and importance to tasks. Each task uses human, material, and capital resources. The people must also be given authority to complete the work. They must understand how their job fits within the overall company activity. Individuals need to know who answers to them. They, likewise, need to know to whom they must answer. Organizing involves three big decisions:

- Who is to do each task?
- How much authority is needed to complete each task?
- How many resources are needed to complete each task?

Directing

Direction begins when goals are set and tasks are organized. Now people must be assigned to do these

Fig. 3-9. This product planning session allows employees to exchange ideas. (Nevada Power Co.)

jobs. However, more is needed. They must be trained and motivated (given a reason) to work efficiently, Fig. 3-10. To be successful, the directing phase must let employees know why each task is important. In addition, they must know how to complete the task, and the rewards (pay and recognition) for doing the job well.

Managers who direct employees will provide proper training. They will also let each worker know he or she is important to success. Each task — large or small — is a step toward moving a product or structure from an idea to the consumer.

Controlling

As work is completed, it must be checked and measured. The results of human effort must be compared to the company goals, Fig. 3-11. This task is called *controlling.*

The quality of the product must be controlled. Raw and finished goods inventories (lists of what is on hand) are controlled. The financial resources, hours worked, and cost of production are also controlled. Hundreds of things about the company operation must be measured and compared to plans. In order to do this successfully, managers:

- Gather performance data (facts) about the sales, production, payroll, etc.
- Compare performance to the plan.
- Determine if changes are needed.
- Decide what action should be taken.
- Begin the right action to correct any problem.

A plan may work the first time. However, management does not stop there. Plans are constantly revised. They challenge the company to

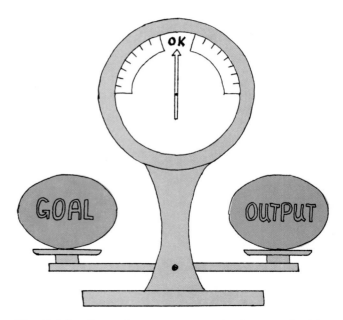

Fig. 3-11. Control compares results (outputs) with the goals of the operation.

become more efficient. Improvements can increase the company's productivity (output for total amount of labor). A more-productive company can pay its workers more or sell its products for less. A healthy company can finance new products and plants. It can grow larger and employ more people.

Levels of Management

Managers must organize the company. They will establish levels of authority. Some people are given more responsibility than others. Some employees have greater decision-making powers than other employees. There is a "pecking order" within the company. This is true of all organizations.

Think about the school you are in. There are many citizens in your school district. They probably do not have the time or ability to run the schools. So, most likely, voters elected a school board. The board then hired a superintendent. He or she manages the day-to-day operation of the school district. Larger districts have several assistant superintendents. Each manages a certain area such as curriculum, personnel, and business affairs.

Principals are hired to manage individual schools. Often, people are assigned to oversee (supervise) departments, such as technology education, science, and history. Instructors teach the classes offered by the departments. The students are offered a chance to learn. They are the consumer of the school's product.

Production companies are very much like schools, Fig. 3-12. They also have an organization.

Fig. 3-10. These employees receive training as part of management's directing role. (General Motors)

Let's look at a typical construction or manufacturing corporation.

Most corporations have many *stockholders* (owners). They, like the voters of the school district, cannot run the company. They probably live all over the country. They may not know how to manage an enterprise. They elect a group to represent them. This group is called the *board of directors.* The board gives the company direction by forming policy. The board hires a full-time manager called a *president.* He or she has several *vice presidents* who are in charge of a major part of the company. There may be vice presidents for sales, marketing, engineering, production, personnel, and other departments.

Let us look at the production level of the company structure. The next level is the *plant manager* in manufacturing or the *project manager* in construction. This individual is in charge of a manufacturing facility or construction project. He or she manages all activities at that site. A manufacturing plant is usually divided into departments such as machining, shipping, accounting, or welding. They are run by *department heads* who are aided by *supervisors.* These individuals assign and supervise the production *workers.*

In construction, a number of superintendents may report to the project manager. Below the superintendents are supervisors who direct the work of the workers—carpenters, plumbers, electricians, and other tradespeople.

Areas of Activities

Managers have functions to carry out. They are given a certain amount of authority to do their job. They also work in certain areas. These areas move a product from the idea stage to completion. When all the work is done, an idea becomes a product. It is then sold to customers for a profit.

There are five major managed areas of activity. These areas, as shown in Fig. 3-13, are:

- Research and development (manufacturing) or Engineering (construction)—Discovers, develops, and specifies new and improved products or structures.
- Production—Engineers (designs and sets up) manufacturing facilities or construction procedures to produce products or structures that meet quality standards.
- Marketing—Identifies (finds) the people who will buy the structures or products. Then marketing promotes, sells, and transfers ownership to them.
- Industrial or labor relations—Operates programs to find and train the company workforce. It also promotes things that make the public and workers feel good about the company.
- Financial affairs—Raises and controls the company's money.

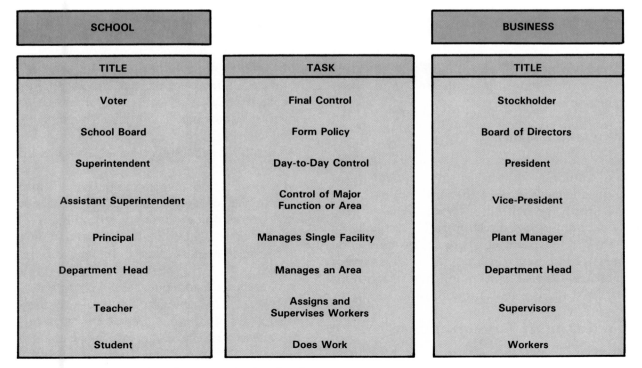

SCHOOL		BUSINESS
TITLE	TASK	TITLE
Voter	Final Control	Stockholder
School Board	Form Policy	Board of Directors
Superintendent	Day-to-Day Control	President
Assistant Superintendent	Control of Major Function or Area	Vice-President
Principal	Manages Single Facility	Plant Manager
Department Head	Manages an Area	Department Head
Teacher	Assigns and Supervises Workers	Supervisors
Student	Does Work	Workers

Fig. 3-12. A comparison between the levels of management and authority in a school and a business.

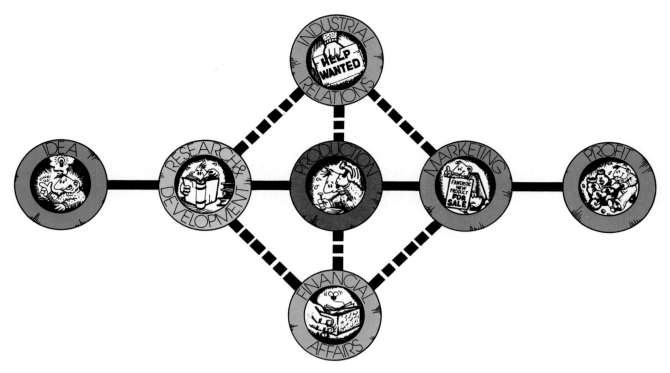

Fig. 3-13. The five managed activity areas move product ideas into reality.

DEVELOPING A MANAGEMENT STRUCTURE

Running a corporation properly takes a team of persons to manage it. For each important function (task) in the company there will be a manager. There may be several levels of managers each with additional managers and staff. This is called a *management structure.* So that everyone knows who is her or his boss, the lines of authority are sketched into a chart. There are a number of organization models. The two most common types are line organization and line and staff organization.

Line Organization

This type of organization is the simplest. A single line of authority flows from the president to the vice presidents, Fig. 3-14. From there, authority flows directly through various levels to the workers. All information and direction flows vertically up and down the structure. There are no horizontal connections between different tasks. This type of organization is also called a military structure. It works well in very small organizations.

Line and Staff Organization

The line and staff organization is used for larger companies, Fig. 3-15. The major line managers have staff officers to advise them. The line officers still have the authority over operations. Staff advice helps them manage more effectively.

DETERMINING FINANCIAL NEEDS

All companies need money to operate. On-going companies can obtain most of their money from sales. New and expanding companies must raise finances from outside sources. Companies find out how much money they need by making up a budget. Budgets are estimates of income and expenses. They detail the costs of operation and sources of income. There are five major types of budgets, Fig. 3-16:

- A sales budget forecasts sales for a specific period.
- A production budget predicts the number of products to be produced to meet the sales budget.
- A production expense budget estimates production costs. They include material, labor, and overhead costs such as equipment, utilities, and rent.
- A general expense budget predicts cost not directly related to the manufacture of products. This includes marketing and administrative costs. Research and development, financial affairs, industrial relations, and top management's expenses are often considered administrative costs.
- A master budget summarizes all other budgets.

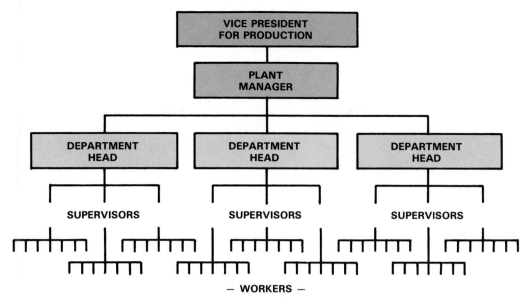

Fig. 3-14. A line organization chart.

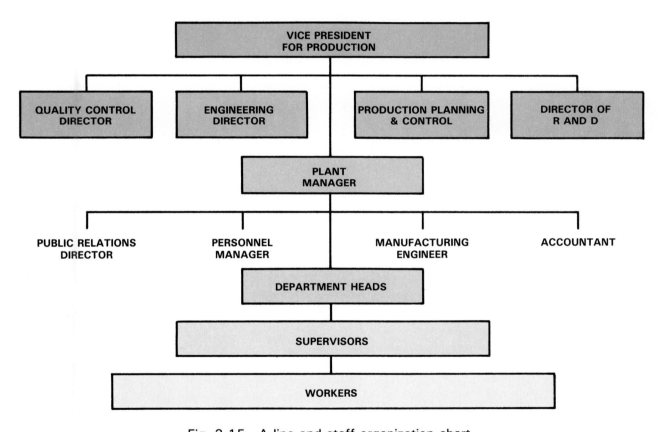

Fig. 3-15. A line and staff organization chart.

GETTING FINANCING

Budgets help managers determine their company's need for money. Often this money must be raised from sources outside the company. There are two main ways to raise outside financing. Ownership rights to the company can be sold. This technique is called *equity financing*. People are sold stock, Fig. 3-17. They become part owners (shareholders) of the company.

Companies can also borrow money. They can use *debt financing*. Basically they agree to "rent" some money. Someone will provide money for a period of time. The company must repay the money plus interest (rent).

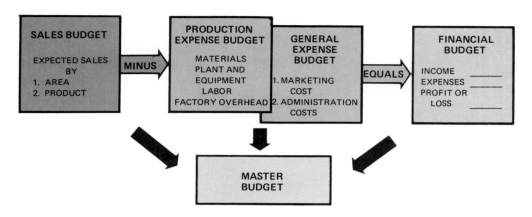

Fig. 3-16. A chart showing the relationships that exists between types of budgets.

Fig. 3-17. A sample stock certificate.

MAINTAINING FINANCIAL RECORDS

Obtaining financing is only part of the financial picture. All companies must manage the use of their money. To do this, they must monitor (review) their financial results. This activity requires financial records. Keeping financial records is often called *accounting*. Many companies keep two types of accounting records. These are general accounting and cost accounting.

General Accounting

Budgets are a prediction of financial activity. *General accounting* records this activity. It involves two major tasks. The first task involves recording financial transactions (dealings). The other task deals with summarizing financial activities.

Recording transactions

Most accounting systems are based on a ledger or journal. Various financial actions are recorded. Each action is described and dated. The amount of the transaction is entered. Money going out is entered in the debit column. These are expenses. Income from sales and other sources is entered in the credit column.

Summarizing financial activities

Ledgers help accountants record financial actions. Other managers want a more general report such as balance sheets and income statements.

A *balance sheet* "balances" assets with liabilities. It lists all the things owned by and owed to the company. These items are called *assets.* They include cash and securities (stocks and bonds), accounts receivable (money owed to the company), inventories (materials and goods in plants and warehouses), and property (plant, and equipment).

Balance sheets also list what the company owes. These are called *liabilities.* They include accounts payable (money owed other companies), salaries and fringe benefits for employees, debts, and deferred taxes (taxes due later).

The assets should exceed liabilites. A company should own more than it owes. The excess is shown as *stockholders' equity.* This is the actual value of the stockholders' ownership (equity). A recent balance sheet is shown in Fig. 3-18.

The second report is an *income statement,* Fig. 3-19. This report is also called a profit and loss statement. It shows the financial success for the year. It lists net (total) sales. The cost of the products sold is then subtracted. The result is *gross profit.* Next, the general expenses are subtracted. The remainder is called *operating profit.* Finally, other income and expenses are entered. The resulting figure is "profit before taxes." Taxes are subtracted giving the *net income.*

Cost Accounting

The second financial record system is cost accounting. It maintains records for each product line, plant, or construction project. The income for each of these is recorded. Also, each expense item is charged to them.

Cost accounting is a valuable tool. It pinpoints plants, projects, or products that are doing well. Others needing attention are also identified.

SUMMARY

All beginning companies must be organized and financed. They become a legal business by meeting certain state requirements. They may be formed as proprietorships, partnerships, or corporations.

The company must establish a managerial structure. Responsibilities and lines of authority for managers must be developed.

Finally, money must be raised to run the company. Budgets are developed to determine financial needs. Money is obtained through equity or debt financing.

Managers must control the company's money. Each financial transaction is recorded. Income and expenses are entered into ledgers. Each product, project, or plant must make money. Cost accounting keeps track of their progress.

KEY WORDS

All the following words have been used in this chapter. Do you know their meaning?

Accounting
Articles of
  incorporation
Assets
Balance sheet
Board of directors
Bond
Budget
Budgeting
Bylaws
Charter
Controlling
Corporate charter
Corporation
Debt financing
Department head
Directing
Dividends
Entrepreneur
Equity financing
Expense
General accounting
Gross profit income
  statement
Level of authority
Line organization
Line and staff
  organization
Liability

Loan
Management
Management structure
Organizing
Partnership
Planning
Plant manager
President
Profit-centered
Project manager
Proprietorship
Retained earnings
Stockholders
Stockholders' equity
Supervisors
Vice president
Workers

CONSOLIDATED BALANCE SHEET
December 31, 19XX and 19YY

ASSETS	19XX	19YY
Current Assets:		
Cash and marketable securities	$ 209,030,000	$ 203,350,000
Receivables	201,610,000	163,380,000
Inventories	248,230,000	243,620,000
Prepaid expenses	10,210,000	11,410,000
Total current assets	669,080,000	621,760,000
Investments in Partially Owned Companies	45,550,000	41,600,000
Receivables and Investments, Related-Party	39,050,000	36,880,000
Other Assets	168,790,000	171,440,000
Property and Equipment	348,940,000	350,480,000
	$1,271,410,000	**$1,222,160,000**

LIABILITIES and SHAREHOLDERS' EQUITY		
Current Liabilities:		
Notes payable	$ 13,530,000	$ 123,890,000
Accounts payable	43,740,000	34,170,000
Income taxes	22,060,000	28,610,000
Accrued liabilities	50,040,000	48,540,000
Total current liabilities	129,370,000	235,210,000
Long-Term Debt	367,640,000	372,540,000
Deferred Income Taxes	45,600,000	25,020,000
Shareholders' Equity	728,800,000	589,390,000
	$1,271,410,000	**$1,222,160,000**

The accompanying notes are an integral part of the consolidated financial statements.

Fig. 3-18. A sample balance sheet.

TEST YOUR KNOWLEDGE

Place your answers on a separate sheet of paper. Do not write in this book.

1. Name and describe the three profit-centered types of company ownership.
2. The _____ _____ _____ is an application form for a state charter.
3. Most bylaws outline six basic directions by which companies run. What is included in these directions?
4. What are the three factors you must study to understand management?
5. From the following list, select those activities which are the functions of management.
   A. Planning (setting goals and courses of action).
   B. Identifying markets.
   C. Organizing (assigning tasks to certain jobs and establishing lines of authority).
   D. Directing (assigning employees to jobs).
   E. Controlling (comparing employees' work with company plan).
   F. All of the above.

CONSOLIDATED STATEMENT OF INCOME
for the years ended December 31, 19XX, 19YY and 19ZZ

	19XX	19YY	19ZZ
Net sales	$1,059,450,000	$855,740,000	$876,530,000
Cost of sales	687,850,000	557,110,000	571,400,000
Gross profit	371,600,000	298,630,000	305,130,000
Selling, general and administrative expenses	183,810,000	150,440,000	139,910,000
Operating profit	187,790,000	148,190,000	165,220,000
Other expense (income), net:			
Interest expense	40,840,000	40,210,000	39,870,000
Other income, net	(29,370,000)	(27,070,000)	(25,390,000)
	11,470,000	13,140,000	14,480,000
Income before income taxes and extraordinary income	176,320,000	135,050,000	150,740,000
Income taxes	69,760,000	57,410,000	62,420,000
Income before extraordinary income ($1.50 per share in 1982)	106,560,000	77,640,000	88,320,000
Extraordinary income from retirement of debentures	–	14,510,000	–
Net income	$ 106,560,000	$ 92,150,000	$ 88,320,000
Earnings per share	$1.93	$1.78	$1.73

The accompanying notes are an integral part of the consolidated financial statements.

Fig. 3-19. A typical income statement.

Matching questions: Match the definition in the left-hand column with the correct term in the right-hand column.

6. Manages a major activity within the production facility.
7. Manages a major segment of the company.
8. Directs the work of production workers.
9. Single line of authority flows from president to vice presidents; from them to workers.
10. Major line officers have staff officers to advise them.

    A. Line organization.
    B. Supervisor.
    C. Line and staff organization.
    D. Department head.
    E. Vice president.

11. What are three major types of financial records kept by manufacturing companies?
12. List and describe the major types of budgets.
13. All the things a company has are called _____; what the company owes is called _____.
14. List the uses for profits.

ACTIVITIES

1. Study the organization of a church, school club, or other group. List the officers (managers) of the group according to the level of authority. Prepare an organizational chart.
2. Assume you are going to organize a group to clean a vacant lot for a playground. List the basic things you would do to:
   A. Plan the activity.
   B. Organize the group.
   C. Direct the group.
   D. Control the activity.

3. Visit a local company and obtain their organization chart. Share it with your class.
4. Assume you and two friends are going to start a lawn care service. What type of ownership would you use and why? What type of steps would you need to take to start the service?
5. Invite an accountant to speak to your class on maintaining financial records.

Production enterprises produce materials and products that make up the human-made world.   (NASA)

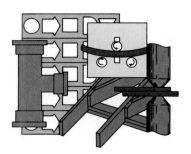

Chapter 4

PROCURING RESOURCES

After reading this chapter, you will be able to:
- ☐ List steps for hiring workers and describe how hiring is done.
- ☐ List the six major steps for buying materials.
- ☐ Describe various personnel and materials forms and state their uses.
- ☐ State reasons why safety on the job is important to yourself and the company.
- ☐ List and discuss the four major phases of a safety program.
- ☐ List four steps in proper job safety training.

Once the company has been organized and financed, production plans can be made. Designers and architects developed product and structure plans. Architectural and engineering drawings have been prepared. Production plans and specifications have been approved. Production equipment and facilities can be developed. Operations are selected and sequenced. However, this is not enough.

The company cannot produce structures or products without more resources. Workers must be hired. Materials must be ordered.

EMPLOYING WORKERS

Employees are people hired to do a specific job. The company matches workers' abilities with its needs. This task is called employment. It requires the six major steps listed in Fig. 4-1.

Determining Needs

The employment official must be told to hire a worker. The process will differ between manufac-

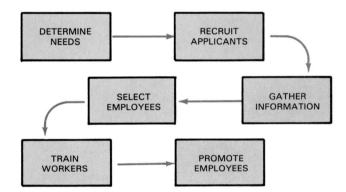

Fig. 4-1. Six steps are followed in the employment and advancement of workers.

turing and construction companies, Fig. 4-2. Manufacturing companies generally hire workers for long periods of time. Construction companies maintain managerial and design personnel for long periods. Construction workers, such as plumbers, carpenters, and electricians, may be hired by the job. Often, they work for the company only as long as they are needed on a specific project.

The employment process often starts with an employee requisition (request) form. This form tells the employment office the job title, skills required, and the date an employee is needed. Receiving a job requisition starts the employment process. It provides basic hiring information.

Recruiting Applicants

People must be found to fill job vacancies (openings). The employment office must find individuals who can do the job. This process is called **recruitment.**

Fig. 4-2. Manufacturing workers (left) generally work for a company for a long time. Construction workers (right) often only work as long as a certain building project lasts.   (Ford Motor Co., Rohm & Haas)

There are four basic ways to recruit employees for manufacturing positions. These are shown in Fig. 4-3, and include advertisements, walk-ins, employment agencies, and schools.

The technique used will vary with the job opening. General factory and office positions and many construction jobs may be filled by walk-ins. These positions are filled by people who come to the company looking for a job. They find the company and the job.

Jobs requiring more skill are filled by other methods. These jobs may include construction and manufacturing managers, technical staff, and skilled operators. Recruiters may visit schools and interview prospective employees.

The company may advertise in newspapers and special technical magazines for trained people. They may also use employment agencies.

A special employment situation is present on unionized construction projects. On-site skilled workers are hired as they are needed for the project. When the work is finished, they are often released by the company. The company uses the union as a source of workers. Each trade (carpenters, electricians, brick masons, etc.) union's business agent maintains a list of qualified workers that are available. People on this list are referred to the contractor as work becomes available.

Gathering Information

Employers need information about an applicant (person seeking a job). They will use the informa-

tion to decide how suited the applicant is for the job. These facts may be gathered in several ways, including:

- Application blank. This is a form that provides basic personal data (facts) and work records.
- Interview. The applicant answers questions about his or her previous work experience, goals, and training, Fig. 4-4.
- Test. An applicant takes a written or performance test to measure her or his ability to do a job.

Fig. 4-3. These four methods may be used to recruit employees.

Fig. 4-4. This prospective worker is being interviewed for a job. (ARO Corp.)

Selecting Employees

It is in a company's best interest to choose the best applicant for each job. Information from the application blanks, interviews, and tests are used to arrive at the best choice. The best applicant is one who can do well on the job and fit well into the company. In addition, the applicant is willing to accept training. He or she also wants to advance (get ahead) in the company.

The person selected is now hired. He or she will receive a job notice or an employment letter. It will tell the worker when to report for work. The job title and pay rate are included in the notice or letter.

Training Employees

Few people can start a job without some training. All workers need some basic information. They should know something about the company itself. An understanding of the company's products, competitors, and plant or construction site locations is also important. Basic rules about hours, pay rates, and work practices must be presented. This information is often given in an induction training session for new employees. They then receive any special training they need.

Production (factory manufacturing and on-site construction) workers may receive training through:

• On-the-job training. This is training at the per-son's workstation. Actual products on the production line are used. A supervisor or another worker does the training.

• Vestibule (off-site, classroom) training. This type of training is done in a special training area. Workers produce actual products or structures. However, the training location is away from the manufacturing line, Fig. 4-5, or construction site. A special instructor is often used.

Fig. 4-5. Vestibule training is conducted in a location away from the manufacturing line. (A.C. Rochester)

- Apprenticeship. Such work preparation combines on-the-job and classroom training, Fig. 4-6. This type is used to prepare skilled construction and manufacturing workers. A skilled worker provides the on-the-job training. Often the classroom instruction is provided by a special teacher.
- Cooperative education. The new worker gets training by attending school part-time and working part-time.

Employees also receive additional training during their work life. Individuals attend conferences and workshops. Often, construction unions conduct member training sessions on new construction techniques. Manufacturing employees receive training in new developments, methods, and equipment, Fig. 4-7. This on-going employee development is essential for company growth.

Advancing in Manufacturing

Employees often change jobs. They develop new skills and knowledge. They are given more responsibility. They advance to better jobs. These jobs are more secure and pay more.

Managers prefer workers who want to get ahead. Workers can show this by their willingness to accept new job and training opportunities.

Progressing in Construction

Those who work hard and are the best trained progress the quickest.

To progress on a job, both pay and job level may change. A worker can progress in four directions.

Fig. 4-6. Workers receiving classroom training.

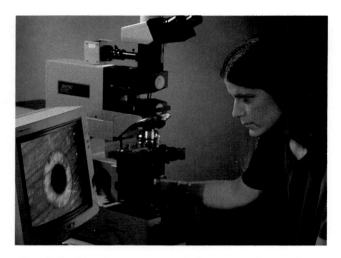

Fig. 4-7. Employees attend classes to learn about new technology. (Goodyear Tire and Rubber Co.)

The first is up. We most often think of progress in this way. A person who moves up will have an increase in pay and job level. Crafters who become supervisors will earn more money. They are in charge of a crew. They will decide things that direct the crew. This is not true for crafters.

Supervisors can progress downward. This may happen because they prefer not to be in charge. A person who cannot handle a crew may be put at a lower job level.

Lateral (movement across) progress results in no change in wages or job level. The transfer of a supervisor to another project is lateral progress. The person may have asked for the transfer. Maybe the home office felt the person knew more about the other job.

Separation is the last way to progress. People leave firms for many reasons. The person may feel that progress in some other firm is faster. The person may not be happy working for the firm. The firm may not be happy with the person. That person may quit or be fired.

PURCHASING MATERIALS

Products are made of many parts and materials. Each of these may be bought. Raw materials must be purchased by steel mills. Steel is bought by appliance manufacturers. Finished parts, like motors, are purchased by power tool manufacturers. Purchasing takes place at each step of manufacture, Fig. 4-8. Likewise, construction companies must purchase basic materials like gravel, lumber, and concrete. They also buy manufactured goods like windows, plumbing fixtures, and electrical supplies.

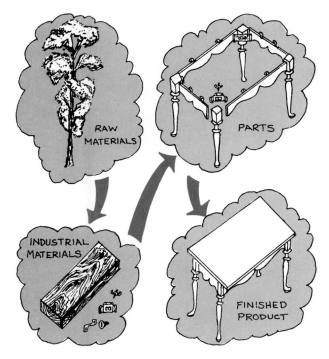

Fig. 4-8. Purchasing takes place at each step in manufacturing.

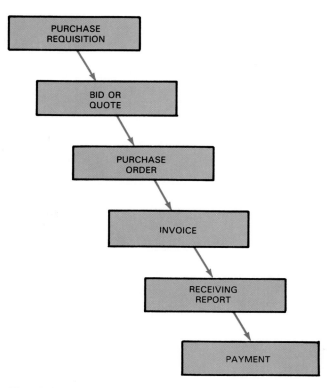

Fig. 4-9. Steps in the purchasing procedure. Filing of proper forms keeps track of each purchase.

Purchasing brings suppliers and users together. This effort involves six major steps. These, as shown in Fig. 4-9, are:
• Requisition (request) materials.
• Get bids or quotes.
• Issue a purchase order.
• Receive shipment and invoice.
• Accept shipment and get receiving report.
• Pay for materials.

Each of these steps involves forms. Paperwork records each activity. These forms are important for controlling purchasing activities. They ensure that the right material or equipment is ordered and received.

Material Requisition

The purchasing office buys materials when told what is needed. This may be done in a material requisition. Proper forms keep track of each purchase. A material requisition lists:
• Material needed.
• Quantity required.
• Delivery date.
• Delivery location (plant, department, and other vital information).

Often production or construction planners fill out the requisition form. It is their job to determine when material and human resources are needed.

Bids and Quotes

Purchasing officers must get costs for requested materials. First, they must find suppliers (vendors). Then, a request for a price is sent to each vendor selected.

The vendors submit their prices for the materials. Some prices must be guaranteed (firm) for a period of time. These are called **bids.** Other prices are current prices. They are the purchase price for that day. These prices are called **quotes.**

Purchase Orders

Purchasing personnel review prices. They study the bids and quotes and choose the best supplier. The choice weighs several factors including price, material quality, delivery date, and the vendor's reputation.

The purchasing people then prepare a purchase order. It is sent to the selected vendor. The purchase order, Fig. 4-10, lists the quantity needed, material description, and price. It also tells where the order is to be sent.

The vendor signs a copy of the purchase order. This copy is returned to the company. The purchase order has become a legal, binding contract. The vendor must supply the materials. The purchaser must pay for them.

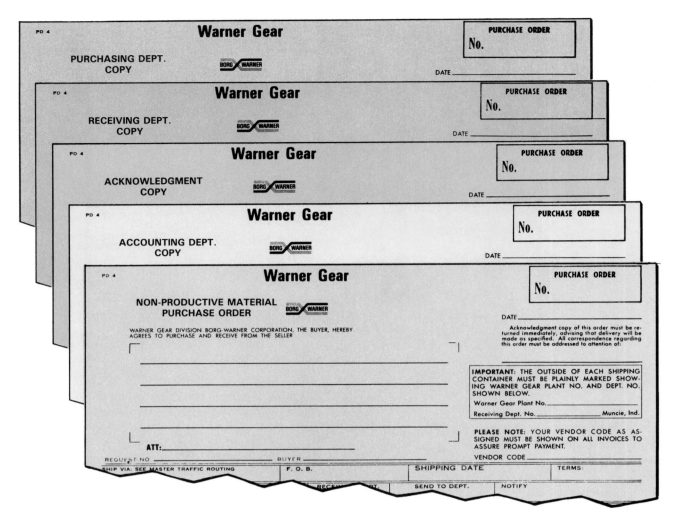

Fig. 4-10. Sample of a large company's purchase order. Note the number of copies needed.

Invoice

When the ordered materials are shipped, a bill is also sent. This form is called an *invoice.* The invoice indicates that the order has been shipped. It also informs the company that they owe the vendor for the materials.

Receiving Report

Often, materials ordered from one location are received in another. For example, an order may come from a Boise construction office, but may need to be delivered to a Kansas City construction site. The order and receipt of materials must be coordinated.

The Kansas City receiving area receives copies of the original purchase order from the Boise office. This tells the receiving area, "These items are ordered. Be ready to receive them." When the order arrives, Kansas City checks the shipment, Fig. 4-11. They compare the purchase order with the materials received. They should match. If they do, Kansas City signs a copy of the purchase order. It becomes a receiving report that is sent to the purchasing office. The signed order tells purchasing officers in Boise that the proper materials have arrived safely.

Payment

The receiving report and the invoice are compared. The materials and prices are checked. The invoice and the purchase order should match. If they do, the invoice is approved for payment. A check is written. The vendor is paid. The purchasing cycle is complete.

MAINTAINING WORKER SAFETY

Safety is an important concern for both the company and the employees. They both suffer when accidents happen. Injured employees suffer

Fig. 4-11. A worker is inspecting newly purchased construction project parts. (American Cast Iron Pipe Co.)

physical pain. They may lose income. Their insurance plan may not cover all their expenses.

Companies, as a result of accidents, can lose the services of valued employees. They cannot use the employees' special skills and knowledge for a period of time. The company will also lose money. Insurance rates are based on accident history. The more accidents a company has, the higher their rates will be.

The Safety Program

Modern construction and manufacturing companies have well-designed safety programs. These programs start with the new worker. They continue throughout the employee's worklife, Fig. 4-12.

These safety programs contain five major phases. The phases are shown in Fig. 4-13.

Safety engineering

Some jobs are safer than others. The person with a desk job is relatively safe. A person on a construction site is more likely to get hurt, Fig. 4-14.

Most jobs can be made safer. The equipment can be engineered to be safely operated, Fig. 4-15. Guards can be placed over cutter heads and saw blades. Controls can be placed in convenient locations. Emergency stop switches can be located within easy reach.

Workers may be removed from very dangerous operations. Mechanical devices may be engineered

to do the job instead. Robots do many dangerous jobs. They are often used to load punch presses, do welding, and apply finishes. Robots are also used to carefully move parts, Fig. 4-16.

Construction sites can be kept free of debris, Fig. 4-17. Equipment can be well-maintained.

Safety education

Workers must be educated about safety. They must be taught its importance. Companies hold

Fig. 4-12. The safety program continues through the worklife of the employee.

Fig. 4-13. The five Es of safety.

periodic meetings to discuss these concepts.

A worker must receive careful safety instruction for his or her assigned job. This instruction includes four steps. Look at Fig. 4-18.

The trainer can never assume a person knows how to do the job safely. Each worker should receive complete instruction on safe practice. They are told how to do the job. Then, safe job practices are demonstrated. They are encouraged to ask questions. Finally, the new worker is observed as he or she does the job for the first time.

Safety Equipment

During training, the worker should be taught about required safety equipment. The need for personal protection is important. Each job has its own equipment requirements. Special protection devices may be provided. These items will protect the worker's sight, hearing, lungs, and skin.

Encouragement

Working safely is a habit. It is developed over time. Therefore, workers must always be en-

Fig. 4-15. This high-speed metal stamping press was designed with safety in mind. Note the clear plastic door in front of the ram. Also, the controls are on a stand to the left. The operator is away from the actual press operation.
(American Metal Stamping Assn.)

couraged to work safely. Most large companies have an on-going safety program. Posters remind workers to work safely. Company newsletters have articles on safety. Signs announce the number of days worked without an accident. Safe workers may win special recognition. Often, safety awards are given to individuals or departments.

Fig. 4-14. A desk job (left) is usually safer than a construction job (right).

Fig. 4-16. Robots are capable of carefully moving parts and products. (Adept Technology, Inc.)

Fig. 4-17. A safe construction site is well-organized and clean.

Employees should also be encouraged to report unsafe conditions. Alert workers can always see ways to improve operations. They should be encouraged to share their ideas.

Enforcement

Everyone becomes careless over time. We start to take chances. We drive too fast or run yellow lights. Police will remind us that this is wrong. They give us a traffic ticket.

The same is true about safety. Workers often have jobs where they must do the same task over and over again. The job becomes routine. Boredom

1. **TELL** HOW TO DO THE JOB SAFELY...

2. **SHOW** HOW TO DO THE JOB SAFELY...

3. HAVE WORKER **ASK** QUESTIONS ABOUT DOING THE JOB...

4. HAVE WORKER **SHOW YOU** HE/SHE CAN DO THE JOB SAFELY...

Fig. 4-18. The steps in educating workers in job safety.

can creep in. With it comes carelessness.

An alert supervisor will remind workers of careless acts. All workers must be required to work safely. Unsafe workers are a hazard (danger). They can hurt themselves and others.

The unsafe worker, like the unsafe driver, may need to be disciplined. She or he must be made to understand that unsafe practices will not be accepted.

SUMMARY

Production depends upon human and material resources. People are hired to do work. Their abilities are matched with jobs. This is the task of employment. First, the need for workers is determined. Applicants are then recruited. Information about them is gathered and studied. The best applicants are hired. New employees receive training about the company and job. Sometime during their employment they are likely to receive additional training.

Materials for production are purchased. The best supplier is found. The material is ordered and received. The vendor receives payment for the materials. These tasks are the job of people in purchasing. They buy the correct materials at the best price. They also see that they are received on time.

Safety is everybody's job. Employees must be provided a safe work environment. The operations must be engineered to be safe. Proper safety education and equipment must be provided. All workers must be encouraged to work safely. Finally, safety rules must be constantly enforced.

KEY WORDS

All the following words have been used in this chapter. Do you know their meaning?

Apprenticeship
Bids
Cooperative
  education
Employment
Hazard
Invoice
Material requisition
On-the-job training
Personnel

Purchasing
Quotes
Receiving report
Recruitment
Safety education
Safety enforcement
Safety engineering
Safety equipment
Training
Vestibule training

TEST YOUR KNOWLEDGE

Place your answers on a separate sheet of paper. Do not write in this book.

1. What are the major steps used to employ workers?
2. Name the four basic ways workers can be recruited.
3. Which of the following are methods companies use to gather information about people looking for jobs with them?
   A. Have person demonstrate skills by giving them a test.
   B. Ask questions about their work experience, education, training, and goals.
   C. Have persons fill out a job application.
   D. All of the above.
   E. None of the above.
4. Training a person at an actual workstation is called _____ _____ _____ training.
5. Apprenticeship training combines on-the-job training with special classes. True or False?
6. List the steps in a typical purchasing system.
7. List and discuss the five phases of a safety program.

ACTIVITIES

1. Invite a personnel director from a company to tell your class about the employment process used by his or her company.
2. Invite the school purchasing officer to discuss the purchasing procedure with your class.
3. Visit with a worker. Find out how they were hired. Ask about methods used to recruit, select, and induct them. Make a display board to show how it was done.

Chapter 5

MANAGING MANUFACTURING OPERATIONS

After reading this chapter, you will be able to:
☐ Recognize the differences between custom, intermittent, and continuous manufacturing.
☐ Compare these three types of manufacturing.
☐ List the major engineering tasks in organizing a manufacturing operation.
☐ Use production system design forms such as the operation process chart and the flow process chart.
☐ Describe a resource control system.
☐ List the major resources used to manufacture a product.
☐ Name and discuss the two tasks involved in a total quality control system.
☐ List and explain the three major steps in production.
☐ Describe, in general terms, the method and sequence used in managing production.
☐ Explain the difference between repair and maintenance of products.
☐ List and describe the steps in a product use cycle.
☐ Explain the functions of a good advertisement.
☐ List the functions of a good package.
☐ List and describe the three major channels of distribution used for consumer goods.
☐ Explain the two major types of sales.
☐ List the steps in making a sale.

Once products are designed they must be made. Materials must be processed into usable goods. The company uses a manufacturing system to produce products.

Three basic types of manufacturing systems are used today. These are outlined in Fig. 5-1.

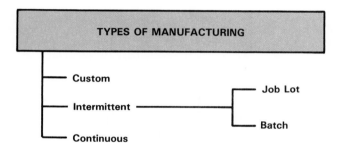

Fig. 5-1. All manufacturing is done by one of these systems.

CUSTOM MANUFACTURING

Custom manufacture is used to make a few products. Often they are one-of-a-kind items, Fig. 5-2. The company produces them to a customer's specifications. The buyer decides the features of the product.

Some people have clothing manufactured to fit them. Kitchen and bathroom cabinets are sometimes built to fit a specific house. Tooling, like the mold in Fig. 5-3, is custom manufactured. (Tooling means to equip a plant with tools, machines, and instruments for production.) They are built to order. The customer's specifications are used.

Custom manufacturing generally requires skilled workers. They must be able to read plans (drawings and specifications). Such workers are often required to set up machines. They operate their own equipment. Each worker checks the quality of his or her own work, Fig. 5-4.

Fig. 5-2. This passenger ship was custom manufactured to the customer's specifications. (National Steel and Ship Building)

Fig. 5-3. Most tooling for manufacturing processes is custom manufactured. (AT&T)

Custom manufacture is the most costly system for manufacture. Workers are more skilled. They are, therefore, paid more. The employees spend much time setting up and checking machines. Only a part of the work time is used for actual production.

Equipment use is also low. Most equipment is not needed all the time. Part of the time it is idle.

Fig. 5-4. Custom manufacturing requires highly skilled workers who are responsible for their own work. Here a potter forms a bowl.

At other times it is being set up. The cost of each machine is charged against products. If it is not used often, more cost is charged to each product.

For these and other reasons, custom manufacturing is not often used. It is chosen only when demand for the product is low but users are willing to pay the added cost.

INTERMITTENT MANUFACTURING

In intermittent manufacturing, products are mass-produced. They are built in large quantities. Intermittent means starting and stopping at intervals (periods of time). The process starts, is completed, then stops. At a later time the cycle is repeated.

You may have seen intermittent manufacturing in your home. A member of your family may have baked a batch of cookies. Perhaps a week later another batch was produced. The same process was used. The two baking activities were separated by a period of time.

Intermittent manufacturing can be used for both primary and secondary processing. Steel, for example, is made in batches. The mill produces and pours a melt of steel, Fig. 5-5. Then another batch

Fig. 5-5. A batch of steel is being poured.
(American Iron and Steel Institute)

is produced. Intermittent manufacture in primary processes is called *batch processing.*

In secondary processing, intermittent manufacturing processes groups of items. A number of parts

move from station to station until they are finished. At each station the entire group, called a lot, is processed. For example, a hole may be drilled at one station. The entire lot is drilled before it moves to the next station. There the hole may be reamed. This type of manufacture is called *job-lot manufacture.* It is pictured in Fig. 5-6.

A company may do intermittent manufacturing for two purposes. Products may be made for the company's own use. The system may also be used to make products for other companies. The specifications, therefore, may be its own or another company's.

Management must do more planning for intermittent manufacture. The job must be scheduled through the plant. Machines and workers must be assigned for each task. The lot must, somehow, be moved from station to station. Inspections must be scheduled.

Also, machines may need to be set up for each operation. Tooling must be installed. The tooling requires checking. The first parts produced have to be carefully inspected.

Intermittent manufacturing is more efficient than custom manufacturing. While skilled machine set-up people are needed, less skilled machine operators can run the equipment. They receive lower pay since they are less skilled. Also, the equipment can produce any number of like parts. Therefore, equipment is not idle as much.

Fig. 5-6. The cabinets are being produced in job lots. Note the stack of parts.   (American Woodwork)

CONTINUOUS MANUFACTURING

Continuous manufacturing produces products in a steady flow. Materials enter the system. Parts are made from them. Products are assembled from the manufactured parts. The process continues at a steady rate.

This method depends heavily on division of labor. This means the task of making the product is divided into jobs. Each worker is trained to do one job. Parts are produced as workers complete their individual jobs, Fig. 5-7. The product takes shape as it moves through the system.

Continuous manufacturing is based on the movement of resources. Most often the worker stays in one place while the product moves to him or her, Fig. 5-8. As a worker completes one job, the product moves on to the next worker.

Not all products are easy to move. In these cases the product is not moved. The workers move to the product. Each worker completes a job. He or she then moves to the next product. There they do their job again. Different employees work on the product at each state of manufacture. Large air conditioners, electric generators, locomotives and aircraft are examples of products which are assembled in one spot. See Fig. 5-9.

Continuous manufacturing saves time. Since workers are trained to do one job, each becomes skilled in completing that one task, Fig. 5-10.

Fig. 5-8. Like these dishwasher cases, many products are moved from station to station during manufacture. (General Electric)

Fig. 5-9. Large products may be assembled without being moved. Workers move to them to complete the jobs. (McDonnell Douglas Corp.)

Equipment is built or set up for a single operation. It is used over a long period of time.

Special tooling and trained workers waste less material. Also, equipment can be developed to perform routine tasks. Automatic equipment can spray finishes, machine parts, and weld assemblies, Fig. 5-11.

Manufacturing changes materials into products. This requires several actions. First the product must

Fig. 5-7. A series of workers assemble a toy. (Ohio Art Co.)

Fig. 5-10. This worker is trained to see defects in kitchen cabinets. (American Woodwork)

be designed to meet a human need or desire. This design process will be discussed in Section III of this book. The product designs represent someone's ideas for a product. These ideas must become reality. This involves the actual production of the product. We call this *manufacturing.* However,

building products is not enough. People have to be able to buy and use them. The product must be moved from the producer to the consumer. This involves *marketing.* Both manufacturing (product production) and marketing (product promotion and selling) are managed activities, Fig. 5-12. Let's look at these two major manufacturing areas separately.

MANUFACTURING PRODUCTS

Producing products takes careful planning and actions. This involves developing a manufacturing facility, designing a production control system, and manufacturing products.

Developing Manufacturing Facilities

A manufacturing facility must be developed. This is the job of manufacturing engineers. They are responsible for five major tasks, as shown in Fig. 5-13.

Selecting operations

Efficient manufacture requires using equipment and workers wisely. The work must be done in an orderly way. The right processes and machines must be used to shape materials and build the product.

Fig. 5-11. The robot is automatically cutting a structural steel part. (Cincinnati Milacron)

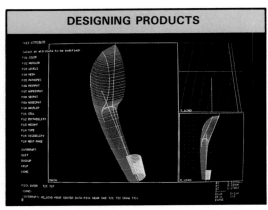

DESIGNING PRODUCTS

PRODUCING PRODUCTS

MARKETING PRODUCTS

Fig. 5-12. Manufacturing includes designing, producing, and marketing products.
(Schlumberger CAD/CAM, Alcan Aluminum, Ohio Art Co.)

This requires several planning tasks. The first one is called a *selecting and sequencing operation*. Simply put, it means deciding the processes that must be done and their order. Generally, this task involves preparing at least two types of documents. The first one is a *flow process chart,* Fig. 5-14. It shows, at a glance, the sequence (step-by-step order) of tasks for producing a single part.

A flow process chart often describes the tasks, provides a code number for each task, identifies the machines to be used, and lists the tooling needed for the task.

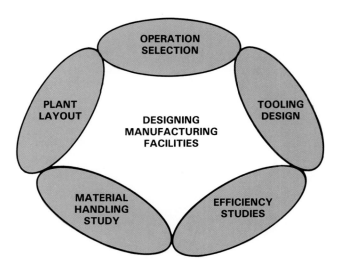

Fig. 5-13. These tasks are completed by manufacturing engineers in designing manufacturing systems.

The second document for sequencing tasks is an *operation process chart.* It shows how each part is to be made. Then it shows how they are assembled into a product. The operation process chart also shows where operations and inspections fit into the sequence. See Fig. 5-15. With the operation process chart, the manufacturing engineer can analyze the overall manufacturing process.

Designing tooling

Many operations cannot be done easily with standard machines. In many cases, special cutters are needed. In other cases, holders and clamps must be built. Sometimes a unique (one-of-a-kind) machine is required. At other times, molds and patterns must be made. All of these devices are called *tooling.*

Tooling helps the machine operator make parts better and faster. It reduces the need to make many machine adjustments. Tooling often fixes the position of the material.

Tooling, as shown in Fig. 5-16, is designed to increase the operation's speed, accuracy, and safety. Speed increases when the operations run smoothly. The tooling can be designed to operate at a set speed. Tooling also increases accuracy of the operations. Operators do not have to position materials. Finally, tooling increases safety. If the tooling holds the part, hands are out of the way and cannot be injured by the machine.

Preparing a plant layout

Selecting operations and designing tooling are not all the tasks that are performed by manufac-

FLOW PROCESS CHART

PRODUCT NAME		FLOW BEGINS	FLOW ENDS	DATE
RECIPE HOLDER		Upright O-1	Upright T-2	

PREPARED BY:	A.B. COMBS	APPROVED BY:	D.E. FRY

PROCESS SYMBOLS AND NO. USED	⬤ OPERATIONS __4__ ◼ INSPECTIONS __1__ ⬅ TRANSPORTATIONS __2__
	◗ DELAYS _____ ▽ STORAGES _____

Task No.	Process Symbols	Description of Task	Machine Required	Tooling Required
O-1	⬤⬅◻◗▽	Cut top angle	Back saw	Jig U-1
O-2	⬤⬅◻◗▽	Cut base angle	Back saw	Jig U-1
T-1	◯⬅◻◗▽	Move to sanding		
O-3	⬤⬅◻◗▽	Face sand		
O-4	⬤⬅◻◗▽	Edge sand		
I-1	◯⬅◼◗▽	Inspect		Gage I-1
T-2	◯⬅◻◗▽	Move to assembly		
	◯⬅◻◗▽			

Fig. 5-14. A sample flow process chart.

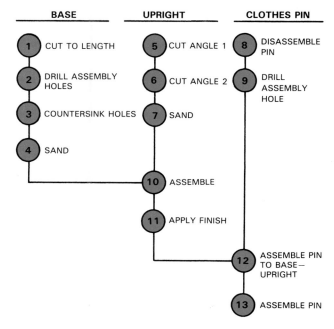

Fig. 5-15. A typical operation process chart.

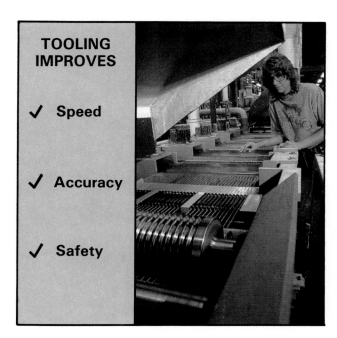

TOOLING IMPROVES

✓ Speed

✓ Accuracy

✓ Safety

Fig. 5-16. Advantages of tooling.

turing engineers. They must also be concerned with resource flow. This means moving materials and people through the factory efficiently, Fig. 5-17.

Workers need to get to their workstations easily. Movement to and from restrooms, cafeterias, and other support areas must also be considered. There must also be rapid movement out of the plant in case of fire, storm, earthquake, or other natural disaster.

For good plant layout, manufacturing engineers must plan:
• Where machines should be placed.
• How material will move.
• Where aisles should be located.
• Location of utilities (electricity, water, gas, etc.)

Designing material handling systems

The fourth part of a manufacturing system is a way to move materials. This is called *material handling,* Fig. 5-18.

The materials must be moved from storage to the manufacturing area. During processing, the material must be moved from workstation to workstation. Finally, finished parts and products must be moved into storage or to transportation (truck, train, ship, etc.).

Material handling devices are of two major types:
• Fixed path — These are devices that move a product from one fixed point to another. Examples of fixed path devices are conveyors, elevators, pipes, and chutes.
• Variable (steerable) path — Variable path devices can be steered. They can move in a number of

Fig. 5-18. This robot is being used as a material handling device. (Cincinnati Milicron)

directions. Common variable path devices are forklifts, overhead cranes, tractors, and hand trucks.

Improving Manufacturing Systems

The last task of a manufacturing engineer is improving the manufacturing system. Like products, they can be improved. They can be redesigned. Operations can be refined. New ones can replace older inefficient ones. Better material flow can be introduced. New material handling devices can be installed. More efficient machines and tooling can be developed or purchased.

DEVELOPING CONTROL SYSTEMS

Good managers use resources efficiently. Machines owned by the company must be used as much as possible. People must be kept busy with productive work. Materials should not be wasted. The word for this management task is *resource control.*

The outputs of the system must also be controlled. Waste, scrap, and pollution must be kept to a minimum. Also, product quality must be assured.

Control Systems

As you can see, all manufacturing activities need controlling. They must be carefully managed. Control systems are developed to do this. These systems, shown in Fig. 5-19, have four phases—

Fig. 5-17. Plant layout deals with the movement of people, materials, and products. (Ford Motor Co.)

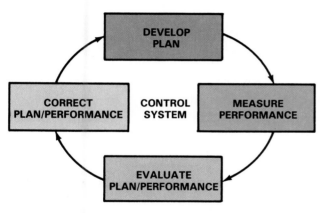

Fig. 5-19. Phases of a control system.

planning, measuring performance, evaluating performance, and corrective action.

- Planning—There are two basic types of manufacturing plans—long-range and short-term. Long-range plans are usually three to five year projections that direct overall business activities. Short-term plans are more concrete (real). They outline performance goals (work to be done) for a given day, week, month, or year. Typical short-term plans include production schedules, budgets, and sales quotas.
- Measuring performance—Manufacturing activities are controlled. That is, their performance is measured. Some method is used to record the use of machines, labor, and material. Records are kept of time worked, products produced, and material used. These measurements provide the basis for management decisions.
- Evaluating performance—Collecting data is not enough. Manufacturing performance must be rated against some standard. This base is often the company's plan. The number of products produced is measured against production plans. Worker output (amount of work done) and product quality is measured.
- Corrective action—Evaluation often points out shortcomings. Performance may not live up to the plan. The company must correct the problems. Management must decide what action to take.

Factors to control

Everything a company does is controlled. Sales are controlled. Raw material and finished goods inventories are controlled. Income and expenses are controlled. Control is the basis for success. Two major concerns of any company are the use of resources and quality of its products. These can be controlled.

The major resources used to make products are:
- Human labor.
- Machine time.
- Materials.

These resources must be managed. They must be used efficiently.

Controlling quality

Quality is important to everyone. Customers want products that work. Retailers want to sell good products. Manufacturers also want quality products. Returned products cost money to process. Sales can be lost by creating dissatisfied customers.

Quality, then, is everybody's business. Every stage in manufacturing must be concerned with quality. Products must be designed with quality in mind. Facilities (space and equipment) must be engineered to turn out quality products. Training programs must stress quality. Customer service must be alert to quality problems.

The key to producing a quality product is *quality control*. It ensures that the product meets standards. This function of a company has two tasks. The first task is to motivate workers to produce quality products. The second task of quality control is to inspect products to remove substandard items.

Motivation. Humans generally do what they think is important. For many years, production was emphasized by companies. Numbers of products manufactured was stressed. Workers reacted as expected. They produced products. Not all of them were good.

However, times have changed. Quality is not very important, Fig. 5-20. A number of programs

Fig. 5-20. These workers are completing a quality audit as part of a total quality control system.

have been developed to encourage quality. Workers are asked to help improve manufacturing systems. They are invited to join *quality circles.* These are voluntary groups that meet weekly. They discuss ways to improve the company. New production methods, management activities, and other ideas are discussed. The goal is to improve quality of both products and work life.

Inspection. Murphy's Law suggests that "if something can go wrong, it will." This is not exactly true. However, no person or machine is perfect. A poor product or part can be produced. They must be taken out of the manufacturing line. This is the job of inspection.

Inspectors are hired to ensure that only good-quality products leave the plant, Fig. 5-21. They check:
- Materials entering the plant.
- Purchased parts.
- Work-in-progress.
- Finished products.

These items are compared with engineering standards. They are often tagged to indicate the condition. Good items receive an "accepted" tag. Other parts are marked for either rework or scrap. Rework parts have their defects corrected. They are then inspected again.

MANUFACTURING PRODUCTS

Finally, when the manufacturing system is ready, actual production can begin. Manufacture of products involves three major steps. These, as seen in Fig. 5-22, are scheduling production, producing products, and controlling production.

Scheduling Production

Scheduling production means to organize a manufacturing production line so products or parts are produced on time. It must be done efficiently. Good products must be produced with the least use of time and materials.

People who do this kind of work are called *production planners.* To plan properly, they must know the number of parts or products that must be built and the deadline (when the parts and products must be ready). Using this information, they organize the workforce, equipment, and materials to do the job.

Production planning

Production planners' work can be divided into four phases:
- Routing—Determining the production path for each product going through the plant.
- Scheduling—Deciding when each production activity will take place and when it will be finished.
- Dispatching—Giving orders for completing scheduling tasks.
- Expediting (follow-up)—Ensuring that the work stays on schedule.

Producing Products

Once developed, the schedules are given to line management (production supervisors). These managers assign workers to complete specific tasks. They must also supervise and motivate the workers.

Line management must see that products are produced on schedule (time). This involves:

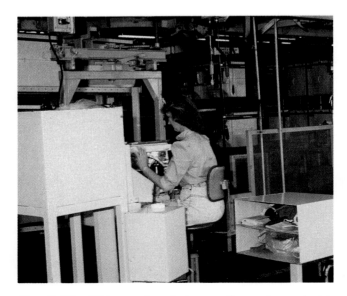

Fig. 5-21. This worker is inspecting a household appliance. (General Electric)

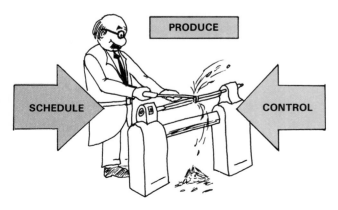

Fig. 5-22. The three major steps in producing products.

- Making parts.
- Making subassemblies.
- Making final assembly.

Pilot run

Often, these production activities are tried out first to see if they work. The system is tested before full manufacture starts. This test is called a *pilot run.* It is designed to "debug" (correct) the system. The line runs for a short time to produce a few products. The output is then evaluated. Design errors are caught. Corrections can be made before high-volume manufacture begins.

The pilot run can turn up a number of problems. These could cause changes to be made in the:
- Product design.
- Tooling.
- Materials used.
- Plant layout.
- Material handling systems.
- Type and sequence of operations.

Full production starts after the pilot run. Products are produced in keeping with production orders and quality control standards, Fig. 5-23.

Fig. 5-23. Manufacturing systems produce products that meet quality standards. (Goodyear Tire and Rubber Co.)

Controlling Production

Once production is started it must be checked often for problems. This activity is called *control.*

Three basic types of data (information) are important for controlling production. These are:
- Product output data.
- Quality control data.
- Labor utilization (use) data.

Product output data

A production department schedules levels of product manufacture. Each plant, department, and worker is expected to complete certain tasks on time.

Production data is collected during manufacture. Various reports are prepared to tell whether production schedules are being met.

A production record may be kept for each worker. These records are often summarized on departmental production reports. The plant manager will review each report. Then she or he prepares a plant production report. This report usually goes to the corporate office.

Daily production reports show areas needing corrective action (change in plan). Overtime can be scheduled to keep from falling behind. More workers may be hired. New equipment or tooling may be installed. Production reports are not just a record of what happened. They are also a record for future action.

Quality control data

Success or failure in producing quality products is shown by quality control reports. These reports tell about three major activities:
- Receiving material.
- Processing materials.
- Testing final products.

Labor data

Workers expect to be paid for their work. Records for pay purposes are kept. The type of records depends upon the pay systems. The two basic systems are:
- Standard pay systems—Workers are paid for time spent on the job.
- Incentive pay systems—Workers receive a base pay for time worked. The company may pay a bonus for production beyond a set number of units. Workers are encouraged to be more productive. They receive additional pay for extra production.

Standard pay systems generally require the worker to keep a time card. A time clock is used for recording starting and quitting times.

Incentive systems use time cards and production records. The workers' starting and ending times are recorded. Also, the output of each worker is recorded. Any rejected parts produced are subtracted from the output. The result is then used to calculate the pay.

MARKETING PRODUCTS

Manufacturing useful products will not make money for a company. Money is earned only when the products are sold. This is the task of marketing. This managed area of activity promotes, sells, and distributes the product.

Promoting Products

All purchases require a choice. This is where product promotion enters the scene. It is designed to encourage sales. Product promotion can be done many ways. Two very important methods are advertising and packaging. Both attract our attention.

Advertising

Advertising is a nonpersonal message. No person is actually there. The message is given by print or electronic means. You must read, view, or listen to it. The customers can decide to receive the message or not. They are in control of the communication.

Functions of advertising. Advertisements call us to act. They are saying, "buy this product," or "believe in this company." Advertisements fulfill a function. They take the potential customer through four steps, Fig. 5-24. The advertisement must:
- Attract attention — The person must want to read, see, or hear the message.
- Inform — The customer is introduced to the product and told of its features and advantages.
- Persuade — The customer must want to use the product.
- Cause action — The customer must seek the product and purchase it.

Creating advertising. Advertising is created by people with special training. They generally follow three basic steps. First, the message is developed. A story is developed from a marketing theme. Facts and ideas are chosen to describe the product or idea. Second, the presentation is designed. A message is not enough. The advertisement must at-

Fig. 5-24. An advertisement should attract attention, provide information, persuade customers, and cause action.

tract and hold attention. Third, the advertisement is produced. If the message will be in print, type will be set. An artist or photographer will provide drawings or photos. The two combine to make up a printed advertisement. If the media is radio or television, actors are selected and the commercial is recorded.

Packaging

A second way to promote a product is with its package. A package can serve three main functions. It can, as shown in Fig. 5-25:
- Protect and contain the product.
- Promote the product.
- Provide information for the customer.

Some products can be damaged during shipment. Others are small and easily lost. A package can protect and contain the product. It can keep it from being broken, or damaged by moisture. Products like toothpaste, corn flakes, and orange juice need to be contained and protected. In fact, most products need some protection as they travel from the factory to you.

Package designers can choose from a large number of package types. Bottles, tubes, cans, cartons, bags, and trays are just a few of the types.

Selling Products

Products must move from the manufacturer to the consumer. They may follow any of several

Fig. 5-25. Packages protect and promote products.

paths. These paths are called *channels of distribution.* Consumer goods follow one of three main routes. These are shown in Fig. 5-26.

The simplest route is called *direct selling.* Manufacturers sell products directly to the customer. You buy the product from the producer. Many encyclopedias, cosmetics, and vacuum cleaners follow this channel. Mail order and catalog sales are also considered direct selling.

Some manufacturers sell directly to *retailers.* These stores then sell the product to the customers. An "authorized" or "franchised" dealer is this type of retailer. They are the only retailers allowed to sell the product. Almost all new automobiles are sold this way.

Most consumer products follow a third route. They are first sold to *wholesalers.* These firms become the owners of the product. They resell the products to retailers. The retail stores make the final sale.

Sales

Each step in the channel of distribution involves sales. Ownership of goods changes hands. Products move from warehouses to stores. The products then move from the stores to customers.

Types of sales

There are two major types of sales—industrial sales and retail sales. These are shown in Fig. 5-27.

Industrial sales involve several types of action. Raw materials may be sold to primary processors. Industrial materials are sold to secondary manufacturing companies. Finished products move to wholesalers and retailers. These are all examples of industrial sales.

Fig. 5-26. Three typical distribution channels for consumer goods.

Fig. 5-27. Sales are classified as industrial and retail.

Retail sales means selling to the final consumer. The customer pays for the products. He or she receives them immediately.

The sales force

Manufacturers hire a special sales force. This includes salespeople who do the selling. Sales managers are also hired. They manage the sales effort. The sales effort takes three major steps—developing the sales team, directing salespeople, and controlling the sales effort.

Developing the sales team. Salespeople are developed in the same way as other workers. They are first recruited. Qualified people are sought for the sales jobs. Applicants are screened. They complete applications. Employment officers interview them. The best applicants are hired. The salespeople then receive special training. They learn the art of selling.

Directing salespeople. In large companies, regional or district sales managers direct the work of the sales force. They supervise and motivate. They assign salespeople to regions often called *territories.* A territory may cover a city, several counties, an entire state, or several states.

Another part of directing is to get people to do their best. This is called *motivation.* Sales managers must find ways to encourage better sales efforts from salespeople.

Controlling the sales effort. All managed activities need to be controlled. An important part of this control is the *sales forecast.* This is the sales budget. The company estimates overall expected sales for each reporting period. Each salesperson works toward a sales quota so the sales forecast is met. Failure to reach quotas will call for action. New motivation techniques may be required. Some salespeople might be replaced. Better training may be provided.

Selling products

Selling is an art; it takes talent. Good salespeople are skilled in several activities. First, the approach to a customer is critical. The salesperson must attract the buyer's attention. Then an interest in the product must be developed.

Second, the salesperson must present the product. The presentation must be designed for the customer. One type of customer may buy a product to resell it. Another may be buying for his or her own use. The presentation must take this into account.

Finally, the salesperson must be able to close the sale. When you buy a product in a store the close is simple. You just pay for it. Usually the clerk gives you the product. An industrial sale does not work this way. The salesperson takes the order. The order information goes to the factory. Often, the order is filled from inventory. The items are shipped to the customer. Some products are not built until they are ordered.

THE CONSUMER AND THE PRODUCT

When a customer buys a product, its life cycle (time it will be used) begins. The manufacturer's work is not done, however. The customer must know how to properly operate the product. The manufacturer provides directions for use and maintenance. Service information or facilities are also made available.

Product Use Cycle

Products usually follow a common life cycle, Fig. 5-28. First the product is *installed.* It is set up where it will be used. It is *maintained* from time-to-time to keep it in working order. After a given period, the product is *repaired;* worn and broken parts are replaced. Finally, the product is taken out of service when it is not possible or economical to repair. It is *replaced.*

Installing products

Some products are not ready to use when they leave the factory. They must be installed. The product must be set in place. It is often permanently

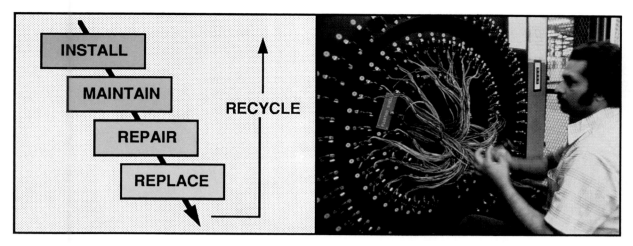

Fig. 5-28. The four stages in product life.

located. Many products connect to utilities. Installers must run water lines, electrical wiring, or natural gas lines. They also may need to attach drains to sewers.

Product testing comes after installation. A dishwasher is run through its cycle. A furnace is operated for a period of time. The installed product is then turned over to the customer.

Maintaining products

Often, products require attention to keep them working. Durable products require the most maintenance. Automobiles have service schedules as do many industrial machines. They must be lubricated and controls must be adjusted.

Nondurable products are also maintained. Dishes and clothing are washed. Hiking boots are coated with silicone. Shoes are polished and carpets are vacuumed.

All service is designed to make the product last longer. Wear and breakage are reduced.

Repairing products

Products will not work forever, however. Parts go out of adjustment. Sometimes they break. The product stops working. It needs repair.

Repair puts the product back into working shape. It is made as much like a new product as possible. There are three major steps in repairing a product. These are shown in Fig. 5-29.

- Diagnosing—You cannot fix something unless you know what is wrong. Finding the defect is called *diagnosing*. The cause for the breakdown is found. The owner or repairer studies the defect. The cost of repair is estimated. The owner must then make a decision. Is the product worth fixing? If it is, the defect is repaired.

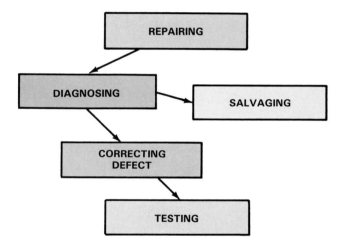

Fig. 5-29. Steps in repairing products.

- Correcting defects—Most defects can be corrected. Repair people can put the product into working order. They order replacement parts for the product. They install and adjust parts. Sometimes, entire subassemblies are replaced.
- Testing—All repair work must be tested. The repaired product should meet operating standards. Testing is the "quality control" step for repair.

Replacing products

Sometimes it costs too much to repair the product. Usually, the repair costs are higher than the product's value. Customers may decide they do not need the product that much. The cost of repair is greater than their need.

Other times a new product is cheaper than repairing the old one. Products not repaired must be recycled. Sometimes they are used for parts. The product is taken apart and good parts are saved.

Other products are thrown away. They are put into landfills. Still other products are *recycled.* They are ground up, shredded, or melted down. They become raw materials for primary processing. Many steel, aluminum, glass, and paper plants use scrap material.

SUMMARY

Manufacturing involves designing, producing, and selling products. This requires efficient manufacturing systems that can produce good-quality products. These products must be marketed. They must be promoted, sold, and distributed.

Finally, many products need servicing and maintaining. They must be kept working until they wear out. Then they should be recycled or properly discarded.

KEY WORDS

All the following words have been used in this chapter. Do you know their meaning?

Advertising	Pilot run
Diagnosing	Productivity
Direct selling	Production planners
Dispatching	Quality circle
Expediting	Quality control
Fixed path	Recycle
Flow process chart	Repair
Industrial sales	Resource control
Inspection	Rework
Install	Routing
Inventory control	Sales forecast
Maintain	Salesperson
Maintenance	Scheduling
Manufacturing	Scrap
engineer	Selecting and
Marketing	sequencing operation
Material handling	Territories
Operation process	Tooling
chart	Variable path
Package	Wholesale
Packaging	

TEST YOUR KNOWLEDGE

Place your answers on a separate sheet of paper. Do not write in this book.

1. What are the major engineering tasks?

Matching questions: Match the definition in the left-hand column with the correct term in the right-hand column.

2. Selecting process tasks to be done and putting them in the order they must be done.
3. Person who organizes people and machines for efficient manufacture.
4. Form listing operations, machine to use, and tooling needed.
5. Shows at a glance the sequence of tasks for producing a single part.
6. Movement of part through manufacture.

A. Operation process sheet.
B. Flow process chart.
C. Manufacturing engineer.
D. Selecting and sequencing operations.
E. Transportation.

7. _____ refers to special tools or devices which make manufacturing operations more efficient.
8. List the four phases in developing and using a control system.
9. Which three of the following are resources for making a product?
   A. The building that houses the factory.
   B. The workers' labor.
   C. Machine time.
   D. Materials.
   E. Capital (money for running business).

Matching questions: Match the definitions in the left-hand column with the correct term in the right-hand column.

10. Selling products to a wholesaler.
11. Area to which a salesperson is assigned.
12. An estimate of the future sales volume.
13. Getting customer's attention.
14. Explaining product and features.
15. Getting customer to buy.
16. Place to record an order.

A. Order form.
B. Closing the sale.
C. Territory.
D. Product presentation.
E. Sales approach.
F. Sales forecast.
G. Industrial sales.

ACTIVITIES

1. If you had an order for two book racks of the same design, which manufacturing system would you use? Which system would you use if your order was for 25 racks per month for two years?

2. Visit a local industry. Describe the manufacturing system being used.
3. Prepare a flow process chart for a simple task such as washing a dish.
4. Invite a manager from a company to class to discuss systems used by his or her company to control the use of resources and quality.
5. You have decided to manufacture track hurdles. What are the various elements that you will have to control? How would you control them?

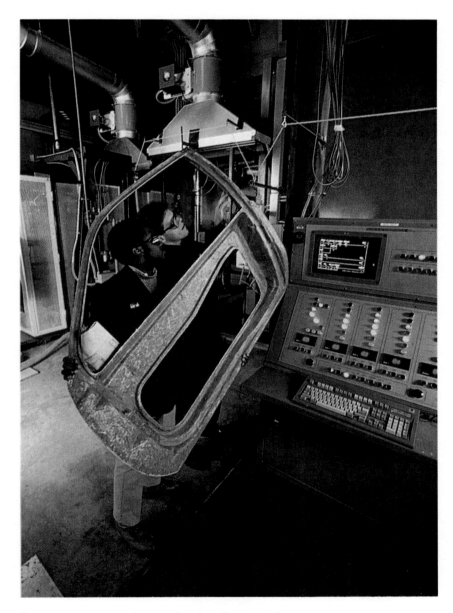

Computers are an integral part of production systems. (E. I. duPont de Nemours and Co.)

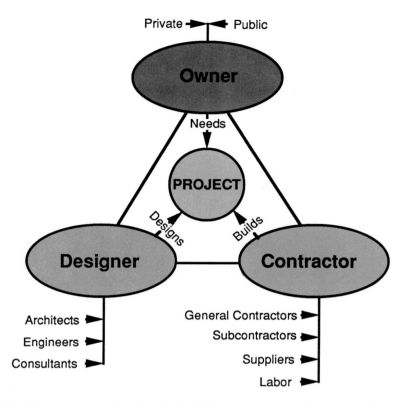

Fig. 6-1. The construction triangle includes owners, designers, and contractors.

THE FOCUS OF TEAMS

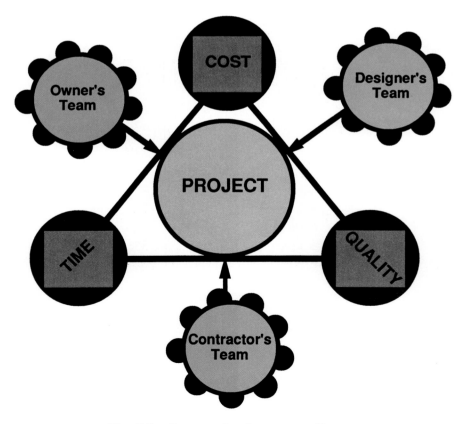

Fig. 6-2. Construction is a team effort.

Chapter 6

MANAGING CONSTRUCTION PROJECTS

After reading this chapter, you will be able to:
☐ Describe the Project Delivery Process.
☐ List and describe three Project Delivery Approaches.
☐ Describe the difference between a home office and a field office.
☐ Compare a general contractor, subcontractor, and supplier.
☐ Discuss the bar chart and critical path methods.
☐ Explain the purpose of a master schedule and how it is made.
☐ List and describe several management careers in construction.
☐ Tell how lead time affects purchasing.
☐ Define the following terms: materials, equipment, and workers.
☐ List three things that are inspected.
☐ Discuss the process of closing the contract.

The building process is both exciting and complex. People involved in construction design build and use the structures. See Fig. 6-1. Each has a major role. Private and public owners have a need for the structure. It is designed by architects, engineers, and consultants (people with special knowledge). Many people are involved in building the structure. All of these people work as a team, Fig. 6-2. Their goal is to produce high-quality structures at a reasonable cost, and on schedule.

How well people manage a project affects the amount of profit or loss. Well-directed projects are of high quality, done on schedule, and stay within budget. This is sometimes hard because a great deal of construction work is performed in the open. Bad weather can stop the work or make it difficult to complete a job on schedule, Fig. 6-3.

Builders work hard to get a good reputation. A *reputation* is what people think about a person as a builder. Good builders do not exploit (overwork) the workers. Correct and safe methods are used to complete the project.

THE PROJECT DELIVERY PROCESS

The *Project Delivery Process (PDP)* gives order to a complex job. The PDP has six phases, Fig. 6-4. In all phases, graphic and written documents are made and the price is estimated. The phases are as follows:
• Phase I—Predesign. The problem is defined in the Predesign Phase. A program, financial

Fig. 6-3. Rain can bring work on this site to a halt.

package, schedule, and budget are prepared.

- Phase II—Schematic Design. Generating schematics (different ideas) is the first step in finding a solution to a design problem. Sketching accounts for a major portion of this stage.
- Phase III—Design Development. Design development is the heart of the design phase. More concern is given to the details.
- Phase IV—Construction Document Phase. After the design is approved, the design team's focus is on producing drawings rather than creating. Working drawings, specifications, and the bidding package are produced in this phase.
- Phase V—Construction Phase. The project is built during this phase. Contractors play the major role. Architects and engineers help the owner by managing the bidding process and inspecting the project.
- Phase VI—Occupancy/Use Phase. In the Occupancy/Use Phase owners move into the structure and begin to use it. Owners must learn how to operate and maintain equipment. Long-range plans will soon be made for future building.

THE PROJECT DELIVERY APPROACH

Three project delivery approaches (PDAs) are used. They are the linear (in a straight line), fast-track, and design/build approaches. Each has its own risks and rewards.

Linear Approach

The *linear approach* is the most common, Fig. 6-5. Each step of the project is completed before the next one is started. Predesign, design, construction documents, construction, and occupancy phases are done in order. The work for each step is finished before the work in the next is started. This approach is the most easily understood and managed. However, this approach requires more time to complete the project.

Fast-Track Approach

The *fast-track approach* is used to shorten the length of time to deliver the project, Fig. 6-6. With this approach the predesign and design phases are completed. Then, the project is divided into separate contracts. There may be separate contracts to do site work, design and build the structure, and design and landscape the structure. The amount of time before occupancy is shortened because construction on early phases can start before design work is finished on other phases.

Design/Build Approach

There may be owners with a well-defined project, and who want to work with just one firm. They

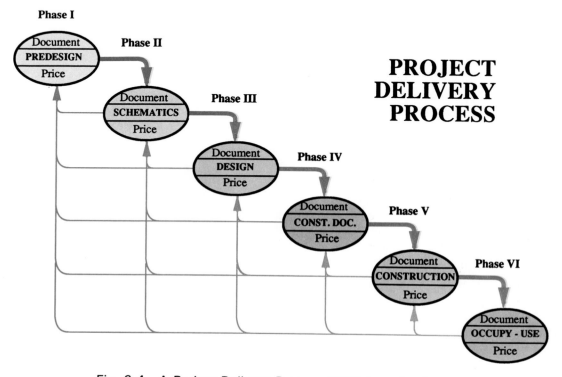

Fig. 6-4. A Project Delivery Process (PDP) has six phases.

LINEAR APPROACH

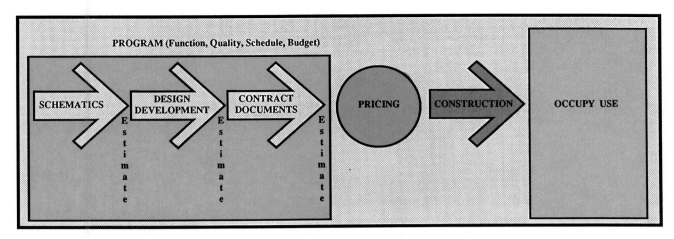

Fig. 6-5. The linear approach is simple but takes more time than others.

FAST-TRACK APPROACH

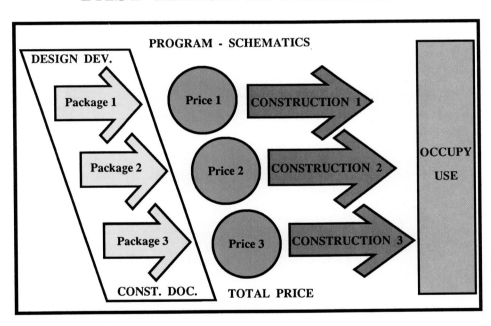

Fig. 6-6. The fast-track approach is faster than the linear approach. Design and construction phases overlap.

often use the *design/build approach,* Fig. 6-7. The client receives a firm price to create and construct the project. The predesign work is done early and does not change much throughout the project.

GETTING THE CONTRACT

A *contract* is a detailed agreement between two parties (people or firms). The contract has *terms* that describe the requirements of both parties. One of the terms describes the work. Working draw-

ings and construction standards describe that work. The price is another one of the terms. The price is the amount of money paid to get the work done. It is set before work begins.

Projects are built by owners, architects/ engineers, or contractors. Most of the work done by owners relates to repairing (fixing), altering (changing the use), or modifying (changing the size) of their structures. A *constructor* is a firm that designs and builds a project for a fee, Fig. 6-8. Most projects are built by *contractors* who compete for the projects.

DESIGN/BUILD APPROACH

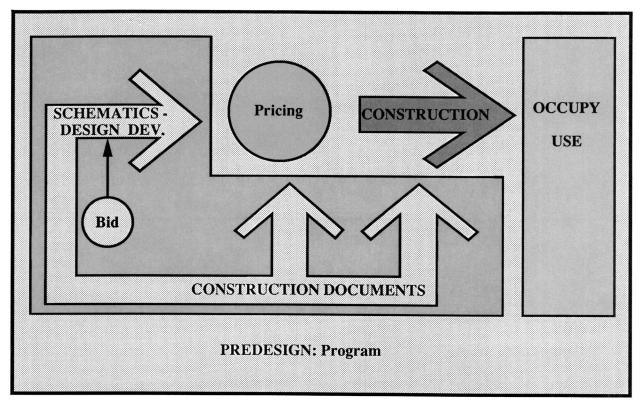

Fig. 6-7. In the design/build approach, either the designer or builder reports to the owner. Both report to the owner with other approaches.

Fig. 6-8. This new port was built by a constructor. The volume and kinds of cargo to be handled were given to the constructor's engineers. Then, the firm designed and built the port.   (Raymond International, Inc.)

Kinds of Contractors

There are three kinds of contractors: general contractors, subcontractors, and suppliers. **General contractors** get the overall contract that includes all work done, Fig. 6-9.

Subcontractors generally perform only one kind of work, Fig. 6-10. A subcontractor may erect steel frames. Another may build concrete forms, place concrete, and remove the forms.

Suppliers provide materials and equipment. A contract states the price and delivery schedules. In Fig. 6-11, a supplier is making a delivery.

Kinds of Contracts

Verbal agreements are made with words and a handshake. The written contract is signed by each party. If a contract is written correctly, it will hold up in a court of law. Verbal contracts may not.

Negotiated contracts result when the owner and contractor talk about the work and price. This kind of contract is common to private owners. Time used for the bidding process is saved. Money can be saved because the project can be finished and used sooner.

In **competitive bidding,** two or more contractors offer to build the project. Each contractor tries to get the job by bidding the lowest and finishing the project the quickest. They are said to "compete" for the job.

Fig. 6-10. The general contractor for this highway project built the roadbed and paved the road. A subcontractor built the bridges. (U.S. Department of Transportation, Federal Highway Administration)

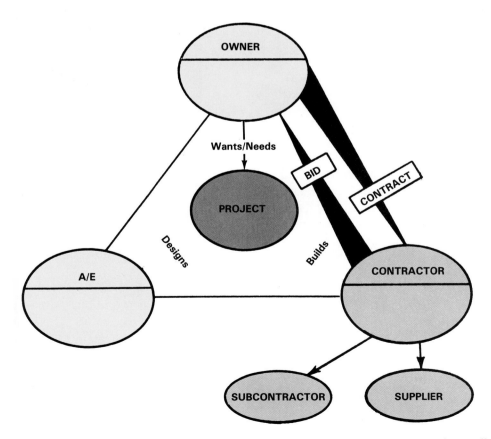

Fig. 6-9. The general contractor decides what the subcontractors and suppliers do.

Fig. 6-11. This concrete supplier must supply the right amount of the right mix when and where the contractor wants it. (DYK Prestressed Tanks, Inc.)

Private owners may feel it is best to use competitive bidding to find a builder. Since the money they spend is their own, they try to get the most value from it. Public owners are bound by local, state, and federal laws. The common competitive bidding process has seven steps. See Fig. 6-12.

The *notice to proceed* lets the contractor begin planning to build, and sets the starting and ending days for the project.

Estimating

Early in the planning stages, owners and the A/Es make rough cost estimates. An *estimate* is the amount of money a person thinks it will take to build the project. The contractor arrives at the estimate by adding up all of the costs for materials, labor, equipment, overhead (office expense), and profit. Whether the project is a home or a dam, the process is the same. First, the estimator looks at the working drawings. Second, they break down all work into a sequence of units. A unit is a part of the project. Third, an estimator computes the cost of each unit of work.

Materials

An estimator figures the materials by counting the number of each piece that is needed in the project. Concrete is bought by volume. The estimator will need to compute the number of cubic yards (a space 3 feet × 3 feet × 3 feet) of concrete needed in the project. Fig. 6-13 shows you how to figure the volume of a sidewalk that is 4 inches thick, 3 feet wide and 54 feet long. To find the cost for the

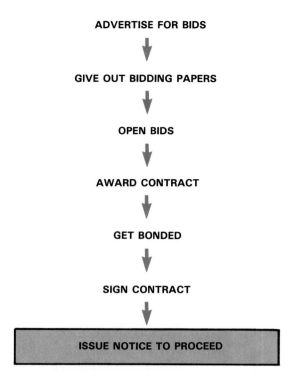

Fig. 6-12. Competitive bidding for public projects follows a procedure.

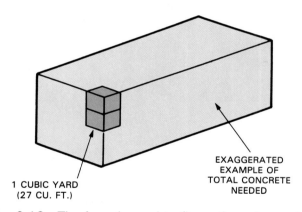

Fig. 6-13. The formula used to figure the volume of concrete for a sidewalk.

concrete, multiply the number of units (cubic yards) times the cost per unit.

Labor

Cost of labor is found by estimating the number of hours it takes to do a job. This number is taken times the rate per hour paid to each worker. Time estimates can be taken from *labor*.

Productivity Tables

Equipment

The cost to run equipment to produce a unit of work is used to figure equipment costs. See Fig.

6-14. If the equipment is rented, the contractor pays for rent, fuel, repairs, and any steps needed for moving it. Owners of equipment must figure the cost of depreciation (loss of value), interest, taxes, insurance, storage, fuel, and repairs.

Overhead

Overhead is the cost of running a firm. There are two kinds of overhead. The first is *home office overhead costs.* See Fig. 6-15. This includes the payroll for those who manage and work in the home office. Office rent, telephone service, and utilities add to overhead expense, as does advertising and travel.

Field office overhead costs are added to each job, Fig. 6-16. This includes the payroll for everyone except the workers. Surveys, office space, testing, site preparation, insurance, storage, building permits, and payments for bonds add to field office overhead costs.

Profit

If a contractor is to stay in business, he or she needs to make a profit. The difference between what the contractor gets paid for building the project and the builder's costs is profit.

Fig. 6-15. These people work in the contractor's home office. Their salaries are part of the overhead. (Honeywell, Inc.)

Fig. 6-14. The cost of digging this trench is estimated in dollars per foot. The estimator adjusts the estimate for the kind of soil and depth of trench. (Caterpillar, Inc.)

Fig. 6-16. Getting power to the site and setting up the field office takes money. These costs and others are field office overhead. (DYK Prestressed Tanks, Inc.)

An estimator computes the cost of material, equipment, subcontractor's quotes, and overhead. Top management decides on the amount of *markup* and prepares the bid. Fig. 6-17 shows this concept.

Computing building costs is a matter of following procedures. The profit decision is a matter of strategy. A *strategy* is a plan to reach a goal.

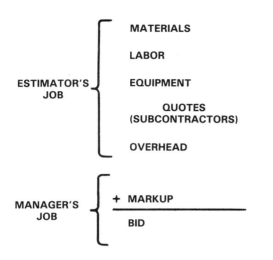

Fig. 6-17. The work of the estimator is routine. Top management decides on the amount of markup and prepares the bids.

MANAGERS OF CONSTRUCTION WORK

Firms are set up in many ways. The line and staff chart shown in Fig. 6-18 is used to describe large firms. One person may do more than one job in a small firm. Larger firms may have more than one person working in each office at each level. People manage from both the home office and field office.

Home Office

Those who lead from the home office make up the master schedule for the project. A *master schedule* consists of a list of tasks and the schedule to get them done. The owner, designer, and contractor help make the master schedule.

In the home office, work on the site is led by a *project manager.* The project manager may be in charge of one large project or more than one smaller projects.

The *architect/engineers (A/Es)* inspect the project while it is being built. The A/Es work for the owner. The A/Es cannot change the methods used

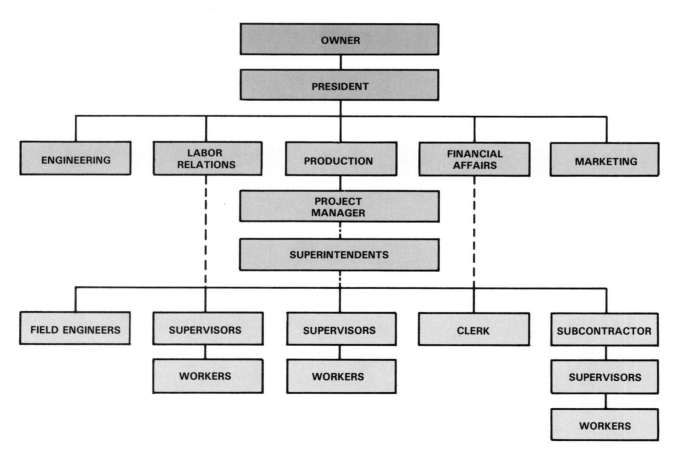

Fig. 6-18. A construction firm has a home office and a field office. The levels of authority are shown for all of the leaders and workers.

by the builder. They only make sure that the builder follows the drawings and specifications, and manage changes that are made.

Field Office

The *superintendent* works on the master schedule with the people in the home office. On the site, the superintendent manages the field office and leads each of the major tasks on the master schedule. Fig. 6-19 shows the results of a superintendent's work.

The project manager and the superintendent keep in close contact. Facts about costs, schedules, and equipment are given back and forth to keep work moving ahead. They look for places where progress on the site and the master schedule are not the same. The work that is behind schedule becomes a priority. *Priority work* is done before other work. In this way, the project can be brought back onto schedule.

Large projects will have a *field engineer.* They may design the building site, and conduct land soil surveys. A field engineer may also conduct tests on site.

A *clerk* takes care of receiving reports, payrolls, time cards, and other paperwork in the field office.

Each trade may have a *supervisor.* This means that plumbers, carpenters, electrical workers, and concrete workers each have a supervisor. The supervisor gets orders from the superintendent. They, in turn, instruct their workers.

Subcontractors receive orders from the superintendent. If they are a large subcontractor, they may have their own supervisor. The workers receive orders from the supervisor.

Construction *workers* must be able to adjust to new work rules and a new supervisor on each job. The duties that construction workers perform often change daily, Fig. 6-20.

Workers in construction perform four kinds of work. They do site work, build the structure, do the mechanical work (plumbing, electrical, heating), and perform finish work on the structure.

SCHEDULING CONSTRUCTION PROJECTS

There are three methods used to manage projects: experience, the bar chart method, and the critical path method. The first is not a planned method. The other two are more formal.

Fig. 6-19. What do you think the superintendent did to make this job run smoothly? (Maine D.O.T.)

Fig. 6-20. This is an example of finish work. Can you explain why? (SENCO Products, Inc.)

Experience

Those who have been builders for many years acquire a "sense" for planning. They know how things need to be done. They have a "feel" for scheduling. They know when work is lagging behind. This method is best used on small projects.

Bar Chart Method

A bar chart is easy to read. The chart shows the schedule for work to be done. It shows what is done and where there are delays. You can compare the planned schedule with the work on the site. The bar chart shows how much money has been spent on the project. It will, also, forecast income from the project. Fig. 6-21 shows a bar chart for a basketball goal project.

Critical Path Method

The Critical Path Method (CPM) shows the sequence of each task. Times are easy to add. The total time to build the project is easy to figure.

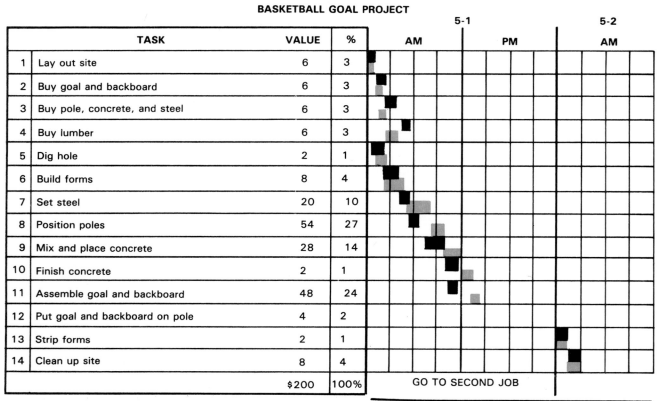

BASKETBALL GOAL PROJECT

	TASK	VALUE	%
1	Lay out site	6	3
2	Buy goal and backboard	6	3
3	Buy pole, concrete, and steel	6	3
4	Buy lumber	6	3
5	Dig hole	2	1
6	Build forms	8	4
7	Set steel	20	10
8	Position poles	54	27
9	Mix and place concrete	28	14
10	Finish concrete	2	1
11	Assemble goal and backboard	48	24
12	Put goal and backboard on pole	4	2
13	Strip forms	2	1
14	Clean up site	8	4
		$200	100%

GO TO SECOND JOB

—— PLANNED WORK SCHEDULE

—— ACTUAL WORK SCHEDULE

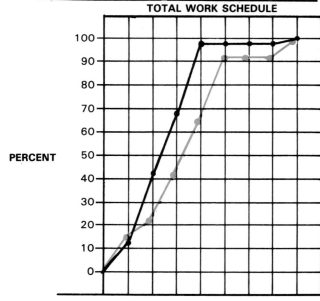

TOTAL WORK SCHEDULE

PERCENT

Fig. 6-21. A bar chart for a basketball goal project.

A CPM chart is an arrow chart. Fig. 6-22 is an arrow chart for the basketball goal project. Each arrow is a task. The circles with numbers in them are events.

A *path* is a series of events that are done in order. The path that takes the longest time to complete is the *critical path (CP).* This path controls the length of time needed to complete the project. If the job superintendent is able to shorten the CP, a second path may become critical.

MANAGING PURCHASES

Builders plan to obtain materials and equipment, and to involve subcontractors early. Even before the contract is signed, they schedule their buying.

As soon as a verbal award of the contract is given, purchasing begins. The *notice of award* is sent to the builder. This paper serves as the contract until the real contract is drawn up and signed.

Leaders in the home office obtain materials, equipment, and employ workers. See Fig. 6-23.

Fig. 6-23. The home office workers have the expertise to purchase materials at low prices, read technical specifications, and schedule the arrival of materials at the building site. Lists of suppliers used in the past help speed up the process. (International Conference of Building Officials)

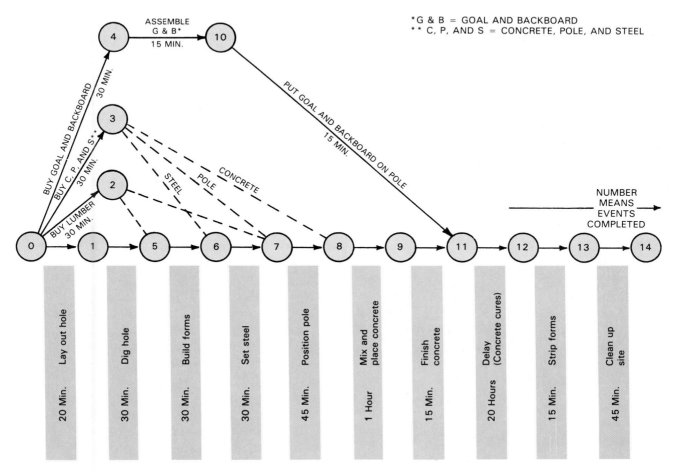

Fig. 6-22. A critical path method (CPM) chart for the basketball goal project.

Leaders in the builder's firm have a planning meeting. This master schedule includes all tasks and lead times. *Lead time* is the time it takes a firm to deliver its product or service to the site.

GETTING MATERIALS AND EQUIPMENT USED IN THE PROJECT

There are different kinds of materials and equipment used in a given structure. The method of getting them also varies.

Kinds

Materials used in the project are new and meet standards stated in the specifications. Materials used to build the projects (form bracing, scaffolds, etc.) may be used more than once. The purchasing agent orders new materials or schedules used materials.

The lumber in Fig. 6-24 is standard stock. It could be bought from a local building supply store. Only a few hours lead time is needed.

Special materials require more lead time than standard items. Any special items need to be put into the supplier's work schedule. The 48-inch butterfly valve in Fig. 6-25 was made just for that project. A few weeks lead time was needed.

Equipment used in a project is often a prime concern. Some owners request that the vendor build

Fig. 6-25. Lead time was needed to get these parts. How was it used? (American Cast Iron Pipe Co.)

a model of the equipment. The models prove that the product will work. Fig. 6-26 is a picture of one such model. Making a model may extend the lead time to over a year. Lead time on equipment can delay the entire project.

Early planning helps subcontractors. They must purchase materials and schedule equipment, too. The builder should select subcontractors as soon as possible.

Methods

Builders have at least five options for obtaining materials. They can get them from stock, buy as needed, buy with lump sum contracts, use a job account, or let a subcontractor buy their own materials.

Materials can be obtained *from stock.* In time, a surplus of materials grows in the stockyard. Materials come from other projects. In either case, they can likely be used on other projects.

The most common way to get materials is to *buy as needed.* The material is used soon after it is placed on the site. The faster it is used, the less chance there is for loss and damage.

With *lump sum contracts,* all materials are sent to or through a central supply. This method gives better control over the materials and shortens lead time.

Fig. 6-24. Lumber comes in standard sizes. It can be bought in any city. (Maine D.O.T.)

Fig. 6-26. This is a model of an electrostatic precipitator. It will clean the dirt out of smoke at a generating plant. The builder must prove to the owner that it will work. (Dresser Industries, Inc.)

Fig. 6-27. What about the machine that moves the concrete to the footings? Is it rented or owned by the contractor? (Morgen Manufacturing Co.)

A superintendent has a set amount of money on hand in a *job account.* The money can be in the form of cash, a checking account, or credit. It is used to pay bills that cannot wait. Freight and other charges are paid through this account. A receipt or invoice is used to show how the money was used.

Other materials, or *submaterials* are used by the subcontractor. The subcontractors order, check, store, and move their own materials.

Getting Equipment

Construction equipment is very costly. A major task is to keep it in use. Idle equipment does not earn the builder any profit. Equipment is owned and scheduled from other projects, bought new, or rented.

Project leaders prefer to schedule equipment they own. There is little problem if the builder owns idle machines. Machines being used on other projects present a bigger problem. One project must wait until another is finished. The time before machines can be used is lead time. The time needed to transport it to the job site must be added.

A firm buys its own machines for big jobs. This is more true when the work is common to the firm. Fig. 6-27 shows a machine that was purchased by the contractor. Firms buy equipment when there is enough lead time. It takes time to buy it, make it, and ship it. The machine in Fig. 6-28 was made

Fig. 6-28. Some projects such as this one, require special machines.

just for that project. Lead time is reduced when a machine is built right on the site and when standard parts are used to build it.

Equipment is rented when it will be needed right away or will be used for a short time. The machine shown in Fig. 6-29 was rented. Can you guess why?

Getting Workers

In construction, there are two kinds of workers. There are the workers who work for a general contractor and those who work for the subcontractors.

The superintendent schedules the firm's workers and subcontractors. The challenge is to maintain the best work group size with the right trade skills.

Fig. 6-29. The truck in the center is used to pump concrete. It was rented because the contractor seldom needs one. (Morgen Manufacturing Co.)

It is common for construction workers to be hired five to eight times each year. Contractors try to schedule their work so that skilled workers can work all year.

Workers may live locally or be from out of town. Workers with special skills may travel a long way to get the job.

MAKING INSPECTIONS

Inspections are made throughout construction. Officials start by looking over the set of plans before a building permit is issued. Inspection continues throughout construction to see that plans and specifications are followed. See Fig. 6-31. A final

Fig. 6-31. Work is inspected as it's done. (Honeywell, Inc.)

If the group is too large or too small, costs will increase. Costs will go up when workers are not doing what they are trained to do.

Contractors try to find good people and keep them as long as they can. Fig. 6-30 shows this concept. The superintendent is most often a full-time employee of the firm. This person is assigned to a new project when the last one is complete.

The superintendent in a small firm hires the workers. In large firms, people from the personnel office do the hiring.

Most construction work is short-term. When the project is done, the worker has to find a new job.

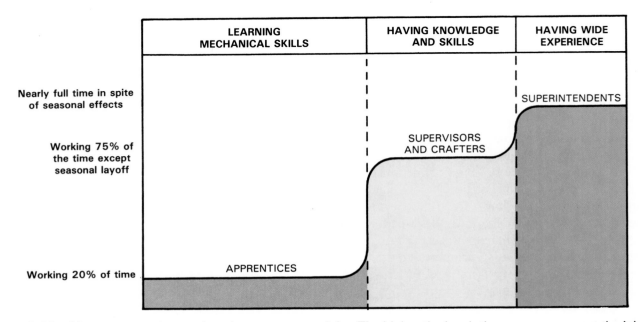

Fig. 6-30. Most construction workers have temporary jobs. The higher the level, the more permanent the jobs.

inspection of the construction phase is done before transferring the project. Inspections end when the structure is taken out of service.

Who Inspects?

Contractors must satisfy a contract, Fig. 6-32. They will not get paid until they do. Future contracts depend on past work. There are five main groups of people who inspect the work:
- Public officials who are concerned for public safety.
- Project designers who inspect to see that the design was carried out.
- Lenders inspect the project to be sure it works well.
- Owners inspect the project to be sure they are getting what they are paying for.
- Suppliers check that shipments of their products are what the customer ordered.

INSPECTING THE PROJECT

Inspectors are concerned about many things. They check the materials, methods, and quality of work.

Fig. 6-32. The contractor (center yellow hard hat) is checking on a step in the construction process. The owner (right), engineers (white hard hats), and superintendent (left yellow hard hat) are consulted. (Southern Company Services)

Materials

Materials are checked on the plans before the building permit is issued. Inspectors then must see that the specified materials are used.

Methods

There are many ways to do any given job. Specifications describe the preferred methods to be used. Inspections ensure they are used, Fig. 6-33.

Quality of Work

The quality of work is checked in several ways. See Fig. 6-34. Inspectors look to see if it works, is the right size, and looks good.

A *certificate of substantial completion* is issued when the project is nearly complete. In the *final inspection,* materials and quality are checked. The defects are listed on a *punch list.* Each item on the punch list must be corrected by the responsible firm. After each item is corrected, an *approval form* is signed by the inspectors and a *certificate of completion* is issued.

CLOSING THE CONTRACT

When all work is complete, the project's ownership is transferred from the contractor to the

Fig. 6-33. Inspections are made at various times during the construction process. (Republic Building Corp.)

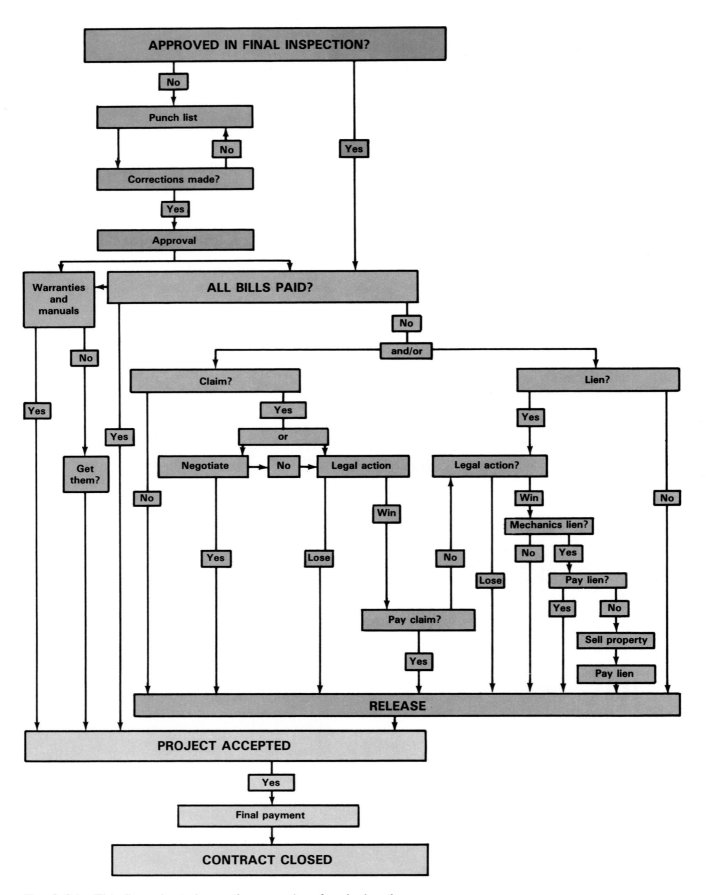

Fig. 6-34. This flow chart shows the procedure for closing the contract. The procedure moves from the top to the bottom.

owner. At the contract closing, the owner pays the contractor and receives documents. The owner makes the final payment to the contractor. The contractor must provide signed approvals, releases, warranties, and manuals.

Complaints of nonpayment are of two types. They are called the claim and lien. A *claim* arises when extra work needs to be done. For example, let's say that a contractor is building a house. When digging for the foundation wall, a dump site is found. The contractor has to pay extra money (money not included in the contract) to remove the trash. The contractor feels that the owner owes him or her more money to clear the site. A *lien* arises when an owner owes money on the building. For example, money can be withheld because the owner is not happy with the materials or work quality, and the owner does not pay the contractor. A *release* frees a person of a complaint.

A *warranty* is a document giving a guarantee that there are no defects. New owners also receive the *manuals* that describe how to operate and maintain the equipment.

Now the owner makes the *final payment.* The contractor is released from the performance and payment bonds. The contractor's responsibility ends except for the warranties. The contract is said to be "closed."

SUMMARY

Contracting is complex and involves many kinds of contracts. A contractor must follow a set process to get a public contract.

Keeping on schedule is not easy. It is impossible if materials and equipment are not on the site. Experience, bar charts, and the critical path method help builders schedule projects.

It is the purchasing agent's job to select the best vendors. Lead time is crucial in choosing a vendor. Contractor's either own, buy, or rent equipment.

Inspections are used to find defects in the project. A release assures the owner that there are no claims or liens on the project. Warranties and manuals are given to the owner. When the project is complete, a certificate of completion is signed, a final payment is made, and the contract is closed.

KEY WORDS

All the following words have been used in this chapter. Do you know their meanings?

Approval form
Bar chart
Buy as needed
Certificate of completion
Certificate of substantial completion
Clerk
Closing the contract
Competitive bid
Constructor
Contractor
Critical path method (CPM)
Design/build approach
Equipment
Estimating
Experience
Fast-track delivery approach
Field engineer
Field office
Final inspection
Final payment
From stock
General contractor
Home office
Job account
Labor
Labor productivity tables
Lead time
Linear delivery approach
Lump sum contract
Manuals
Markup
Master schedule
Negotiated contracts
Notice to proceed
Overhead
Priority work
Profit
Project delivery approach (PDA)
Project delivery process (PDP)
Project manager
Punch list
Quality inspection
Release
Strategy
Subcontractor
Submaterials
Superintendent
Supervisor
Supplier
Terms
Warranty
Workers

TEST YOUR KNOWLEDGE

Place your answers on a separate sheet of paper. Do not write in this text.

Matching questions: Match the definition in the left column with the correct term in the right column.

1. Costs of surveys, site preparation, insurance, and building permits.
2. A plan to reach a prearranged goal.
3. Includes office payroll and telephone.
4. An estimate used to plan profit level.
5. Receipts minus costs.

A. Home office overhead costs.
B. Field office overhead costs.
C. Profit.
D. Markup.
E. Strategy.

6. List five phases of the Project Delivery Process (PDP).
7. Describe the following:
   A. Linear approach.
   B. Fast-track approach.
   C. Design/build approach.

8. A designer/builder is called a _____.
9. List the three types of contractors.
10. What do you call the amount of money a contractor thinks it will take to build a project?
11. There are three mehods used to manage projects. They are experience, the _____ _____ method, and the _____ _____ method.
12. The time it takes a firm to deliver its product or service to the site is called _____ _____.
13. Machines that are needed right away are often _____.
14. When the project is nearly complete, a Certificate of _____ _____ is issued.
15. In the final inspection all defects are placed on a _____ list.
16. When a problem in payment is resolved, a _____ is signed.

ACTIVITIES

1. Do you or the people you live with have contracts with employers or unions? Make a list of them. Include the terms.
2. Let us say you need a new garden shed. Plan it out and make some sketches. How much will the materials cost? How much time will it take to build it? Are there any overhead costs such as gas for a car to pick up supplies?
3. Visit with a worker. Find out how they were hired.
4. Develop a bar chart or CPM chart for a new mailbox at your house.
5. Talk with the owner(s) of a new structure. Have them explain their contract closing procedure. How long do warranties last? How long can a payment schedule term last?

Teamwork is vital to an efficient construction project.   (AMAX Corp.)

Section III
DESIGNING PRODUCTS AND STRUCTURES

Chapter 7

ESTABLISHING NEEDS

After reading this chapter, you will be able to:
☐ Define and describe three approaches production companies use in developing new products and structures.
☐ Explain how companies can identify good, profitable ideas.
☐ Describe several processes companies might use in developing new, profitable ideas.
☐ Develop some methods of your own for finding profitable ideas your class can produce and sell.

All products or structures must start with an idea, Fig. 7-1. Ideas usually start with needs. Someone conceives (thinks) of something people need. A person may think of a product or structure they need.

DESIGN APPROACHES

Three basic approaches are used to design products and structures, Fig. 7-2. The approach used depends on the desired output.

Production Approach

The *production approach* to product design stresses producing products. A design staff develops a product. It is then produced in quantity. Major advertising campaigns try to convince people they need the product.

Many high-volume consumer goods are developed by the production approach. Cosmetics, soaps, toothpaste, and designer clothing are examples of products using this approach. It is doubtful that large numbers of people were asking for crockpots or electric pencil sharpeners to be

Fig. 7-1. All products or structures start with an idea.

developed. They were first designed and produced. Then we were told that we needed them through advertising.

Consumer Approach

The *consumer approach* first identifies products people need. Then, the products are designed and produced. This system is widely used in developing industrial goods, Fig. 7-3.

Boeing Airplane Company carefully collects data from airlines before they design a new aircraft.

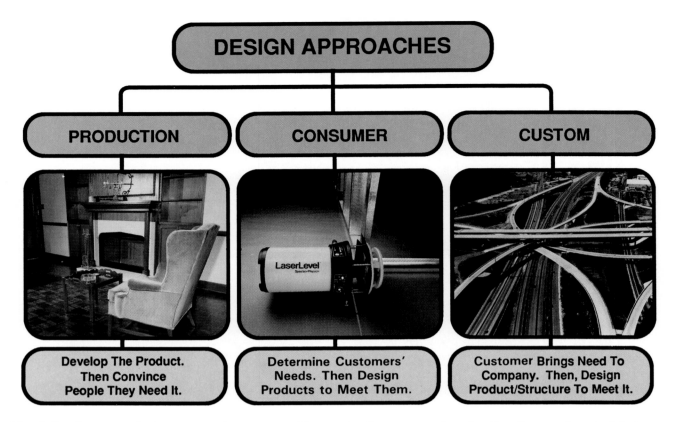

DESIGN APPROACHES

PRODUCTION

Develop The Product. Then Convince People They Need It.

CONSUMER

Determine Customers' Needs. Then Design Products to Meet Them.

CUSTOM

Customer Brings Need To Company. Then, Design Product/Structure To Meet It.

Fig. 7-2. Common design approaches are used by production companies. A—Furniture and materials to finish a house. B—LaserLevel used on construction projects. C—Highway interchange.
(Pease Flooring Co., Inc.; Spectra-Physics; U.S. Department of Transportation, Federal Highway Administration)

Fig. 7-3. This machine was developed using a consumer approach.   (Caterpillar, Inc.)

They try to include all the features requested by the many different airlines.

Another company asked boat builders and casket makers "What kind of sander do you need?" Their answer was "A small machine that will sand curves and small surfaces." This research led to the handheld oscillating sander.

Until recently, most products you bought were designed using the production approach. Growing competition has caused more companies to use the consumer approach.

Custom Approach

The *custom approach* is used by manufacturing companies for special-purpose equipment. Usually, only one or a few custom-designed products or structures are produced.

Construction uses this approach most of the time. Large buildings, highways, dams, pipelines, and airports are all examples of custom-produced structures. The companies who produced the bridge in Fig. 7-4 used the custom approach. A manufacturing company used the approach to produce the equipment that is lifting the concrete section in place.

The owner or customer may have a need for a structure. It will be stated in a set of requirements and limitations called a *program.* An architectural firm or engineering firm will be selected to do the design work. Another division of the company may

Fig. 7-4. A custom approach was used to design both the bridge and the lifting equipment. (U.S. Department of Transportation, Federal Highway Administration)

build the product or structure. Joint ventures are common on these large projects. A *joint venture* is when two or more companies work together on one project.

IDENTIFYING PROFITABLE IDEAS

Developing products and structures is hard. It must balance the needs of the customer with the strengths of the company, Fig. 7-5. Customers must need or want the products or structures. Likewise, the company must have the resources to design, produce, and market the product.

A company cannot produce a product or structure just because it is a good idea. It must fit the company's area of operation. A metal machining company will not be very interested in an idea for a wood desk.

Determining Consumer Needs and Wants

Each of us has needs and wants. You may want a new bicycle. You best friend may want a stereo

Fig. 7-5. Products must be designed to meet customer need and use company strength.

system. This difference causes a problem for companies. They cannot manufacture a product just for you. They need to produce products many people want (mass appeal).

The company must decide what a group of people will buy. This is done in many ways. It will depend on how the company develops products and structures.

Some companies are imitators. They produce a product much like those of other companies. They let someone else identify and build the market. The basic information they need is sales figures. Assume Company D (developer) is selling many widgets. Then, Company I (imitator) will also want to make widgets. *Imitation* is a common product development technique. Think of products that are widely imitated. How about home computers, stereo receivers, clothing styles, and toys?

Another technique is *adaptation.* This means a product is "improved" by changing it. The manual typewriter was adapted to be an electric typewriter. Now we have electronic typewriters, Fig. 7-6. The 10-speed bicycle was a modification of the normal bike. Adapted products are all around us.

The last technique is *innovation* (something new). A totally new product is developed. The video recorder, microchip (Fig. 7-7), and polyester fibers are recent innovations.

The *image* of an architectural or engineering design firm is seen in the structures or products they design. Fast, reliable, low-cost basic service is given by "delivery firms," Fig. 7-8. They provide routine, but very efficient service. "Service firms" use widely accepted ideas to solve complex and special problems, Fig. 7-9. They tailor their service to each client. "Idea firms" are known for the unique struc-

A

B

Fig. 7-6. A—Electric typewriter was adapted from a common typewriter. B—Electronic typewriter is a further adaptation. (IBM)

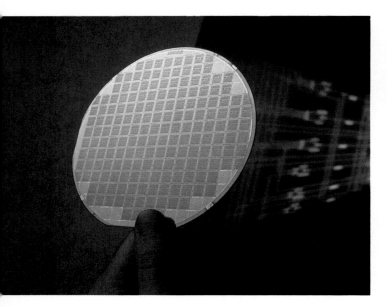

Fig. 7-7. This silicon wafer is a recent innovation. Each small square on the wafer contains a custom-designed integrated circuit. (AT&T)

Fig. 7-8. An efficient "delivery firm" would be selected for this project. The tunnel is shallow. Soil conditions are uniform. The construction methods are well known.
(Martin K. Eby Construction Co., Inc.)

Fig. 7-9. A strong "service firm" designed this structure. Well-understood knowledge about geodesic domes was used to solve this unique problem. (TEMCOR)

tures they design, Fig. 7-10. These firms search out the brightest professional to find creative solutions.

Responding To Customer Needs

Most construction projects are initiated by public and private owners. They are asking for projects that are becoming larger and more complex. New and unique ways to meet these needs are being

Fig. 7-10. An "idea firm" designed the first cable stayed bridge.   (HNTB Engineers)

found by architects and engineers. Contractors are being challenged to build these new structures.

Construction projects are usually one of a kind, Fig. 7-11. That means owners, designers, and builders must work closely as a team. A *design program* is vital to team building and to producing structures. The program describes the physical requirements, delivery schedule, and project budget. The program serves three purposes:

- It acquaints the project team with each person's role and to the project.
- It directs the design process.
- The design program is used to secure support for the project. The project needs support from its users, investors, designers, and the government.

SOURCES OF PRODUCT IDEAS

Each of the methods for product development starts with ideas. These ideas come from both inside and outside the company. They basically arise from studying the three sources shown in Fig. 7-12.

Market Research

Market research is used to study people's thinking about products. It may tell the company what products people want. It may test people's feelings about a product the company already has in its line. The information gathered is used for either product development or improvement.

Market research gathers information in three major areas as seen in Fig. 7-13. It gives the company information about people's choice of product size, color, style, and function. This information is the starting place for good product design or redesign.

Some kinds of research collect information about the market itself. A company learns things about its customers: their age, sex, where they live, their occupation, and income.

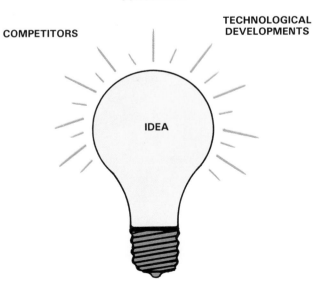

Fig. 7-12. New product ideas come from many sources.

Fig. 7-11. The owners, designers, and builder worked as a team on this building.   (HNTB Engineers)

Fig. 7-13. Market research helps identify product ideas by gathering information about the product, market, and market system.

Finally, a company gathers data on the value of its marketing activities. Information is obtained on types of stores where the product is purchased.

More detailed information about the product is obtained by surveys. Individuals are often asked to use or taste the product, Fig. 7-14. They then are questioned. The actual questions try to bring out the following information:

- Feelings about the product.
- Evaluation of product quality.

Fig. 7-14. Some product ideas are tested through customer surveys.

- Whether the person would like to own or use the product.
- Reaction to product color, size, and function.
- Expected selling price.
- Number of products that would be purchased in a year.
- Use for the product—gift or personal.
- Improvements that could be made.
- Comparison to other similar products on the market.
- Type of store in which the product would be expected to be found.

The warranty card, Fig. 7-15, is often used to gather data. Warranty cards are usually packaged with new products. Basic information is usually needed on:

- Name and address of purchaser.
- Sex and age of the new owner.
- Income of customer.
- How the customer heard about the product.
- Type of store in which the product was purchased.
- Whether the product was purchased for a gift or for personal use.

Competitive Analysis

All companies carefully study the products of their competitors. A company can determine the need to improve its own product from this study. This is called *competitive analysis.*

Product imitators can determine trends in product development. They can identify areas where they want to develop similar products.

Each company, of course, must ensure that they do not break patent laws. They must develop their own technology, pay to use someone else's ideas, or use nonpatented technology. There are thousands of ideas not patented. The patents of many other products have expired.

Technological Developments

The last source of product ideas is *technological developments.* Advancements in science and technology can give designers product ideas. New materials may suggest new products. The development of composites gave us fiberglass fishing poles and lightweight aircraft parts. The invention of the laser and glass fibers gave us fiber optic communication systems.

Companies never stop gathering information about new developments. They may produce the advancement in their own research labs, Fig. 7-16.

OWNER INFORMATION CARD

Seal card here

Model

0234351 (4600 EFU)

IMPORTANT: Please complete the information below and mail this card right away.

1. ☐ Mr. 2. ☐ Mrs. 3. ☐ Ms. 4. ☐ Miss   **41D**

Name (First/Initial/Last)

Street

City   State   Zip

Date of Purchase: ___/___/___
                  Mo   Day   Yr

Serial Number _____

A) Where was this product purchased?
1. ☐ Camera store
2. ☐ Department store
3. ☐ Discount store
4. ☐ Mail order
5. ☐ Military (PX, etc.)
6. ☐ Catalog showroom
7. ☐ Received as gift
8. ☐ Other (specify: _____)

B) This product will primarily be used for:
1. ☐ Commercial/Industrial/Govt.
2. ☐ Scientific/Medical
3. ☐ Photo journalism
4. ☐ Creative hobby
5. ☐ Family/Travel

C) Who/What was the greatest influence in your final decision to purchase this product?
1. ☐ Advertising
2. ☐ Vivitar brand name
3. ☐ Product features
4. ☐ Friend/relative
5. ☐ Price
6. ☐ Product brochure/literature
7. ☐ Salesperson
8. ☐ Other (specify: _____)

D) Check the one which is appropriate:
1. ☐ This is the first time I have owned a product of this type.
2. ☐ I own another Elite product of this type.
3. ☐ I own another product of this type, but not an Elite
4. ☐ I already own other products of this type—both Elite and other brands.

E) User's highest level of education completed:
1. ☐ High school
2. ☐ Some college
3. ☐ College graduate
4. ☐ Post graduate

F) Which of the following do you read/see/listen to regularly?
1. ☐ Newspaper
2. ☐ Television/Radio
3. ☐ *Modern Photography*
4. ☐ *Petersen's Photographic*
5. ☐ *Playboy Magazine*
6. ☐ *Popular Photography*
7. ☐ *Readers Digest*
8. ☐ *Sports Illustrated*
9. ☐ Special Interest magazines
10. ☐ *Time/Newsweek/U.S. News*
11. ☐ *TV Guide*

G) What brand of 35mm SLR do you own?
1. ☐ Conar   4. ☐ Xbrand
2. ☐ Mito   5. ☐ Mbrand
3. ☐ Noko   6. ☐ Other

H) What model do you own? _____

I) Which of the following have you done in the past 6 months? (check all that apply)
1. ☐ Redeemed a product coupon
2. ☐ Ordered an item from mail order catalog
3. ☐ Sent in product inquiry card from magazine
4. ☐ Bought item from offer received in mail
5. ☐ Entered sweepstakes/contest

J) Month and Year of your birth:
☐☐   1 9 ☐☐
Month   Year

K) Do you have any children in any of the following age groups who are living at home?
1. ☐ Under age 2   5. ☐ Age 11-12
2. ☐ Age 2-4   6. ☐ Age 13-15
3. ☐ Age 5-7   7. ☐ Age 16-18
4. ☐ Age 8-10

L) Marital status:
1. ☐ Married   2. ☐ Unmarried

M) Which group best describes your family income?
1. ☐ Under $10,000   6. ☐ $30,000-$34,999
2. ☐ $10,000-$14,999   7. ☐ $35,000-$39,999
3. ☐ $15,000-$19,999   8. ☐ $40,000-$44,999
4. ☐ $20,000-$24,999   9. ☐ $45,000-$49,999
5. ☐ $25,000-$29,999   10. ☐ $50,000 & over

N) Do you:
1. ☐ Own your home?
2. ☐ Rent your home?

(over)

Fig. 7-15. Study the questions on this warranty card. How would the information help a product designer or an advertising person?

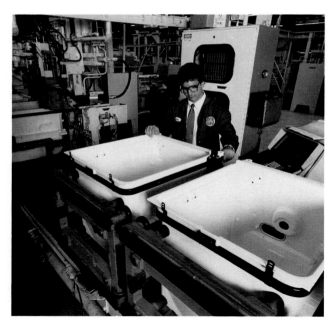

Fig. 7-16. Engineers monitor production processes. (General Electric Co.)

Other data are obtained by outside sources. These sources include:
- Other companies.
- Government agencies.
- Universities.
- Private research centers.
- Private inventors.

COMPANY PROFILE

Production ideas, as mentioned, must be matched to the company strengths. These strengths are often contained in a list called a *company profile.* Five main elements are included in a company profile. These are the:
- Market the company knows.
- Type of products or structures the company produces.
- Sales volume the company expects.
- Cost to develop and engineer the product or structure.
- Financial resources available.

SUMMARY

Products and structures are designed by using either production, consumer, or custom approaches. They start the design process with ideas. The ideas may be imitations (copies) of other products. Some ideas adapt or improve on existing prod-

ucts. Few ideas are truly new. They are called innovations. A future owner of a structure may have a program to describe a construction project.

Profitable ideas are generated by studying (1) consumers, (2) competitors, and (3) technological developments. All ideas must fit the company. They must fall within a profile of the company's strengths.

KEY WORDS

All the following words have been used in this chapter. Do you know their meaning?

Adaptation	Innovation
Company profile	Joint venture
Competitive analysis	Market research
Consumer research	Program
Custom approach	Technological
Image	developments
Imitation	

TEST YOUR KNOWLEDGE

Place your answers on a separate sheet. Please do not write in this text.
1. Explain the difference between the consumer approach, production approach, and custom approach to product and structure development.
2. Adaptation means producing a new product by _____.
   A. improving an old design so the product does the job better
   B. changing a product so it looks different
   C. making product of cheaper materials to make more profit
   D. stealing another company's product idea
3. _____ _____ is studying people's thinking about products.
4. List the three sources of ideas for product development.
5. Describe two methods of getting information from users of a company's product.
6. When a company studies the products of its competitors to see how it can or should improve its own products, the method is called _____.
   A. comparison shopping
   B. competitive analysis
   C. technological development
   D. patent search

ACTIVITIES

1. List 10 products or structures that were developed using a:
   A. Consumer approach.
   B. Production approach.
   C. Custom approach.

2. Visit a company and interview a product designer. Find out how she or he finds new product ideas.

3. Interview a retail store manager. Ask him or her to discuss products that were:
   A. designed to meet a basic customer need.
   B. first designed and then the need was developed by advertising.

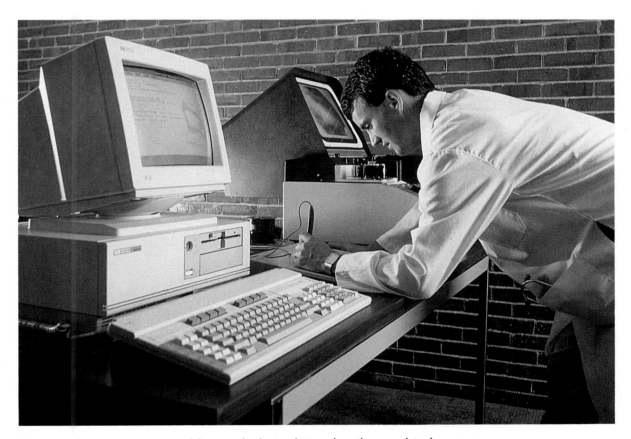

A company can use competitive analysis to determine the need to improve its own product.   (Photo courtesy of Hewlett-Packard Company)

Thorough research and design is a vital part of a product's life.   (Goodyear Tire and Rubber Co.)

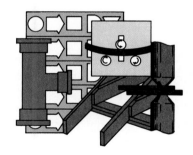

Chapter 8

DESIGNING AND ENGINEERING PRODUCTS

After reading this chapter, you will be able to:
□ List and describe the objectives of design.
□ Explain factors of industrial design.
□ List and describe steps in a design process.
□ Explain different types of models used in presenting designs.
□ Explain how products are engineered.
□ Recognize different types of engineering drawings and tell how they are used.
□ Describe a bill of materials and explain its use.
□ Discuss specifications and describe their form and contents.

Product ideas must be developed to meet product needs. Product designers change words into products. They convert need statements into product ideas.

To do this, designers use a process called *ideation.* They sketch many ideas to meet the product need. Then, the best ones are selected. They move "ideas-in-mind" to "ideas-on-paper."

The act of product design has objectives, and is a process. It has goals and is a method (way of doing).

DESIGN OBJECTIVES

All product design activities are aimed at meeting a goal. The major goals are to develop products that customers want. In addition, these products must meet or beat competition, and make a profit for the company.

Successful designers always keep three major factors in mind. They design for function, manufacturing, and selling, Fig. 8-1.

Fig. 8-1. Products are designed with three factors in mind. They must fill a need (function), be easy to make (manufacture), and customers must want them.

Designing for Function

All products are designed to do a job. A train must move freight, Fig. 8-2. A picture must decorate a wall. A washer must wash clothes.

The ability to do a job is called *function.* Designers consider the product's purpose, operation, and safety. For example, a designer of toy trucks must consider several factors related to function. These might include:
• Where is the toy going to be used? Will it be an indoor or outdoor toy?

Fig. 8-2. Trucks are designed to move freight. This is their function. (Freightliner Corp.)

- Is it designed for educational purposes?
- What type of surface must it roll on?
- What age of child will use it? What safety features are required for this age group?

Every product's worth is measured in terms of function. It must operate under typical conditions.

Designing for Manufacture

It is not enough to have a functional product. The company must be able to build it efficiently. This means that designers must consider *ease of manufacturing*, Fig. 8-3.

Fig. 8-3. Designers considered manufacturing and assembly when they designed this airplane. Design for manufacture allows the aircraft skin to be easily mated with the frame. (Boeing)

Designers also consider the number of parts needed. Usually, the fewer parts the better. They will also use standard parts and materials whenever possible. Why make a bolt if you can buy it cheaper?

In addition, the number of different parts are considered. A designer would not use a 5/8-16UN screw in one place and a 5/8-28UN screw in another. They are the same diameter. Only the number of threads per inch is different. Using one size reduces inventory costs.

The ability to process the part is another consideration. Look at Fig. 8-4. The part on the left would be more difficult to cut out and sand. The design on the right would be easier to manufacture.

Designing for Selling

Product function and manufacture are important. However, the product must also *sell*. Customers must see that the product meets their needs. These needs include function, appearance, and value.

We buy products to do a job for us (function). We also want them to be attractive. Even a table saw is designed to look good. Finally, the product must have value. We must feel that it is worth the selling price.

DESIGN PROCESS

Product designers follow a few basic steps in developing product ideas. These steps, shown in Fig. 8-5, include:
- Developing preliminary (beginning) designs.
- Refining designs.
- Preparing models.
- Communicating designs.
- Obtaining approval for designs.

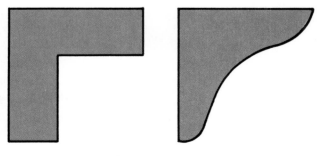

SHELF SUPPORT

Fig. 8-4. The part on the right would be easier to manufacture than the one on the left.

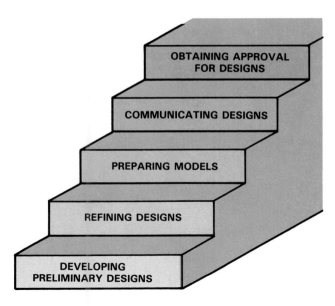

Fig. 8-5. There are five steps in the design process.

Preliminary Designs

Generating ideas is the first step in product design. Designers quickly sketch as many ideas as they can, Fig. 8-6. Often these sketches are simple "doodles." They are designed to record what the mind dreams up.

Fig. 8-6. Designers develop rough sketches for their "library of product ideas."

These first sketches are often called *thumbnail,* or *rough sketches.* They serve the same purpose as notes do for writers. They are assorted pieces of information.

You might think of the rough sketches as a "library of product ideas." A large library will more likely have good ideas. Therefore, it is important for a designer to develop many rough sketches.

Refining Designs

The designer selects the best ideas from the many rough sketches. These ideas are then improved upon. Details are added. Several sketches may be fused (put) together to form a better idea. The sketches, as they become more complete, are called *refined sketches.* The refined sketch shows shape and size. It gives a fairly accurate view of the designer's ideas.

Many designers use computers to develop ideas, Fig. 8-7. Computer systems allow the designers to quickly change lines and shapes. The drawings can then be stored for later use. Also, copies can be produced using printers and plotters. These design systems are called *computer-aided design (CAD).*

Preparing Models

Many times sketches do not show enough detail. They are two-dimensional (have width and height only). The mind has to imagine the third dimension. Therefore, models are often built.

There are two major types of models: mock-ups and prototypes. A *mock-up* is an appearance model, Fig. 8-8. It shows what the product will look

Fig. 8-7. This 3-D CAD drawing allows the designer to study an automobile suspension system. (Daimler Benz)

Fig. 8-8. This designer is working on a scale model of a new automobile. (Ford Motor Co.)

Fig. 8-9. This engineer is testing a toy prototype for safety and durability. (Ohio Art Co.)

like. Mock-ups are usually made of materials that are easily worked. Cardboard, balsa wood, clay, Styrofoam™, and plaster are commonly used.

Prototypes are working models. They generally show the product in full size. Prototypes use the same material the product will use. Their purpose is to check the operation of the final product. Fig. 8-9 shows a typical prototype.

Models allow the design to be viewed more completely. It can be seen from all angles. The appearance and operation of the product can be checked carefully.

Communicating Designs

Developed designs must be communicated to management. In many cases, managers want to study the idea's size, shape, color, and details. Typically, completed designs are shown in two ways: models and renderings.

These *models* are usually final prototypes or mock-ups. Earlier models were used for the designer to check ideas. Now, new models are made which include all design changes.

Renderings are also used to show final designs. They are usually colored pictorial sketches showing the overall detail of the design. Fig. 8-10 shows renderings of four television cabinet designs.

Getting Management's Approval

The final step for the design process is approval. Management must give its "OK" to continue developing the product. Management evaluates the product design against several factors. These include the competition, manufacturing cost, market size, profit margin, and resource requirements.

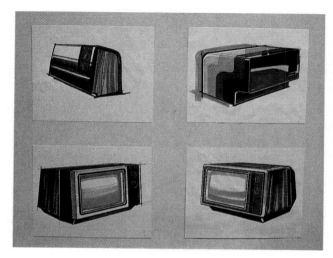

Fig. 8-10. Renderings showing four television cabinet designs. (RCA)

The managers usually receive preliminary cost estimates. They also review the design sketches and models, Fig. 8-11. Managers decide the fate of the product ideas. If the designs are approved, they will be sent to product engineering.

ENGINEERING DESIGNS

Product designs show how the product will look and work. However, the product is not ready to be produced. The design must be refined. This final preparation is called *product engineering*.

Product engineering modifies (changes) and specifies the design. Specifying means to give the size, material, and quality requirements for the product. Product engineers also test the product. They check its operation and safety, as well as other important features.

SPECIFYING DESIGNS

Most products have several parts, Fig. 8-12. These parts must fit and work together. Often, the product has parts from several sources. Standard items are bought from suppliers. Others may build special parts. Suppliers may bid to product parts of the product. The company, itself, may produce many different parts. All of them must fit together to make the product, Fig. 8-13.

Each supplier must know the exact size, shape, and properties of the components they make. This information is found in the specifications. Product engineers specify product characteristics (features) in three ways:
• Engineering drawings.
• Bill of materials.
• Specification sheets.

Engineering Drawings

Engineering drawings tell how to make the product. The drawings include specifications for individual parts. Information needed to assemble the product is also given. This basic information is placed on three types of drawings: detail drawings, assembly drawings, and schematic drawings.

Fig. 8-12. Like this television cabinet, most products have several parts. (Zenith Electronics Corp.)

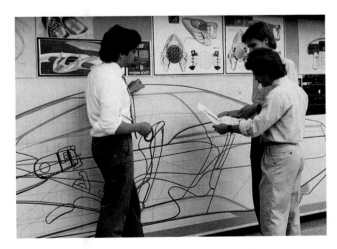

Fig. 8-11. A management team reviewing sketches for a new automobile. (Ford Motor Co.)

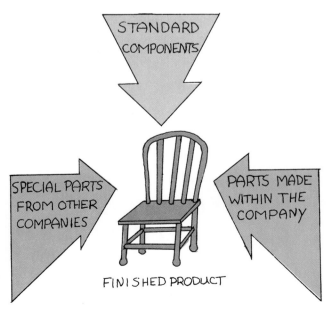

Fig. 8-13. Parts from several sources must fit together to make a typical product.

Detail drawings

Engineering will prepare a detail drawing for each different part. *Detail drawings* give the exact size of the part, as well as the size and location of all features. These features may include holes, notches, curves, and tapers. The features give the parts their final form.

Detail drawings are usually multiview (many view) drawings. They show the part from several sides. These drawings use a system called *orthographic projection*. This system generally shows the part in two or three views, Fig. 8-14. Round parts are commonly shown in two views—a front view and a side view. Other shapes are shown in three views: front, top, and right side. You see each view in two dimensions, height and width. It is as though you are looking directly at that side of the part.

Many detail drawings are now prepared using CAD systems. These systems allow the drafter (a person who prepares drawings) to quickly draw and change a drawing, Fig. 8-15.

A detail drawing must give all the information needed about a part. The manufacturer (maker of parts and products) must be able to make the part from the drawing. Look at Fig. 8-16. Could you

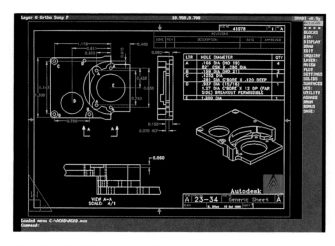

Fig. 8-15. Many drawings are first prepared on a CAD system. They can then be stored or printed out. (Autodesk, Inc.)

make the table leg from the information given? What additional information might you need? Remember we are talking about making many parts that are alike. Could you make the curves identical on each part? Does the drawing give you that information? You can easily see why drawings must be complete. Parts cannot be accurately produced without good detail drawings.

Assembly drawings

Parts must be put together to make many products. *Assembly drawings* show how these parts mate. These drawings identify the parts by a code (number, letter, etc.). They then show the position of each part.

Assembly drawings may be a two-dimensional (width and height) drawing showing the parts in their final assembled position.

Pictorial (picture-like) drawings are also used. 8-17. The parts are pulled apart to show better how they fit together.

Schematic drawings

Schematic drawings are used to show electrical, pneumatic (air), and hydraulic (fluid) systems. They show the location and connections of parts in the system.

Schematic (also called systems) drawings give information needed for assembly and servicing. Workers can easily see how components fit in the system.

Bill of Materials

A second tool of the product engineer is the *bill of materials.* It is a list of all materials needed to

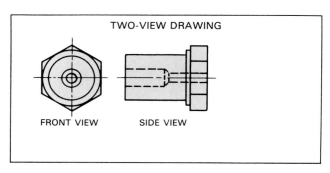

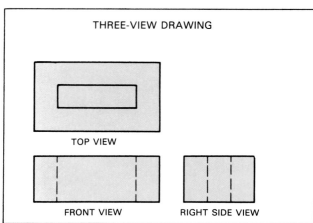

Fig. 8-14. Orthographic projections are "straight on" drawings of parts. Two types are shown.

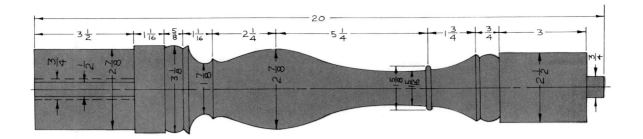

Fig. 8-16. This is a simple detail drawing.

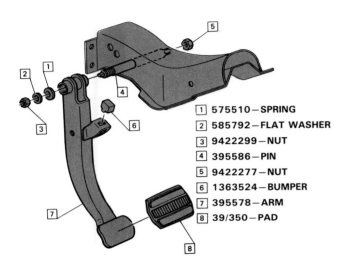

1	575510 — SPRING
2	585792 — FLAT WASHER
3	9422299 — NUT
4	395586 — PIN
5	9422277 — NUT
6	1363524 — BUMPER
7	395578 — ARM
8	39/350 — PAD

Fig. 8-17. An exploded assembly drawing is pulled apart so you can better see where each part belongs.

MASTER BILL OF MATERIALS

PRODUCT: _____

PRODUCT CODE NUMBER: _____

Part No.	Part Name	Material	Qty.	Size T W L

Fig. 8-18. A sample bill of materials lists sizes of and quantities of materials in orderly fashion.

make one product. A bill of materials, shown in Fig. 8-18, includes:

• Part number.
• Part name.
• Material to be used.
• Quantity of each part needed.
• Size of each part.

The sizes are given in logical order. The thickness is listed first, then the width is given, and finally the length.

A bill of materials is a valuable form. It is used to determine the material to order. It is also used to estimate the cost of manufacturing the product.

Specification Sheets

Some items and certain qualities cannot be shown on a drawing. How would you show adhesives (glues) on a drawing? A drawing of a piece of sheet steel would be of little value.

The important qualities of these materials is not size and shape. Instead, its mechanical, electrical, thermal, or chemical characteristics are important. Product engineers need to know or specify these various properties.

Small manufacturers cannot afford to have materials developed for them. An adhesive may be needed to bond an aluminum sheet to plywood. A small manufacturer would call an adhesive manufacturer and describe the need. The adhesive company would provide *technical data sheets.* These sheets describe adhesives that would do the job. The product engineer reviews the data sheets. Then, she or he picks the best adhesive for the job.

Larger companies may specify the material qualities they want. They prepare a *specification sheet* for the material. Suppliers offer to supply the material. It would be produced to meet the customer's specifications (specs).

Testing Products

Product engineers also test designs. They make sure that the product works. Just as important, they will test it for safety, Fig. 8-19. The product is put

Fig. 8-19. A cylinder head is tested in a laboratory. (General Motors)

under actual conditions of use and closely watched. The data gathered helps engineers to decide if the product works. Also, testing information is one source of ideas for product improvement.

One more use of product testing is to answer customer complaints. Broken products may be returned; they may have quit working. Testing can determine if the product design has flaws. It can find out if customer misuse caused the failure. If so, new instructions for use may be needed.

SUMMARY

Designing products involves careful consideration of function, manufacture, and selling. Creating a successful design involves several steps. Ideas must be generated through rough sketching activities. These ideas are further developed. Refined sketches and models are prepared. The refined ideas are communicated to management for approval.

Approved ideas are then engineered. Product engineers must specify their characteristics. This is done with detail drawings for each part, assembly drawings that show how the parts go together and schematic drawings to describe electrical, pneumatic, and hydraulic systems.

Also, bills of materials that list all parts needed to make a product are prepared. Finally, the properties of a material or product are specified. They are contained in technical data sheets and specification sheets.

KEY WORDS

All of the following words have been used in this chapter. Do you know their meaning?

Assembly drawing
Bill of material
Computer-aided design (CAD)
Detail drawing
Ease of manufacturing
Engineering drawing
Function
Ideation
Mock-up
Model

Orthographic projection
Product engineering
Prototype
Refined sketch
Rendering
Schematic drawing
Sell
Specification sheet
Technical data sheet
Thumbnail sketch

TEST YOUR KNOWLEDGE

Place your answers on a separate sheet of paper. Do not write in this book.
1. Give the steps for the process of ideation.
2. Describe what is meant by:
   A. Designing for function.
   B. Designing for manufacture.
   C. Designing for selling.
3. Arrange the following design steps in their proper order:
   A. Obtaining approval for designs.
   B. Developing preliminary designs.
   C. Communicating designs.
   D. Refining designs.
   E. Preparing models.
4. What are the two types of models used by product designers? What is the difference between them?
5. Using computers to draw up designs is known as _____. The term stands for _____ _____ _____.
6. A rendering is a _____.
   A. final prototype
   B. colored pictorial sketch
   C. final mock-up that has been painted
7. _____ drawings are used to give the exact size of a part.
   A. Schematic.
   B. Assembly.
   C. Detail.

8. If you want to show all the features of a drawing (including holes, notches, curves, and tapers) you would use a(n) _____ drawing.

9. An orthographic projection (select all correct answers):
   A. Allows you to see height, width, and depth in a single view.
   B. Generally shows parts in two or three views.
   C. Shows each view in two dimensions, height and width.
   D. Shows round parts in two views.
   E. Often shows three views: front, top, and right side.

10. A drawing which presents the parts as though it were a picture is called a _____ drawing. It shows the part in _____ dimensions, _____, _____ and _____.

11. List the information included on a bill of materials.

12. If a small company asked an adhesive manufacturer to supply information on a glue to meet the company's needs, would the adhesive manufacturer supply the information on a technical data sheet or a specification sheet?

13. When are specification sheets used?

ACTIVITIES

1. Visit a product designer to see samples of product sketches. Ask about the design process (steps) used. Find out about the way products are designed and approved for manufacture.

2. Select three simple products in your home. Evaluate their designs in terms of function, manufacture, and selling.

3. A maple book rack has three major parts—a large end which is 3/4 × 6 × 8, a small end which is 3/4 × 6 × 3, and a shelf which is 3/4 × 6 × 14.
   A. Prepare a bill of materials for the product.
   B. Prepare a drawing for the large end.

4. Interview a drafter to find out:
   A. Types of drawings he or she prepares.
   B. Methods used to prepare the drawing.
   C. Basic requirements for the job.

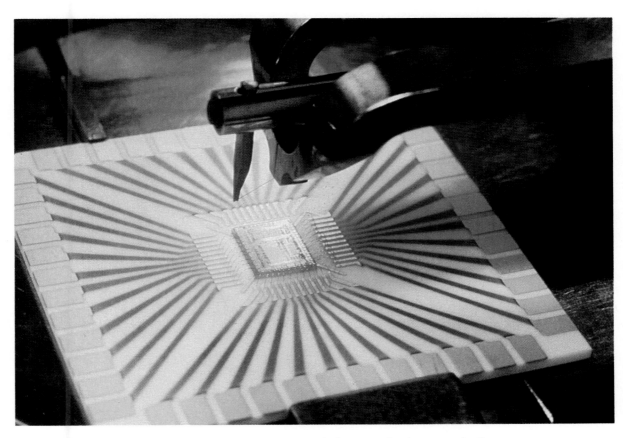

Some designs are very detailed. Here, cold wires are being attached automatically to the semiconductor.   (Photo courtesy of Hewlett-Packard Company)

Fig. 9-1. Designing large buildings is complex. (Cambridge Seven Associates, Inc.)

Chapter 9
DESIGNING AND ENGINEERING STRUCTURES

After studying this chapter, you will be able to:
☐ Contrast an architect's work with that of an engineer's.
☐ List the five factors designers must consider.
☐ Describe the design process.
☐ List what is found in the bid package.
☐ Describe what is found in a set of drawings.
☐ State the purpose of written specifications.

Designing is an activity that finds a solution to a problem. Suppose that you are going to build a birdhouse. You would need to have an idea how to build it. Then, you buy and cut lumber.

Designing large structures such as skyscrapers, bridges, dams, and roadways requires the same steps as you would follow in designing the birdhouse. The larger the project, of course, the more complex the designing process becomes. See Fig. 9-1.

Designing large projects takes a long time. The time is well spent because construction projects are used for a long time. It is hard to change them once they are built.

WHAT IS DESIGNING?

Creative designers must be able to see a problem and find the best way to solve it. Solutions to problems are usually unique (one of a kind). They are unique because each problem differs slightly.

As you travel on a highway, many bridges look alike, Fig. 9-2. If the bridges are studied more

Fig. 9-2. All bridges may look alike, but they are not. Each is unique.

closely, you will find that each is unique. The span, grade, and foundations differ for each bridge. The designers used standard materials and methods. They used them in different ways for each bridge. A unique design was the result.

People can build on knowledge. We can save knowledge in our brains, books, and many other ways. One of the best ways is in computers. What we learn, we record. We can then retrieve (get) it back again.

For example, the longest suspension bridge in the world has a main span of 4,626 feet. The principles used to build this bridge are the same as early people used. The principles were built upon. New materials were used. A longer bridge that supports more weight was the result, Fig. 9-3.

Fig. 9-3. Architects and engineers build on knowledge that already exists. This bridge is an example.   (HNTB Engineers)

Fig. 9-4. Much of these engineers' time is saved by using computers to produce drawings. This field of work is called computer-aided design (CAD). (LeMessurier Consultants)

Computers have helped a lot in designing structures. They store information in an organized form. It is easy to retrieve and use the information. Best of all, computers do things quickly. See Fig. 9-4.

Architects and engineers (A/Es) take knowledge and build on it. They use what has been learned to build taller buildings, larger dams, longer bridges, and bigger harbors.

WHO DESIGNS CONSTRUCTION PROJECTS?

Who designs a project depends upon what needs to be built. Small projects at home are designed by people like you and your parents. Fathers and mothers can design complete homes, Fig. 9-5, or design changes in their homes.

Architects and engineers are design professionals. *Design professionals* are trained people who are paid for their services. They are hired by the project owner. The person who pays for the service is known as the client. A *client* is an owner, represents an owner, or is a civic leader, Fig. 9-6.

Architects are hired to design buildings and to do *master planning*. A master planner sets the main theme for a large, complex project. See Fig. 9-7. A shopping center is made up of many stores, walking malls, parking lots, and roadways. The master planner sees that all parts of the project fit together.

Construction projects are designed by architects. Housing and commercial and public buildings are examples. For larger buildings, engineers design the

Fig. 9-5. This family designed their own home. Now they are choosing the windows to put in it. (Pella/Rolscreen)

foundations, framework, and mechanical systems. Architects consider the appearance and function of the building and select materials. Engineers consider strength, utilities, and drainage. Engineers are chief designers of dams, pipelines, roadways, water control projects, and utility systems, Fig. 9-8.

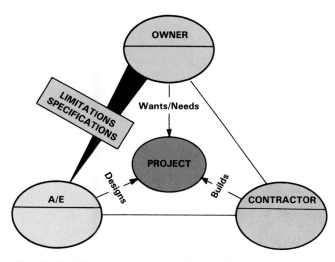

Fig. 9-6. The project is the focus of the owner-A/E-contractor triangle.

WHAT ARE THE CONCERNS OF THE DESIGNER?

Architects and engineers are always aware of five factors, Fig. 9-9. They should always consider the following factors:

- Function — Will the project do what it is supposed to do?
- Appearance — Does the project look good and does it blend with the area around it?
- Cost — Will the project be within the budget?
- Strength — Will the project withstand the forces of nature?
- Materials — Which materials will be the best for the purpose?

The A/E must keep all factors in mind at all times. No single factor stands alone. One material may look right, but if it costs too much, it is a poor choice. A strong, yet low-cost framework is not a good choice if it obstructs the floor plan.

THE DESIGN PROCESS

Designing starts in the early stages of the project. It continues throughout the life of the structure. The goal is to get the most value for the cost. A/Es try to find and remove items that add cost without helping the function. The further designers get into the project, the less impact (effect) they

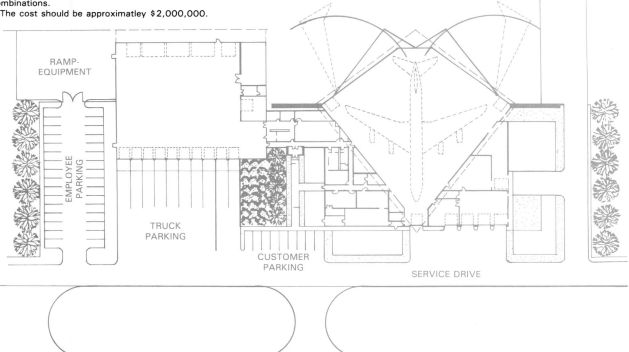

The problem is to design a prototype one-bay hangar. The hangar is to have:
1. Space to enclose either a Douglas PC-8 or Boeing 727 aircraft, (18,000 sq. ft.).
2. Support space for line maintenance (14,000 sq. ft.).
3. Cargo facilities for air freight (18,000 sq. ft.).
   The one-bay hangar is to be designed so that it can be built singly or in combinations.
   The cost should be approximatley $2,000,000.

RAMP-EQUIPMENT

EMPLOYEE PARKING

TRUCK PARKING

CUSTOMER PARKING

SERVICE DRIVE

Fig. 9-7. Architects developed the master plan. An engineering firm designed the special roof. A second engineering firm designed the mechanical systems. (Miller-Dunwiddie Architects, Inc.)

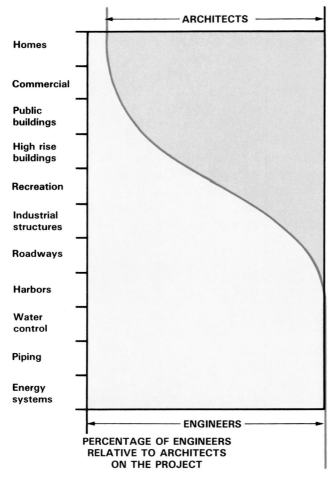

ARCHITECTS

Homes

Commercial

Public
buildings

High rise
buildings

Recreation

Industrial
structures

Roadways

Harbors

Water
control

Piping

Energy
systems

ENGINEERS

PERCENTAGE OF ENGINEERS
RELATIVE TO ARCHITECTS
ON THE PROJECT

Fig. 9-8. Who designs what projects? This chart will help.

have on the project. See Fig. 9-10.

An A/E approaches a problem in many ways. Good architects and engineers use a planned approach to solving problems. Recall the birdhouse. It was a simple problem. The approach used for large projects requires much more of the same kind of planning. The design of a dam and lake, for example, takes more planning than the design of a farm pond. More planning is needed because large projects are more complex and more people are involved. Many A/Es use the steps shown in Fig. 9-11.

Step I — Predesign — Identify the Problem

In the predesign phase, the problem is identified. Predesign work defines the project. It usually consists of:
- Program — What goals are to be met with the structure?
- Financial package — Will the structure earn a profit for the owners?
- Schedule — When is the project to be finished?
- Budget — How will the money be spent?

Step II — Schematic Design — Generate Ideas

During the schematic design step, A/Es generate as many solutions as possible. Little concern is

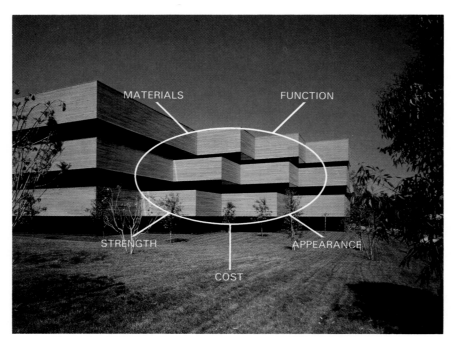

MATERIALS FUNCTION

STRENGTH APPEARANCE

COST

Fig. 9-9. Can you state how the five concerns influenced this building? (California Redwood Association)

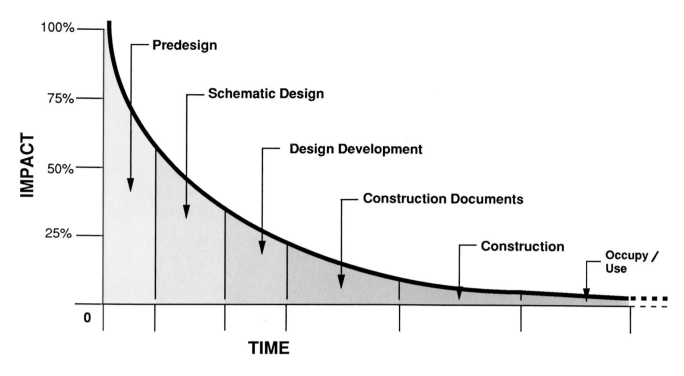

THE IMPACT OF DESIGN

Fig. 9-10. Designing goes on throughout the life of a structure. Designers affect the project most in the early stages.

Design Process

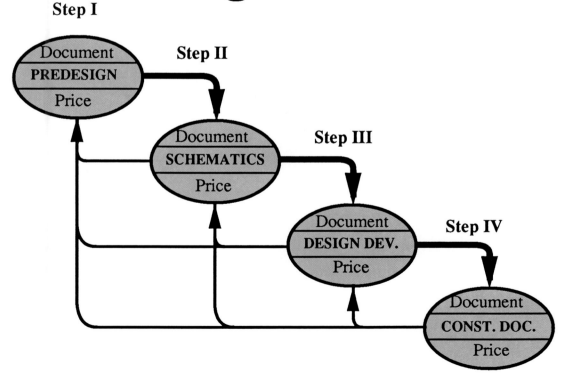

Fig. 9-11. An organized approach is used to define a problem and find a solution.

given to details. Every thought that comes to mind is written down. Sketches and notes are used. It is easy to change and improve your ideas. You need only an eraser and pencil.

Brainstorming is a way to encourage everyone to share good ideas. There are three rules to brainstorming. People who use the method:

1. Come up with as many ideas as they can. (The more, the better.)
2. Think up unique ideas. (The wilder, the better.)
3. Avoid judging the ideas. (All thoughts are good.)

It is likely that a lot of new ideas will come out. Perhaps they can be combined to meet the needs of the project.

Step III — Design Development

The design development step has two tasks. They are to refine the ideas and to select the best design.

Task 1 — Refine ideas

Two or more of the best ideas are chosen. The A/E refines and improves them in the design development phase. Structures are drawn to scale on a site plan. Details and sizes are added to the drawings. As A/Es refine the ideas, they can see if the ideas will work, Fig. 9-12.

If the A/Es develop more than one idea, they will have a choice. If they compare and combine ideas, better solutions can be found. Each is judged on how well it meets the needs of the design.

Large and complex projects require models. A *model* is a small likeness of the project. Fig. 9-13 is a model of a refinery. Models make it easier to study each design feature. The analysis of an idea may show that it is not a good one. If it does not work, the A/E selects, refines, and analyzes a second choice.

Task 2 — Select the best idea

The next step is to select the best design. The design is selected by the designer or the client. Each idea is shown to the people who make the choice. Models, pictures, slides, drawings, charts, and graphs help to show the features of each design, Fig. 9-14. Complete drawings may be used for small

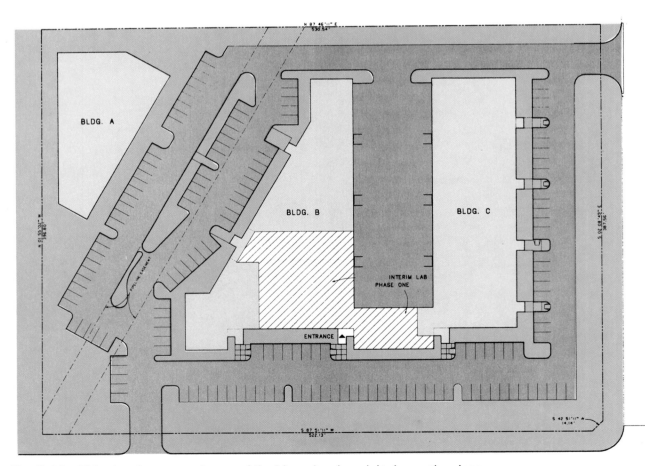

Fig. 9-12. This site plan was only one of the ideas developed. It shows the placement of the building and parking spaces. An interim (temporary) structure is sometimes part of the plan.   (Pierce, Goodwin, and Alexander)

Fig. 9-13. This is a model of a refinery. A model lets the designer see how things fit. It is easier to change the model than a new refinery.
(Combustion Engineering, Inc.)

Fig. 9-14. Models make it easy to show a client the features of a design.
(Ball State University)

projects. Drawings for large projects would have less detail. The site, shape, and placement of the structure are shown. See Fig. 9-15. Site plans may be made to show buried utility lines or pipes. Details would not be on the drawings.

When shown the design, the client may decide to:
• Accept one design.
• Combine two or more designs into one.
• Reject all designs.

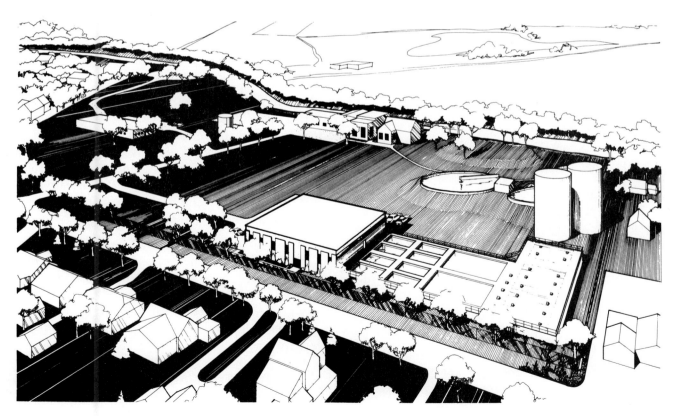

Fig. 9-15. An artist's rendering (drawing) is used to show how structures fit into the surroundings. (Indiana-American Water Co., Inc.)

If they reject all designs, the process is stopped, or it starts over again with new ideas.

Step IV — Construction Documents — Implement Design

When the design has been chosen, the A/E prepares construction documents. Construction documents include the working drawings and specifications.

Working drawings give the facts needed to build the project. Drawings are used to describe the shape, size, and placement of the parts. *Specifications* describe, in words, those things that cannot be shown in drawings. Other documents are added to make up the bidding documents.

PREPARING THE BIDDING DOCUMENTS

Bidding documents are the link between the A/E and the builder. See Fig. 9-16. Contractors first use bidding documents to guide them in submitting bids. A set of bidding documents consist of:
- Bidding Requirements.
- Contract Forms.
- Contract Conditions.
- Specifications.
- Drawings.
- Addenda.

Bidding Requirements

Bidding requirements describe how contractors are to submit their bids. A formal *invitation to bidders* comes first. It describes the nature of the project. It is followed by specific *instructions to bidders.* All of the *bid forms* a prospective bidder will need are included.

The size and kind of bid bond is described. A *bid bond* is a form of insurance. The bidder has to write a check for a set amount. The check is sent in with the bid. The owner does not cash the check. If the bidder is awarded the contract, but is not able to provide the service, the owner can then cash the check.

Contract Forms

A copy of the *agreement* (contract) between the owner and contractor is enclosed. Many kinds of standard agreement forms are published.

The nature and size of bonds the contractor must have are described. These *bonds* protect the owner

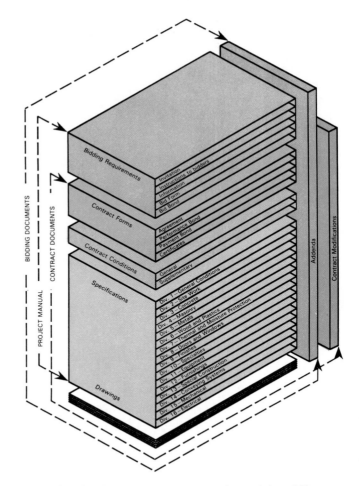

Fig. 9-16. Documents are packaged in different ways. Bidding documents are different than contract documents. (Construction Specifications Institute)

if the contractor defaults (breaks) the contract. They assure the owner that the project will be finished and that all bills will be paid.

Copies of all *certificates* used to show that the work is started, approved, and finished are attached.

Contract Conditions

The rights and responsibilities of the owner, designer, and contractor are stated in the contract conditions. These written conditions have been revised and improved over a period of many years. *General conditions* apply to nearly all construction projects. *Supplementary conditions* vary from project to project.

Working Drawings

Working drawings and specifications tell the builder how the A/Es want the project built. They must be approved by the owner. In many cases, the drawings are developed on a computer and output on a plotter. See Fig. 9-17. *Working drawings* show the shape and size of each part and where it goes. See Fig. 9-18.

Construction projects are too large to be drawn full-size. Working drawings are drawn to scale. That means they are smaller than the actual project. Each dimension is put on the drawing and it is made easy to read. This saves the workers some time and they make fewer mistakes.

Small projects

Small projects, such as a house, have all drawings in one *set*. A site plan, foundation plan, floor plan, elevations, and sections with details are in the set.

The *site plan* shows the horizontal dimensions (size, shape, and location) of the land, Fig. 9-19. The site plan includes the boundary lines. Bench marks are placed at each corner. *Bench marks* are used to determine the elevation. The placement of structures is found on the site plan. Streets, driveways, utilities, and easements (strips of land used by utility companies) are drawn on the plan. On house plans, the roof line may be shown on the drawing.

The final shape of the site is shown with contour lines. The placement of trees, shrubs, and fences, and the locations of other landscape features are found on the site plan. If the landscape drawing is complex, a *landscape plan* is added to the set of drawings.

The *foundation plan* shows the support structure of the building. See Fig. 9-20. Footings are

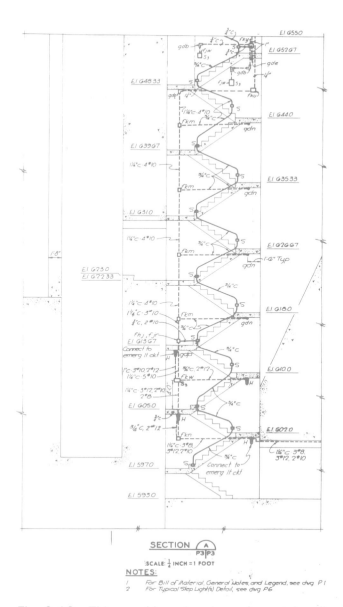

Fig. 9-18. This working drawing of a stairwell shows location of conduit, fixtures, and switches.

Fig. 9-17. Graphics produced on computers save a lot of time. Engineering data is fed into the computer. The plotter outputs the drawings. (Stran Buildings)

the base on which the foundation rests. Footings for piers and columns are also shown. Dimensions help show the size, shape, and placement of all footings and other parts of the foundation.

Section views of the footings and foundation are used to show more detail. A section view is a drawing of an imaginary cut through the foundation. These details show exact dimensions and shapes.

Concrete is made stronger by placing steel rods in it. These rods are called reinforcing bar or rebar. The size and placement of steel reinforcement in the concrete is shown in the section view.

The *floor plan* is a fully dimensioned room layout of each floor, Fig. 9-21. All openings such as doors, windows, and walls are shown. The

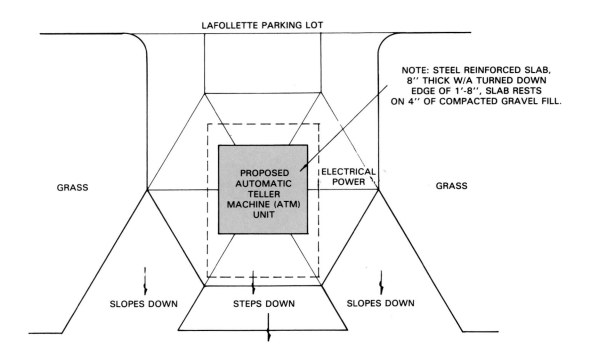

Fig. 9-19. Site plans describe the site where the structure is placed. This structure is for an automatic bank teller unit. (Mutual Federal Savings Bank)

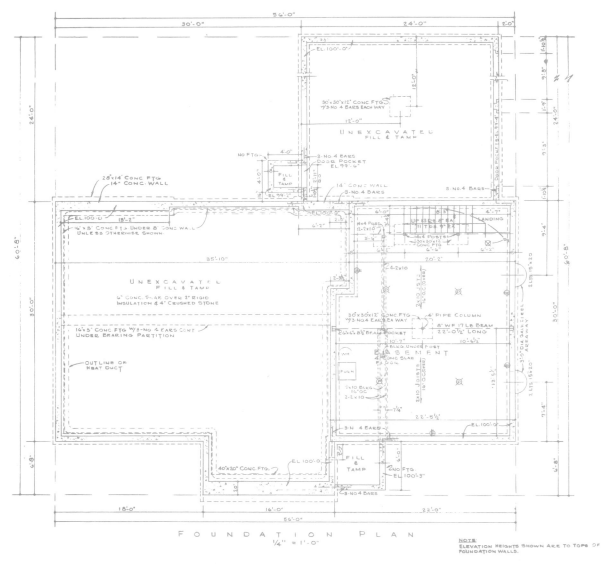

Fig. 9-20. A foundation plan including footings. (L. F. Garlinghouse)

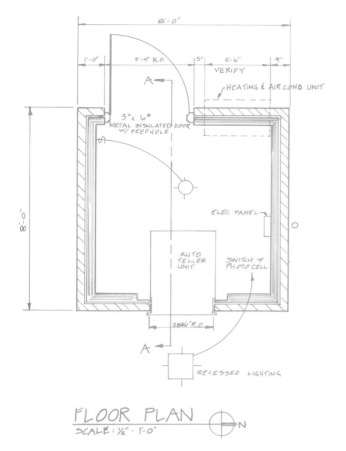

FLOOR PLAN
SCALE: ½" = 1'-0"

Fig. 9-21. A floor plan shows room placement and size. (Mutual Federal Savings Bank)

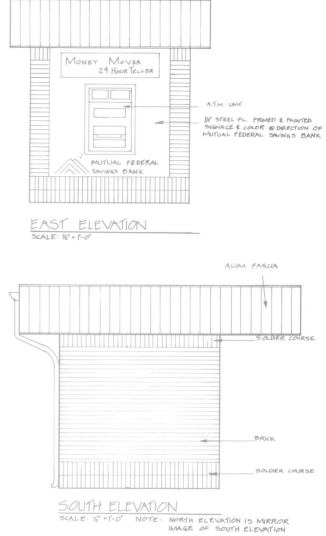

EAST ELEVATION
SCALE: ½" = 1'-0"

SOUTH ELEVATION
SCALE: ½" = 1'-0"   NOTE: NORTH ELEVATION IS MIRROR IMAGE OF SOUTH ELEVATION

Fig. 9-22. Elevation drawings show what the building looks like from the outside. (Mutual Federal Savings Bank)

mechanical systems may be on the floor plan, too. They include the electrical, plumbing, and heating/cooling/ventilating systems. A floor plan is made for each level. The basement is drawn if it is to be finished. A finished basement has floor, wall, and ceiling surfaces added to it.

Elevation drawings are drawn to show the outside of the structure. These drawings appear as though you are looking straight at the structure. See Fig. 9-22. An idea of how the finished structure will look is shown in an elevation. They show the length and height of a house. All sides that are different are shown. Elevations of buildings show all grade, floor, and ceiling levels.

Sections and details show how the walls, ceiling, and roof are built. See Fig. 9-23. Detail drawings show areas such as fireplaces, stairways, and finish millwork.

Schedules are lists and descriptions of standard items in a structure. Fig. 9-24 is a door schedule for a dentist's office. Typical schedules for a building include windows and doors, wall treatments, floor coverings, ceiling materials, and light fixtures.

Shop drawings show a part of a structure in greater detail. Detailed drawings were probably made of the built-in cabinets in your technology lab. The drawings were made by either the contractor or subcontractor. Subcontractors use shop drawings to guide their work, Fig. 9-25.

Large projects

More than one set of working drawings is needed for large projects. Such projects will have a set of civil, site, architectural and engineering, mechanical and electrical, and structural drawings.

Civil drawings describe the site before building begins. Earthmoving and site preparation are described in Fig. 9-26. Civil drawings show changes in the course of a stream or road.

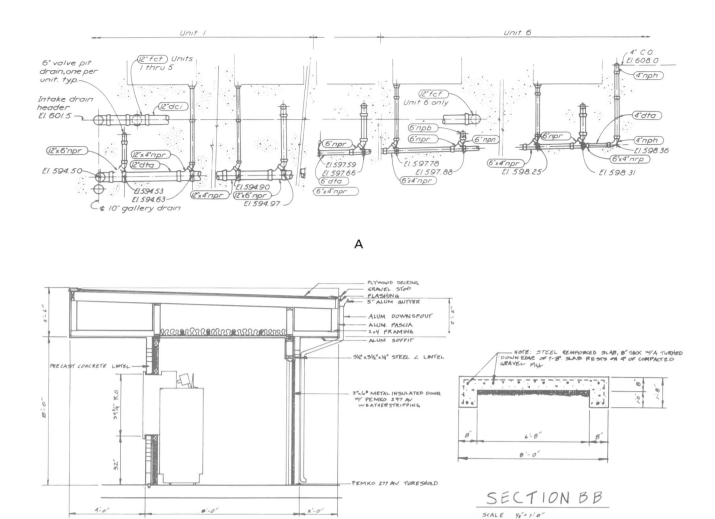

Fig. 9-23. Sections and details show how parts of a structure are shaped and placed. A—Detail of a plumbing system. B—Section AA shows a cut through the automatic teller building. Section BB shows a side view of a cut through the footing.   (Mutual Federal Savings Bank)

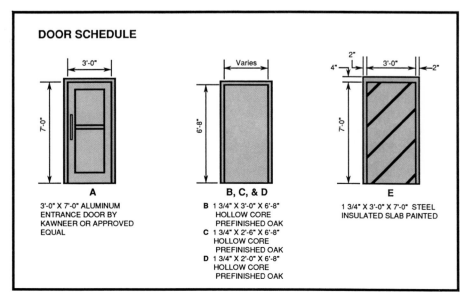

Fig. 9-24. Door schedules describe the doors used in a project. The letters A, B, C, D, and E are placed on the floor plan to show where the doors are installed.

Fig. 9-25. This electronic track system is for a mail room in a large corporate office. The workers used shop drawings to guide their work. The shop drawings were made by the subcontractor. (Translogic Corp.)

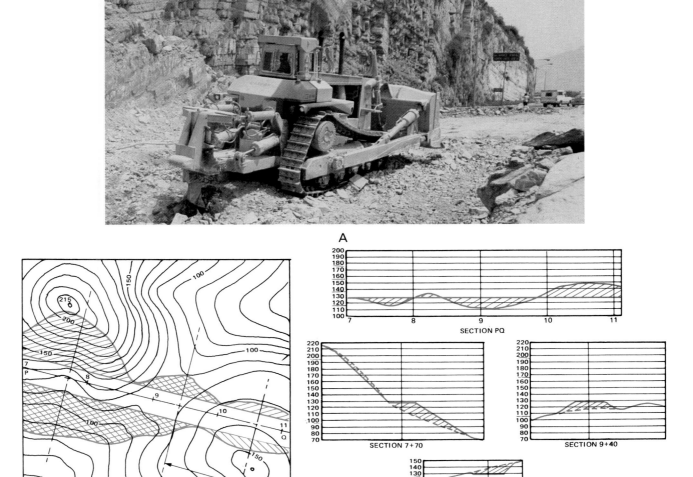

Fig. 9-26. A—This machine operator is moving earth. B—The kind of earth and where to put it are shown on the civil drawings. (Caterpillar, Inc.)

Site plans show drainage of excess water from the site. They include building placement and grading elevations. The final contour and landscape plan are in this set. See Fig. 9-27.

Architectural and engineering drawings are made to show the physical form of the project. Many detail drawings are needed. *Architectural drawings,* Fig. 9-28, are used to check the structure itself and add detail to master plans. *Engineering drawings* are used for utilities, roads, pipelines, and other long, narrow projects.

Mechanical and electrical drawings are used by electricians, plumbers, and heating/cooling contractors. Mechanical drawings are important for large projects. *Mechanical drawings* describe the heating, ventilating, and air conditioning (HVAC) and plumbing systems. Elevators and moving stairs are common to public buildings with more than two floors. Mechanical drawings are used to describe these transportation systems. *Electrical drawings* show the kind and size of electrical circuits and where to run wires, Fig. 9-29. The type, size, and location of each electrical fixture is shown.

Structural drawings describe the main support system for a structure, Fig. 9-30. Many detailed

Fig. 9-27. The operators (equipment drivers) are building a roadbed. A site plan shows where to remove and dump the soil. (Caterpillar, Inc.)

drawings are used. They show the size and shape of parts, and how the parts are joined.

Specifications

Specifications are details about the project that are easier to put into words than into drawings.

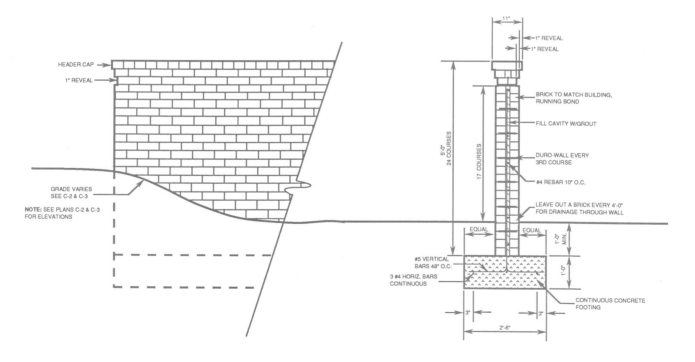

Fig. 9-28. These architectural drawings describe the details for a brick wall that surrounds a residential community. (Niles Bolton Associates)

Fig. 9-29. Electrical drawings were used by this electrician. They showed him where to put this light and how to wire it. (Leviton Manufacturing Co., Inc.)

If drawings and specifications do not agree, specifications are followed.

Specifiers write the specifications. They are guided by the project designers. Specifiers need to be fast, clear, and thorough. Methods have been developed to reach these goals. Specifiers can use copies of earlier work or use standard forms. Computers save a lot of time. Skilled specifiers are able to do the work right on the computer screen.

Organizing specifications

The Construction Specifications Institute (CSI) describes how to organize and write specifications.

A list of titles and numbers are used to organize specifications. The system has 16 *divisions.* Division 1 describes general procedures. The other 15 divisions relate to special trades. Refer back to the specification section in Fig. 9-16.

Writing specifications

Specifiers must decide on the method, scope, and the level of restrictiveness (control) to use. The methods determine how the quality will be stated. Will it be based on performance of the product, a standard, or a brand name of a product?

The scope is used to describe the breadth of the system. A broad scope system may be the entire ventilating system for a highway tunnel. A narrow scope would refer to the intake and exhaust grates for the system.

The level of restrictiveness can limit or broaden the number of bidders. Flooring materials for a gym may be restricted to wood only. This would exclude all other kinds for flooring materials.

Matching drawings and specifications

Drafters and specifiers try hard to reduce errors. They work to reduce duplication. Duplication means to state something in more than one place. Details may differ if they are stated twice. Identical terms are used in both drawings and specifications.

Ways are found to resolve conflicts. Specifications generally are used when they differ from the drawings. An A/E may also be asked to put a ruling in writing.

Coordination guides are stated and followed to prevent errors. They list all standard terms and symbols that are to be used. The procedures used to check work and to settle conflicts are described.

Addenda

Many people study the documents during the bidding process. This often reveals oversights. These things need to be explained, corrected, or added. The addenda section describes all of the changes that are made in the documents.

SUMMARY

The design process begins soon after the decision to build is made. A project designer's goal is to find the best way to meet the program for the project.

Architects/Engineers (A/Es) design construction projects. They are concerned with the function, looks, cost, strength, and materials of the project. A planned approach is used by those who design projects. The more complex the project, the more important it is to use a planned approach.

The bidding documents are the link between the designer and the builder. Bidding documents describe the project in detail, how to submit bids, and copies of the forms used.

Working drawings and specifications describe how to build a project. They are used by contrac-

A

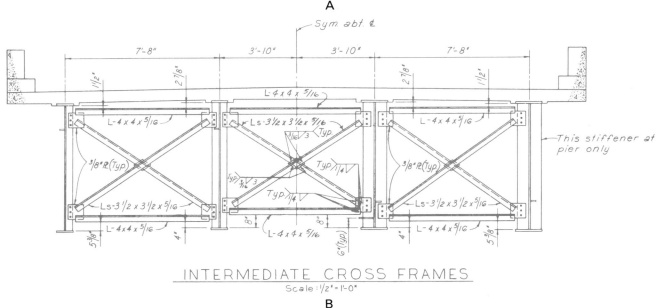

INTERMEDIATE CROSS FRAMES

Scale: 1/2"=1'-0"

B

Fig. 9-30. A—Structural drawings describe these beams. Details show how they are joined. B—Structural drawing of a bridge crossframe. (Corps of Engineers, Kansas City District)

tors to estimate and bid a project. They become a part of the contract when it is signed. Working drawings are put into sets. The set describes how to prepare the site, the form of the project, the mechanical systems, and the structural framework. Shop drawings are made for the subcontractor. Specifications are written out. They describe such things as levels of quality that are easier to write than to draw.

KEY WORDS

All of the following words have been used in this chapter. Do you know their meaning?

Addenda
Agreement
Appearance
Architects
Architectural drawings
Bid bond
Bid forms
Bidding documents
Bidding requirements
Bonds
Brainstorming
Budget
Certificates
Civil drawings
Client
Contract conditions
Contract forms
Cost
Designing
Design development
Construction documents
Design process
Design professionals
Divisions
Elevation drawings
Engineering drawings
Engineers
Financial package
Floor plan
Footing and foundation plan
Function
General conditions
Instructions to bidders
Invitation to bidders

Landscape plan
Master planning
Materials
Mechanical and
  electrical drawings
Model
Program
Schedules
Schematic design

Sections and details
Site plan
Specifications
Specifiers
Strength
Structural drawings
Supplementary
  conditions
Working drawings

TEST YOUR KNOWLEDGE

Place your answers on a separate sheet. Please do not write in this text.

1. The chief designer for a bridge is a(n) _____.
2. The person who pays for the professional design service is called the _____.
3. List and briefly describe the four steps of the design process.
4. Contractors use bidding documents to guide them in _____ _____.
5. During brainstorming, you avoid _____ any ideas.
6. What is the purpose of a model?
7. What does the abbreviation CAD mean?
8. An artist's _____ shows how a structure fits into the surroundings.
9. An offer to build a project at a stated price is a(n) _____.
10. A contractor may make shop drawings for a(n) _____.
11. Which of the following is not shown in a site plan?
    A. Final shape of the site.
    B. Section view of foundation.
    C. Placement of structures.
    D. Boundary lines.
    E. Easements.
12. A(n) _____ drawing describes the site before building begins.
13. Specifications are organized into 16 _____.

ACTIVITIES

1. Think of a project you would like to build at home. Go through the four steps of the design process. Repeat the process with a friend. Are two heads better than one?
2. Talk with an A/E and find out how he or she designs a project.
3. Use the four step process to earn more money or to plan a trip.
4. Visit an architect or engineer. Ask to see a set of drawings for a small project.
5. Visit the waterworks or waste water treatment plant in your community. Ask to see a set of bidding documents for a planned project. Read through the specifications. Can you find Bidding requirements? Contract forms? Contract conditions? Drawings? Specifications?

Section IV
MANUFACTURING PROCESSES

Chapter 10

INTRODUCTION TO MANUFACTURING PROCESSES

After reading this chapter, you will be able to:
☐ Identify manufacturing processes as primary or secondary.
☐ List and discuss major steps in the manufacturing processes.
☐ Define primary and secondary processes.
☐ Describe six types of secondary processes.
☐ Name outputs of manufacturing activities.
☐ Discuss the impact of manufacturing processes on the environment.

Throughout history, people have changed the size, shape, and looks of materials. They have tried to make materials better fit their needs. In so doing, people have manufactured products.

The actual changing of the form of material is one part of manufacturing. This activity is called *material processing*. Management, you remember, is the other part of successful manufacturing.

Changing the form of materials takes three major steps. These stages, as shown in Fig. 10-1, are:
1. Obtaining natural resources.
2. Producing industrial materials by changing raw materials into them.
3. Making finished products from industrial materials.

Keep in mind that we are going to talk mostly about materials. However, this is only one resource in manufacturing. People, energy, time, knowledge, capital, and finances are also important. However, converting materials into products *is* the task of manufacturing. The other resources (inputs) support this activity.

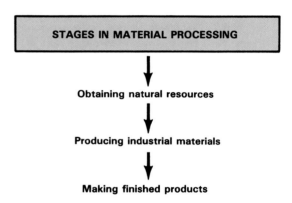

Fig 10-1. There are three stages of material processing.

OBTAINING RESOURCES

We cannot build a product without materials. The material must be located and gathered. The typical processes for collecting materials are listed in Fig. 10-2. These are:
- Mining—Digging the material from the earth by means of a hole or tunnel.
- Drilling—Pumping material from below the earth's surface through a narrow, round shaft.
- Harvesting—Cutting a mature, renewable resource from the land.

PRIMARY PROCESSING

Once raw materials are obtained, they are moved to a mill. Here the resource is changed into an

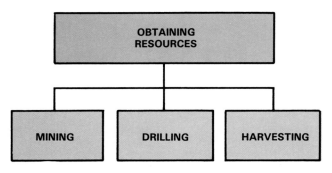

Fig 10-2. Resources are gathered in three ways.

industrial material. Trees are made into lumber, plywood, fiberboard, and particleboard. Iron ore, limestone, and coke are used to produce steel. Natural gas is a feedstock (source) for many plastics. These outputs are called standard stock. They are the products of primary processing.

Primary processing is the first major step in changing the form of materials. Three major processes are used to convert raw materials into industrial materials. These, Fig. 10-3, are:

- Thermal (heat) processes.
- Chemical processes.
- Mechanical processes.

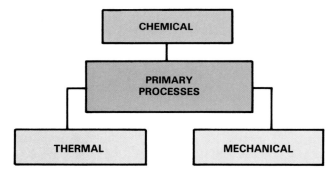

Fig 10-3. Types of primary processing. Sometimes more than one type is used to produce a primary material.

These are not entirely separate. *Thermal processes* heat crushed (mechanically processed) ores. The hot ores enter into a chemical reaction. This reaction separates the metal from the undesirable impurities. However, heat is essential (needed) for the process.

Mechanical processes cut or crush resources. Trees are cut into lumber, veneer, and chips. Rocks are crushed into gravel. Wool is sheared from sheep. All are mechanical processes. They use mechanical force to complete the activity.

Chemical processes use chemical reactions to refine raw materials. Plastics are formed by chemical reactions. Simple compounds are combined to form the complex polymer chains we call plastics. Fig. 10-4 lists some resources that basically use each type of primary process.

SECONDARY PROCESSING

Industrial materials (standard stock) must be changed into finished products. Lumber must be made into furniture and houses. Leather is made into shoes and belts. Steel is used in cars, appliances, and reinforcing bars for concrete. Thousands of products are made from the outputs of primary processing.

Finished products are produced by *secondary processes*. These activities, as shown in Fig. 10-5, are:

- Casting and molding—Pouring or forcing liquid material into a prepared mold. The material is allowed to become solid. Then, it is removed from the mold.
- Forming—Using force to cause a material to permanently take a shape. A die, mold, or roll is used to shape the material.
- Separating—Converting material to size and shape by removing excess material. The material is cut or sheared by these processes.

PRIMARY PROCESSES		
THERMAL	CHEMICAL	MECHANICAL
Steelmaking	Aluminum refining	Lumber manufacture
Copper smelting	Polymer formation	Plywood manufacture
Zinc smelting	Gold refining	Particleboard making
Lead smelting	Papermaking	Rock crushing
	Leather tanning	

Fig 10-4. Resources processed by each type of primary processing.

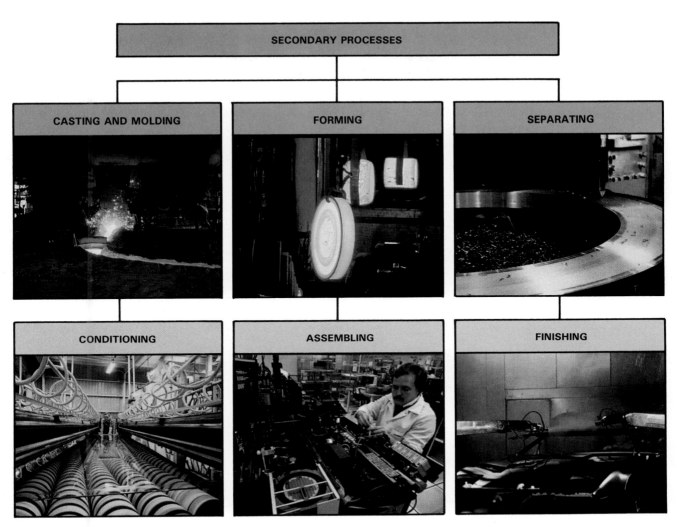

Fig 10-5. Secondary processes are casting and molding, forming, separating, conditioning, assembling, and finishing. (Rohn & Haas; Bethlehem Steel; Inland Steel Co.; PPG Industrial; AT&T; DeVilbiss)

- Conditioning—Using heat, mechanical force, or chemical action to change the internal properties of a material.
- Assembling—Temporarily or permanently holding two or more parts together.
- Finishing—Protecting or adding beauty to the surface of a material.

PRODUCTS, WASTE, AND SCRAP

Almost all manufacturing activities create unwanted by-products. Many create holes in the ground. Logging requires roads into the peaceful woods. Foundries give off fumes, dust, and wastes. Machining activities create chips and shavings. There are no scrapless, pollution-free manufacturing activities. People must plan to control undesirable outputs.

The protection of the environment is the responsibility of all citizens. We need clean air, water, and soil. Each of us must do our part to save our precious natural resources. Also, we should expect—even demand—that industry help. Companies must consider:

- Their practices in obtaining raw materials.
- Are they efficient?
- Is the land returned to use, Fig. 10-6?
- Pollution caused by manufacturing processes.
- If not, can it be controlled and cleaned up?
- Scrap and waste.
- Do the manufacturing processes produce unnecessary scrap and waste?
- Is every effort being made to recycle scrap? See Fig. 10-7.
- Is unusable waste material disposed of properly?

Our future will be more secure with industrial and personal resource conservation. You and tomorrow's children can have the "good life," too.

Fig 10-6. This is land that was once an open pit mine. (American Electric Power)

Fig 10-7. Scrap metal can be recycled and used in the steelmaking process.

SUMMARY

Manufacturing materials are converted from raw materials to finished products through three stages, Fig. 10-8. Raw materials are first located. They are then obtained from the earth by harvesting, drilling, or mining. Secondly, the raw materials are converted into standard stock. Thermal, chemical, and mechanical processes are used. Finally, the industrial goods are changed into finished products. The form change is done through casting and molding, separating, forming, conditioning, assembling, and finishing processes.

Throughout the processing, the ecology must be protected. Resources must be used wisely. Scrap and waste must be kept to a minimum. Pollution needs to be controlled.

With environmental concern and efficient manufacturing, we can all live better. We will have useful products and a clean world.

KEY WORDS

All of the following words have been used in this chapter. Do you know their meaning?

Chemical processes

Material processing

Mechanical processes

Primary processes

Secondary processes

Thermal processes

TEST YOUR KNOWLEDGE

Place your answers on a separate sheet. Please do not write in this text.

1. Changing the form of materials takes (three, four, five) major steps.
2. List and describe three ways of obtaining natural resources.
3. Which of the listed processes are called primary processes?
   A. Chemical processes.

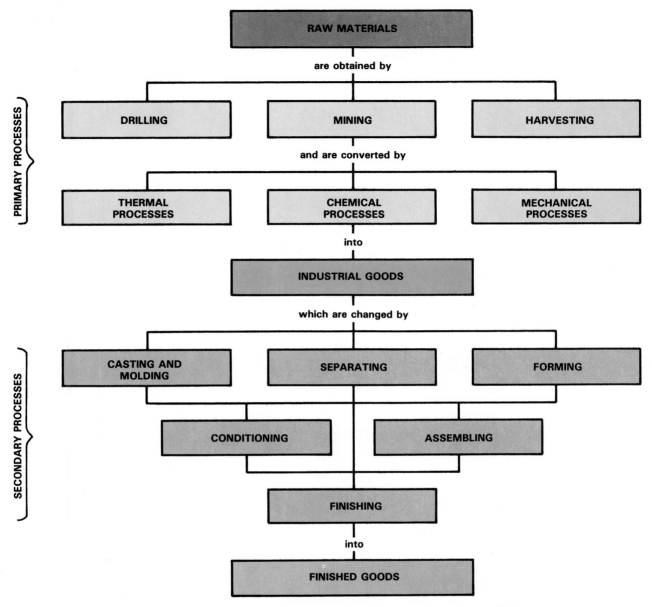

Fig 10-8. A summary diagram of the material processing activities.

B. Heating processes.
C. Mechanical processes.
D. Electrical processes.
E. Extracting processes.
4. Crushing is a primary process called _____ processing.
5. List and describe the six types of secondary processes.
6. Name the three outputs of manufacturing activity.
7. Protection of the environment is _____ responsibility.

ACTIVITIES

1. Invite a person from a manufacturing company to discuss the inputs, processes, and outputs of manufacturing.
2. View a film on primary manufacturing processes (steelmaking, lumber manufacturing, aluminum refining, etc.). List and describe the major steps in the process.
3. Go on a field trip to a manufacturing company. Observe and list the resources, sequence of operations, and outputs.

Proper forestry techniques can be used to ensure an adequate supply
of lumber for the future.   (U.S. Department of Agriculture)

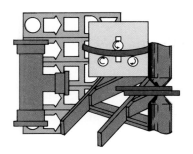

Chapter 11

OBTAINING RAW MATERIALS

After reading this chapter, you will be able to:
□ Define renewable and exhaustible resources and give examples of each.
□ Describe three different methods for mining raw materials.
□ Define and describe two methods of drilling for oil or gas.
□ Describe three methods of harvesting forests.
□ Explain methods by which raw materials are moved to mills and refineries.

Most products are made from many different materials. All of these materials were once in a *raw* condition. They were a natural resource found on or in the earth or seas.

All manufacturing starts with raw materials. These materials are of two basic types, Fig. 11-1. They are renewable or exhaustible.

RENEWABLE RESOURCES

Renewable resources are biological materials (growing things). Each growing unit (plant or

RESOURCES	
RENEWABLE	**EXHAUSTIBLE**
Trees	Metal ores
Cotton	Petroleum
Wool	Natural gas
Flax	Coal
Animal hides	Clays

Fig. 11-1. There is no limit to the supply of renewable resources. Exhaustible resources will be gone one day and cannot be replaced.

animal) has a life cycle. First, it was planted or born. It then grows through stages to maturity (full size). Finally, it becomes old and dies.

A tree is a good example of a renewable resource. It is planted by nature or people. It grows and, after a number of years, reaches its full size. Then, growth slows and finally stops. Limbs die and fall off. Insects, wind, and decay attack the tree. In time, it dies and falls to the forest floor. There it decays, providing nutrients (food) for other plants.

Managing Resources

Managing a resource means making sure that there is always a supply to use. It means seeing that future generations will have its use, too.

Even though some resources are renewable, managing them is still important. People must plan and work at growing new resources and knowing when and how to harvest them. For instance, a forester should not cut down all the trees in a forest without planting new ones.

We depend on many renewable resources for manufactured products. They provide us with wood products (such as furniture), leather, and natural fibers (wool, cotton, silk, and linen) for making cloth.

Exhaustible resources, discussed next, also must be managed. Unlike renewable resources, we cannot replace them. Management means collecting and using them carefully so they are not wasted.

EXHAUSTIBLE RESOURCES

Not all natural resources are renewable. Some have a limited supply. There is a fixed amount of it on earth. Once used up, there will be no more.

These resources are called *exhaustible* (can be used up). Like the dodo bird, a material can become extinct.

For example, there is only so much petroleum, gold ore, natural gas, or iron ore on this earth. If we use it all, that's it. All resources must be used wisely.

Locating Raw Materials

Obtaining raw materials for manufacturing is a three-step process. This includes:

1. Locating resources.
2. Gathering resources.
3. Transporting (moving) resources.

A large part of getting raw materials is finding them. Aerial mapping (using a plane to take pictures) can help locate trees. Geological (under the ground) searches will find minerals and petroleum. See Fig. 11-2.

Other resources are easier to find. They are grown commercially (for money). Trees in the south are often grown like a crop. Livestock provides us with leather.

The search for raw materials can be costly and disappointing. For example, our future supplies of petroleum cause us concern. Oil companies spend millions of dollars searching for new pools of oil. Often they come up dry. Several multimillion dollar dry holes have been drilled off the east coast of the United States. No oil was found.

On a smaller scale, some persons spend a lifetime looking for minerals. The gold prospectors (hunters) of old still live. They use better equip-

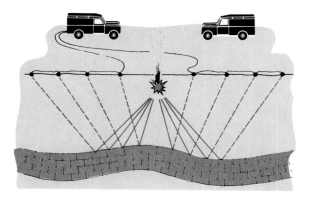

Fig. 11-2. Seismic studies send shock waves into the earth to detect promising locations for raw materials. (Shell Oil Co.)

ment, but are still unlikely to "strike it rich." Along with them, trained geologists (people who study the structure of the earth) from mining companies constantly look for gold, silver, uranium, and other metal ores.

Even with all the scientific knowledge and equipment available, finding underground resources is hard. Yet it is necessary. Our life is built on materials. Our society must have a continuing flow of raw materials.

GATHERING RAW MATERIALS

Once found, raw materials must be gathered. This is done using three major methods. These methods were introduced in Chapter 10, and are shown in Fig. 11-3.

Fig. 11-3. Materials are collected by mining, drilling, and harvesting. (AMAX Corp.; Boise-Cascade Corp.)

Mining

Mining involves digging resources out of the earth. If the raw material is close to the surface, it can be mined from the surface. The topsoil is removed and often stored. The mineral is then scooped up by giant power shovels and put in huge trucks. They haul the material to a conveyor or to the surface, Fig. 11-4. This is called *open-pit* or *surface mining*.

Often the mineral is in a narrow vein (strip) like many coal deposits. In this case, the topsoil is replaced. The land is returned to productive use. Lakes, pastureland, and farms are developed over the mine pit.

In other cases, the mineral is in a very deep (thick) deposit. As it is removed, a huge pit is produced. The Bingham Canyon copper mine in Utah is over 1/2 mile deep and 2 miles wide. Over 2,000,000,000 (two billion) tons of material have been removed since the mine opened in 1904.

Other ore deposits require digging tunnels to reach the material. This is called *underground mining*. There are three major underground mining methods. As seen in Fig. 11-5, these are:

1. *Shaft mining.* This method is used for deeply buried mineral deposits. A shaft is dug down to the level of the deposit. These shafts can extend several thousand feet into the earth. The main vertical (up-and-down) shaft is used to move people and equipment in and out of the mine. The mineral is also lifted out through the vertical shafts. Other vertical shafts are dug to bring in fresh air and remove stale air and gases. The material is mined by digging horizontal (level) tunnels from the vertical shaft.

2. *Drift mining.* This method is used when the mineral vein comes to the surface at one point. A tunnel is dug at that point. The tunnel follows the ore vein into the earth. People and materials are moved by rail cars which travel along the drift shaft.

3. *Slope mining.* This method is used for a shallow mineral deposit. A sloping tunnel is dug down to the deposit. Workers can walk or ride motorized cars down to the deposit. There they dig the mineral out of the vein. The materials are often carried to the surface on a moving platform called a conveyor.

Drilling

Drilling involves cutting a round hole deep into the earth, Fig. 11-6. A drilling rig or derrick is brought to the site. A drilling bit is attached to a drill pipe. The pipe is clamped in a rotary table in the middle of the drilling floor. The table turns and

Fig. 11-4. An open pit mine in operation. This type of mining is suitable when ores are near the surface. (AMAX Corp.)

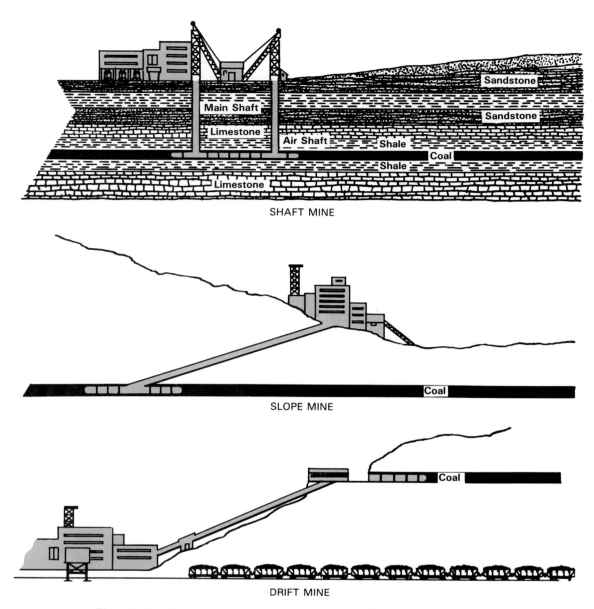

SHAFT MINE

SLOPE MINE

DRIFT MINE

Fig. 11-5. Types of underground mines. (National Coal Assn.)

the hole is drilled. More drill pipe is added as the hole deepens.

Throughout the drilling, "mud" is pumped down the drill pipe. It comes out through the drill bit. The mud is forced to the surface, carrying with it the cuttings from the bit. Casing (pipe the diameter of the hole) is forced into the hole to keep it from caving in.

Drilling stops when the hole reaches the underground reservoir (pool). The drilling rig is removed. Valves to control the flow and a pump are attached. The well is ready to supply petroleum, water, natural gas, and other liquids.

Drilling may be done either on land or in the water, Fig. 11-7. Generally, the drill produces a straight hole. This type of drilling is called *vertical drilling.* Newer techniques allow the drilling of a curved well. This method is called *directional drilling.* It allows us to reach a reservoir which would be hard to get to with vertical drilling. Also, several wells can be drilled from a single platform.

Harvesting

Harvesting is a method used to collect a growing resource. Trees are the major "growing" resource that produce engineering materials. Trees are harvested using one of three methods. These, shown in Fig. 11-8, are:

1. *Selective cutting.* Mature trees are selected and cut. This method is used for trees that can grow

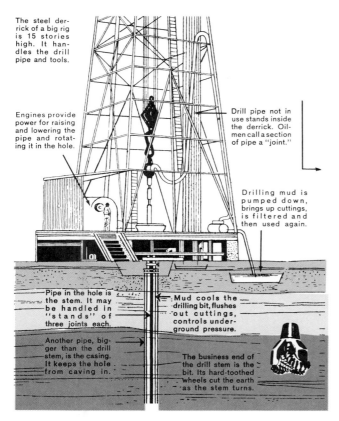

The steel derrick of a big rig is 15 stories high. It handles the drill pipe and tools.

Engines provide power for raising and lowering the pipe and rotating it in the hole.

Drill pipe not in use stands inside the derrick. Oil-men call a section of pipe a "joint."

Drilling mud is pumped down, brings up cuttings, is filtered and then used again.

Pipe in the hole is the stem. It may be handled in "stands" of three joints each.

Mud cools the drilling bit, flushes out cuttings, controls underground pressure.

Another pipe, bigger than the drill stem, is the casing. It keeps the hole from caving in.

The business end of the drill stem is the bit. Its hard-toothed wheels cut the earth as the stem turns.

Fig. 11-6. A typical oil drilling rig. The derrick supports a block and tackle for raising and lowering drill pipe.   (Shell Oil Co.)

in the shade of others. The stands will have all ages of trees present. Selective cutting is used in western pine areas and in hardwood forests.

2. **Clear-cutting (Block cutting).** All trees in a block of about 100 acres are cut. Trees in areas around the block are left alone. They will provide the seed to reforest the area. This technique is used for trees that will not grow in the

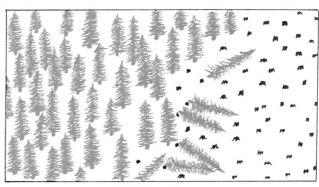

CLEAR-CUTTING

SEED TREE CUTTING

SELECTIVE CUTTING

Fig. 11-8. Types of tree harvesting.

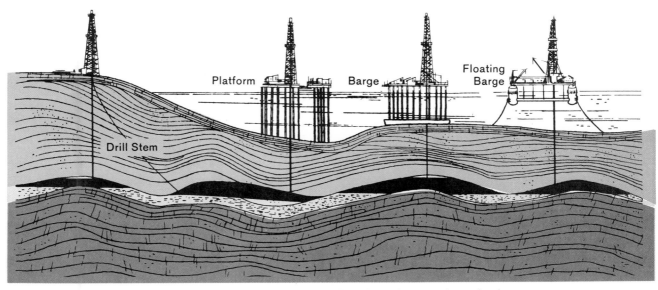

Fig. 11-7. Some common drilling locations and methods.

shade, such as Douglas fir. Clear-cutting is widely used in the western coastal forests.

3. *Seed tree cutting.* All trees in an area, except for four or five large ones, are cut. The large trees reseed the area. This technique is used in the southern pine forests.

Harvesting requires several steps. First, either trees or the area to be harvested must be selected. Fallers then fell (cut down) the trees, Fig. 11-9. A bucker removes the limbs and top. The tree is cut to standard lengths for the mill.

The lengths, called logs, are moved to a central location for loading on trucks or rail cars. This task is called *yarding*. From the yard, the trees are hauled to the mill. They are placed in a pond to help retain their moisture and reduce insect damage.

Newer practices are now using more of the tree. Chippers are placed in the woods. Limbs and tops are chipped up for boiler fuel, hardboard, and paper.

TRANSPORTING RESOURCES

Nearly every type of land and water transportation is used to move raw materials. Pipelines move petroleum and natural gas. Coal can be ground up and mixed with water, forming a *slurry,* for pipeline transport. Trucks of all kinds and sizes

Fig. 11-9. A tree is cut or felled by a skilled worker. (Boise-Cascade Corp.)

move mineral and forest products. Barges and ships are used on inland waterways and oceans. In short, the most economical method is used to move raw materials from mine, well, or forest.

SUMMARY

Raw materials are the foundation for all manufactured goods. These materials are either a renewable or an exhaustible resource. They are located, gathered, and transported to primary processing mills or refineries.

Commonly, raw materials are gathered through mining, drilling, and harvesting. The gathered resources move over land and on water. There they are transformed (changed) into industrial materials.

KEY WORDS

All the following words have been used in this chapter. Do you know their meaning?

Clear-cutting	Renewable resource
Directional drilling	Seed tree cutting
Drift mining	Selective cutting
Drilling	Shaft mining
Exhaustible resource	Slurry
Harvesting	Underground mining
Mining	Vertical drilling
Open-pit mining	Yarding
Raw materials	

TEST YOUR KNOWLEDGE

Place your answers on a separate sheet. Please do not write in this text.

1. A material that is still in its natural form is called a _____ material.
2. Explain the difference between a renewable and an exhaustible resource.

Matching questions: Match the definitions in the left column with the correct term in the right column.

3. Sloping tunnel is dug to get at shallow deposit.
4. Tunnel follows surfaced ore vein into earth.
5. Deep shaft is dug straight down to deposit.
6. Deposit is dug from open-pit.

   A. Shaft mine.
   B. Surface.
   C. Drift mine.
   D. Slope mine.

7. List ten renewable resources.
8. List ten exhaustible resources.

9. _____ searches are used to find underground resources such as petroleum, coal, copper, and other mineral resources.
10. If you want to drill for oil on a certain spot but cannot because a lake is in the way, which of the following methods would you use?
    A. Vertical drilling.
    B. Directional drilling.
11. Describe the difference between the following methods of harvesting trees: selective cutting, clear-cutting, and seed tree cutting.

ACTIVITIES

1. Write to a company that uses drilling, mining, or harvesting to obtain natural resources. Request information about their techniques.
2. Bring a newspaper or magazine article that describes a resource conservation practice or action. Share the article with your class.

Drilling is one method used to obtain raw materials. (American Petroleum Institute)

Perfectly formed slabs of steel are cut to length by automatic flame torches. A two-strand continuous slab caster is capable of converting 300 tons of molten steel into solid slabs in 45 minutes. (Bethlem Steel)

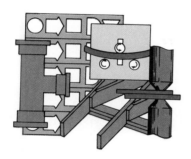

Chapter 12

PRODUCING INDUSTRIAL MATERIALS

After reading this chapter, you will be able to:
☐ Explain primary processing.
☐ Define and identify various kinds of standard stock.
☐ Describe four major types of synthetic wood composites.
☐ List forms of plastic standard stock.
☐ Describe steps in making iron and steel stock.
☐ Explain how forest products are converted to standard stock.

When raw materials arrive at the mill, they are ready for a change in form. They will be refined or converted into standard stock. Trees will become lumber or plywood. Natural gas will be changed into polyethylene (a type of plastic). Bauxite will become aluminum sheets. Lime, silica sand, alumina, iron, and gypsum are processed into Portland cement. This first step in manufacturing is called *primary processing,* Fig. 12-1. Raw materials are processed into industrial materials. Another name for them is standard stock.

STANDARD STOCK

What is standard stock? *Standard stock* is a material that has been changed so it has certain characteristics (qualities). It has a particular grade, size, and shape.

Each type of material has its own standards. Let's look at some major types of standard stock.

Standard Forest Products

Forest products include all things made from wood. Even in its natural state, wood is a com-

Fig. 12-1. The primary processing system changes materials from a natural state to one more suitable for a useful product.

posite. It is made up of fibers held together by lignin, a natural adhesive. The common natural wood composite is *lumber.*

Fiberboard, particleboard, and laminated boards make up the synthetic wood composites. Paper is also a synthetic wood composite, but is not an engineering (structural) material.

Hardwood lumber standards

Hardwood is cut to standard thickness—4/4 (four quarters of an inch), 5/4, 6/4, 8/4, and so on. The boards are random (varying) widths and lengths. The diameter and length of the log determine the width and length of the lumber. Other manufacturing steps may produce standard hardwood products. Examples of these are flooring and interior trim for houses.

Softwood lumber standards

Softwood lumber is generally produced to standard sizes for all of its dimensions. Boards are cut to set thicknesses, widths, and lengths. For example, you can buy a 2 × 4 × 8 (1 1/2 inches thick by 3 1/2 inches wide by 8 feet long) or a 1 × 8 × 16 (3/4 inch thick by 7 1/4 inches wide by 16 feet long). Do you remember that the material is sold by its nominal (in name only) size?

Synthetic wood composites

The typical synthetic composites, as shown in Fig. 12-2, are:

- *Plywood.* A panel composed of a core, (middle layer), face layers of veneer (thin sheets of wood), and usually crossbands. The grain of the core and the face veneers run in the same direction. Except in thin plywood, the crossbands are at right angles to the face veneers, Fig. 12-3. Three-ply material has a core that is at right angles to the face veneers. Most plywood is made entirely from a series of layers of veneer. Other plywoods have cores of particleboard or solid lumber (lumber-core), Fig. 12-4.

- *Particleboard.* A panel made from chips, shavings, or flakes of wood. The actual name of the material comes from the type of particles used. The most common types are called standard particleboard, waferboard, flakeboard, and oriented strand (placed in a certain direction) board. The

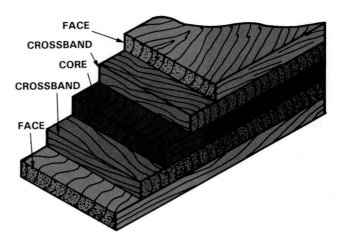

Fig. 12-3. A diagram of plywood construction. Note the crossbanding that gives it strength.

particles are held together with a synthetic adhesive (glue).

- *Fiberboard.* A panel made from wood fibers. The most common fiberboard is hardboard, commonly referred to as Masonite™. This material is very dense. Fibers are held in place by natural glue (lignin).

- *Laminations.* Heavy timbers produced from a series of layers of veneer or lumber. The grain of all layers run in the same direction. The member is held together by synthetic adhesives. Many wood beams in churches and other buildings are laminations.

Except for laminations, synthetic wood composites are produced in sheets. The most common sheet size is 4 feet by 8 feet. Materials are made in a number of standard thicknesses. Fig. 12-5 lists the most common ones.

STANDARD METAL STOCK

Like wood, metals also come in several standard sizes and shapes. Basically, the standard determines

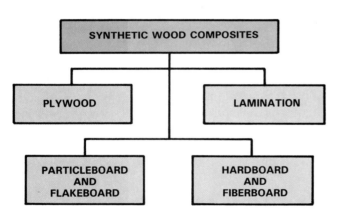

Fig. 12-2. Synthetic wood composites can be classified.

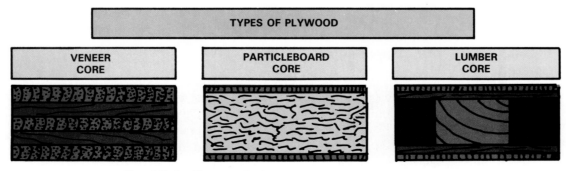

Fig. 12-4. Types of plywood are named for their core.

SIZE	PLYWOOD	PARTICLEBOARD	HARDBOARD
1/8			*
1/4	*	*	*
3/8	*	*	
1/2	*	*	
5/8	*	*	
3/4	*	*	
1	*	*	

Fig. 12-5. Standard sheet sizes for wood composites.

the cross section and the length of the material. Typical shapes are shown in Fig. 12-6.

STANDARD PLASTIC STOCK

Plastic materials are typically produced in pellets and powders, or as sheets and film. Pellets and powders are sold by the pound. They are the inputs for many molding processes.

Sheets and films are used for thermoforming processes and in packaging. These materials are sized by thickness and width. The thickness is given in mils. A *mil* is 0.001 in. thick. Width for these materials is given in inches.

Films are sold in single thickness sheets, tubing, and folded forms, Fig. 12-7. Folded film is used for shrink packaging, such as is seen on compact disc packages. Tubing can be made into bags.

Single thickness film has many uses. These include vapor barriers (between wallboard and insulation in homes), heat-sealing wraps (meats and vegetables in grocery stores), and temporary storm windows.

PRODUCING STANDARD STOCK

Each material has its own primary processing method. Aluminum is refined differently than is copper. Lumber is produced by techniques not used for manufacturing plywood. Each plastic is produced by a special chemical process.

It would be impossible to cover all primary processing systems. It would take many books. Instead, two common primary processing activities—steelmaking and forest product manufacturing—will be presented. This will give you an idea what a raw material goes through to become standard stock.

SHAPE	APPEARANCE	HOW SIZED	LENGTHS*
Sheet	Less than 1/4" thick	Gage No. (thickness) x width Lengths to 12 ft.	To 12 ft.
Plate	more than 1/4" thick	Thickness and width	
Band		Thickness and width	
Rod		Diameter	
Square		Width	12-20 ft.
Hexagonal		Width across flats	
Octagonal		Width across flats	
Angle		Leg lengths (2) x thickness of legs	
Channel		Width x height x web thickness	to 60 ft.
I-beam		Height x flange thickness x web thickness	

*Special orders (not standard) can be in many other lengths.

Fig. 12-6. Standard metal shapes and their names.

Steelmaking

Steelmaking started in North America over 300 years ago. It is now a big industry. The process is a complex science. Complicated chemical actions occur at high temperatures. We say that the processes are *thermally activated.*

Steelmaking requires three basic raw materials. These are iron ore, coke, and limestone. Other materials are added as alloys (mixtures of metals) are manufactured. Steelmaking is a four-step process:
 1. Preparing raw materials.
 2. Making iron.

SHEET	TUBING	FOLDED

 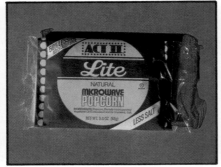 

Fig. 12-7. Plastic film shapes.

3. Making steel.
4. Producing standard stock.

Preparing raw materials

Steelmaking is a process of removing impurities from iron ore. The early processes used high-grade iron ores. These ores then contained large amounts of iron. Now, such deposits are hard to find. Instead, low-grade ores called *taconite,* are often used. They must be preprocessed at the mines. The iron content is increased by removing many unwanted minerals. The remaining material is *sintered* (heated to high temperatures) and made into pellets. The pellets contain about 65 percent iron.

Coke also must be produced. It is a clean-burning carbon product made from coal. The coal is loaded into chambers in a coke oven. The ovens, seen in Fig. 12-8, look like a series of drawers set on edge. Each chamber is about 18 inches wide, 20 feet high, and 40 feet deep. The coal is heated by gases burning between each chamber.

As the coal is heated to 2400 °F (1316 °C), gases, oils, and tar are driven off. These materials are caught and used for many products such as lipstick and plastics.

After being heated for about 18 hours, the door of the chamber is opened. The coke is pushed into a quench (rapid cooling) car. The cooled coke is a high-carbon fuel.

The final ingredient of steel—limestone—must be mined and purified (made pure). It is crushed and screened. At the same time, impurities are removed by magnets and the screens.

Environmental protection (reducing pollution) is considered during the preprocessing of the iron

Fig. 12-8. This 80-slot coke oven battery can produce 850,000 tons of coke a year. (Bethlehem Steel)

ore, coke, and limestone. Land and water are reclaimed at the mine sites. Dust is controlled at the taconite mines and limestone crushers. Coal gases are carefully collected at the coke ovens. Workers are careful to collect as many pollutants as possible. Some are useful by-products.

Making iron

Iron is the first product of the steelmaking process. Most iron is made in a blast furnace like the one shown in Fig. 12-9. Layers of coke, limestone, and iron ore are loaded in the top. They move slowly down to the furnace. The coke is ignited by super hot gases moving upward.

Fig. 12-9. This blast furnace produces iron. It towers 270 feet into the sky. (American Iron and Steel Institute)

Burning coke removes oxygen from the iron ore. (Iron ore is really iron oxide, a combined form of iron and oxygen.) The limestone now combines with impurities in the molten (liquid) iron. It produces a substance called slag, which is drawn off.

The iron ore, by this time, is a mixture of iron and carbon (from the coke). This material collects at the bottom of the blast furnace. Now and then it is drawn off into railcars. These cars, shown in Fig. 12-10, move the iron-carbon (pig iron) mixture to steelmaking furnaces.

Making steel

Steel is made from pig iron and steel scrap. It can be produced in one of two major furnaces:
- Basic oxygen furnace.
- Electric furnace.

The older open hearth furnace is being rapidly replaced by these.

Most steel is produced by the *basic oxygen process,* Fig. 12-11. The furnace is charged with steel scrap and hot iron from the blast furnace, Fig. 12-12. A water-cooled lance is lowered into the furnace. Pure oxygen is blown through the lance into the metal. The oxygen burns (combines with) the extra carbon and any impurities in the iron. They form gases that are collected and cleaned. Also, lime and other materials are added to absorb more impurities. They form slag which is drawn off. Alloying elements (other metals) are added to the molten steel. The resulting steel is drawn off into a ladle.

Fig. 12-13 is a flowchart for the steelmaking process. You can study it to see the steps in produc-

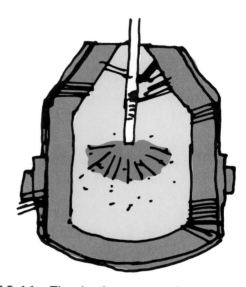

Fig. 12-11. The basic oxygen furnace in cross section.

Fig. 12-10. This 330 ton capacity car carries molten iron away from the blast furnace. (Bethlehem Steel)

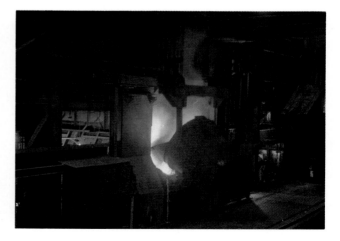

Fig. 12-12. Molten iron from a blast furnace is charged into a basic oxygen furnace. (Bethlehem Steel)

a flowline of steelmaking

From iron ore, limestone and coal in the earth's crust to space-age steels — this fundamental flowline shows only major steps in an intricate progression of processes with their many options.

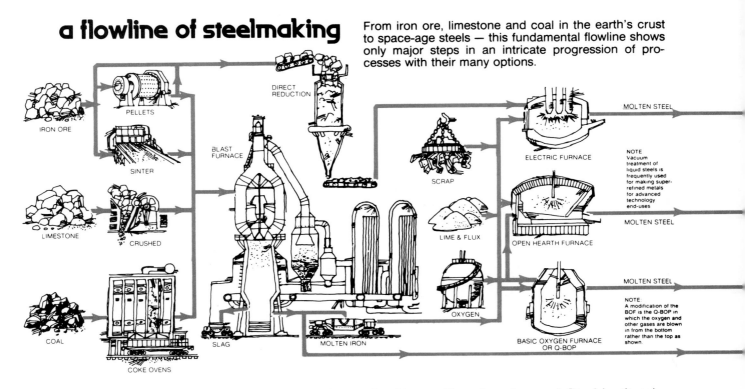

Fig. 12-13. A flowchart summarizing steps for steelmaking. (American Iron and Steel Institute)

ing steel as standard stock. Note the environmental control systems used at each step.

The electric furnace, seen in Fig. 12-14, is used to recycle (reuse) steel scrap. These furnaces are generally smaller than basic oxygen furnaces. Many high-alloy steels are produced in them. The output is typically stainless, tool, and specialty steels. Recently, larger electric furnaces have been developed to produce carbon steels.

Producing standard steel stock

The molten steel from the steelmaking furnaces must be processed further. It is usually cast into a workable shape first. Then, the steel is rolled into a final shape (standard stock).

Older mills first cast an ingot, Fig. 12-15. This is a solid casting that will be shaped in later processes. The ingots are first cooled in soaking pits to solidify the steel. Then, they are reheated to a rolling temperature.

More modern mills use a continuous casting process, as shown in Fig. 12-16. The metal is cast and cut into slabs, Fig. 12-17. The hot slabs move directly to the rolling mills. This process saves large amounts of time and energy (fuel).

Workers in control centers, Fig. 12-18, oversee many rolling processes. These processes change slabs into many shapes, Fig. 12-19.

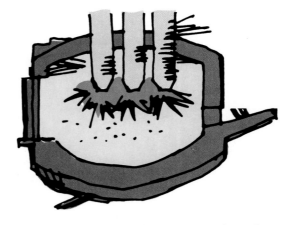

Fig. 12-14. The electric furnace uses heat from an electric arc to melt the charge.

Forest Products Manufacturing

All forest products start with logs. These logs are debarked (bark removed) and enter the mill, Fig. 12-20. In the mill, they move through one of four distinct paths. They can be used to make lumber and sheet materials.

Lumber manufacturing

The lumber manufacturing process varies slightly according to the size of the log. Basically, the logs go through seven steps, as seen in Fig. 12-21:

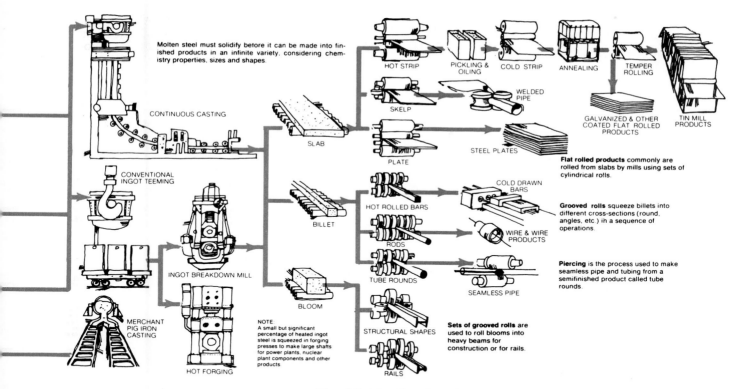

Molten steel must solidify before it can be made into finished products in an infinite variety, considering chemistry properties, sizes and shapes.

CONTINUOUS CASTING

CONVENTIONAL INGOT TEEMING

INGOT BREAKDOWN MILL

MERCHANT PIG IRON CASTING

HOT FORGING

NOTE:
A small but significant percentage of heated ingot steel is squeezed in forging presses to make large shafts for power plants, nuclear plant components and other products.

SLAB

BILLET

BLOOM

HOT STRIP

PICKLING & OILING

COLD STRIP

ANNEALING

TEMPER ROLLING

SKELP

WELDED PIPE

GALVANIZED & OTHER COATED FLAT ROLLED PRODUCTS

TIN MILL PRODUCTS

PLATE

STEEL PLATES

Flat rolled products commonly are rolled from slabs by mills using sets of cylindrical rolls.

HOT ROLLED BARS

COLD DRAWN BARS

RODS

WIRE & WIRE PRODUCTS

Grooved rolls squeeze billets into different cross-sections (round, angles, etc.) in a sequence of operations.

TUBE ROUNDS

SEAMLESS PIPE

Piercing is the process used to make seamless pipe and tubing from a semifinished product called tube rounds.

STRUCTURAL SHAPES

RAILS

Sets of grooved rolls are used to roll blooms into heavy beams for construction or for rails.

Fig. 12-13. Continued.

Fig. 12-15. Molten iron is poured into ingot molds. (Bethlehem Steel)

1. Larger logs are squared at a head rig. The outer slabs produce wider boards that are fairly knot-free.
2. The square center, called a *cant,* and smaller logs are cut into boards at a gang saw.
3. The edges of the boards are sawed parallel with the edger. This process removes wane (sloping edges). Wider boards may also be cut into two or more narrower boards at this step.

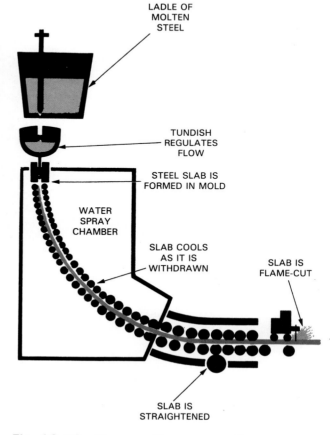

LADLE OF MOLTEN STEEL

TUNDISH REGULATES FLOW

STEEL SLAB IS FORMED IN MOLD

WATER SPRAY CHAMBER

SLAB COOLS AS IT IS WITHDRAWN

SLAB IS FLAME-CUT

SLAB IS STRAIGHTENED

Fig. 12-16. The continuous casting process. Molten steel moves from ladle, to mold, to rollers in an unbroken flow.

Fig. 12-17. A steel strand from a continuous caster is flame cut to length. (Bethlehem Steel)

Fig. 12-20. Logs enter a mill after debarking.

Fig. 12-18. Modern electronics helps this technician in an elevated pulpit to control the steel rolling process.

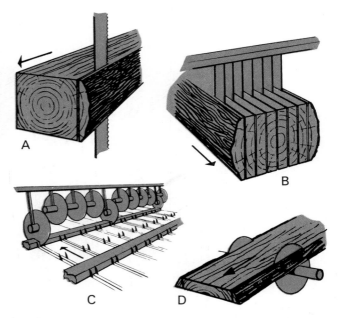

Fig. 12-21. Major steps in the lumber manufacturing process. A—Squaring up large logs. B—Sawing a cant into boards. C—Trim saws cut out defects. D—Board moves through the edger.

4. Trim saws cut out defects and square the ends of the boards. They also produce standard length boards.
5. The lumber is graded as it moves down a conveyor called a green chain. Different grades are piled in separate stacks.
6. The lumber is air and/or kiln (oven) dried.
7. The dry lumber is often planed and edged (smoothed) to a standard thickness and width, Fig. 12-22.

Plywood manufacturing

Most plywood is made from softwood. Douglas fir and southern pine are the main species (types)

Fig. 12-19. A steel plate is being rolled in a 160 inch wide plate mill. (U.S. Steel)

Fig. 12-22. Dry lumber is planed and edged to a standard size. It is then sorted and graded. (Weyerhauser Co.)

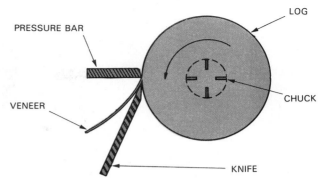

Fig. 12-24. A diagram of a veneer lathe. (American Plywood Association)

used. Logs are steamed so they can be cut more easily. They are then placed in a veneer lathe, Fig. 12-23. The lathe turns the log against a sharp knife, as shown in Fig. 12-24. A thin sheet of wood, called *veneer,* is cut from the log. The log is simply "unwound" much like paper from a roll.

The veneer is dried and graded. The better pieces will have knots and defects cut out. Patches are placed in the holes.

The veneer is then laid up into plywood. The inner layers, as shown in Fig. 12-25, are coated with glue. Veneer strips for outer layers are edge-glued to produce a single sheet. They are placed on top of the inner layers. The "veneer sandwich" is placed

Fig. 12-25. Veneer is coated with an adhesive. The curtain glue spreader is in the center of the picture. (American Plywood Association)

in a heated press. Heat and pressure squeeze the sheet together and cure the glue.

After a set curing time, the panel is removed from the press. When the sheet has cooled, saws trim it to size and sanders smooth and reduce it to a standard thickness. Finished sheets are grade marked and shipped to customers.

Particleboard manufacturing

Particleboard is a sheet material made from logs and mill waste. Chips and flakes are mixed with a glue. The mixture is formed into a mat, Fig. 12-26. The mat is pressed while heat is applied. The heat cures the glue, producing a rigid sheet. The cured sheet is sanded to thickness and cut to a standard size.

Hardboard manufacturing

Hardboard also uses mill waste and chips. These materials are defibered (broken down to single fibers). This process is shown in Fig. 12-27. The fibers are then formed into mats. The mat is placed

Fig. 12-23. A veneer lathe "unpeels" a log section to make veneer. (Weyerhauser Co.)

Fig. 12-26. A particleboard mat is formed by a machine. (American Forest Products Industries)

Fig. 12-27. Defibered wood is the basic ingredient of hardboard. (American Forest Products Industries)

in a heated press. Pressure is applied. The natural lignin on the fibers bonds them. The result is a very hard, dense sheet. It is cut to a standard width and length. The sheet is so smooth as it leaves the press that it does not need to be face sanded.

SUMMARY

Raw materials are converted into standard stock. Each material has its own standard sizes, shapes, and compositions. These standards determine the materials that are available to small manufacturers and individuals.

All standard stock is produced by primary processing practices. Each material has its own processing methods. The basic processing activities for steel and forest products are presented. You may want to check books out of a library to read about other materials.

KEY WORDS

All the following words have been used in this chapter. Do you know their meaning?

Basic oxygen process	Forest products
Cant	Hardboard
Coke	Hardwood lumber
Lamination	Sinter
Lumber	Softwood lumber
Particleboard	Standard stock
Plywood	Taconite
Primary processing	

TEST YOUR KNOWLEDGE

Place your answers on a separate sheet of paper. Do not write in this book.

1. List and describe the three major types of structural synthetic wood composites.
2. Describe the major steps in making iron. . . in making steel.
3. List the steps in manufacturing lumber from logs.
4. How is plywood made?

ACTIVITIES

1. Write to a producer of forest products or steel. Request information describing their manufacturing processes. Share these materials with your class.
2. Visit a library and research the manufacture of a major standard stock. Prepare a short report on the manufacturing process.

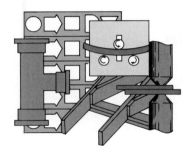

Chapter 13

LAYOUT AND MEASUREMENT

After reading this chapter, you will be able to:
☐ State the meaning of the terms "measurement" and "layout."
☐ Identify surfaces of a part.
☐ Identify special features on a part.
☐ Identify measuring and layout tools.
☐ List principles of measurement for round and flat stock.
☐ Describe how to lay out a part.

Before any part or product can be made it has to be measured and laid out. You need to measure to find the distance between two points. Measuring also tells you how thick, wide, and long a part is. It tells you the diameter and depth of any holes. You also find the width and depth of grooves and dados by *measurement.*

When you hear the word *layout*, you will know that it means to measure and mark a part so that it can be made. The markings tell you where every feature (hole, notch, etc.) should be on the part. It also shows where a part is to be cut from a larger piece of material. The difference in these terms is shown in Fig. 13-1.

Before you can lay out or measure parts and features you must know:
1. Names of the surfaces on a part.
2. Special features or cuts.
3. Basic measuring and layout tools.
4. Layout practices.

SURFACES OF A PART

There are some basic terms that describe a part. Everyone must know these terms so they can communicate with other workers. These terms, as

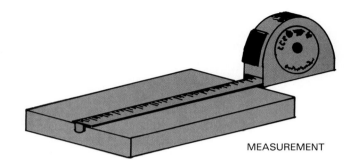

MEASUREMENT

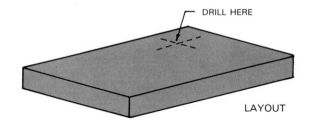

DRILL HERE

LAYOUT

Fig. 13-1. The difference between measurement and layout.

shown in Fig. 13-2, are:
1. Length—Largest dimension of a part.
2. Width—The second largest dimension.
3. Thickness—The smallest dimension of the part.
4. Diameter—The distance across the end of a round part.
5. Face (or side)—The largest surface.
6. Edge—The second largest surface.
7. End—The smallest surface.

Dimensions are all the size measurements of a part. They are always given in a certain order. For rectangular pieces, the order is "thickness × width × length." A round part's diameter is given first followed by its length.

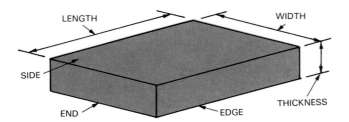

Fig. 13-2. Common terms used in most layout and measurement.

Wood Measurement

These basic terms are a little different for wood and wood products with grain. Length is always measured along the grain. Width is measured across the grain.

It is possible, as shown in Fig. 13-3, to have a board wider than it is long. Whenever you see a dimension listed, you can tell grain direction. A piece of wood, 3/4 × 6 × 24, has the grain parallel with the longest dimension. However, a part 1/2 × 12 × 6 is a board with the grain parallel to the 6 inch measurement.

SPECIAL FEATURES

Special features are the cuts that change a part from a square or rectangle. They are holes, cuts for joints, and specially shaped cuts. There are many special features. The most common are pictured in Fig. 13-4.

MEASURING TECHNIQUES

Measuring determines sizes of parts and features. Typically, we measure the external (outside) sizes and angles or the internal (inside) sizes and angles.

External measurement basically determines the thickness, width, and length of a part. It also measures the outside diameter of round parts. Special features that change external features, such

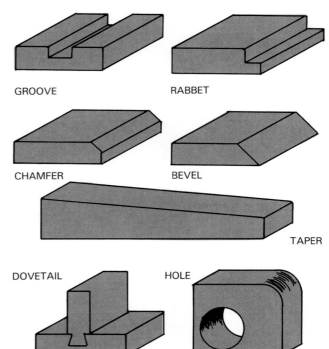

Fig. 13-4. Common features on parts change them from a basic square or rectangular shape.

as angled or shaped edges, must also be measured, Fig. 13-5.

Internal measurements determine the sizes of holes, grooves, slots, and other "inside" features. Typical internal measurements are width, inside diameter, angle, and depth. Fig. 13-6 shows some common internal dimensions.

These measurements are generally either standard or precision (very accurate). In *standard measurement*, you would measure to the nearest fraction of an inch. *Precision measurement* is generally given in thousandths of an inch (0.001").

Standard measurement is used for most woodworking, carpentry, and sheet metal work. Preci-

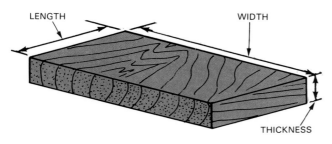

Fig. 13-3. Measurement of wood. Length is always with the grain of the wood.

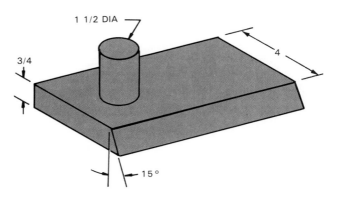

Fig. 13-5. Samples of external measurements. They are on the outside surfaces of parts.

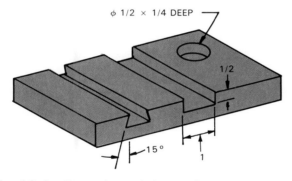

Fig. 13-6. Examples of internal measurements. They are on the inside surfaces. The ϕ means diameter.

sion measurement is commonly used in metal machining, plastic molding, and material-forming practices. The type of measurement to be used depends on the accuracy needed and the stability of the material.

SI Metric Measurement

SI metric measurement is used by some U.S. industries and by most other countries of the world. In this system, standard measure is taken to the nearest millimeter, which is much smaller than the inch (1mm = 0.0394 in.). Precision measurement is accurate to the nearest tenth or hundredth of a millimeter (0.1mm = 0.004 in.; 0.001mm = 0.0004 in.).

The more accurate a part must be, the more precise the system of measurement is needed. Engine cylinders or transmission gears must be very accurately manufactured. Therefore, these are held to thousandths (0.001) or ten-thousandths (0.0001) of an inch.

However, some materials do not lend themselves to that type of precision. Wood, for example, is not very stable. It expands and contracts as the humidity of the air changes. It is useless to measure wood in thousandths. It will vary in size from day to day as the weather changes.

MEASURING AND LAYOUT TECHNIQUES

Layout and measuring is always done with the aid of tools and gages. The basic measuring tools may be grouped by what they measure:
• Linear (length) distances.
• Diameters.
• Angles.

Linear Distance Measuring Tools

Certain tools measure distances between two points in a straight line. They will determine the basic size measurements: thickness, width, and length. The most common measuring tool is the *tape rule.* It provides an easy way to measure long parts. Shorter parts may be measured with *machinist's rules* and *bench rules,* Fig. 13-7. Machinist's rules usually have scales (markings) which will measure down to 1/64 inch.

A *micrometer,* Fig. 13-8, makes precision measurements. The most common type is an outside micrometer. They come in various sizes. The 0-1 inch micrometer, that measures in thousandths of an inch, is typical. Others measure larger sizes, but within a one inch range. For example, a 1-2 inch micrometer is available. So is a 3-4 inch.

Calipers and *dividers,* Fig. 13-9, can also be used to measure linear distance. The caliper is set against

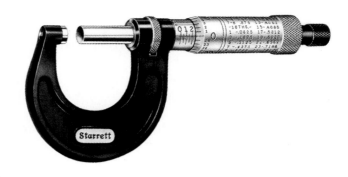

Fig. 13-8. A common outside micrometer. It measures accurately to one-thousandth of an inch (0.001''). (The L.S. Starrett Co.)

the two parallel surfaces. It is then removed from the part. The distance between the caliper legs is measured with a rule.

Depth is also a linear measurement. It may be the depth of a hole, groove, or other feature. They can be measured with a rule if it will fit into the feature. Also, special *depth gages,* as shown in Fig. 13-10, are available.

Diameter Measuring Tools

Rules can be used to measure diameter. However, accurate measurements are hard to make. Typically, outside diameters are measured

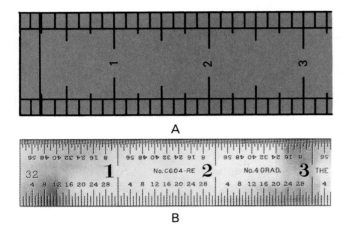

A

B

Fig. 13-7. Rules such as these measure distance along a straight line. A—Bench rule. B—Machinist's rule. (The L.S. Starrett Co.)

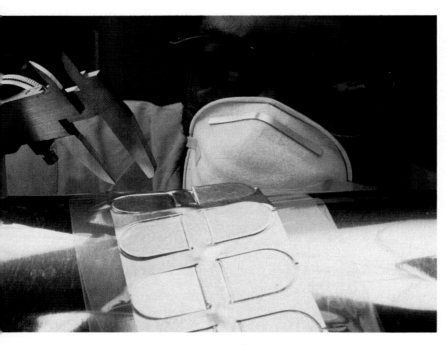

Fig. 13-9. Calipers and dividers can be used for measuring. (The L.S. Starrett Co., Goodyear Tire and Rubber Co.)

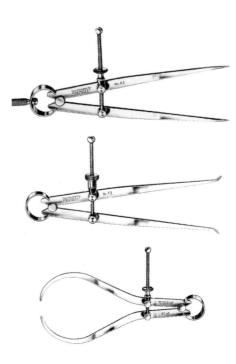

Fig. 13-10. A direct reading depth gage is used to check depth of a tire mold. (Goodyear Tire and Rubber Co.)

with a micrometer, Fig. 13-11, or calipers. Micrometers provide precision measurements while calipers are accurate up to 1/64 inch.

Inside diameters can be measured with inside micrometers or inside calipers, Fig. 13-12. Again, micrometers are more accurate than calipers.

Angle Measuring Tools

Angles can be any value either greater or smaller than 90 degrees. The common 90 degree or right angle is checked with a *square.* There are many kinds of squares, as shown in Fig. 13-13. These include rafter squares, try squares, and combination

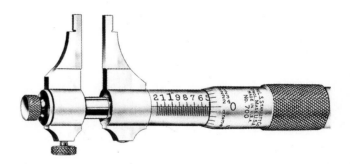

Fig. 13-12. Inside micrometers and calipers are used to check the size of internal features. (The L.S. Starrett Co.)

squares. Combination squares will check both 90 degree and 45 degree angles.

Angles other than 90 degrees or 45 degrees can be checked with a *protractor,* Fig. 13-14. This may be a separate tool or part of a combination set. The *combination set* has a 45/90 degree head, a protractor head, and a center-finding head. All the heads will fit on a single rule, Fig. 13-15, but are used separately.

LAYOUT PRACTICES

One principal use of measuring tools, as shown in Fig. 13-16, is layout. The part itself must be laid out (drawn) on the standard stock. Layout should

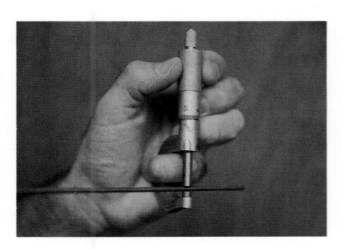

Fig. 13-11. A micrometer is being used here to measure the diameter of a wire. (Western Electric)

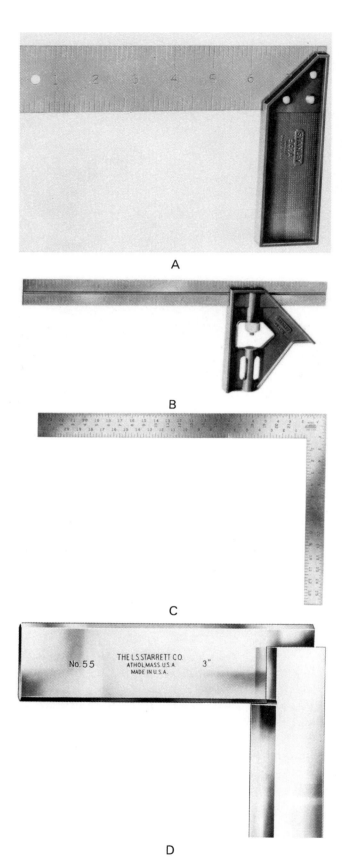

A

B

C

D

Fig. 13-13. Types of common squares. A—Try square. B—Combination square. C—Steel square. D—Machinist's square.
(Stanley Tools; The L.S. Starrett Co.)

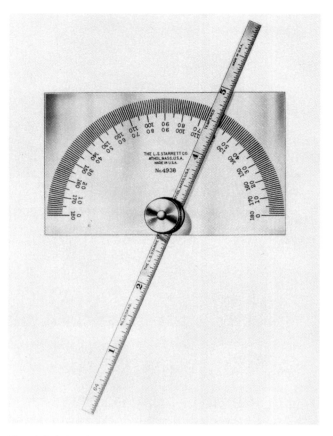

Fig. 13-14. A protractor can check many angles. (The L.S. Starrett Co.)

follow some basic steps.

First, the part size is measured off on the stock. Lines for length and width are scribed or drawn on the material. Fig. 13-17 shows a way to use the square to do this. The part blank is then cut out.

Second, features should be located on the blank. Centerlines for holes and arcs are drawn first. Rules and squares are used to make these lines square and parallel.

Holes and arcs are then located. Dividers or a compass are used to lay out the circumference of (distance around) circles.

Centers of holes should be marked. A prick punch or center punch is used for this task. Tangent lines (lines which connect circles) are then drawn. Finally, straight cuts are laid out. Fig. 13-18 shows a typical layout process.

SUMMARY

Layout and measurement are important for all manufacturing processes. Measurement determines sizes of a manufactured part. Layout determines the location of features and the size of parts to be

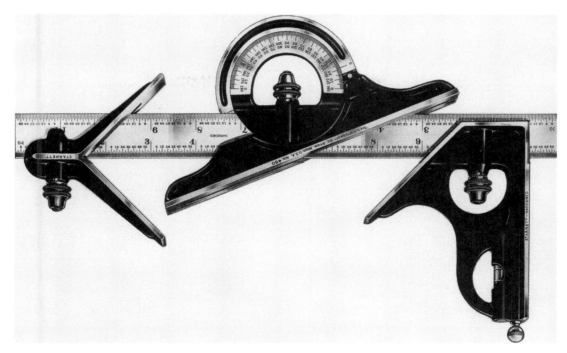

Fig. 13-15. A typical combination set has three different kinds of heads.   (The L.S. Starrett Co.)

Fig. 13-16. A worker uses a square to lay out a piece of wood.

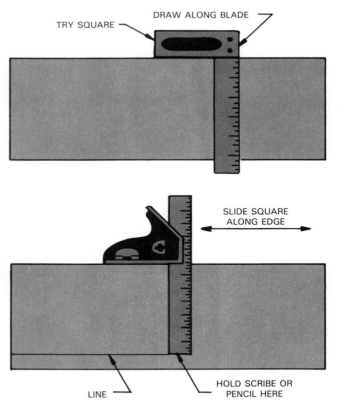

TRY SQUARE

DRAW ALONG BLADE

SLIDE SQUARE ALONG EDGE

LINE

HOLD SCRIBE OR PENCIL HERE

Fig. 13-17. Laying out the length and width of a part. Top. Marking the length. Bottom. Using a combination square to scribe a parallel line for width.

produced. We lay out something to be made. We measure the part after manufacturing operations are completed.

The principal surfaces of a part are its face, edge, and end. They are measured as a width and thickness (or a diameter) and a length.

Measurement may be very accurate (precision) or simply in fractions of an inch. These measurements may be for internal or external sur-

faces and features. All measurements are done with tools which measure linear distances, diameters, and/or angles.

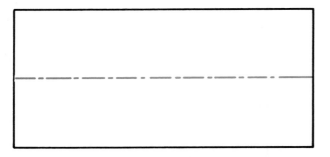

1. LOCATE CENTERLINE FOR PART

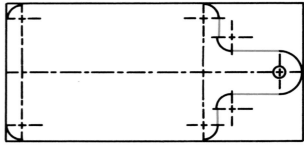

2. LOCATE CENTERLINES FOR ARCS AND CIRCLES

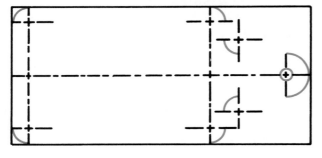

3. DRAW ARCS AND CIRCLES

4. CONNECT ARCS

Fig. 13-18. Procedure for laying out product features.

KEY WORDS

All the following words have been used in this chapter. Do you know their meaning?

Bench rule
Calipers
Combination set
Depth gage
Diameter
Dimensions
Edge
End
Face
Layout
Length
Machinist's rule

Measurement
Micrometer
Precision
  measurement
Protractor
Square
Standard
  measurement
Tape rule
Thickness
Width

TEST YOUR KNOWLEDGE

Place your answers on a separate sheet. Please do not write in this text.
1. What is meant by precision measurement?
2. Which measuring tool would you use to measure the following features?
   A. Diameter of a hole in thousandths.
   B. Length of a board.
   C. Diameter of a wood dowel.
   D. Diameter of a steel shaft in thousandths.
   E. Length of a metal part in 1/64ths.

3. The proper order for listing the dimensions of a part is _____.
   A. For rectangular parts: thickness × width × length; for round parts: diameter × length.
   B. Always length × width × thickness.
   C. Always list in descending order of size.
4. _____ are the cuts that change a part from a square or a rectangle.
5. In laying out and measuring a part, which would you do first?
   A. Locate features on the piece of stock.
   B. Saw off the piece of stock to right length.
   C. Lay out the length and width of the part on the stock.
6. _____ of holes should be marked before they are drilled. A _____ is used for this task.

ACTIVITIES

1. Measure some common items in your home using a ruler. Have someone who lives with you check your work.
2. List 10 parts or products that you think would be manufactured using precision measurement.
3. List 10 parts or products that you think would be measured using fractions of an inch.

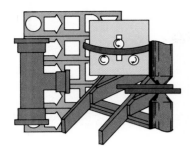

Chapter 14

CASTING AND MOLDING PROCESSES

After reading this chapter, you will be able to:
☐ Identify the parts of a mold.
☐ Describe how patterns and cores are used.
☐ List ways to make materials liquid.
☐ State requirements for removing parts from a mold.

The first step in secondary processing is giving a material size and shape. The dimensions (size) of the part must be worked out. Also, the part must be produced in the right shape, Fig. 14-1.

Three processing activities can be used to make the part. These are casting and molding, forming, and separating. This chapter explores how casting and molding techniques can shape and size materials into parts or products that each of us use everyday.

WHAT IS CASTING AND MOLDING?

What is casting? Have you ever eaten an ice cube? Have you washed your hands in a sink or seen an automotive engine? If you have experienced any of these things, you have come into contact with or used a cast product, Fig. 14-2.

Casting and molding are a family of processes in which an industrial material is first made into a liquid. The liquid material is poured or forced into a prepared mold. Then, the material is allowed or caused to solidify (become hard). The solid material is finally extracted (removed) from the mold.

Casting and molding are really terms that describe the same general process. *Casting* is the

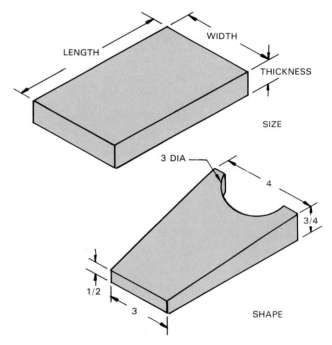

Fig. 14-1. Establishing size and shape. Casting and molding, forming, and separating produce size and shape characteristics.

word generally used when working in metal and ceramic materials. The term *molding* is used when working with plastic.

Steps in Casting

All casting processes have five basic steps. They are used no matter what material (clay, metal, plastic, wax, or glass) is being cast. These steps are:
1. A mold of proper shape is produced.
2. The material is prepared for casting.
3. The material is introduced (poured or forced)

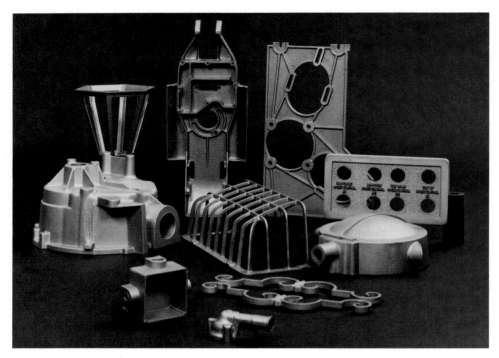

Fig. 14-2. Typical cast products.

into the mold.

4. The material is allowed or caused to solidify (harden).

5. The finished item (a casting or molded part) is extracted (removed) from the mold.

Some products come from the mold almost finished. They need little extra processing. Others need cleaning, machining, heat treating, assembling, and/or finishing.

In all cases, their basic size and shape has to be set in the first step. Other processing simply adds features, trues surfaces, or completes other similar shaping activities.

Molds

A casting process needs a container for the liquid material. The material must be held in the right shape as it solidifies.

The container for casting processes is called a **mold.** The mold is a carefully prepared **cavity** (hole). The cavity, as seen in Fig. 14-3, must be of proper size and shape. Molds for castings are of two basic types: expendable molds and permanent molds.

Expendable molds

Expendable molds are so-called because they are used only once. They must be broken to remove the casting. Inexpensive materials like sand or plaster are used to make expendable molds.

Expendable molding requires two items. First, a pattern is needed. A **pattern** is a device that is the exact shape of the finished casting. Patterns are usually slightly larger than the finished product.

SAFETY WITH CASTING AND MOLDING PROCESSES

1. Do not attempt a process that has not been demonstrated to you by the instructor.
2. Always wear safety glasses, goggles, or a face shield.
3. Wear protective clothing, gloves, and a face shield when pouring molten material.
4. Do not pour molten material into a mold that is wet or contains water.

5. Carefully secure two-part molds together.
6. Perform casting and molding procedures in a well-ventilated area.
7. Do not leave hot castings or molded parts where other people could be burned by them.
8. Constantly monitor the material and equipment temperatures during casting or molding processes.

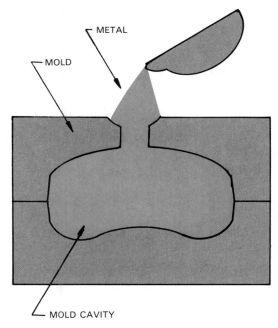

METAL

MOLD

MOLD CAVITY

Fig. 14-3. Mold cavity must be the proper size and shape.

Remember, most materials shrink as they cool. Therefore, you need a mold cavity that is bigger than the finished product.

The second item you need is a molding material. It is something to place around the pattern to form a mold.

Casting process

It is easier to understand the use of patterns and molding materials by studying an actual casting process. Let's look at *green sand casting,* Fig. 14-4.

The first step is to make a pattern. Patterns are usually made from wood, Fig. 14-5. If they are to be used many times, they may be made from metal or epoxy.

The pattern must have *draft* (sloped sides). Otherwise it could not be removed from the sand mold without causing damage to the mold.

The green sand mold is produced in a two-part flask. Each part of the *flask* is a four-sided container without a top or bottom. The bottom half is called the *drag.* The *cope* is the top half.

The molding process starts by placing the drag on a board. Half of the pattern is placed in the drag. The pattern is coated with a thin layer of powder called *parting compound.* It makes removing the pattern easier.

Next, molding sand is *riddled* (sifted) into the drag. The sand is rammed (packed) against the pattern with a special tool. The drag is filled and receives a final ramming.

The drag is then turned over and the cope is put on top. The other half of the pattern is placed exactly over the first half. Again parting compound is applied. Sand is riddled into the cope and rammed as before. The top is then *struck* (leveled off).

The cope and drag are now separated. Pattern parts are carefully removed. The *gating* (a path into the cavity for the molten metal) is then cut. Finally, the mold is put back together. Metal can now be poured in. When the metal is solid, the sand mold is shaken apart.

Other one-shot molds are:
1. Plaster investment molds, Fig. 14-6.
2. Glass molds.
3. Shell (baked sand and resin) molds, Fig. 14-7.

Permanent Molds

Permanent molds can be used over and over again. They will produce many castings before they wear out. Most permanent molds have cavities that are machined into them. This makes permanent molds more expensive.

Permanent molds are either gravity or pressure molds. *Gravity molds* are filled by pouring the material into the mold from the top.

Pressure molds must be built to allow the material to be forced into the cavities. The molds must be much stronger than gravity molds. They must withstand the force of a strong clamping system that holds the mold together. Also, pressure is produced from inside by the material being forced into the molds.

Preparing the Material

Casting requires a liquid or semi-liquid material. Several methods are used to prepare the materials for casting, Fig. 14-8.

Most plastics and metals are heated to the molten or flowable state. Often this is done in a furnace. The metal, as shown in Fig. 14-9, is then moved to the mold in a ladle.

Some casting processes use a machine that first melts the material. It then causes the material to flow directly into the mold. Most pressure molding processes use this system, Fig. 14-10.

Other materials are not melted. Instead they are suspended (dissolved) in a liquid. The mixture is poured into molds where it hardens. Clays and certain plastics are cast as a *suspension.*

Finally, some materials are already a liquid. Water is a good example. Another widely used liquid material is liquid acrylic (casting plastics).

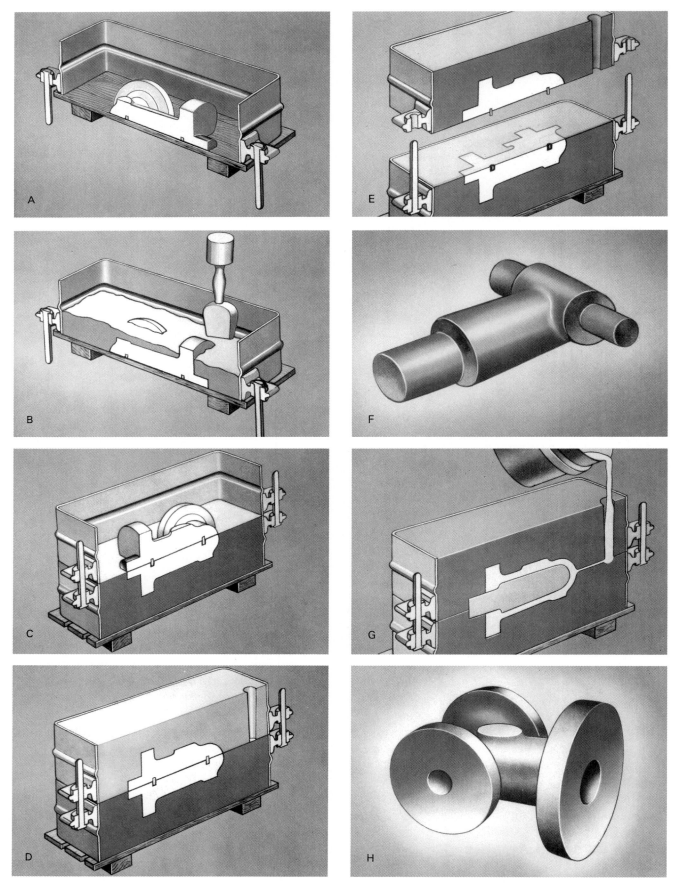

Fig. 14-4. Cutaway drawings show how a green sand mold is prepared. A—Pattern is placed in the drag and dusted with parting compound. B—Sand is riddled and packed around the pattern. C—Drag is filled and then turned over. The cope and second half of the pattern are put in place. D—Parting compound is sifted over pattern. Cope is rammed full of sand. E—The flask is separated and the pattern is removed. F—A core of baked sand is placed in the cavity. G—The mold is assembled and molten metal is poured into the cavity. H—The finished casting is removed from the mold.   (Gray and Ductile Founders' Society)

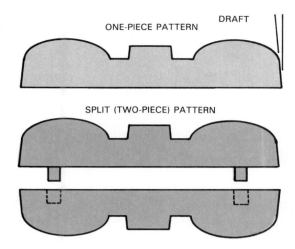

Fig. 14-5. Two types of patterns.

ONE-PIECE PATTERN
DRAFT

SPLIT (TWO-PIECE) PATTERN

Fig. 14-7. Sand-resin core (inserts) and a shell mold drag is in place. (Brush Wellman Co.)

Fig. 14-6. Wax patterns are dipped in plaster as the first step in producing an investment (lost wax) casting. (Arwood Co.)

Many liquid materials must have a hardening agent compounded (mixed) into them. They will then harden by a chemical reaction.

Introducing Materials in the Mold

Once the mold is produced and the material is prepared, they need to be brought together. The material must be put into the mold. Two basic techniques are used to do this. The material may be poured into the mold as was shown in Fig. 14-9. Gravity causes the mold to be filled. Most sand molds, slip casting molds, and nonpressure permanent molds are gravity filled.

Materials may also be forced into a mold. Several casting techniques use pressure to fill molds, including die casting and injection molding.

In *die casting,* nonferrous (not iron or steel) metals are melted in a "pot." A ram then forces some of the molten metal into the mold. The mold is water-cooled and, therefore, cools the metal. The dies (molds) open and the solidified part is *ejected* (pushed out). A typical die casting process is shown in Fig. 14-11.

Injection molding is another very important process. In principle it works exactly like die casting. The difference is in the material being molded. Die casting uses metals while injection molding works with plastic. Fig. 14-10 shows an injection molding machine. Cold plastic pellets enter a heating chamber. The chamber softens the plastic. Then, a pneumatic (air-driven) ram forces the plastic into the mold. There the plastic solidifies. The mold opens and automatically ejects the molded part, Fig. 14-12.

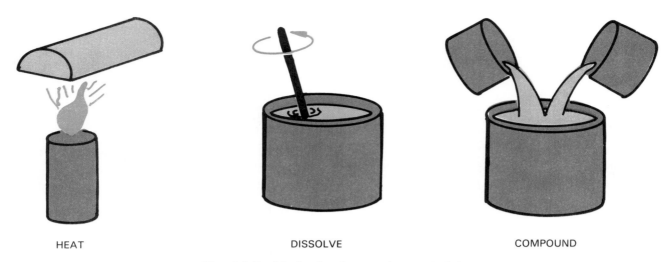

HEAT   DISSOLVE   COMPOUND

Fig. 14-8. Methods of preparing materials.

Fig. 14-9. Precious metals are poured from a ladle into a mold.   (FMC Corp.)

Solidifying the Material

Liquid or soft material in a mold must become hard. One way to cause this is to remove heat. If the material was melted, cooling will solidify it. Liquids harden as heat is removed.

The heat can also be allowed to radiate (escape) into the air. This is natural cooling. It is the method used by most expendable molding techniques.

High-speed permanent molding processes require rapid cooling. Water or other liquids are commonly used for cooling. Channels in the molds allow cooling liquids to circulate and remove excess heat. Suspended materials must dry. The liquid must evaporate or be drawn off.

Slip casting of clay, shown in Fig. 14-13, uses this method. The slip (water/clay suspension) is poured into plaster molds. The molds absorb water.

Fig. 14-10. Injection molding machines use pressure to fill molds with plastic.   (Stokes)

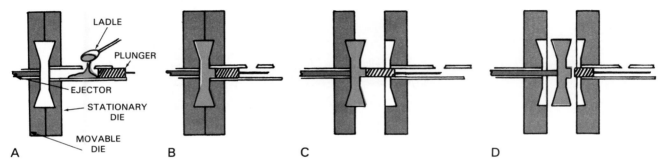

Fig. 14-11. Steps in cold chamber die casting. A—Metal is placed into the chamber. B—Metal is forced into the die. C—Die is opened. D—Casting ejected from die.

Fig. 14-12. This computer-controlled plastic press produces one dishwasher tub every 68 seconds. The tubs are robotically removed from the press. (Whirlpool Corp.)

As a result, clay against the mold starts to become a solid. As additional water is absorbed, the outside wall of clay thickens. The center material is still liquid. When the wall reaches the correct thickness, the slip left in the center is poured out. This results in a hollow clay product.

The clay is allowed more time to dry. Then, the mold is opened and the casting is removed. It continues to dry under controlled conditions. The clay is then fired (heated to harden) in a kiln. The plaster mold must also be dried before it can be used again. Many clay products, such as figurines, cream pitchers, lavatories (sinks), and toilets are produced using slip casting.

The last method of hardening a material is through chemical action. This process is really a conditioning technique (discussed in detail in Chapter 17). A chemical reaction is caused by a hardener. This process is generally used with plastics. It causes simple organic molecules to form rigid, complex molecules.

Removing the Casting

After a cast material is solidified (hardened) it must be extracted (removed) from the mold. The method to remove castings is directly related to the type of mold used. One-shot molds are broken up to remove the casting, Fig. 14-14.

Permanent molds are opened. The parts (castings or molded items) are removed. Often ejection pins built into the mold automatically push the parts out.

SUMMARY

Casting is the only process that directly converts an industrial material into a finished part in one major step. It moves from a liquid to a sized and shaped part in a single process. Casting and molding involves producing an expendable or a permanent mold. The material to be cast is then prepared. It is melted, dissolved, or compounded with hardeners. The prepared material is then poured or forced into the mold.

The material is caused to solidify by cooling, drying, or chemical action. The solid part is then removed by destroying the expendable mold or opening the permanent mold.

KEY WORDS

All the following words have been used in this chapter. Do you know their meaning?

Casting	Draft
Cavity	Drag
Cope	Eject
Die casting	Expendable mold

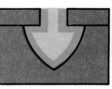
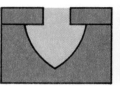
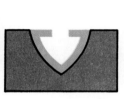
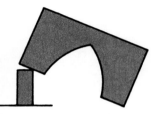

A. Mold filled with slip. | Wall thickness builds. | B. Excess slip poured out. | C. Casting removed. Mold opened. | D. Mold is dried.

FILLING MOLD

BRACING MOLD

PULLING BODY CORE

REMOVING FULL MOLD

Fig. 14-13. Top. Major steps in slip casting. Bottom. Photos showing slip casting of a toilet.

Fig. 14-14. Expendable molds are destroyed to remove the casting. (Crouse-Hinds Co.)

Flask
Gating
Gravity mold
Green sand casting
Injection molding
Mold
Molding
Parting compound

Pattern
Permanent mold
Pressure mold
Riddle
Slip casting
Struck
Suspension

TEST YOUR KNOWLEDGE

Place your answers on a separate sheet of paper. Please do not write in this text.

1. What is the difference between "size" and "shape?"
2. List the five major steps in casting.
3. _____ and _____ are the two major types of molds.

4. List and describe the three main ways of preparing materials for casting or molding.
5. Molten materials are forced into the mold by _____ casting and _____ molding.
6. Indicate which of the following are methods of solidifying material cast into a mold:
   A. Freezing of the material.
   B. Natural cooling by radiation.
   C. Drying and/or evaporation.
   D. Chemical action.
   E. Pressure.

ACTIVITIES

1. List 10 parts or products that were manufactured using casting or molding.
2. List three casting activities used in preparing food in a typical home.

Injection molding is used to create these razor handles.   (Gillette Co.)

A drawing die is used to form the beverage cans shown
in this photograph. (Reynolds Metals Co.)

Chapter 15

FORMING PROCESSES

After reading this chapter, you will be able to:
□ Define the term "forming."
□ Identify the major stages of forming and describe what happens in each stage.
□ List various shaping devices and explain the process to which each is related.
□ Discuss the relationship of a material's temperature to forming.
□ List the types of force used in forming.

Forming is a second method of giving a part size and shape. This family of processes changes the size and shape, but not the volume of the material. The material will weigh the same before and after a forming process.

STAGES OF FORMING

Forming uses pressure. All engineering materials being formed go through two major stages as stress (pressure or force) is applied. These stages, Fig. 15-1, are:

1. *Elastic stage.* Stress will stretch the material in this stage. However, when the stress (load) is removed, the material will return to its original size and shape. At the end of the elastic range is the *yield point.* Beyond this point, additional stress will permanently deform (change shape of) the material.
2. *Plastic stage.* This stage starts at the yield point. The material starts to give in (yield) to the stress. It will be permanently stretched into a new shape. Added stress (pull) will cause more stretching. The plastic stage continues up to the *fracture point.* Then the material breaks into two or more parts.

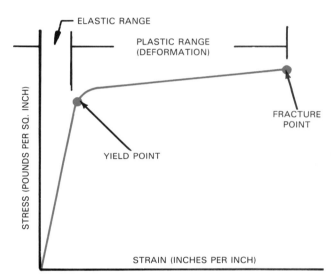

Fig. 15-1. A simple stress-strain curve showing material-forming stages. The part of the curve that is nearly vertical marks the first stage limits. Up to the yield point, material will still return to its original shape if the stress is removed.

Forming is always done between the yield point and the fracture point. Pressure is applied to cause permanent reshaping (deformation) without breaking the material.

All forming practices have three major things in common:
1. A shaping device is used.
2. A material forming temperature is established.
3. There is a method for applying force.

SHAPING DEVICES

The shaping tool is to forming as the mold is to casting; it gives size and shape to the material.

1. Do not attempt a process that has not been demonstrated to you by the instructor.
2. Always wear safety glasses, goggles, or a face shield.
3. Always hold hot materials with a pair of pliers or tongs.
4. Place hot parts in a safe place to cool, keep-

ing them away from people and from materials.
5. Follow correct procedures when lighting torches and furnaces.
6. Never place your hands or foreign objects between mated dies or rolls.
7. Always use a spark lighter to light a propane torch or gas furnace.

There are two basic types of shaping devices used in forming processes: dies and rolls.

Dies

Dies are flat pieces of hard materials. They must be harder than the material they are forming. Tool steel is used for metal and many plastic-forming dies. Plaster can be used for ceramic dies. Certain plastic-forming processes can use wood, ceramic, or epoxy dies.

The dies generally have a shape cut into them. This may be a cavity or raised portion, Fig. 15-2. Three major types of dies can be used:
1. Open dies.
2. Die sets.
3. Shaped dies or molds.

Open dies

This is the simplest type of die. An *open die* is basically two flat, hard plates. One die half is stationary (unmoving). The other moves to hit (hammer) or put pressure (squeeze) on the material between the dies.

The blacksmith's hammer and anvil work like open dies. The anvil is the stationary half of the die. The hammer is the striking force. Today, open dies (smith forging) are used to form special

material, Fig. 15-3. These materials cannot be shaped easily by other processes.

Die sets

Die sets have shapes machined or engraved on their faces. Usually the shape on one half of the die fits the shape on the other half. Fig. 15-4 shows the two types: closed and mated. These dies either fit together or mate with each other.

Some important processes use die sets to shape material. Forging squeezes material into a shape. First, a heated metal workpiece is placed between shaped die halves. The upper die is pressed or dropped on the work. The material is forced to take the shape of the dies, Fig. 15-5. The dropping die process is called *drop forging*. Many wrenches, sockets, and pliers are drop forged.

Press forging also uses squeezing action. It is used to shape many automotive and aircraft parts. Included are camshafts, piston rods, and crankshafts.

In many cases, a single die will have several cavities, also known as *stations*. The material is

Fig. 15-2. An example of a two-piece die with cavities machined in them.

Fig. 15-3. A steel ingot is forged with an open die forging press.   (Bethlehem Steel)

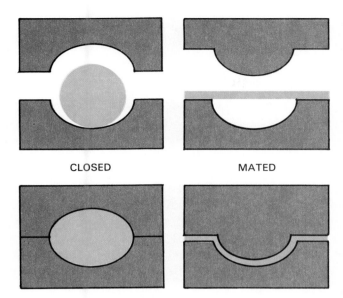

CLOSED   MATED

Fig. 15-4. Examples of two-piece closed and mated dies. Top. Dies are open. Materials are ready to be shaped. Bottom. Dies are pressed shut to shape the part.

Fig. 15-5. This forged steel truck axle was produced with closed dies. (Forging Industry Assn.)

moved from one station to the next. At each station, Fig. 15-6, a single forming act is completed. When the part leaves the die it is completely formed.

Drawing is another shaped die process. One die pulls sheet metal into the other die. This makes pan-shaped products such as automotive body parts, dry cell battery cases, and baking pans. See Fig. 15-7.

Many times drawing is called *stamping.* Many stamping processes combine shearing (cutting) with drawing (bending). Fig. 15-8 shows a complex progressive (several stations) stamping die. The part

Fig. 15-7. Stamped pieces coming off a production line. These pieces will be used in automobile production. (Ford Motor Co.)

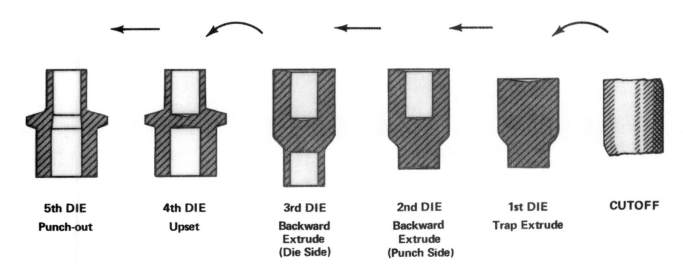

5th DIE	4th DIE	3rd DIE	2nd DIE	1st DIE	CUTOFF
Punch-out	Upset	Backward Extrude (Die Side)	Backward Extrude (Punch Side)	Trap Extrude	

Fig. 15-6. Steps in cold forming a part. The part was formed on a single die with five stations. (National Machinery Co.)

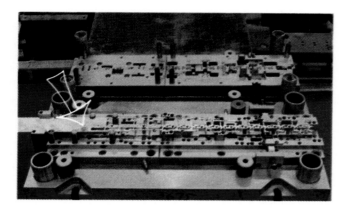

Fig. 15-8. A progressive carbide stamping die. The workpiece (indicated with the arrow) is partly formed. (Alton Tool Co.)

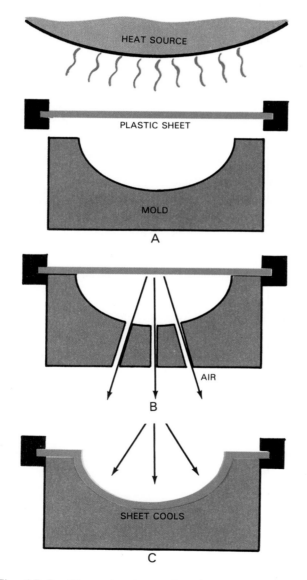

HEAT SOURCE

PLASTIC SHEET

MOLD

A

AIR

B

SHEET COOLS

C

Fig. 15-9. Steps in thermoforming. A—Sheet is heated. B—Heat source removed and air drawn out of mold. C—Atmospheric pressure forces sheet into mold.

on the lower die is partly shaped. A die like this one can cost over $100,000.

Shaped dies or molds

Shaped, or *one-piece dies* and molds are used when air or liquid pressure forms the part. Pressure or vacuum forces the material against the die. This type of die is called a *mold.*

This process is called *thermoforming,* Fig. 15-9, when it is used to make plastic parts or products. The material is held in a frame and heated. The hot material is lowered over the die. The air in the mold cavity is drawn out. Atmospheric pressure forces the plastic into the cavity. After the part is cool, it is removed from the mold. Fig. 15-10 shows some thermoformed products.

Metal spinning

Another process that uses one-piece molds is *metal spinning.* A spinning disc of metal is forced over a spinning mold called a *chuck,* Fig. 15-11. Large lighting reflectors, satellite antennae, and tank ends are formed using the metal spinning process.

Blow molding

A third one-piece die process is called *blow molding.* This process actually uses a multipiece (several parts) die. The die, Fig. 15-12, forms the outside shape of the product. A *parison* (heated

Fig. 15-10. Typical thermoformed products. (Packaging Industries, Inc.)

Fig. 15-11. Metal spinning workpiece is rotated as tool forces it over a chuck (pattern). (Alcan Aluminum)

glob) of material is placed in the mold. Air is blown into the parison. The glass or plastic material expands and takes the shape of the mold. Blow molding produces light globes, Christmas ornaments, and bottles and jars of all shapes, Fig. 15-13.

Extrusion

Extrusion also uses a one-piece die. In the *extrusion process,* the material is forced through a shaped hole in the die, Fig. 15-14. As the material flows through the die, it takes on the shape of the opening. As shown in Fig. 15-15, extrusion can produce different shapes in metals, plastics, and ceramics.

A DIAGRAM OF PARISON AND BOTTLE FORMING CYCLE BY BLOW AND BLOW PROCESS

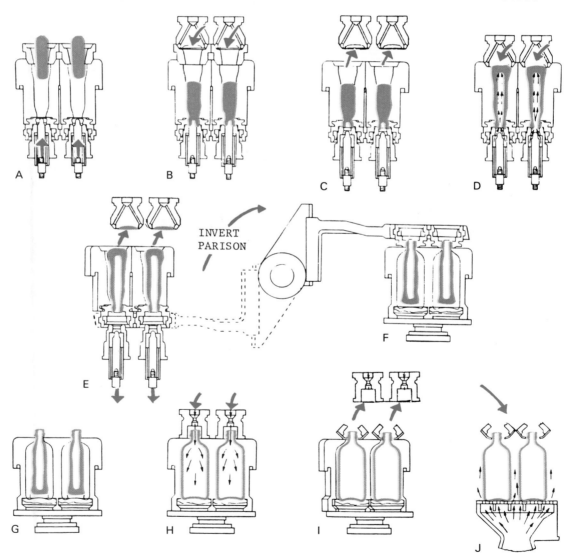

Fig. 15-12. Diagram of a two-step blow molding process for producing glass bottles. A—Gob of heated glass is delivered into closed blank molds. B—Subtle blows, pushing glass downward onto plunger. C—Gob reheats. D—Air from plungers shapes parison (gob). E—Blanks open; parison allowed to reheat. F—Parison released into blow molds. G—Parison reheats and gets longer. H—Bottles formed to blow mold shape. I—Molds open. Bottles taken out. J—Bottles released and swept off onto conveyor. (Owens Illinois)

Fig. 15-13. Glass blowing process. A—Product being moved. B—Gob being placed in mold. C—Closed mold.

ROLL FORMING

Rolls are a second type of shaping device. They can be either smoothed or formed. Smooth rolls will curve a straight piece without changing its cross

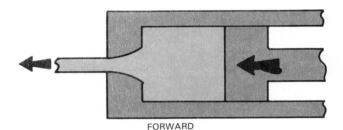

FORWARD

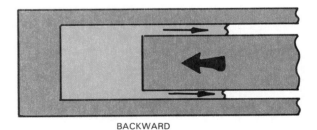

BACKWARD

Fig. 15-14. Diagrams of two major types of extrusion. Top. Hydraulic extrusion. Material is heated to soft, but not molten state, and is forced through opening under pressure. Bottom. Impact extrusion. This process is used to make such products as cans and tubes.

Fig. 15-15. A bundle of aluminum shapes produced using an extrusion process.   (Reynolds Metal Co.)

section. For example, *roll forming* will produce a curved I-beam. However, the "I" shape of the beam will not change, Fig. 15-16. Curved members for storage tanks, rocket bodies, and large-diameter pipe are roll formed.

A set of matched rolls can also be used to produce formed sheets. The "quilting" on aluminum foil is produced by matched roll forming. Metal barn siding and roofing is also produced using

Fig. 15-16. A heavy-duty roll former bending an I-beam. Note that the other features of the beam are not changed. (Buffalo Forge Co.)

matched roll forming. Fig. 15-17 shows corrugated sheet material being formed.

MATERIAL TEMPERATURE

Material temperature is an important factor in all forming processes. It is at room temperature,

Fig. 15-17. A series of matched, shaped rolls form corrugated aluminum roofing. Note the position of the rolls at each stage. (Reynolds Metal Co.)

or it is hot or cold. The material must flow, under pressure, into a new shape.

Forming is usually listed, by temperature, as:
1. Hot forming.
2. Cold forming.

Hot forming is the name given all processes done above the point of recrystallization. The *point of recrystallization* is the lowest temperature at which a material can be formed without causing internal stress. At this point, the material will form easily. Upon cooling, the material reforms its original stress-free crystals.

Forming below the point of recrystallization is called **cold forming**. The material may be at room temperature or it may be heated. Sometimes the term, *warm forming,* is used. This describes forming heated materials which are not above the point of recrystallization.

Both hot and cold forming have advantages and disadvantages. These must be considered in choosing material temperature. The advantages of each are shown in Fig. 15-18.

KINDS OF FORCE

Forming processes use three kinds of force: *compression* (squeezing), *drawing* (stretching), or *bending*. These forces are developed in a number of ways. Most common techniques use one of four types of machine tools. These, as shown in Fig. 15-19, are:
1. Hammers.
2. Presses.
3. Draw bench.
4. Rolling mill.

Hammers

Hammers and presses are alike in some ways. This fact can be seen in the diagrams. The hammer pounds the material into shape. It produces a sharp blow.

COLD FORMING	HOT FORMING
No heat required.	Hardness not changed.
Close dimensional control.	Porosity eliminated.
Smooth oxide free surface.	Less force required.
Increased hardness.	Smaller machines needed.
Improved strength.	Large shape changes possible.
	Clean surfaces not required.

Fig. 15-18. Both hot and cold forming have advantages that may lead to choosing one over the other.

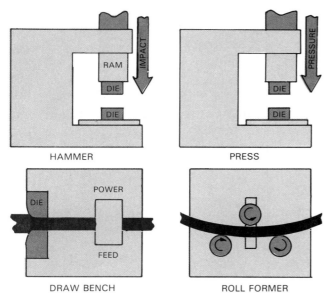

Fig. 15-19. Diagrams of typical forming machine tools.

Many forging operations require this type of force. A hard blow is delivered. A movable ram and die hit a stationary die, Fig. 15-20. Some hammers use gravity to move the upper die. The die is raised and drops onto the lower die. These hammers are called **drop hammers**. Steam or air hammers use force to produce the quick impact needed.

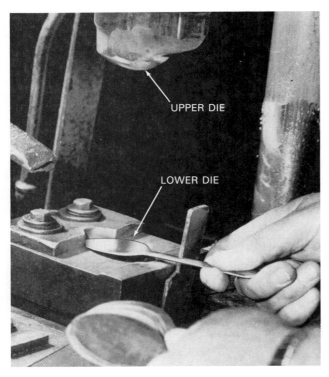

Fig. 15-20. The bowl of this spoon is cold forged by a set of mated dies. (INCO)

Presses

Presses have movable upper dies and stationary lower dies similar to hammers. The upper die is moved in a uniform powered stroke to produce a squeezing action. Typical processes using presses are drawing, bending, shearing, and press forging, Fig. 15-21.

Sheet metal and band metal can be bent on machines that act like presses. They have two dies (bending leaves, radius posts, etc.). The machine applies uniform pressure to cause the material to bend, Fig. 15-22.

Fig. 15-21. Giant press used to press forge a part. (Bethlehem Steel)

Rolling Machine

A rolling machine has two or more rolls. They may be smooth or shaped. The material bends as the rolls apply pressure. As the rolls turn, they draw material between them. This squeezes and bends the material.

Draw Bench

A **draw bench** is a forming machine with a shaped one-piece die and a drive mechanism. It can:
1. Stretch a bar or sheet over a die. This process, shown in Fig. 15-23, is called **stretch forming**. The draw bench pulls the material beyond its elastic limit. Then, a convex (curved outward) die is pushed into the material. The aircraft industry uses stretch forming to make airplane skin and structural parts.
2. Pull a wire or bar through a hole in a die. Metal rod is pulled through smaller and smaller die openings. The material is finally drawn into the proper diameter. Reducing the diameter causes the length of a material to increase, Fig. 15-24.

Fig. 15-22. Common press-like machines. Top. Box and pan brake. Middle. Press brake. Bottom. Band metal bender. (DiAcro)

Fig. 15-23. Powerful stretch forming press can lengthen a 40 foot sheet of aluminum another 4 feet. Its seven huge jaws shape sections of an aircraft fuselage (body). (Alcan)

Fig. 15-24. A draw bench (wire drawing machine) produces wire by drawing rod through a series of forming dies. (The Wire Assn.)

Other Forming Systems

Other forces are used to form certain materials. As mentioned earlier, air pressure can mold plastics and glass (blow molding). Vacuum is used to form thermoplastics (thermoforming).

High energy sources are also used. These include:
1. Explosive materials.
2. Rapidly changing electromagnetic fields. These and other *high-energy rate (HER) processes* are used in special applications.

SUMMARY

Forming is changing the size and shape, but not the volume, of a material. The change is caused by applying a force above the yield point and below the fracture point. The force causes the material to take the shape of a die or forming roll.

All forming processes consider material temperature. Some use heated materials while others operate at room temperature.

Forming processes must have a source of pressure. The most common source is a machine tool. Four machine tools are used: hammers, presses, rolls, and draw benches. Other sources of pressure, such as air, vacuum, and high energy rate systems are used to produce forming pressure.

KEY WORDS

All of the following words have been used in this chapter. Do you know their meaning?

Bending	Mold
Blow molding	One-piece die
Cold forming	Open die
Compression	Parison
Die	Plastic stage
Die set	Point of
Draw bench	recrystallization
Drawing	Press forging
Drop forging	Roll forming
Elastic stage	Rolls
Extrusion process	Stamping
Forming	Station
Fracture point	Stretch forming
High-energy rate	Thermoforming
(HER) process	Warm forming
Hot forming	Yield point
Metal spinning	

TEST YOUR KNOWLEDGE

Place your answers on a separate sheet. Please do not write in this text.

1. When a material has been stretched so that any additional load will cause it to permanently deform, the material has reached its _____.
   A. elastic stage
   B. plastic stage
   C. change of shape stage
   D. yield point

2. The shaping tool or device is to forming what the _____ is to casting.

Matching questions: Match the terms on the right-hand column with the correct definition in the left-hand column.

3. Two hard, flat plates; one is stationary, the other is movable.
4. Usually, shape on one die half fits the shape on other die half.
5. The several cavities found in die sets.
6. Used when air or liquid pressure forms the part.
7. The shape or pattern used when forming a part by metal spinning.
8. One-piece die process used for forming bottles, glass, and ornaments.
9. In _____, rolls are used to shape metal sheets, beams, or pipe.
10. What are the four major types of machines used to produce forming forces?
11. Two high energy forming sources are _____ materials and rapidly changing _____ fields.
12. List five parts or products that were manufactured using forming processes.

A. Open die.
B. Stations.
C. Shaped die or mold.
D. Die sets.
E. Chuck.
F. Blow molding.

ACTIVITIES

1. List some common forming processes used in the home.
2. Prepare a report describing a forming practice of your choice.
3. Collect pictures of common formed products. Prepare a bulletin board or scrapbook using the collected materials.

Chapter 16
SEPARATING PROCESSES

After reading this chapter, you will be able to:
☐ List and describe the three elements common to all separating processes.
☐ Define and give examples of cutting motion, feed motion, and depth of cut.
☐ List six types of separating machines and describe how they work.

Separating processes remove excess (extra) material to change the size, shape, or surface of a part. There are two major groups of separating processes, Fig. 16-1.
 1. *Machining*. Changing size and shape by removing excess material such as chips or particles.

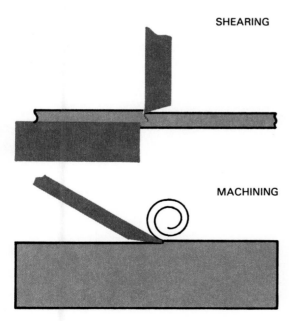

Fig. 16-1. The two types of separating processes—machining and shearing.

 2. *Shearing.* Using opposed edges to fracture (break) the excess material away from the workpiece.

Manufacturing would not be possible without separating processes. They shape and size parts so they are *interchangeable.* This means that all parts that are alike will fit in each other's place in an assembly.

Separating processes are also used to build jigs, fixtures, patterns, and templates. These devices, called *tooling,* are used in manufacturing many products. Separating machines are used to build other machines and tools. They are the machines building machines, otherwise known as *machine tools.*

ESSENTIALS OF SEPARATING

Every separating process has three elements. These are:
 1. A tool or cutting element.
 2. Movement between the workpiece and the cutting element.
 3. Tool and the workpiece are clamped or held in position.

Tool or Cutting Element

Separating processes use several kinds of cutting elements or tools. See Fig. 16-2. Shearing and chip-removing machines generally use hard steel or ceramic tools. New machining (nontraditional) methods use other cutting elements such as light, sound, and electric sparks. Flame cutting uses burning gases to separate the scrap material from the workpiece.

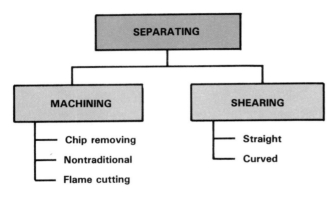

Fig. 16-2. Types of machining and shearing processes.

Chip removing tools

Many manufacturing processes depend on the major property of all materials: hardness. A harder material will form, shear, or cut a softer material. This works better if the hard material has the proper shape. In separating, the hard, properly shaped material is called a *tool*.

When the tool moves against a softer material it will form a chip. A particle of material will be cut (separated) from the workpiece. If the cutting action continues, additional chips will form. The excess material will be cut away. This leaves a properly shaped and sized part.

Two major groups of cutting tools exist: single-point tools and multiple-point tools.

Single-point tools. Single-point tools are the simplest. They have one cutting edge, Fig. 16-3.

Fig. 16-3. A single-point tool is the simplest type. It has one cutting edge.   (Inland Steel Co.)

A number of machines and hand tools, Fig. 16-4, use single-point tools. The most common of these are as follows:

1. Hand tools—Chisel, plane, gouge, and scraper.
2. Machines—Lathe, metal shaper, and metal planer.

Multiple-point tools. Multiple-point tools are merely two or more single-point tools that form one unit, Fig. 16-5. Having several cutting surfaces speeds up the cutting action.

Multiple-point tools have either uniformly (evenly) spaced or random (no pattern) cutting edges, as seen in Fig. 11-6. Most cutting tools have teeth spaced uniformly around or along the tool. Abrasive cutting tools and materials have randomly spaced cutting elements.

Multiple-point cutting is used for both hand tools, Fig. 16-7, and machine cutters. Typical examples of each are:

Fig. 16-4. The jack plane is a typical single-point hand tool.

Fig. 16-5. A multiple-tooth tool, such as this table saw blade, increases cutting speed.

UNIFORM	RANDOM

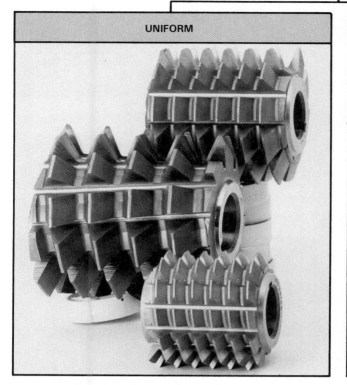 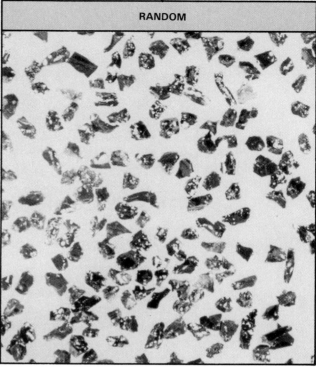

Fig. 16-6. Multiple-point tools may have uniformly spaced or randomly spaced teeth. The gear hobs on the left have uniform teeth. The magnified abrasive grains on the right form random cutting element.

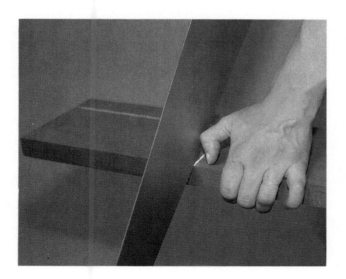

Fig. 16-7. A crosscut saw is a typical multiple-point hand tool. (John Walker)

Uniformly spaced teeth

1. Hand tools — Saw, file, tap and die, and hand drill.
2. Machines — Milling machine, drill press, wood shaper, router, jointer, and surfacer.

Randomly spaced cutter

3. Hand tools — Abrasive paper.
4. Machines — Abrasive machines and grinders.

Cutting tool designs. Cutting tools come in many sizes and shapes. However, they are basically either straight or round. On straight tools, the teeth may be set along the edge or at the end of a straight piece of material. Bandsaw blades and handsaws have teeth along a strip of metal. Chisels and lathe tools have a point at the end of a flat strip.

In some tools, the teeth are located around or on the end of a cylindrical (round) tool. Drills have cutting lips at the end of a round "rod." Milling cutters and circular saw blades have teeth spaced on the circumference (edge) of a disc or drum.

Each tooth on a tool must be properly designed. These designs follow certain rules:

1. Tooth or cutting surface shape must be correct. Each surface to be machined needs a certain shape, Fig. 16-8. A rounded edge on a board would require one shape of cutter. A straight edge would need another shape.
2. Sharp corners must be avoided whenever possible. They wear or break easily. Sharp points

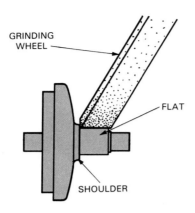

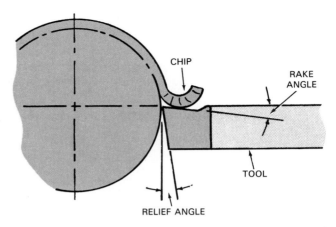

Fig. 16-8. This grinding wheel machines the flat and the shoulder of this product at one time. (Landis Tool Co.)

Fig. 16-10. Rake and relief angle are shown on a common metalworking lathe tool.

give a rougher cut than a rounded edge. Does a knife cut more smoothly on its point or its edge?

3. The cutting edge must be able to enter the workpiece. This requires *relief angles* for clearance behind all cutting parts of the tool, Fig. 16-9. Relief angles also keep most of the tool from rubbing on the workpiece. This keeps the tool cooler and stops it from burning the workpiece.

4. *Rake* must be shaped into the tool. This is a slope of the tool face away from the workpiece, Fig. 16-10. Rake causes the chip to curl away from the cut. It also reduces the power needed to make the cut.

Other cutting elements. *Nontraditional machining* and *flame cutting* do not use a "tool" as we generally use the word. They use heat, light, chemical action, or electrical sparks to produce a cut.

The oldest of these "nontool" separating practices is flame cutting. This process uses an oxyacetylene system with a special tip. (This system will be discussed in Chapter 18.) The material is first heated. Then, a blast of oxygen burns the material away, Fig. 16-11.

Fig. 16-11. Flame cutting separates metal parts from a workpiece.

Heat is also used for cutting plastic materials. Instead of a flame, a hot wire or strip can be used to melt the plastic apart.

A number of processes use an electric arc to cut material. *Electrical discharge machining (EDM)* was the first process of this type.

EDM, as shown in Fig. 16-12, uses a carbon electrode or "tool." It is attached to a movable head. The workpiece is placed in a tank of dielectric (nonconductor) material. The workpiece is attached to one terminal (side) of an electric circuit. The tool is attached to the other side. When the tool is lowered, a spark will jump from it to the workpiece. The spark will dislodge (break away) particles of the workpiece. As the tool continues to be lowered, a cavity is machined. EDM is used

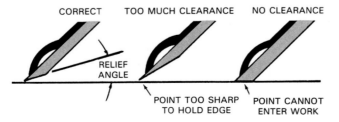

Fig. 16-9. Cutting edges must have the correct relief angle.

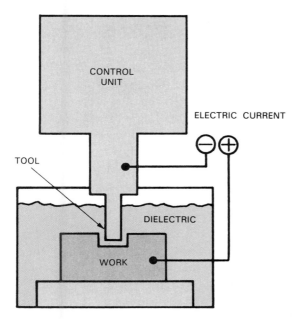

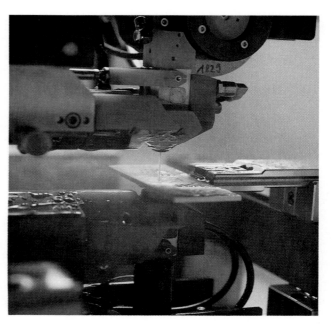

Fig. 16-13. An electric discharge sawing machine. (DoAll Co.)

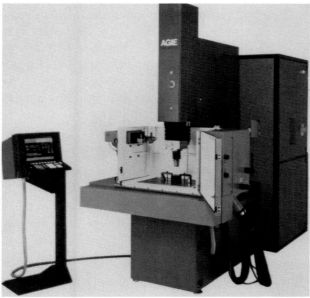

Fig. 16-12. Diagram and photo of typical electrical discharge machining (EDM) equipment.

to cut holes in metal. Also, it is widely used to produce cavities (holes and recesses) in various steel-forming molds and dies.

Newer machines, Fig. 16-13, produce electric sparks between moving wires, bands, and wheels. These processes are called electric discharge wire cutting, electric discharge sawing, and electric discharge grinding.

Intense light is also used for cutting. The process uses a *laser* (Light Amplification by Stimulated Emission of Radiation). A laser changes electromagnetic radiation (energy waves) into light of a single color. It then amplifies (makes stronger)

the light. This strong light produces heat when it strikes a surface. The heat will cut a workpiece, as shown in Fig. 16-14.

Other processes use chemicals and a combination of chemicals and electrical current. These processes accurately cut parts from various materials.

Movement

In all separating processes there is movement between the workpiece and tool. This movement,

Fig. 16-14. A general-purpose laser cutting system. (Strippit, Inc.)

shown in Fig. 16-15, consists of two types: cutting motion and feed motion.

Cutting motion. Cutting motion is the movement between the workpiece and the tool that creates a chip. The motion is created by three basic patterns which are shown, Fig. 16-16. These are:

1. Rotating—The workpiece or tool turns.

2. Reciprocating—The workpiece or tool moves forward and backward.

3. Linear—The workpiece or tool moves forward in a straight line.

All machines can be grouped into some basic classes according to their cutting motion. We will talk about these groups later.

Feed motion. Cutting motion alone will not separate a material. New material must be constantly brought into contact with the tool. This movement, called feed motion, is usually in a straight line. It is created by either moving the workpiece into the tool or the tool into the workpiece.

The terms, *feed motion* and *cutting motion,* may be a little hard to understand. To see the difference between them, study the photograph of a bandsaw in Fig. 16-17. The cutting motion is created by teeth moving downward through the workpiece.

Imagine what happens if you placed a board against the blade. If you turned the machine on, the first tooth would create a chip as it moved through the board. It would cut away wood fibers. However, the second tooth would follow the exact path of the first one. There would be no more wood to cut. However, if the board were pushed forward, new material would be there for the second tooth to cut. The forward movement of the workpiece is the feed motion. This action brings the new materials into contact with the tools.

Depth of cut. Depth of cut is another important term in separating activities. It is related to feed. The *depth of cut* is the difference between the original surface and the newly machined surface. The depth of cut and the rate (speed) of feed will determine the amount of material removed in a minute.

Clamping Devices

Most separating processes use devices to hold both the tool and the workpiece. These devices give the support necessary for accurate cuts.

The type of cutting motion dictates the tool

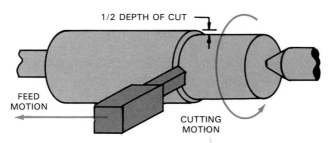

Fig. 16-15. Cutting and feed motions of a lathe.

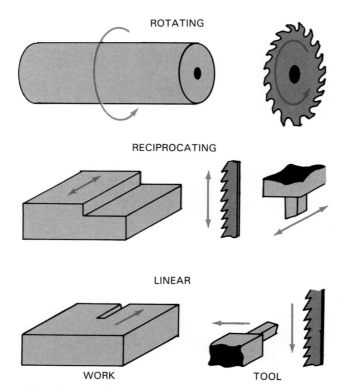

Fig. 16-16. Types of cutting and feed motion.

Fig. 16-17. Guide blocks guide the blade of a bandsaw. (DoAll Co.)

clamping devices used. Linear cutting motion is usually produced by a band that rotates around two large wheels. The wheels tension the blade to give it support. Guide blocks keep the blade cutting in a straight line, Fig. 16-17.

Rotating workpieces are clamped between lathe centers as shown in Fig. 16-18. It is held on a chuck or a faceplate. Its jaws hold the workpiece. Centers hold the ends of the material and allow it to rotate. Chucks and faceplates hold and rotate various shaped parts as seen in Fig. 16-18.

Vices, clamps, and magnetic tables can also hold workpieces during machining. Special jigs and fixtures, Fig. 16-19, are built when many similar parts are to be machined. Generally, all these devices are attached to the table or bed of the machine. They are then moved to produce feed motion.

Fig. 16-19. Parts are being held by a clamping fixture. (Cincinnati Milacron)

SEPARATING MACHINES

There are six basic types of separating machines. These machines, as shown in Fig. 16-20, are:

1. Turning machines.
2. Drilling machines.
3. Milling and sawing machines.
4. Planing and shaping machines.
5. Grinding and abrasive machines.
6. Shearing machines.

In addition to these basic machines, there is special equipment for nontraditional separating and flame cutting.

Turning Machines

Most turning machines rotate (turn) the workpiece against a tool. The tool generally has a single cutting point. Some wood-turning operations use a rotating multipoint tool (cutter).

The rotating workpiece is the cutting motion. The feed motion is developed by slowly moving the tool along or into the workpiece (linear motion). These movements are shown in Fig. 16-21.

Common turning machines are wood lathes, metal cutting (engine) lathes, and potter's wheels used for ceramic forming.

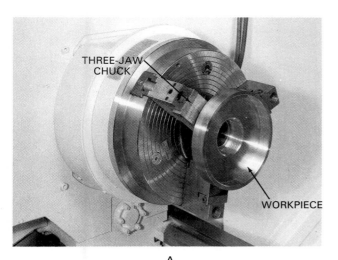

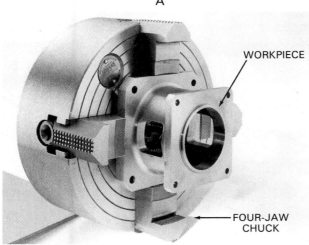

Fig. 16-18. A—A three-jaw chuck grips round stock. B—A four-jaw chuck can grip square stock or hold round stock off center. (LeBlond Makino Machine Tool Co., Cushman Co.)

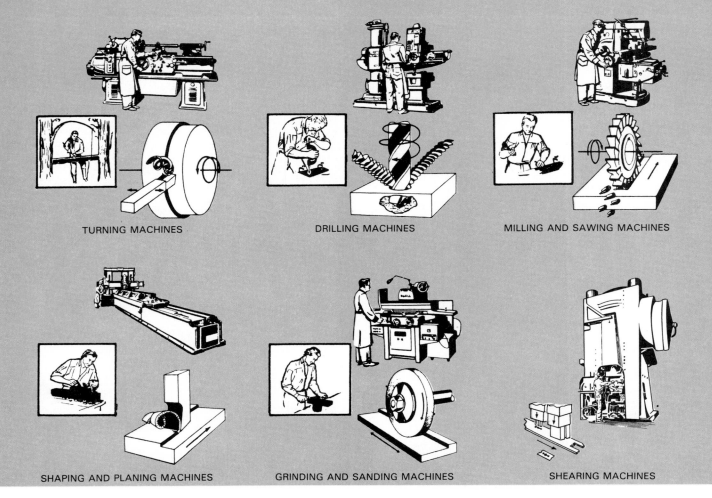

TURNING MACHINES

DRILLING MACHINES

MILLING AND SAWING MACHINES

SHAPING AND PLANING MACHINES

GRINDING AND SANDING MACHINES

SHEARING MACHINES

Fig. 16-20. Six basic types of machines. (DoAll Co.)

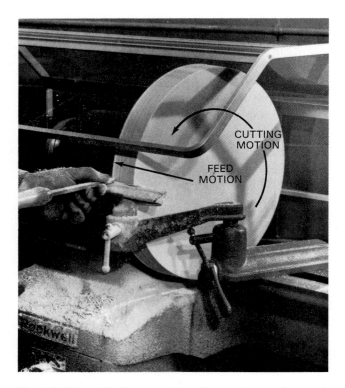

Fig. 16-21. A lathe operation shows the cutting and feed motions.

Drilling Machines

Drilling rotates a pointed tool (drill) to create a hole. The movement of the drill produces both the cutting and feed motion. The drill is held in a chuck and rotated. This action produces the cutting motion. The rotating drill is moved into the workpiece, creating the feed motion, Fig. 16-22.

The drill press is the most common drilling machine. A number of hand tools and portable electric tools also perform drilling operations. These include hand drills, braces, and automatic drills. Some common hand drilling tools are shown in Fig. 16-23.

Drilling machines and tools use a number of drills and bits. Some of these are shown in Fig. 16-24. They include auger bits, twist drills, countersinks, plug cutters, hole saws, and special-purpose bits.

Milling and Sawing Machines

All early saws had teeth arranged on a straight piece of metal like a handsaw. Later the teeth were arranged on discs that rotated. These two ar-

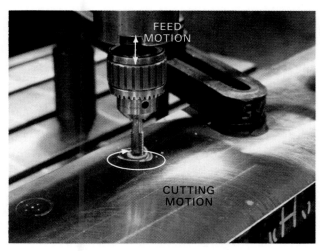

Fig. 16-22. The cutting and feed motions of a drill press. The bit rotates and can be moved down by the machine operator. (Inland Steel Co.)

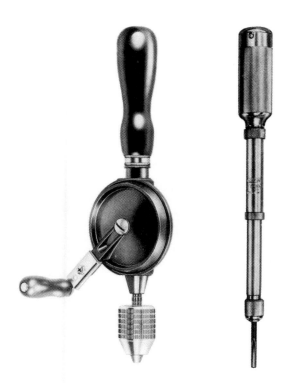

Fig. 16-23. Common drilling tools include hand drills. (Stanley Tools)

rangements make up the common milling and sawing tools.

A number of machines use rotating cutters. Among them are the milling machine, table saw, jointer, surfacer, wood shaper, and router. All of the machines have three things in common:
1. They use a multitooth or knife cutter.
2. The rotating cutter generates the cutting motion.
3. The feed motion is produced by moving the

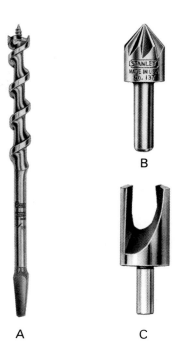

Fig. 16-24. Some common cutting tools used for drilling. A—Auger bit. B—Countersink. C—Plug cutter.

workpiece into the cutter in a straight line.

Look at the two pictures in Fig. 16-25. Notice the feed and cutting motions.

Other sawing machines use evenly spaced teeth on a band or strip. The cutting motion is created

A

B

Fig. 16-25. Cutting and feed motions. A—Milling machine. B—Wood planer. (Inland Steel Co.; Delta International Machinery Corp.)

by passing the teeth over the stock in one direction. Some machines use reciprocating (forward and backward) motion. The cut, however, is in only one direction. The backward stroke simply returns the blade for the next cutting stroke. Machines that use this action are the hacksaw, Fig. 16-26, and the scroll (jig) saw. Handsaws and saber saws cut the same way. Files also work on the same reciprocating principle.

A bandsaw continuously feeds teeth past the workpiece. As the band travels around its track, the teeth are always on a downward path as they contact the workpiece, Fig. 16-27.

Planing and Shaping Machines

The action of planing and shaping machines is similar to that of a hand plane, shown earlier in

Fig. 16-26. Cutting and feed motions for a power hacksaw. (Armstrong-Blum Mfg. Co.)

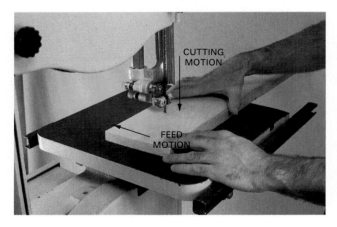

Fig. 16-27. Cutting and feed motions of a bandsaw. The blade is like a belt. It moves in only one direction.

Fig. 16-4. A single-point cutter is used to remove a continuous chip.

The metal shaper and hand plane operate exactly alike. The tool is moved forward, creating a chip. At the end of the stroke, pressure on the tool is released. It is moved back to the starting point. Another cut is then made. This reciprocating action is repeated until the surface is completely machined, Fig. 16-28.

The metal planer also uses reciprocating action. Only the cutter is stationary (stays in one place). The workpiece moves beneath it to create the cutting motion.

Grinding and Abrasive Machines

Grinding and abrasive machines are adapted from other basic machines. An abrasive disc, drum, or belt is substituted for the cutter. Look at Fig. 16-29.

Sanding with portable electric tools and hand sanding use similar principles. The portable belt sander is much like a stationary belt sander. Pad sanders and hand sanding are like the metal shaper. Abrasive paper is moved back and forth to machine the material.

Fig. 16-28. Cutting and feed motions of a tracer metal shaper. Note the model on the left side. (Rockwell Machine Tool Co.)

ABRASIVE MACHINE	RELATED MACHINE	CUTTING ACTION
Disc sander Grinder Drum sander	Milling machine	Rotating cutter Work fed into cutter (linear)
Belt sander	Band saw	Downward moving (linear) Cutting band. Work fed into abrasive belt (linear)
Surface grinder	Metal planer	Stationary rotating tool. Work reciprocates under tool

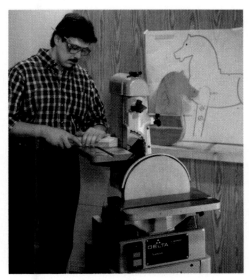

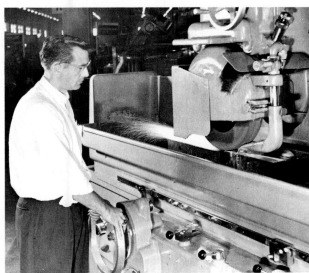

Fig. 16-29. Top. Comparing grinding with traditional machining. Middle. Combination disc and belt sander. Bottom. Surface grinder.
(Delta International Machinery Corp., Norton)

Shearing Machines

The last major type of separating machine is the shearing machine. The other five types of machines use a tool to cut away a portion of the workpiece. Chips of material are cut from the stock. Shearing does not remove stock. It breaks material into parts. Shearing uses two opposing edges, like on tin snips, to fracture the material. In this process, material is not lost. The resulting parts weigh the same as the original piece. Also the sum of their lengths will equal the original length.

Most shearing machines have a moving blade or die and a stationary edge. A *die* is a blade designed to cut special shapes such as curves, circles, or whole outlines, Fig. 16-30. The material is placed between the shearing elements (blades or die). The movable element travels downward. The material is fractured (broken) as the two elements pass each other.

Typical of machines that use this process are the squaring shear, corner notcher, and hole punch. Tin snips, chisels, and punches work on the same basic principle. Chisels and punches use the bench top or a back-up (scrap) board as an opposing edge.

SUMMARY

Separating is a very common process. All of the techniques use a tool or cutting element, movement between the tool and workpiece, and support devices for both workpiece and tool.

Fig. 16-30. Special shapes can be cut using dies. (Strippit, Inc.)

SAFETY WITH
SEPARATING PROCESSES

1. Do not attempt a process that has not been demonstrated to you.
2. Always wear safety glasses or goggles.
3. Keep your hands away from all moving cutters and blades.
4. Use push sticks to feed small pieces of stock into wood-cutting machines.
5. Use all machine guards.
6. Stop machines or equipment when making measurements and adjustments.
7. Do not leave a machine until the cutter has stopped rotating.
8. Clamp all work when possible.
9. Unplug machines from the electrical outlet before changing blades or cutters.
10. Remove all chuck keys or wrenches before starting machines.
11. Remove all scraps and tools from the machine before turning on the power.
12. Remove wood scraps with a push stick. Use a brush to remove metal chips and particles.
13. Keep your hands behind the cutting edge of chisels and punches and behind screwdriver points.
14. Obtain the instructor's permission before using any machine.
15. Keep all work areas clear of scraps and unneeded tools.
16. Use only sharp cutting tools for separating operations.

The tools are either single- or multiple-point. They are designed to provide a smooth cut with the least tool wear and power.

The movement in all separating acts can be classified as either cutting motion or feed motion. Cutting motion actually produces the chip. Feed motion brings new material into contact with the workpiece.

The workpiece and the tool are generally supported or held. Centers, chucks, or clamping devices are commonly used.

A combination of feed and cutting motions are built into six basic machines. These are turning, drilling, milling and sawing, shaping and planing, grinding and abrading, and shearing machines.

KEY WORDS

All the following words have been used in this chapter. Do you know their meaning?

Cutting motion	Machining
Depth of cut	Nontraditional
Die	machining
Electrical discharge	Rake
machining (EDM)	Relief angle
Feed motion	Separating
Flame cutting	Shearing
Interchangeable	Tool
Laser	Tooling
Machine tool	

TEST YOUR KNOWLEDGE

Place your answers on a separate sheet. Please do not write in this text.

1. Indicate which of the following are elements common to all separating processes:
   A. Tool or cutting element.
   B. Tool has a single point.
   C. Cutting element always uses a shearing operation.
   D. Movement occurs between the workpiece and the cutting element.
   E. Tool and workpiece are either clamped or held in place.
2. Describe cutting motion, feed motion, and depth of cut.
3. A _____ point tool has one cutting edge.
4. Which of the following are examples of multiple-point cutting tools or machines?
   A. File.
   B. Lathe.
   C. Tap and die.
   D. Chisel.
   E. Jointer.
   F. Saw.
   G. Abrasive paper.
5. What is rake and why is it important in a tool?
6. What do the following have in common: flame cutting, hot wire for cutting plastic, electrical discharge machining, and laser machining?

7. A die is a specially shaped blade for cutting various shapes. True or False?

ACTIVITIES

1. Look at a workbench in your technology laboratory. Prepare a list of the separating processes you think may have been used to manufacture it.

2. List the cutting tools found in a typical home. Indicate which type of separating machine each is most like.

3. Prepare a list of cutting tools and machines in the technology laboratory. Group them according to their type (turning, drilling, sawing, etc.). Indicate the type of tool they use (single-point or multiple-point).

Computer programs can be used to lay out holes, notches, and other openings in sheet metal. (Strippit, Inc.)

Conditioning changes the internal structure of a material.　(ARO Corp.)

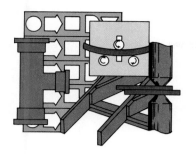

Chapter 17

CONDITIONING PROCESSES

After reading this chapter, you will be able to:
☐ Explain what conditioning does to a material and give at least one simple example of a conditioning method.
☐ State three reasons why materials are conditioned.
☐ List and explain the three types of material conditioning.

Casting and molding, forming, and separating processes only change the size and shape of a workpiece. They change the outside of the product but not the inside.

Sometimes, however, the material itself needs changing to make it better suited for its purpose. Think of what happens when someone in your family makes cookies. After the flour, sugar, butter, eggs, and other materials are mixed into a dough, it does not taste like much—certainly not like cookies. Bake the dough for a few minutes and it becomes crunchy and tastes very good. What has happened is that the heat of the oven changed the internal structure of the dough. The cookie now does its job. Its taste pleases you and it satisfies your hunger.

When you do the same thing to an industrial material it is called *conditioning*. Look at Fig. 17-1. Before curing (like baking), the rubber on the tire is very soft and will not wear well. As with the cookies, heat changes the internal structure of the rubber and makes it tougher so it does its job better.

HOW WE CHANGE MATERIALS

Most often, conditioning is needed to change the physical or mechanical properties of a material. In

Chapter 2, it was stated that:
1. Physical properties mean the size, weight, or condition of a material. They describe what the material is like when no outside forces are making changes in it.
2. Mechanical properties describe a material's ability to support a load. Common mechanical properties are: strength, elasticity, plasticity, hardness, toughness, and fatigue resistance.

Fig. 17-1. "Green" or uncured truck tires are ready to be conditioned. They will be vulcanized (heat cured). (Goodyear Tire and Rubber Co.)

STEPS IN CONDITIONING

Before any conditioning is done, a manufacturer must consider the three things shown in Fig. 17-2. Let's go back to the cookie. What properties do you want in a cookie? What should the inside of the cookie be like? What process will change the cookie dough to what you want?

The cookie should be tasty and crunchy, not mushy as it is before baking. The inside should be hard but not so hard that it will not crumble when you bite into it. The way to process the cookie is to put the dough into a hot oven and bake it for a few minutes.

Other Examples

Any number of physical properties can be improved by conditioning. An important physical property for wood products is moisture content. Lumber cut from logs (green lumber) may have from 30 to 300 percent moisture content. Green lumber is not a good material for making furniture. The furniture would soon fall apart as the wood begins to lose moisture and shrinks.

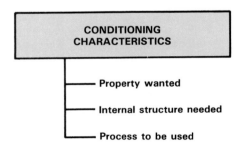

Fig. 17-2. Conditioning considerations. Think of a simple product and study these characteristics.

Natural or kiln (large oven) drying is a conditioning process that reduces the moisture content and makes the wood better for furniture making. Shrinking and warping would be slight compared to the green wood. Strength is one of the mechanical properties often changed in a material. This is the ability to withstand a load without breaking. Conditioning is used to improve the tensile (pulling), compression, shear, and torsion strength of the material.

Conditioning can also make a material harder. Internal changes will help it resist wear and denting. However, in making the material harder you also increase its brittleness. A hard material fractures more easily under load.

Plasticity can also be changed by conditioning. A material can be made softer and easier to form. Its ability to be hammered into form (malleability) can be improved. So can its ability to be stretched or rolled (ductility) to shape.

These are some examples of the properties that can be affected by conditioning. Other properties include elasticity, stiffness, fatigue resistance, and toughness.

Structure of Materials

The properties of materials are directly related to their chemical structure. Some plastics are strong and rigid because of the way the molecules are linked together. Other plastics, whose molecules are loosely linked, can be reformed any number of times.

Round and widely spaced grains make a metal more ductile. A strong steel has flat, packed crystals. Also, fine-grained metals are harder and stronger than coarse-grained metals.

SAFETY WITH CONDITIONING PROCESSES

1. Do not attempt a process that has not been demonstrated to you.
2. Always wear safety glasses or goggles.
3. Wear protective clothing, gloves, and face shield when working around hot metal or other materials.
4. Do not leave hot products or parts where other people could be burned.
5. Constantly monitor material temperatures during conditioning processes in which heat is used.
6. Use care when working with chemicals used for conditioning.
7. Use a holding tool such as pliers or tongs to hold metals that are being heat treated.
8. Use a spark lighter to light a heat-treating furnace.
9. Stand to one side of the quench solution when quenching hot metals.
10. Place a "Hot Metal" sign on any parts that are air cooling.

The length and arrangement of wood fibers also affect the strength. Longer fibers make for stronger wood. Hardwoods usually have longer fibers and are generally stronger than most softwoods.

TYPES OF CONDITIONING

A manufacturing industry conditions a material for a number of reasons. Three main reasons are shown in Fig. 17-3.

These goals may be met using one of three types of conditioning acts. These are thermal (heat) conditioning, chemical conditioning, and mechanical conditioning, Fig. 17-4.

Thermal Conditioning

Thermal conditioning uses heat to change the physical or mechanical properties of a material. There are a number of different thermal conditioning techniques. Three important ones are:
1. Drying.
2. Heat-treating.
3. Firing.

Drying

Drying removes moisture from a material. It is used to solidify clay slip. It changes a liquid suspension into a solid. The physical property of the material is changed.

A widely used drying sequence reduces moisture in wood. Wood expands, contracts, and warps (twists or bends) as its moisture content changes. The wood is often stabilized by drying it. This process is called *seasoning.*

Two types of seasoning are used. One is *natural,* or *air drying.* The lumber is carefully stacked. Stickers (spacers made from strips of wood) are placed between each layer, Fig. 17-5, so the air can circulate. The wood will naturally lose some of its moisture content this way. The lowest level that can be obtained with air drying is about 15 percent.

Air-dried lumber is suitable for some construction applications. However, it is not good for interior construction, cabinets, or furniture. Lumber for these uses is *kiln dried,* Fig. 17-6. The stacks of lumber are placed in a kiln. Air circulation, heat, and humidity are carefully controlled as the lumber

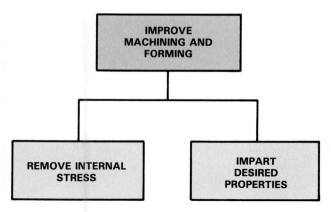

Fig. 17-3. Reasons for conditioning manufacturing materials.

Fig. 17-5. Lumber being air dried uses spacers between boards for good air circulation.

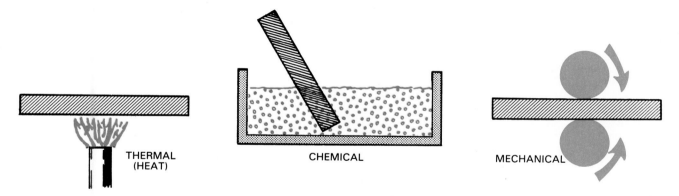

THERMAL (HEAT)   CHEMICAL   MECHANICAL

Fig. 17-4. Methods of conditioning materials.

Fig. 17-6. Lumber awaiting its turn at a drying kiln.

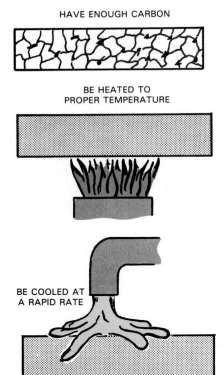

Fig. 17-8. Conditions necessary to harden steel.

is dried. Kiln-dried lumber will have a moisture content of 6 to 12 percent.

Heat treating

Heat treating is thermal conditioning of metals. It is a process of heating and cooling solid metal to produce certain mechanical properties. Heat treating includes the three major groups shown in Fig. 17-7. These are:

1. Hardening—Increasing the hardness of a material.
2. Tempering—Removing internal stress.
3. Annealing—Softening a material.

Hardening steel. As shown in Fig. 17-8, it is necessary to:

1. Have a proper carbon content (0.08 to 1.5 percent).
2. Heat the metal to a proper temperature of 1400° to 1500°F (760° to 816°C) in a furnace like the one shown in Fig. 17-9.

Fig. 17-9. Hot parts leaving the heat-treating furnace. (Bethlehem Steel)

3. Cool the hot steel rapidly to obtain a fine grain structure, Fig. 17-10.

Other hardening processes produce a layer of hard metal on a soft core. Low-carbon steels are soaked in special material. The steel absorbs a layer of carbon from the other material. The metal is then heated and quenched. This process is called *case*, or *surface hardening*. It is used for gears, shafts, and other parts that must be tough and long-wearing.

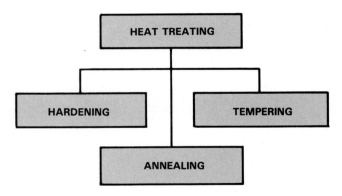

Fig. 17-7. Types of heat treating.

Fig. 17-10. Hardened and tempered alloy steel magnified 400 times. Note the fine grain structure of the metal. (Bethlehem Steel)

Tempering. Fine-grained steel is hard but has internal stresses. It is very brittle and fractures easily. Therefore, after hardening, metals must be *tempered.* The parts are heated to a temperature between 300° to 1200°F (149° to 649°C). (The actual temperature depends on the type of steel and the hardness needed.) Then, the heated metal is allowed to cool slowly. The result is a slightly softer but stronger metal.

Annealing. Metals can also be softened. This process is called *annealing.* The material is heated to its hardening temperature. Then, it is slowly cooled. The result is a stress-free metal with larger grain size as shown in Fig. 17-11.

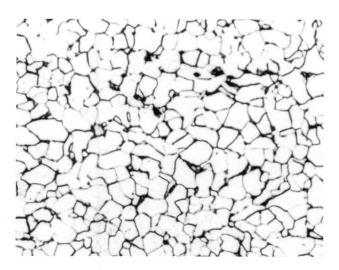

Fig. 17-11. Annealed, cold rolled steel magnified 400 times. Compare this grain structure with the grain structure shown in Fig. 17-10. (Bethlehem Steel)

Firing

Firing is a thermal conditioning process used in ceramics. It melts the glassy part of the ceramic. Upon cooling, the product will be clay particles held together by the glassy material.

The products are loaded on carts or conveyors, Fig. 17-12. The loaded carts are then moved into the kiln, as shown in Fig. 17-13. The material is heated to between 1650° and 2550°F (899° to 1399°C) then cooled. The result is a very hard material.

Chemical Conditioning

Materials can be conditioned using chemicals. Catalysts (materials which start chemical actions) can be added to cause internal change. For exam-

Fig. 17-12. Workers are loading dinnerware on kiln cars. Note the refractory molds (right) that hold plates from warping during firing. (Lennox China)

Fig. 17-13. Loaded cars ready to enter the kiln. (Syracuse China)

ple, a catalyst called a hardener, added to liquid polyesters causes the liquid to become a solid. In scientific terms, this is called polymerization action. Crosslinks form between the polymer chains.

Water added to plaster of paris or Portland cement starts a chemical conditioning process. The material will set (harden), Fig. 17-14.

Chemicals are also used to treat animal hides. Their organic fibers are made to change. The tanned leather is a more usable product than was the hide.

Mechanical Conditioning

Cold forming operations change the internal structure of metals. The pounding or squeezing action changes the basic grain structure. Round, soft grains are changed into long, flat, hard grains, Fig. 17-15. This action is called *work hardening*.

Shot (steel pellets) may be sprayed against a part to mechanically condition it. The surface is purposely hardened. The result is a part that can withstand constant flexing. Its fatigue resistance is improved.

Fig. 17-14. The concrete in this slab sets by chemical conditioning.

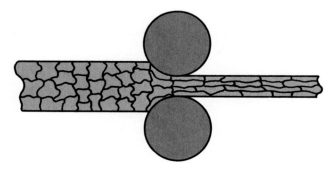

Fig. 17-15. Effects of work hardening on the grain structure.

SUMMARY

Not all processes change the external characteristics of material. Some change the material's internal structure. These processes are called conditioning. They use heat, chemicals, or mechanical forces to change the physical and mechanical properties of materials.

KEY WORDS

All the following words have been used in this chapter. Do you know their meaning?

Air drying
Annealing
Case hardening
Chemical
   conditioning
Conditioning
Drying
Firing
Hardening

Heat treating
Kiln drying
Mechanical
   conditioning
Seasoning
Tempering
Thermal conditioning
Work hardening

TEST YOUR KNOWLEDGE

Place your answers on a separate sheet. Please do not write in this text.

1. State, in your words, what the word "conditioning" means.
2. Which of the following are not a reason for conditioning a product?
   A. Changing the shape of a product.
   B. To improve mechanical properties (strength, hardness, fatigue resistance, etc.)
   C. To remove internal stress and strain.
   D. To make a material easier to shape or cut.
   E. To make the material or product more attractive.
3. Conditioning is done by three processes. What are they?
4. Drying is one of the conditioning _____ processes.
5. Hardening, annealing, and tempering are chemical conditioning processes. True or False?
6. Sometimes, shot is sprayed against a part to harden the surface of the metal. The purpose of this conditioning is to _____.
   A. improve appearance of the surface
   B. make the surface resistant to corrosion
   C. increase ability to withstand flexing of part
   D. improve fatigue resistance

ACTIVITIES

1. List some conditioning processes used in the home.
2. Look around the technology laboratory. List five items that you think were conditioned during manufacture. Why were they conditioned?
3. Identify ten items around your home that you think were conditioned during manufacture. Divide these items into groups based on whether you feel they were thermally conditioned, chemically conditioned, or mechanically conditioned. State reasons why you placed them in that particular group.

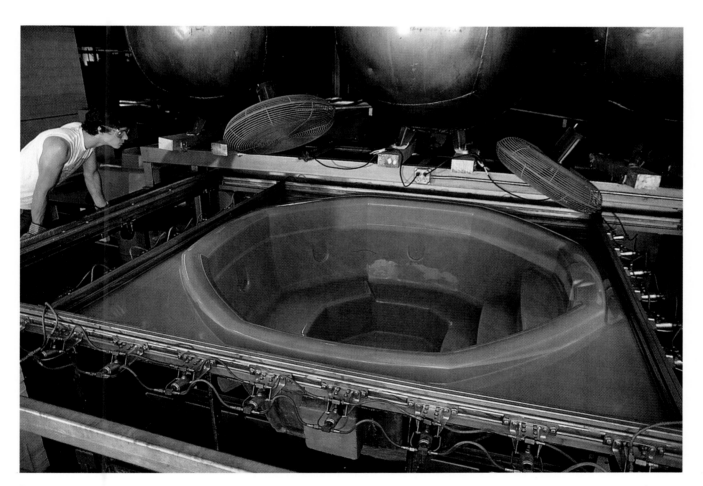

Chemical action is used to harden the plastic material that binds the fiberglass in this hot tub.   (Rohm & Haas)

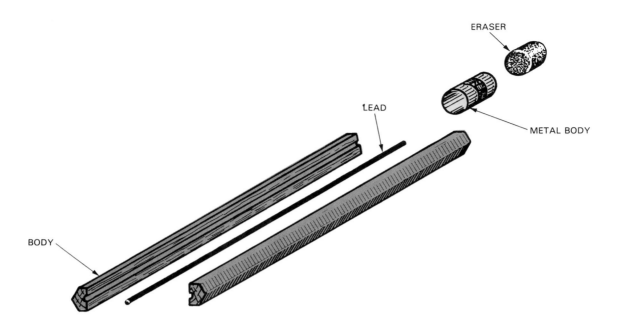

Fig. 18-1. A simple pencil has at least five different parts that must be assembled.

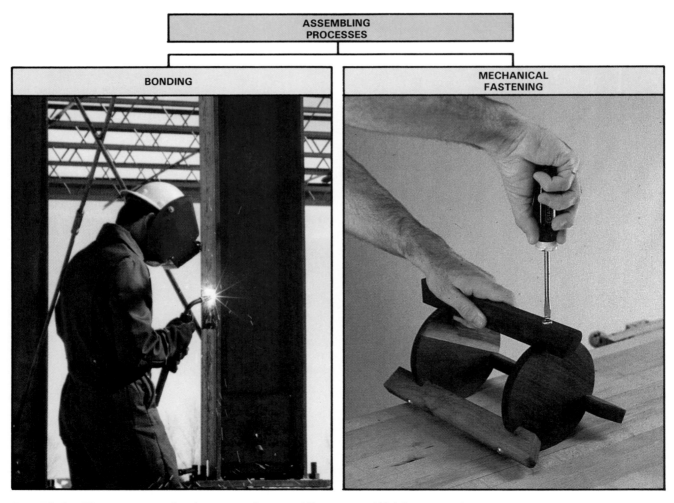

Fig. 18-2. There are two basic ways of assembling parts. Welding uses heat for a permanent assembly. A screw is a temporary type of fastener. (Miller Electric Mfg. Co.)

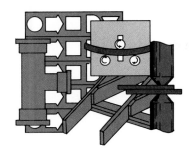

Chapter 18
ASSEMBLING PROCESSES

After reading this chapter, you will be able to:
☐ Demonstrate an understanding of the importance of assembling processes in manufacturing.
☐ List the two major assembly processes and cite examples of each.
☐ List and describe methods of bonding.
☐ Define three types of mechanical fastening and describe the process for each.
☐ Recognize and name five different types of joints.

Almost every product you use was put together out of several parts. This is called *assembling.*

If you have a lead pencil, look at it. How many parts are there? The simplest pencil, Fig. 18-1, has at least five parts. In addition there is a layer of glue holding the wood together. A layer of paint and some printing finish it off. Even the simple pencil is an *assembly.*

Assembling is the manufacturing process which permanently or temporarily fastens parts together. There are two major ways to assemble parts into products. These, as shown in Fig. 18-2, are:
1. *Bonding.* Permanently fastening parts together using heat, pressure, and/or a bonding agent (like glue).
2. *Mechanical Fastening.* Permanently or temporarily holding parts together using mechanical devices (like screws) or mechanical force.

ASSEMBLING BY BONDING

Bonding can be used with metals, plastics, wood products, and ceramics. In each bonding process, three basic things must be considered:

1. The *bonding agent* (substance) to be used to hold the parts together.
2. The method used to create the bond.
3. Kind of joint used at the bonding point.

Bonding Agents

Bonding requires "atomic closeness" between two parts. *Atomic closeness* means the atoms of matter across a joint must be very close together. In fact, they must be as close together as are atoms inside each part.

Two basic types of bonding elements are used for bonding: self-bonding and bonding materials. These are shown in Fig. 18-3.

Heat and/or pressure can be used to make the two parts flow together. The material becomes liquid or plastic. When the parts cool, they appear as one. Fig. 18-4 shows two parts that were bond-

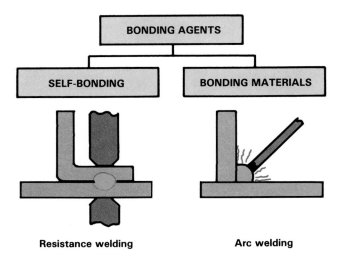

Resistance welding   Arc welding

Fig. 18-3. Self-bonding or bonding materials are used as bonding agents.

Fig. 18-4. Self-bonding uses no additional fillers. This photo shows an inertia (friction) welded part. (Caterpillar, Inc.)

ed by friction welding. The disc was held still. The ball-shaped part was rotated against the disc. The rubbing action created heat and atomic closeness. The parts were welded by self-bonding.

Bonding materials are often used as bonding agents. These bonding materials may be:

1. The same material as that being bonded. For example, using a mild steel rod to weld mild steel parts.
2. The same type of material, but a different composition. For example, using solder (tin-lead alloy) to bond copper sheets.
3. A totally different material with bonding properties. For example, using an adhesive (glue) to bond wood parts.

Methods of Bonding

There are hundreds of different bonding techniques. They can be grouped into five basic types:

1. Heat bonding.
2. Heat and pressure bonding.
3. Pressure bonding.
4. Solvent bonding.
5. Adhesive bonding.

These methods differ both in the bonding agent used and the techniques for applying the agent.

Heat Bonding Processes

Several major techniques use heat for bonding. These processes use no pressure. Welding is an example. Heat bonding processes melt the edges of the parts to be joined. The molten material flows between the parts. Often, additional material from

a filler rod is added to the weld area. Upon cooling, the part is a solid metal.

Heat bonding processes include two groups. One is fusion bonding, the other flow bonding.

Fusion bonding. Fusion bonding can use the base metals themselves to create the weld. However, if the part is thicker than 1/8 inch, a filler rod is used. This rod is made of the same material as the base metal. It simply provides more metal to produce a strong weld, Fig. 18-5.

The common fusion welding methods get their names from their heat source. Heat to melt the base metal and filler material comes from one of two basic sources.

1. Burning gases.
2. Electric arc (spark).

The most common burning gas welding uses oxygen and acetylene. Fig. 18-6 shows a typical oxy-acetylene welding outfit. The oxygen and acetylene are kept in separate tanks. Gauges on the tank regulate the pressure and flow of gases to the torch. The torch mixes the gases. The gas mixture flows out the tip where it is ignited. The burning gases will produce temperatures up to 6300 °F (3482 °C).

Most fusion welding techniques in industry use an electric arc as a heat source. The source of energy can be either alternating current (AC) or direct current (DC). One lead from the welder is attached to the work. The other goes to the electrode (rod) holder, Fig. 18-7.

When the electrode is brought close to the workpiece, a spark will jump. This electric spark generates about 11,000 °F (6093 °C) of heat. The heat from the spark melts both the base material and the electrode. These form a puddle of molten metal. As the puddle cools, the base metals are bonded together.

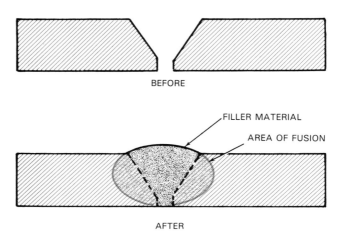

BEFORE

FILLER MATERIAL

AREA OF FUSION

AFTER

Fig. 18-5. Fusion bonding creates a part that appears to be one piece.

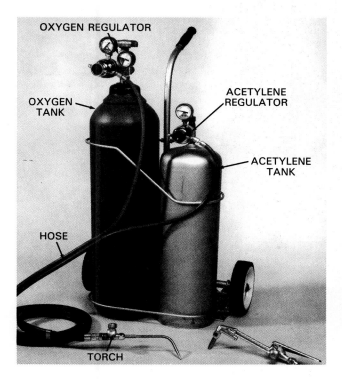

Fig. 18-6. A basic oxyacetylene welding outfit can be used for gas welding and flame cutting. (Airco Welding Products)

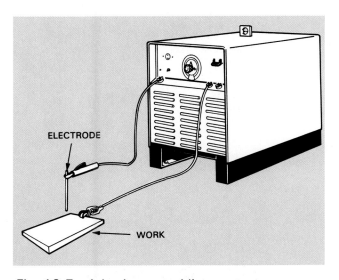

Fig. 18-7. A basic arc welding system. (Miller Electric Mfg. Co.)

It is often necessary to keep oxygen away from the weld arc. This is the case when welding aluminum or other nonferrous metals. The heat from the arc and the oxygen in the air causes the metal to burn (vaporize). To weld these metals, an envelope (cloud) of inert gas is used to shield the weld area. The base metal and filler rod are melted in this cloud to form the bond, Fig. 18-8. The

Fig. 18-8. A worker welding an aluminum frame with an inert gas system. (Miller Electric Mfg. Co.)

typical processes that use this system are Gas Tungsten Arc Welding (GTAW) and Gas Metal Arc Welding (GMAW).

Flow bonding. Flow bonding heats, but does not melt, the base metal. The heated metal is bonded by melting a different material into the joint.

The two common methods for flow bonding are *brazing* and *soldering.* Both work on the same principle. A close-fitting clean joint is first prepared. Then the base metals are heated. Flux is applied to remove oxides. It helps the bonding material to flow. The bonding material is then melted on the joint area. Capillary action (the same action which causes water to soak uphill through a paper towel) draws the bonding agent into the joint. There it hardens and bonds the parts together. This action is shown in Fig. 18-9.

The main difference between soldering and brazing is the material used as a bonding agent. Soldering uses a tin-lead alloy which melts below 800 °F (427 °C). Brazing is done with copper, silver, and aluminum alloys. These melt at temperatures above 800 °F.

Heat and Pressure Bonding Processes

Bonding processes that use heat and pressure do not use filler materials. The base materials form the bond themselves. There are several processes like this; the most common is resistance welding.

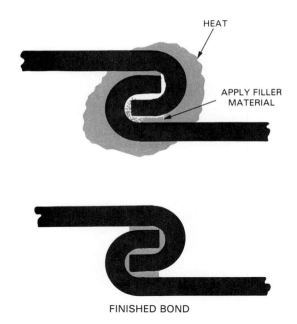

Fig. 18-9. The flow bonding process. Filler is drawn into the joint by heated metal.

Resistance welding

Resistance welding uses resistance to electric current to melt the material. The material is then squeezed to form the weld. A widely used resistance welding technique is *spot welding.* It uses a special welding machine, Fig. 18-10. A transformer (device to change voltage) delivers electric current to the copper electrodes (terminals). The metal to be welded is placed between the electrodes. Then a four-stage cycle begins:

1. Pressure is applied to the metal parts.
2. Electricity flows between the electrodes. The electrical resistance of the metal parts causes them to heat up. A spot (kernel) of molten metal forms between the two parts, Fig. 18-11. The kernel forms at the point of maximum electrical resistance.
3. The current is stopped, but the pressure is held. The melted spot cools.
4. The electrodes release the work.

One spot welding process uses rolling electrodes. The rolls perform the same four steps as a regular spot welder. The process produces a continuous weld, Fig. 18-12, called a *seam weld.*

Resistance welding is used to assemble sheet metal parts. The home appliance and automotive industries, Fig. 18-13, are its major users.

Impulse sealing

A special type of resistance welding—*impulse sealing*—is used on plastic films. It is used to seal packaging films for bags and shrink packs. The

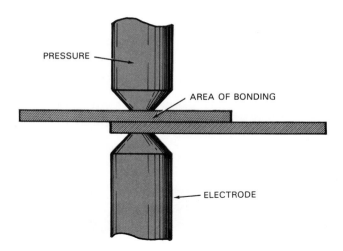

Fig. 18-11. The spot welding process. Material is placed between the electrodes.

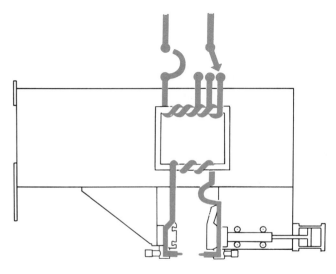

Fig. 18-10. A diagram of a spot welder. (Taylor Winfield)

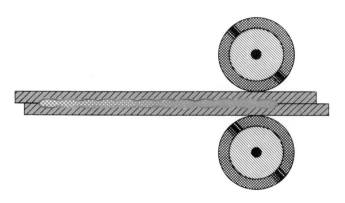

Fig. 18-12. A diagram of a seam welding process. Rollers act as electrodes. (Taylor Winfield)

Fig. 18-13. Automobile bodies at an assembly plant move through a robotic welding line.

films are held between two pressure bars. A wire recessed in one bar is heated by a pulse of electricity. The hot wire softens the plastic sheets. The pressure bar causes them to bond.

Pressure Bonding Processes

Pressure or cold bonding uses great pressures to get the necessary atomic closeness, Fig. 18-14. This method works only on very ductile materials such as copper and aluminum. Pressures from 50,000 to 200,000 psi (pounds per square inch) are needed.

Solvent Bonding Processes

Solvent bonding uses a chemical to soften the material. The parts are then pressed together. The solvent evaporates or is absorbed into the materials. The material hardens into a permanent bond. Solvents are used to bond plastics together. Also, ceramics are assembled using liquid slip as bonding material, Fig. 18-15.

Adhesive Bonding Processes

Adhesive bonding uses a material which has "tackiness" or "stickiness." The parts are held together by an adhesive or glue, Fig. 18-16.

Fig. 18-15. A worker attaches cup handles to bodies with liquid slip.   (Syracuse China)

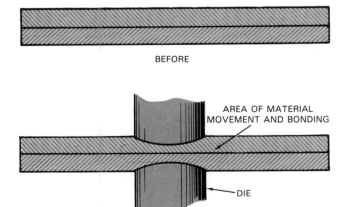

Fig. 18-14. Cold bonding uses heavy pressure to bond ductile materials.

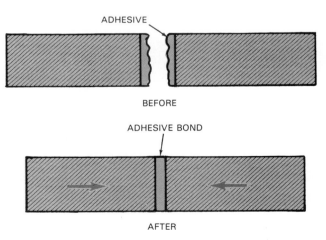

Fig. 18-16. Adhesive bonding uses a tacky substance to hold parts together.

These materials can be natural or synthetic. Early glues were natural. They were made from animal parts, fish, and milk (casein). Most modern adhesives are synthetic polymers. Like all plastics, they can be either thermoplastic adhesives or thermosetting adhesives.

Thermoplastic adhesives

Thermoplastic adhesives are usually resins suspended in water. They form a bond when the solvent evaporates or is absorbed into the material.

Thermoplastic adhesives cannot withstand water or high temperatures. They do absorb a great deal of shock before failing. Most thermoplastic glues are for home and school use.

Thermosetting adhesives

Thermosetting adhesives are powders or liquids that cure by chemical action. The curing action is started by adding water or a catalyst. Heat will often speed the curing of the glue. Thermosetting glues resist heat and water. They are good for cabinet and furniture work.

Elastomers

A third type of adhesive is an *elastomer.* This glue, often called contact cement, is a polymer. Elastomers have low strength. They work well for attaching plastic laminates to panels.

Applying adhesives

Adhesives can be applied by brush, roll coaters, and spraying. Each adhesive has a set life (pot life). The adhesive must be used within this time. Also, there is a maximum time—open time—between applying the adhesive and clamping the parts together. Finally, the parts must be clamped for a minimum period of time (clamp time). These characteristics vary with each glue. A technical data sheet from the manufacturer provides this information.

MECHANICAL FASTENING

The two major techniques using mechanical means are mechanical fasteners and mechanical force.

Mechanical Fasteners

Mechanical fasteners hold two or more parts in a specific position. There are many types of fasteners. Some are designed for general use; others are very special. Fasteners can be divided into groups by their permanency (how permanent they are). As shown in Fig. 18-17, these groups are:
1. Permanent.
2. Semipermanent.
3. Temporary.

Permanent fasteners

Permanent fasteners are meant to be installed and not to be removed. If they are removed, the fasteners are destroyed.

Rivets are the most common permanent fastener used on engineering materials. When properly installed, the rivet is enlarged at both ends, Fig. 18-18.

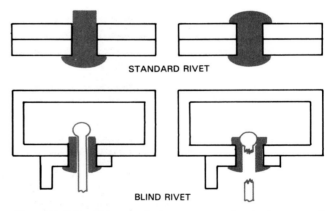

STANDARD RIVET

BLIND RIVET

Fig. 18-18. Types of rivets—standard rivets and blind rivets.

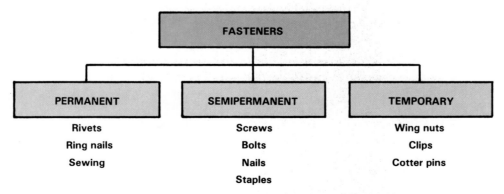

Fig. 18-17. There are three general types of fasteners.

The parts are held by the force created when setting (forming the straight end) the rivet. When correctly installed, the rivet is destroyed when removed. Several head shapes are made for industrial application. As in Fig. 18-19, these are button, countersink, flat, and truss head.

Rivets are widely used for attaching sheet metal to frames. Aircraft and trailer companies are major users of rivets.

Semipermanent fasteners

Two major types of fasteners can be classified as semipermanent fasteners—threaded fasteners and wire fasteners.

Both types depend on friction to hold them in place. Nuts are held on bolts because of friction between the nut and the surface it rubs against. Screw threads create friction with the fibers of wood. Nails also are held in wood by friction.

Threaded fasteners. The three major threaded fasteners are wood screws, machine screws, and bolts. Wood screws are used to attach a metal, wood, or plastic part to a wood member.

Two different hole sizes are required when installing screws. One hole is drilled through the first part. It should be the size of the shank of the screw. A smaller diameter hole—the pilot hole—is drilled into the second member. Also, countersinking or counterboring may be required for the screw head. The screw slips through the first part. The screw threads grip and draw the second part against the first one, Fig. 18-20.

Similar to the wood screw is the *sheet metal screw.* It has threads the full length of its body. A sheet metal screw, as the name implies, is designed to hold two pieces of sheet metal together. The screw should fit easily through the hole in the first member. It will cut threads (self-threading) in the second part.

Screws are sold by their head shape, gage (diameter), and length. The material and finish are also specified. If a special slot is needed it must be listed. A screw might be described as "1 1/4 × 10

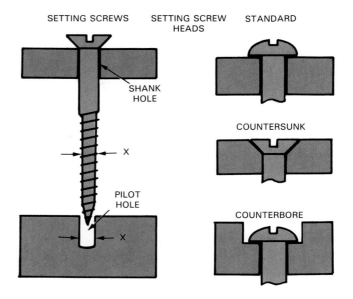

Fig. 18-20. Proper setting of a screw.

flat head cadmium-plated steel wood screw." A catalog will show the typical lengths and diameters available. Note the larger the gage number the greater the diameter. Fig. 18-21 shows the common screw head shapes.

Machine screws are threaded fasteners used to assemble metal parts. They have round, flat, or oval heads. The shank has a uniform diameter and threads along its full length. Machine screws may fit through two parts and be secured by a nut, or they may fit through one part and into a threaded hole in the second part.

Machine screws are sold by diameter, number of threads per inch, and length. The head shape and material must also be listed. A common machine screw is "10-32 × 1 flat head steel screw." It has the diameter of a No. 10 wire, 32 threads per inch, and is 1 inch long.

Bolts are larger threaded fasteners. They are used to assemble heavier members.

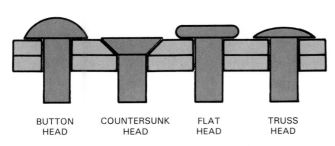

Fig. 18-19. Typical head shapes for rivets.

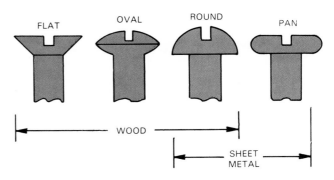

Fig. 18-21. Common screw heads.

Wire fasteners. Wire fasteners are basically nails and staples. Nails are the most widely used. They have two basic head shapes:

1. Flat heads designed to stay on the surface.
2. Ball or tapered head designed to be set (driven) below the surface.

Nails are sold by diameter and length. Small-diameter nails (wire nails and brads) are sized by their actual diameter and length. For example, a 1 1/2-19 is a common wire nail. The 1 1/2 stands for the length and the 19 represents the gage number. A smaller gage number means a larger diameter. A No. 16 wire nail has a larger diameter than a No. 18.

Larger nails are gaged by the penny (d). This is a standard which gives both diameter and length. The greater the penny size the larger the diameter and the length. Fig. 18-22 shows the length and head shapes of some common nails.

HEAD SHAPE	SIZE	
	PENNY	LENGTH
Common	2d	1
	3d	1 1/4
Box	4d	1 1/2
	6d	2
Finish	8d	2 1/2
	10d	3
	12d	3 1/4
Casing	16d	3 1/2
	20d	4

Fig. 18-22. Common nail lengths and head shapes.

Temporary Fasteners

Some assemblies must be quickly and easily taken apart. They require temporary fasteners. Wing nuts on bolts, quick-snap clips, and cotter pins are often used. Also, machine screws and bolts can serve as temporary fasteners.

Fastening by Mechanical Force

Parts may be connected without bonding or fasteners. Mechanical forces can be used to hold them in place.

One fastening technique using mechanical force is *seaming,* Fig. 18-23. It is used widely to fasten sheet metal parts. The parts are bent so they hold themselves together.

Other parts are forced together. The friction between the two pieces keeps them assembled. A shaft

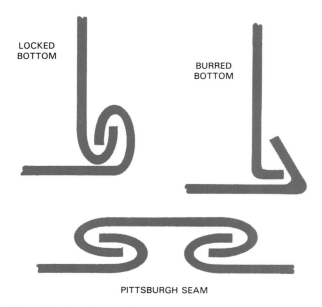

Fig. 18-23. Examples of common sheet metal seams.

SAFETY WITH ASSEMBLING PROCESSES

1. Do not try to complete a process that has not been demonstrated to you.
2. Always wear safety glasses.
3. Wear gloves, protective clothing, and goggles for all welding, brazing, and soldering operations.
4. Always light welding torches with spark lighters, never matches or lighters.
5. Handle all hot materials with gloves and pliers.
6. Perform welding, brazing, and soldering operations in well-ventilated areas.
7. Use proper tools for all mechanical fastening operations. Be sure screwdrivers and hammers are the proper size for the work being performed.
8. Carefully follow instructions for lighting welding torches. Light the gas (acetylene, etc.) first; then turn on the oxygen.
9. When shutting off a welding torch, first turn off the oxygen, then the gas.

may be pressed into a hole. This type of fit is called a **press fit**. Also a part with a hole may be heated. The part and the hole diameter expand. A shaft may be placed in the enlarged hole. As the heated part cools, it contracts. A **shrink fit** is produced between the shaft and the hole.

JOINTS

All assembly operations require joints. The parts must come together at a point. There are five basic types of joints, as shown in Fig. 18-24.

However, additional modifications (changes) have been made to these basic joints. Special cuts have been added to increase strength. Compare the joints in Fig. 18-24 with those in Fig. 18-25. Can you see how they could be stronger? Also, would the parts be easier to line up? These are but a few of the many joints which can be made.

SUMMARY

Assembly involves attaching two or more parts together. Two common ways of assembling parts is bonding and fastening.

Bonding uses heat, pressure, and/or adhesives to hold the materials. Bonds are created by:
1. Melting the parts together without pressure.
2. Melting a dissimilar (unlike) material which bonds (adheres) to both parts.
3. Using heat and pressure.
4. Applying high pressure.
5. Dissolving the bond area.
6. Applying an adhesive.

Parts may also be assembled using mechanical means. Mechanical fasteners may be used to hold parts in place. Self-assembly may use seams or press and shrink fits.

All assembly requires picking a proper joint. It must withstand stress and be attractive.

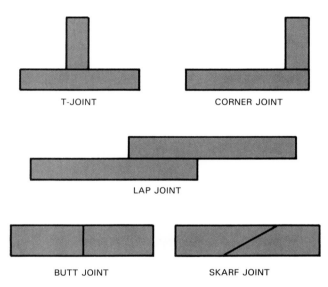

Fig. 18-24. Common types of joints used for many different types of materials.

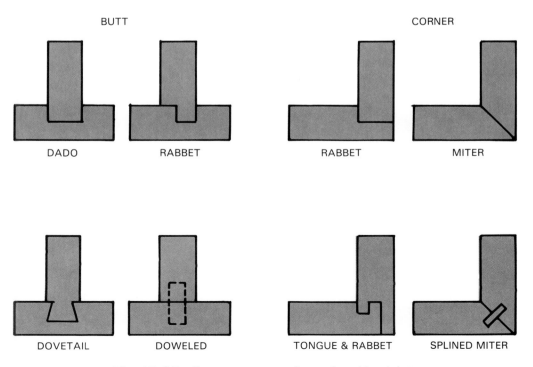

Fig. 18-25. Common types of woodworking joints.

KEY WORDS

All the following words have been used in this chapter. Do you know their meaning?

Agent
Assembling
Assembly
Atomic closeness
Bonding
Bonding agent
Brazing
Elastomer
Fastener
Impulse sealing
Joint
Machine screw
Mechanical fasteners

Press fit
Resistance welding
Seam weld
Seaming
Sheet metal screw
Shrink fit
Soldering
Spot welding
Thermoplastic
  adhesives
Thermosetting
  adhesives

TEST YOUR KNOWLEDGE

Place your answers on a separate sheet. Please do not write in this text.

1. The two types of assembling processes are _____ and _____.
2. Describe each of the methods in Question No. 1.
3. When the atoms of matter across a bonded joint are very close together, they have _____.
4. Which of the following are examples of bonded joints:
   A. Mild steel used to weld mild steel parts.
   B. A hide glue to bond wood parts.
   C. Rivets of mild steel holding tin sheets together.
   D. Solder used to bond copper sheets.
   E. None of the above.
   F. All of the above.
5. List and briefly describe the five methods of bonding.
6. Indicate whether each of the following fasteners is permanent, semipermanent, or temporary:
   A. Nail.
   B. Screw.
   C. Bolt and nut.
   D. Staple.
   E. Rivet.
   F. Bolt and wing nut.
   G. Cotter pin.
7. List the five basic types of joints.
8. Make a sketch of a dado joint and a miter joint.

ACTIVITIES

1. Look around your home. Identify four major joints used in products. Sketch the joint and describe how each is used.
2. List as many different fasteners as you can find in your home. Give one example of how each was used.
3. Find four examples of bonding used on products at home or school. Describe the types of bond and how it was used.

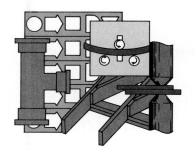

Chapter 19
FINISHING PROCESSES

After reading this chapter, you will be able to:
☐ Explain the two basic purposes of finishes.
☐ Classify finishes under their main types.
☐ Describe methods of surface preparation before application of finishes.
☐ Give brief descriptions of application methods for each type of finish.

Almost every product you use is surface finished. Some products have a coating that makes them more attractive. They are more colorful or glossy than the base material. Such products have more value.

However, finishing is not just for looks. Many engineering materials are attacked by the environment. Metals rust; woods rot; and clay crumbles. These materials must have a protective coating.

Finishing, then, is a surface treatment that protects or decorates a material. Finishing involves three basic steps:
1. Selecting a finishing material.
2. Preparing the part to accept the finish.
3. Applying the finish.

FINISHING MATERIALS

There are a great number of different finishes. However, they fall into two major classes—converted finishes and coating. See Fig. 19-1.

Converted Finishes

The surface of the material may be converted (changed) by chemical action. No material is added as a coating. Instead, the surface molecules are changed to make a protective skin or layer. This layer resists the effects of a normal environment.

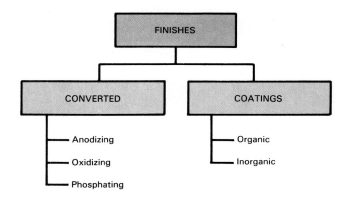

Fig. 19-1. Finishes are either converted finishes or coatings.

Chemicals in the air and water will not damage the material.

Anodizing is a common converted finish. This process is shown in Fig. 19-2. It uses an electrical current and an electrolyte (solution that conducts electricity).

Aluminum parts are placed in the bath. Electricity flows, causing metal on one electrode to ionize and travel through the solution as aluminum oxide. The aluminum oxide attaches itself to the surface of the aluminum product.

The thickness of the coating is controlled by the current and the length of time the parts are in the bath. The pure aluminum develops a "converted" oxide coating. This coating can be colored with a dye. The result is colorful aluminum products like tumblers and ashtrays.

Surface Coating

Surface coatings are a protective layer of material. This material is designed to seal the sur-

Fig. 19-2. The aluminum parts move through a series of cleaning and treatment tanks in this modern anodizing process. (Mirro Aluminum Co.)

face against the environment, Fig. 19-3. In many cases, it also adds color and beauty. Coatings are of two basic types—organic or inorganic.

Organic coatings

Organic (once living matter) *coatings* are the most widely used. They are natural or synthetic

Fig. 19-3. Coatings are a protective layer on top of the base material. This dishwasher case is receiving a dip coating of porcelain.
(Columbus Products Co.)

polymers (chain-like combinations of molecules of organic materials). Organic finishes are classified into a number of groups. Four important ones are paint, varnish, enamel, and lacquer. These are described as follows:

1. Paint—All materials that contain a liquid forming a coating by polymerization (linking of molecules into strong chains). Many paints have a coloring agent added. Special types of paints are *varnish* (a clear oil-based paint) and *enamels* (a colored paint).
2. Lacquer—A material containing a polymer coating and a solvent. A lacquer dries when the solvent evaporates.

Organic coatings are used as undercoats and top coats. Undercoatings improve the bond between the base material and the top coat. They may also smooth the material. Top coats produce a long-lasting, attractive, final surface.

Inorganic coatings

Inorganic (never living matter) *coatings* are metals or ceramic materials. Metal coatings are often applied to other metals or plastics. The common chrome-plated automobile trim is an example. Also, zinc and tin are applied to steel to stop rust. Zinc coating, as shown in Fig. 19-4, is called *galvanizing*. Tin-coated steel is used for food containers (tin cans).

Ceramic coatings are glass-like substances applied to metal or ceramic base materials. These in-

Fig. 19-4. A large steel structure being dipped into zinc. (American Galvanizers Association, Inc.)

clude glaze used on dishes and porcelain enamel applied to ceramic and metal products, Fig. 19-5. The coating is cured by firing at temperatures above 1500°F (816°C). The heat melts the coating and fuses it to the product.

PREPARING MATERIALS FOR FINISHING

A material generally must be cleaned before it will accept a finish. Therefore, industry has special cleaning methods. Two cleaning procedures are mechanical cleaning and chemical cleaning.

Mechanical Cleaning

Mechanical cleaning requires abrasives, wire brushes, or metal shot to remove dirt and roughness. This cleaning may involve simple hand grinding or polishing with an abrasive wheel, Fig. 19-6, or the parts may be tumbled with metal shot or abrasives as shown in Fig. 19-7. In more complex processes, parts may be cleaned or polished with automatic sand blasters or wire brushing machines.

Chemical Cleaning

Chemical cleaning uses liquids or vapors to remove dirt and grease. Chemical cleaning is a basic part of many finishing processes. All plating and surface conversion finishes use cleaning (pickling) steps, Fig. 19-8.

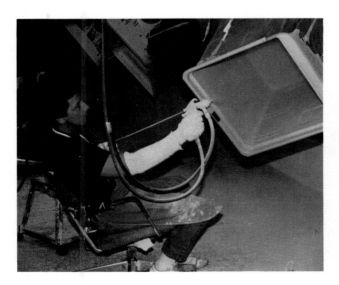

Fig. 19-5. A worker sprays an inorganic coating on this product.

Fig. 19-6. The surface of this metal structure is being prepared for its finish. (ARO Corp.)

Fig. 19-7. A diagram of one type of tumbler. A part is placed on the disc and spun. Shot tumbles over the part's surface to polish it. (Ransburg Corp.)

Fig. 19-8. This row of tanks contains chemicals used to clean parts before finishing them.

APPLYING FINISHING MATERIALS

Application often means adding a coat of material to a surface. This definition is too narrow for our purposes. Converted surface finishes are applied. A chemical or electrochemical (combination of electricity and chemistry) application is used. The protective layer or skin is applied. Therefore, there are two basic technologies.

1. Applying conversion finishes.
2. Applying surface finishes.

Applying Conversion Finishes

Conversion finishes result from chemical action. Each has its own process. Basically, they expose the metal to chemicals. The chemicals react with the metal. The outer surface of the material becomes a protective layer. The basic surface conversion finishes are:

1. Phosphate coatings—Used as primers for organic coatings and chrome plating.
2. Chromate coatings—Provides a decorative or paint-adhering surface.
3. Oxide coatings—Provides an oxide of the metal. A common oxide coating is black iron oxide.
4. Anodic conversion coatings—Electrochemical process that produces an oxide coating on aluminum.

Applying Surface Coatings

Coatings are the most commonly used finishes. They may be applied by a number of processes. The typical methods include brushing, dipping, rolling, spraying, and electroplating.

Brushing

Brushing is seldom used as a manufacturing process. It is slow and requires skilled painters. However, brushing surface finishes (painting) is a common practice of the construction industry.

Rolling

Rolling is also a little-used process in manufacturing. Its primary use is in coating sheet stock like

SAFETY WITH FINISHING PROCESSES

1. Do not try to complete a process that has not been demonstrated to you.
2. Always wear safety glasses when performing finishing processes.
3. Always apply finishes in well-ventilated areas.
4. Do not apply finishing materials near an open flame.
5. Always use the proper solvent to thin finishes and clean finishing equipment.
6. Do not cause finish to flip onto other people or surfaces when you are using a brush.
7. Dispose of all waste finishes and solvents in the proper manner.

steel, hardboard paneling, etc. These techniques first coat a roller with a finishing material. The stock is fed under the roller. The finishing material is then transferred from the roller to the stock. Rolling can coat large areas very quickly.

Spraying

Spraying is a widely used method of applying finish material. Common spraying methods include hand spraying, automatic spraying, electrostatic spraying, and plasma spraying.

In hand spraying, a gun mixes finishing material with air, Fig. 19-9. Air under pressure carries the material to the surface where it sticks and dries. Hand spraying can apply both organic and ceramic material, Fig. 19-10.

Automatic spraying can be used for high-volume production. The spray heads mount in a fixed position. The parts move along on a conveyor or turntable. They are automatically coated as they pass the spray heads. This process is shown in Fig. 19-11.

A big disadvantage of automatic spraying is overspray. *Overspray* is finishing material that misses the product. It is wasted and pollutes the air. *Electrostatic spraying* (from static electricity) overcomes this problem. The part is given an electric charge. The paint receives the opposite charge. Since unlike charges attract, the paint is drawn to the part. It is primarily used for metal parts. Paint will actually wrap around the product. It will even blow past the part then be drawn back. It is possible to paint the whole product while spraying from one side, Fig. 19-12. Note that all sides of the grate are being coated.

Plasma spraying uses a gun that vaporizes metal or ceramic materials, Fig. 19-13. The particles are then carried to the workpiece on hot gases. This process deposits a thin, even coating on metals, plastic, and ceramic parts.

Fig. 19-9. A general-purpose spray gun. Air under pressure mixes with fine particles of finish. (DeVilbiss Co.)

Fig. 19-11. Automatic spraying equipment is used in high-volume production work. (DeVilbiss Co.)

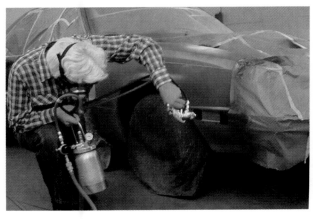

Fig. 19-10. A worker spraying a finish coat. (DeVilbiss Co.)

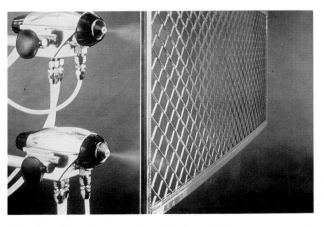

Fig. 19-12. Automatic electrostatic spray guns coat both sides of a metal grate. The paint has a magnetic attraction to the part. (DeVilbiss Co.)

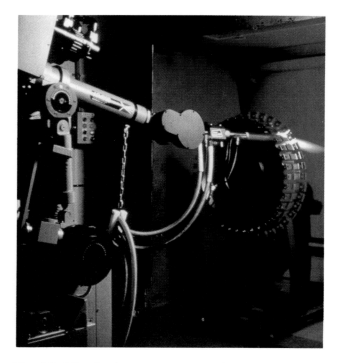

Fig. 19-13. A plasma spray gun in action sprays vaporizing metal or ceramics. (Metco)

Dipping

Dipping is a common way to coat materials. The product is dipped in a vat of finishing materials. The item is then lifted from the vat. The excess material is allowed to flow from the part. Examples of dip coating were shown earlier in Figs. 19-3 and 19-4.

Electrocoating, Fig. 19-14, is a type of dipping process. It uses unlike charges in parts and finishing materials just like electrostatic spraying. The charged part is dipped in a tank of charged finishing materials. The material is attracted to the part. When the part is removed from the tank it is rinsed with water. Then the paint is usually baked (dried) in a continuous oven. (This is an oven that surrounds a moving assembly line.)

Another process like dip coating is *curtain coating.* The surface of the material is flooded with finishing material. The excess runs off into a collecting pan. Curtain coating is often used to coat flat parts or sheet stock.

Electroplating

Electroplating, Fig. 19-15, deposits a layer of metal on a base material, usually steel. It should not be confused with anodizing, which changes the metal on the part's surface.

Often layers of different metals are applied to obtain the desired result. For example, a coat of

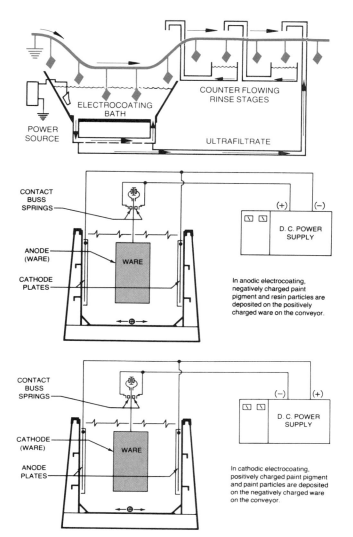

In anodic electrocoating, negatively charged paint pigment and resin particles are deposited on the positively charged ware on the conveyor.

In cathodic electrocoating, positively charged paint pigment and paint particles are deposited on the negatively charged ware on the conveyor.

Fig. 19-14. Diagram of the electrocoating process. (George Koch and Sons)

Fig. 19-15. Automobile trim parts are lifted from a plating tank. (General Motors)

copy may be applied for adhesion. Then a layer of chromium may be added for appearance.

The electroplating process, like anodizing, uses a tank of electrolyte, Fig. 19-16. An electrical lead is attached to the part. The other lead (opposite charge) is attached to a piece of plating metal. The part and the plating metal are lowered into the tank. The direct current charge causes molecules to leave the plating metal. They move across the electrolyte and stick to the part. When the plating is thick enough, the power is turned off. The plated part is removed and rinsed. Electroplating is used on automotive trim, jewelry, and tinplate.

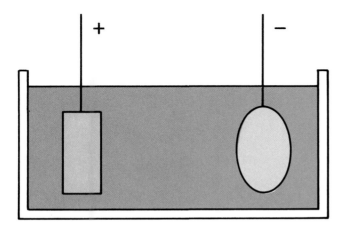

Fig. 19-16. Diagram of a basic electroplating circuit. The process causes new material to coat the part.

SUMMARY

Finishing processes protect and/or beautify materials. The process may change (convert) the outside layer of a material, or it may deposit a protective layer (coating) on top of the base material.

Coatings can be inorganic or organic. They are applied by brushing, rolling, spraying, dipping, or electroplating.

Careful attention to the selection, preparation, and application of finishes produces beautiful and durable products. These products are attractive and serviceable.

KEY WORDS

All the following words were used in this chapter. Do you know their meaning?

Anodizing	Converted finishes
Brushing	Curtain coating
Chemical cleaning	Dipping
Coatings	Electrocoating
Electroplating	Organic coatings
Electrostatic spraying	Overspray
Enamel	Paint
Finishing	Plasma spraying
Galvanizing	Rolling
Inorganic coatings	Spraying
Lacquer	Surface coating
Mechanical cleaning	Varnish

TEST YOUR KNOWLEDGE

Place your answers on a separate sheet. Please do not write in this text.

1. Finishing of products only makes them look better. True or False?
2. The three basic steps for finishing a product are:
   A. Pick a finishing material.
   B. Roughen the surface of the part to accept the finish.
   C. Do what is necessary to prepare the part to accept the finish.
   D. Apply the finish.
   E. Cure the finish.
3. If the finishing process does not add material to the part, it is called a _____ finish.
4. An electrolytic process that uses chemicals and electricity to change the material on the surface but does not add material is known as _____.
   A. painting
   B. electroplating
   C. anodizing
5. A(n) _____ contains a polymer coating and a solvent.
6. A conversion finish is the result of _____ action.
7. Which of the following finishes are conversion finishes?
   A. Paint.
   B. Lacquer.
   C. Phosphate coating.
   D. Oxide coating.
   E. Anodic coatings.
8. Explain what happens in electroplating.

ACTIVITIES

1. List 10 items that are finished. Indicate why you think the finish was applied (protection, beauty, or both).
2. Look around your community. Find and list two items which were primarily finished for protection, beauty, or protection and beauty.

Section V
CONSTRUCTION PROCESSES

Chapter 20
PERFORMING SITE WORK

After reading this chapter, you will be able to:
☐ Explain why builders need to get building permits.
☐ Describe how sites are cleared.
☐ Discuss how centerlines and baselines are used to locate structures.
☐ Suggest ways to design a construction site.
☐ Explain how excavations are stabilized against cave-ins.
☐ Describe some soil removal methods both under water and on land.

Before any site work is started, the contractor must get a building permit. Then, the work on the site can begin. Extra structures and plant growth are cleared. Access roads, security, and utilities are provided. Stakes are set to locate the structure on the site. Finally, earthwork is started.

GETTING A BUILDING PERMIT

People must have permission to use the land. This permission is called a *building permit.* Permits are needed to build, move, or demolish (destroy) structures. They are also needed to enlarge, repair, or convert a building. "Convert" means to change the use of a building. It is the builder's job to get the permit.

The future project must meet certain standards. When the standards are met, a building permit is given. The standards are stated in the *building code.*

Getting a building permit for a new structure requires a complete set of drawings. See Fig. 20-1. Drawings and facts about soil, utilities, materials, and methods are also needed. The fee paid for a

building permit covers the cost of inspecting the plans and issuing the permit. As a rule, the larger the project, the more a permit costs.

A builder must display the permit. Work can be stopped if there is no permit or if construction does not follow the building code. In either case, a *Stop Work Notice* is given, Fig. 20-2. Work is not to proceed on until changes are made.

CLEARING THE SITE

Many building sites may have structures and vegetation on them. If these features are in the way, they must first be cleared. The crew that clears the

Fig. 20-1. Building inspectors check the plans before building begins.
(International Conference of Building Officials)

Fig. 20-2. A Stop Work Notice is legal and binding.

A

B

C

Fig. 20-3. Both structures and plant growth are demolished and salvaged. Salvaging recycles materials. A—Discarding rubble. B—Clearing trees and brush. C—Moving a house. (Caterpillar, Inc.; ASPLUNDAH)

site can either salvage or demolish the features. Fig. 20-3 shows how to take care of some site features.

There are two ways to clear a site. They are to demolish or to salvage the structures or vegetation. Features can be *demolished* by wrecking, breaking, or blasting. Features on a site can be *salvaged* by saving and recycling some of the parts or by moving the structures to another location.

Demolishing

When machines are used to demolish a structure, it is called *wrecking.* The structure in Fig. 20-4 is being wrecked using a bulldozer. A steel wrecking ball is often used. The heavy ball hangs from a crane cable and the crane operator swings the ball against the building. Rubble is loaded onto trucks and hauled away.

In Fig. 20-5, the *breaking* method is being used. Air hammers do the work. They break concrete and rocks into smaller pieces. Then the pieces are loaded onto trucks or put in trash containers and hauled away for disposal.

Blasting uses explosives to destroy a structure. Blasting can reduce a large structure to a pile of rubble. It takes only a few seconds once the explosives are placed. In many cases, the blasting is so well coordinated that a building between two other structures can be demolished without harming them.

Salvaging

The machine in Fig. 20-6 processes rubble from a demolished highway. The materials can then be

Fig. 20-4. Wrecking is often used for small buildings.

Fig. 20-5. An air hammer breaking the concrete. The steel will be salvaged.

Fig. 20-6. This machine crushes old concrete and sorts out the reinforcing steel. In the top right of the photograph, broken concrete is being dumped into the crusher. Can you find a pile of crushed concrete? Where is the scrap steel piled? The crushed concrete is used as the base for a new highway. The scrap steel is to be sold.

recycled. The machine crushes the concrete and separates out the reinforcing steel. The concrete is then crushed and used for the base under a new highway. The steel is sold to a scrap yard.

Some good structures are moved, as was shown in Fig. 20-3. They are placed on wheels. A truck tractor pulls the structure to a new site. This practice saves a lot of materials and labor.

LOCATING A STRUCTURE

Builders need to know where to place a structure on the site. There are two methods used to locate structures. The first method uses a centerline as a guide. The second uses a baseline for control points.

Centerline Method

The *centerline method* is used for locating roadways, tunnels, shafts, and piping systems, Fig. 20-7.

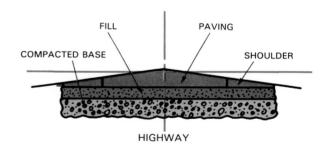

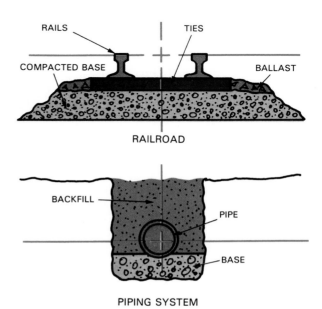

Fig. 20-7. Long, narrow projects are laid out on a centerline. A centerline gives horizontal and vertical control.

A shaft is a vertical opening, while a tunnel is a horizontal opening. A centerline passes through the middle of the project. It describes the horizontal and vertical placement of the project.

A highway is an example that shows how a centerline is used. Fig. 20-8 shows you the process. Notice the procedure used in this process.

Baseline Method

A baseline is used to place a building. A baseline may be on an axis (centerline) or off to one side.

The center baseline passes through the middle of the structure. An offset baseline is set a distance away from the building. This line is parallel to the centerline. (Parallel means that the lines will never meet.)

Follow the process used in Fig. 20-9 to locate a building. The steps are numbered in the drawing. As you read the following steps, refer to each number in the drawing:

1. Locate the boundary lines that currently exist.
2. Locate the center baselines of the structure.

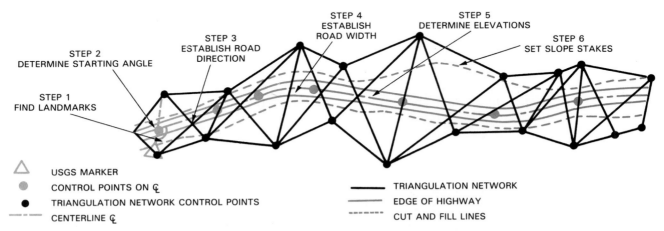

Fig. 20-8. The steps used to lay out a roadway.

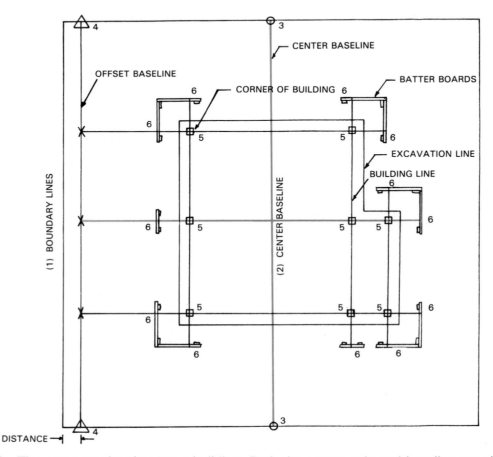

Fig. 20-9. The steps used to lay out a building. Both the center axis and baseline are shown.

3. Clearly mark the centerline.
4. Measure from the centerline to place markers for the offset baseline.
5. Locate the corners of the building.
6. Reference points are placed on batter boards. Fig. 20-10 shows the parts of the batter boards and their relation to the building lines. *Batter boards* are used to locate the building lines.

DESIGNING THE SITE

The engineering section designs the work area layout. They plan how to get in and out of the site. Temporary buildings used by the workers are often placed on the site. Engineers also plan how to get utilities to the site. Lastly, they determine how the site is to be made secure and safe.

Gaining Access

Most buildings are built close to streets and highways. Access to them does not pose much of a problem. *Access* means to gain entry to a work site. Dams, pipelines, power plants, and offshore structures can cause access problems. Special transportation or roads may be needed. Workers on offshore projects ride helicopters and boats to work. Barges bring machines and materials to offshore jobs, Fig. 20-11.

Rerouting

When repairs to roadways are made, traffic must continue. Roadways may be rerouted. Temporary roads may be built along roads under construction. Even streams are rerouted when dams are built.

Providing Temporary Shelter

Projects that take a long time to build need temporary buildings. These buildings may house offices, restrooms, repair shops, and laboratories. (Laboratories are used to test soil and materials.) A building may even be used as a temporary home. Temporary shelter is shown in Fig. 20-12. These buildings may be on wheels. A trailer is often used as an office. Trailers also provide storage space.

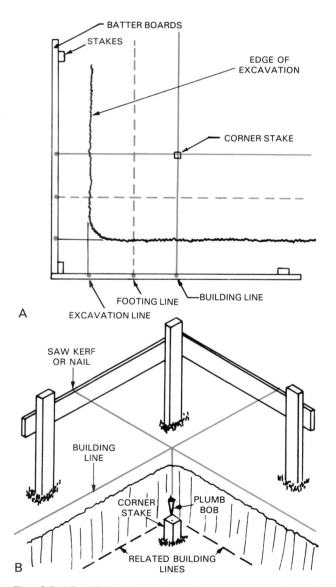

Fig. 20-10. Using batter boards, a corner stake, and plumb bob to establish building lines. A—Plan view. B—Lines must intersect over the nail in the corner stake.

Fig. 20-11. This is a floating work site. A bridge is being built. No fences are needed to secure the site. Where are the offices and materials stored? Where do they get their utilities? (U.S. Department of Transportation, Federal Highway Administration)

Getting Utilities

Building sites need *utilities* such as electricity, water, and telephones. This is not a problem for sites in or near cities. It is easy to get utilities to the site. In remote places, Fig. 20-13, diesel-powered generators are used to provide electricity. Water may be pumped from wells, lakes, or rivers and purified (made clean) for drinking. Communication on the site and to distant places is

Fig. 20-12. Twelve workers live in this van. Each person has a bed, power, and a bathroom with a shower. (Venture Ride Manufacturing, Inc.)

Fig. 20-13. The utilities for this job site are all on board. They generate their own electricity. They communicate with people on land by radio. (Raymond International, Inc.)

needed. Portable telephones and radios are used for this purpose.

Making the Site Safe and Secure

Work sites can be dangerous. They may attract vandals, thieves, and curious observers. The most secure sites are closed off from the outside. Only workers and others bringing materials and equipment can enter them.

Safety for workers is planned in three ways.
1. Safe methods are practiced.
2. Safety equipment is used.
3. Training programs give workers the knowledge.

The workers buy tools, or the firm provides their tools and machines. Safe workers maintain good attitudes.

DOING EARTHWORK

Changes must often be made in the earth when preparing a site for construction. These changes are referred to as *earthwork*. The shape or contour may be changed because it is too hilly or too flat. Poor soil may need replacing. Even after rearranging soil on a site, there may be too much, and some must be removed. Earthwork includes seven different processes:
• Stabilizing earth.
• Loosening soil.
• Excavating.
• Adding earth.
• Moving earth.
• Disposing of earth.
• Finishing earthwork.

Stabilizing Earth

While excavating, soil may need to be *stabilized* (held securely to avoid cave-ins). Stabilized soil will not cave in when soil next to it is removed. Digging large holes can cause footings on nearby buildings to crack. Buildings with shallow footings can slide into the hole beside them.

Builders put slope on the sides of the holes, use retaining walls, build coffer dams, and drive steel sheathing into the soil to prevent cave-ins. See Fig. 20-14.

Loosening Soil

Hard earth has to be loosened. Rock is blasted, Fig. 20-15. Frozen, hard, or rocky soil is ripped. In Fig. 20-16, a steel prong is pulled through the

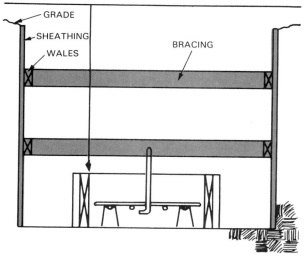

Fig. 20-14. Walls are used to stabilize soil around a pit. Braces and shoring hold it in place. (Morgen Manufacturing Co.)

Fig. 20-15. Holes are drilled and explosives are put into the holes. The blast loosens the soil. (Ingersoll-Rand Co.)

Fig. 20-16. A ripper loosens hard rocky soil. One or two prongs are forced into the ground and pulled forward. (Caterpillar, Inc.)

soil down to 3 feet deep. Scarifying is like ripping but does not go as deep. Air hammers are used to break boulders. One is being used in Fig. 20-17.

Excavating

Excavating means to remove soil to gain space on the site, expose a bearing surface, or bury a structure. Digging a basement is an example of excavating to gain space. The soil taken out is called *spoil,* Fig. 20-18. Spoil is loaded onto trucks and removed, or is saved and used later to finish the site.

Shallow excavations are made by pushing and scraping the earth. Dozers are used to push soil. Scrapers (commonly called pans) can load themselves, haul, and spread the earth. Fig. 20-19 shows a scraper in use.

When harbors and rivers need to be deepened, suction dredges and scoops are most often used, Fig. 20-20. A scow (flat-bottom barge) hauls away the spoil. Soft soil is removed with a hydraulic dredge. Soil is loosened with a cutter, and water at high speed removes the spoil. The water and spoil are pumped to land. The water runs away and spoil stays.

Fig. 20-19. Scrapers are useful in excavating shallow pits or leveling soil. (Caterpillar, Inc.)

Fig. 20-17. This rock breaker is operated with air. Others use direct drive from engines. (Ingersoll-Rand Co.)

Fig. 20-18. Backhoes are useful machines. They can dig trenches for basements, break concrete, or load trees. (Caterpillar, Inc.)

Fig. 20-20. A dredging operation. A round cutter loosens the soil. Spoil and water are mixed. The pump can move the spoil up to 15 miles. (American Dredging Co.)

Tunnels provide useful space below ground. A subway is a typical use of a tunnel, Fig. 20-21. Tunnels dug from below ground start from the ends and from shafts. See Area C in Fig. 20-22. A shaft is a tunnel that extends vertically into the earth. Excavation work then proceeds both ways from the shaft.

Hard rock is drilled and blasted. See Area B in Fig. 20-22. *Muck* is loaded and hauled out. Soft rock and soil are bored by machines at Area C in Fig. 20-22. Steel or concrete liners are pushed out against the tunnel walls. When the tunnel goes below the water table (existing ground water level), the work space is kept under pressure to keep the water out.

A second reason to excavate is to expose a bearing surface. The footings for structures need to be below the frost line. The frost line is the depth the soil freezes during the winter. Backhoes are used to dig footings.

Bridge towers and large buildings require a strong base. Bedrock is the best type of base material. Many feet of soil may often cover the bedrock.

Caissons are driven into the surface of the earth. Caissons are hollow tubes of steel or concrete. Clamshell scoops on a crane are used to remove the spoil. The man in Fig. 20-23 is running a crane with a clamshell scoop.

Drilling makes round holes. In Fig. 20-24, tapered steel piling is driven into predrilled holes. They are later cut to height and filled with concrete.

Holes and trenches are dug to bury structures like tanks and pipes of all kinds. Fig. 20-25 shows a trench for a sewer line. The direction and depth is closely controlled. Replacing the earth after the structure is buried is called *backfilling.*

Cut and cover tunnels are buried structures. A trench is "cut" (dug). The floor, walls, and ceiling are put in place. Utilities are added. The outside of the tunnel is waterproofed and then "covered" (backfilled) with soil. See Fig. 20-26.

Adding Earth

Some sites need to add earth to raise the grade. In some cases, better soil is needed on the site. To raise the grade, soil is taken from a place where

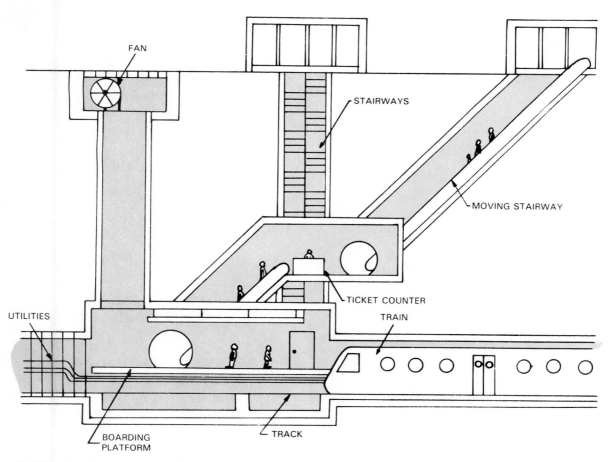

Fig. 20-21. A subway system has track tunnels, ticket counters, fan shafts, utilities, and stairways.

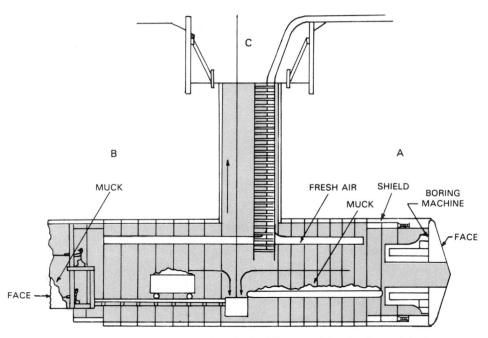

Fig. 20-22. Tunnels are bored from the ends of a shaft. The machine in Area A is for boring into soil. Tunneling into rock is shown near Area B. The shaft is at Area C.

it is not needed and put where it is needed. When building roadways, earth is cut from high spots and used to fill the low spots.

Storms can ruin beaches when the sand is washed away. Hydraulic dredges are used to restore them. Sand and water are pumped from offshore onto the beach. The water runs away and leaves the sand.

The earth in a swamp makes a poor road. A channel can be dredged in marshland. Soil mixed with water is dredged from another place and is pumped to the site. The soil raises the roadbed

Fig. 20-23. Clamshell scoops are used to dig holes in limited space. (Tennessee Valley Authority)

Fig. 20-24. This machine drills and drives tapered steel piling. (Raymond International, Inc.)

Fig. 20-25. A trench for a pipeline is being dug with a rotating scoop wheel. The soil will be pushed back into the trench after the pipe is laid. (Barber-Greene Co.)

Fig. 20-26. Cut and cover tunnels are not deep. (ARMCO Construction Products)

above the marsh. The stronger soil makes the road last longer, Fig. 20-27.

Dirt and gravel will pack and settle. Therefore, concrete and crushed rock are used under piping systems. These materials will not allow the pipes to settle. Pipe encased in concrete is rigid and resists the force of water going around corners in the pipes. Without the bracing, pipes would crack. To make room for the crushed rock fill and concrete, extra soil is removed.

Fig. 20-27. Dredging makes it possible to build roads in problem areas such as marshland. Here cars travel where only small boats could go before. (American Dredging Co.)

Moving Earth

Excavated spoil must be moved. One way is to use conveyors. Conveyors are moving belts or chains. They are suited to moving spoil over a short distance. A conveyor moved most of the soil for the earthen dam shown in the background in Fig. 20-28.

Fig. 20-29 shows a small dredge. The spoil is mixed with water and pumped to a dumping place. Larger machines can pump the spoil over 15 miles away.

Fig. 20-28. Trainload after trainload of soil was moved over rough terrain with the conveyor in the background.
(California Department of Water Resources)

Trucks haul spoil. They are easy to load and dump. They can move over difficult terrain. Fig. 20-30 shows some types of hauling equipment.

Disposing of Earth

Earth is used, dumped, or sold. In doing cut and fill work, the spoil is used rather than dumped or sold. Rivers are dredged so larger ships can use them. The spoil can be used to raise a river bottom to make a preserve for wildlife. Land can be raised higher and used for road and factory sites.

Topsoil is often stripped from the work area and piled somewhere else on the site. Later, it is spread over the site and used for growing grass and flowers. Soil around the tennis courts in Fig. 20-31 was left on site during construction. It was then replaced when the work was completed. Grass and trees were planted.

Spoil is dumped in old pits and other low spots when it cannot be used. In time, the dump site may be filled and made into useful land.

Some people need fill and will pay for the earth and the hauling. People that have low spots in their yards may choose to buy the spoil.

Finishing Earthwork

Washing, trimming, compacting, and grading are used to finish earthwork. Rock is washed to clean its surfaces so concrete will bond better. The holes in Fig. 20-32 were first excavated to the rough size. They were then trimmed to the exact size and shape with hand tools. Compacting takes the air out of the soil. Three types of compacting machines are shown in Fig. 20-33. Grading smooths and

Fig. 20-30. Dump trucks come in a variety of sizes and designs. Even though they are large, they are easy to drive. (Caterpillar, Inc.)

levels soil for a roadbed. The slope in Fig. 20-34 is being graded with a motor grader.

SUMMARY

Getting a building permit must precede the site work. Then site clearing can begin.

The new structures are located by using surveying methods that start with a centerline for highways, or with a baseline for buildings. Temporary shelter is provided for workers and supervisors. Utilities are also provided. Fences and walls help secure the building site and keep it safe.

Earth is stabilized so it will not cave in. Some earth must be loosened before it is excavated. Builders excavate to remove soil from a space. They

Fig. 20-29. The dredge is used to keep the pond clear of soil. The pond is used to cool the water from the power generator. The soil is pumped hundreds of feet away. (Mud Cat Division)

Fig. 20-31. A large concrete water tank is buried on this site. The soil was left at the site during construction. (DYK Prestressed Tank, Inc.)

also excavate because they need soil somewhere else. Builders move the earth they remove. They dump, use, or sell the spoil.

Fig. 20-32. This soil is strong. It serves as the forms for the concrete footings. The holes were trimmed to the exact size and shape.

A

B

C

Fig. 20-33. Many types of machines can be used to compact soil. A—Vibrating plate compactor. B—"Sheep's foot" compactor. C—"Smooth wheel" compactor. (Ingersoll-Rand Co.)

Fig. 20-34. Motor graders can form slopes or level sites. The blade can be set in many positions.

KEY WORDS

All the following words have been used in this chapter. Do you know their meaning?

Access
Backfilling
Baseline method
Batter boards
Blasting
Breaking
Building code
Building permit
Centerline method
Demolish

Earthwork
Excavating
Loosening earth
Muck
Salvage
Spoil
Stabilizing earth
Stop Work Notice
Utilities
Wrecking

TEST YOUR KNOWLEDGE

Place your answers on a separate sheet. Do not write in this text.

1. Sides of trenches in soil can be stabilized against cave-ins by giving them a _____.
2. Soil under water is most often removed with a _____.
   A. clamshell scoop
   B. dredge
   C. backhoe
   D. None of the above.
3. Compacting takes out the _____.
4. Building standards required for a building permit are stated in the local _____.
5. Getting a building permit for a new structure requires a complete set of _____.
6. Living space for workers is provided by _____ shelters.

Matching questions: Match the definitions in the left column with the correct term in the right column.

7. Selling items saved from a site.
8. A survey method used to lay out a highway.
9. A survey method used to lay out a building.
10. Removing a building by striking or bulldozing.
11. A line from an existing survey.
12. Removing a building with timed explosions.

A. Wrecking.
B. Baseline.
C. Boundary.
D. Blasting.
E. Centerline.
F. Salvaging.

ACTIVITIES

1. Sketch out a clubhouse or storage shed. Lay it out at home or at school. Use the centerline or baseline method.
2. Lay out a sidewalk to the clubhouse. Stake the centerline and the edges. What would you use to clear the site? How would you design the workplace? Describe the excavations needed for a sidewalk. What kind of tool would you use? How would you move the spoil and dispose of it?
3. What would you do to make the clubhouse site secure? How long will it take? How much will it cost? Is it worth it?
4. How would you finish the excavations? Do you need to add any earth? Where would it come from? How is it finished?
5. Find out the price you must pay for clean, topsoil. The price is stated for a cube that is 1 yard × 1 yard × 1 yard. (A cube with these dimensions is one cubic yard.)

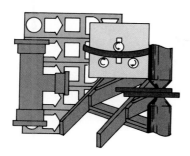

Chapter 21

BUILDING FOUNDATIONS

After reading this chapter, you will be able to:
☐ Explain the purpose of foundations and describe the five types.
☐ List requirements for footings.
☐ Explain how wood can be used in foundations.
☐ List parts of forms for concrete.
☐ Describe drainage systems for footings.
☐ State the purpose of parging and asphalt coating.

A structure consists of a substructure and a superstructure. The substructure is called a *foundation.* The foundation extends from the bearing surface to the main structure. The two parts may meet under the ground, at the grade level, or above the ground. See Fig. 21-1.

A foundation supports the weight of a structure. Structures have to withstand the pressures of wind and water, and other forces. Foundations work like the roots of trees. A stable foundation anchors the structure to the earth, Fig. 21-2.

Two parts are common to all foundations. They are the bearing surface and the footings. These parts are shown in Fig. 21-2. The *bearing surface* is where the structure and the earth meet. Small wooden structures are lightweight. Firm soil that has not been disturbed is a good bearing surface for these types of structures. Sandy or wet soils make poor bearing surfaces. They are too soft.

Large, heavy structures need a strong bearing surface. Bedrock or hard clay are the best types of bearing surface for these types of structures.

The *footing* is the bottom of the structure. Footings are designed to spread the weight of the structure over a greater area. In this way, a bear-

ing surface can support more weight. It is the designer's job to match the footings with the bearing weight.

Most foundations have upright supports. *Upright supports* transfer the pressure of the structure down to the footings. Walls are one type of upright support, Fig. 21-3. Outside walls have to withstand three forces. The weight of the building pushes down. The soil pushes in. Water puts pressure on the wall and soaks through it into basements.

Another type of upright support is the column. Columns are used to support the inner parts of a structure.

KINDS OF FOUNDATIONS

Most foundations can be classified as one of the following:
• Spread foundations.
• Floating foundations.
• Friction pile foundations.
• Bearing pile foundations.
• Pier foundations.
The kind of foundation used depends on two things. They are the forces put on the foundation and its bearing surface.

Spread Foundations

Most small buildings use the spread foundation. See Fig. 21-4. Flat concrete footings are built under foundation walls and columns. The footings are usually twice as wide as the foundation walls. The weight of the building is spread over more surface. More soil is used to resist the pressure.

A

B

C

Fig. 21-1. Foundations can be below ground, at ground level, or above ground. A—Friction pile foundation. Tanks will be installed on concrete caps. B—Bridge foundations extend above water. C—A dam is nearly all foundation. Buildings below the dam are superstructures.   (Raymond International, Inc.; American Institute of Steel Construction; Guy F. Atkinson Co., Ron Chamberlain)

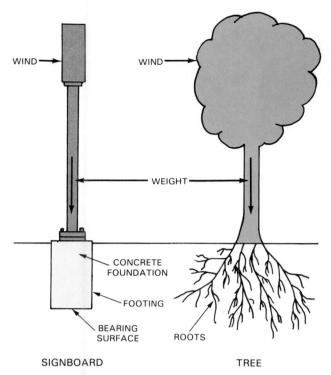

Fig. 21-2. Signboards and trees need a strong foundation. They must resist wind and support weight.

Fig. 21-3. Walls and columns are used in this structure. They transfer weight to the footings.

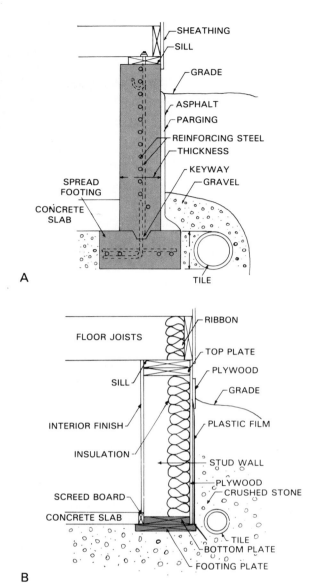

A

B

Fig. 21-4. Spread foundations are used for low structures. They require a firm bearing surface. A—Concrete. B—Pressure-treated wood.

Concrete and pressure-treated lumber are commonly used for foundations. Pressure-treated lumber does not rot. Insects will not affect it.

The foundation wall is built on top of the footings. Cast (poured) concrete or concrete blocks are most often used. Treated lumber and plywood also work well.

The footings are placed below the frost line. The *frost line* is the depth that soil freezes in the winter. When soil freezes, it expands. Soil expands with such force that it will move a structure. Over time, the footings can be broken, resulting in a weakened foundation. Soil does not freeze in the southern states. In northern states, the frost line may extend more than four feet down.

Floating Foundations

Light buildings built on weak soil use floating foundations. See Fig. 21-5. A single concrete slab supports the building. Steel rods or wire are used to strengthen the concrete. The slab needs extra strength under walls and columns. More thickness and steel are added at these points.

Friction Pile Foundations

Friction piles are used in weak soil. See Fig. 21-6. Friction piles never reach firm soil. Long poles are driven into the ground. They may be driven straight or at an angle.

Friction between the piles and the ground makes them stable. Friction can be increased by using more piles. Piling that is longer or thicker has more friction. A wavy surface on the piling also helps create more friction.

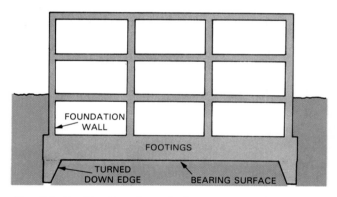

Fig. 21-5. Floating foundations are used in weak soil. The entire area under the building is used for support.

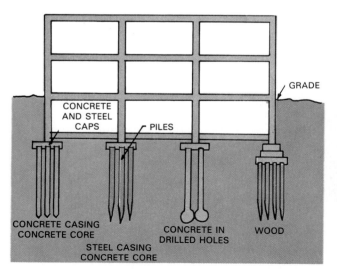

Fig. 21-6. Friction piles are like nails; they are driven into the material. Friction holds them in place.

Friction piles are grouped in rows under walls. A cluster of piles is used under columns. Concrete and steel are used to connect the tops, forming a cap. The *cap* spreads the weight evenly over all of the poles. See Fig. 21-7. Friction tubes are made of concrete or steel. They are driven into the ground. They are cut to height, filled with concrete, and capped.

Some piles are made of wood, Fig. 21-8. Trees are cut and their bark removed. They are then pressure treated so they will not rot or decay.

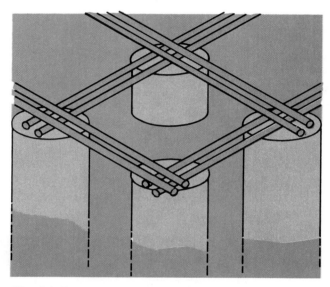

Fig. 21-7. A cap is used to spread the pressure over several friction piles. Concrete will be placed over the steel and piles.

Fig. 21-8. Driving wood piles for a temporary railroad bridge. Wood that is saturated (soaked) with water will not rot. However, it will rot when it is partly dry. Adding chemicals to the wood will keep it from rotting at any time. (Misener Marine Construction Co.)

Bearing Pile Foundations

Bearing piles transmit the weight of the structure to the bearing surface. The bearing surface can be bedrock or firm clay, Fig. 21-9. Bearing piles are longer than friction piles. Some are over 200 feet long. Longer bearing piles are made of concrete and steel. Shorter piles are often made of pressure-treated wood. Bearing piles are used in clusters. A concrete and steel cap is used to spread the load.

Steel beams in the shape of an "H" can be used. They are driven to the bearing surface. Fig. 21-10 shows steel beams being driven. They are driven in sections. Sections are welded together as they are driven.

Steel and concrete pipes are driven in lengths, too. They are later filled with concrete. Steel may be used to strengthen the concrete.

Pier Foundations

Piers transmit the weight of the structure to a bearing surface. See Fig. 21-11. Many shapes are used. They are larger in diameter than most piles.

Piers are made by removing a column of earth. See Fig. 21-12. Drills are used for small round piers.

Fig. 21-10. A cluster of steel "H" piles is being driven to bedrock. They will support a bridge. (Pennsylvania Department of Transportation)

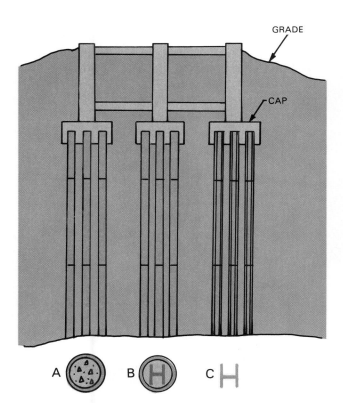

Fig. 21-9. Bearing piles are driven down to firm soil or bedrock. A and B—Hollow pipes made of steel or concrete are filled with concrete after they are driven. C—Steel "H" piles.

Fig. 21-11. The cable towers for this bridge sit on piers. They extend down to solid rock. (U.S. Department of Transportation, Federal Highway Administration)

Clamshell scoops are used for larger ones. The earth is replaced with concrete and steel. During excavation, steel or concrete liners are used. A caisson (liner) keeps water out and keeps the sides from caving in. A single pier is used to replace a cluster of piling. Therefore, no cap is needed.

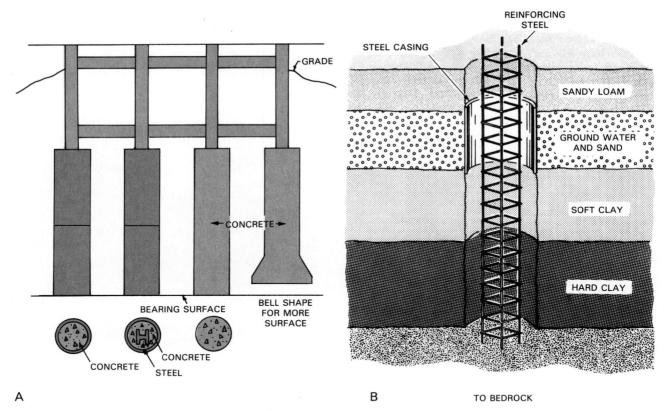

Fig. 21-12. Piers are used to support buildings or utility projects. A—Earth is removed to reach or to form a solid bearing surface. B—A caisson holds wet, loose soil in place until concrete is placed.

Some piers do not reach a firm bearing surface. A special drill is used to remove the soil. It spreads out when it gets to the desired depth. See Fig. 21-12A. The bottom of the hole is bell-shaped. The larger base spreads out the load. It can, then, support more weight.

HOW SPREAD FOUNDATIONS ARE BUILT

The spread foundation is the most common type of foundation used today. Spread foundations are made from concrete or pressure-treated wood. In both cases, a trench is dug. The trench should reach below the frost line. If the structure will have a basement, an excavation is dug. A retaining wall is used if the soil is weak. What happens after the excavation is made depends on which material is used for the footing.

Building Concrete Foundations

As discussed before, a foundation consists of two parts—the footings and the foundation walls. The footings must be constructed prior to building the foundation walls.

Footings

If there is any water in the trench, it must first be pumped out. The bottom of the trench is trimmed. All loose soil is removed. Layout lines are restrung on the batter boards at the footing marks on the boards. A plumb bob dropped from the layout lines locates the footing forms. See Fig. 21-13. Recall that the same string system was used to place marks on the batter boards for later use.

Footing forms are commonly made of 2 inch (1 1/2") lumber. The boards are placed on edge. A form board is placed on both the outside and inside. Footing forms are held in place with stakes driven into the ground. The top edges of the forms are set level and at the exact height. Double-headed nails hold them in place. These nails are easy to pull when the forms are removed. In many cases, the form boards and stakes are strengthened using braces.

Reinforcing steel is placed next. The working drawing shows the size and location. Cast foundation walls require special bent steel rods. They project above the form and become a part of the foundation wall. A *keyway* (groove) is put down the center of the footing when concrete foundation walls are to be used. See Fig. 21-14. A wooden

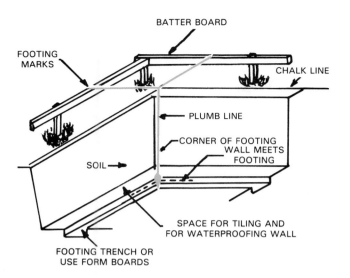

Fig. 21-13. The corner of the footing is found by dropping a plumb line from the building lines.

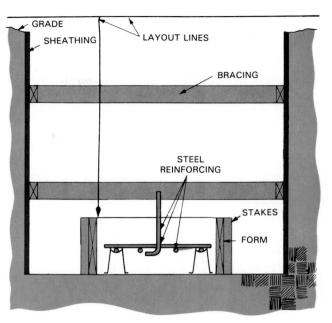

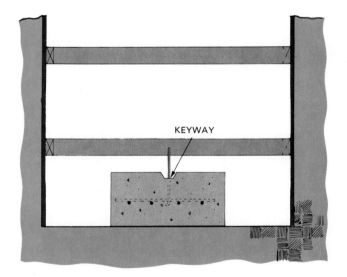

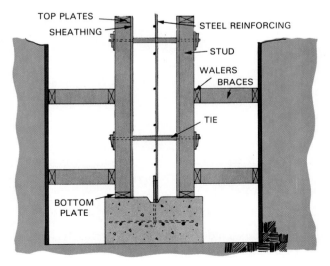

Fig. 21-14. Wall forms consist of plates, studs, walers, ties, braces, stakes, and sheathing.

strip with slanted sides forms the keyway. The keyway strengthens the joint between the footing and the wall. In other foundations, the tops of the footings remain flat, as when concrete blocks are used for the wall.

Concrete is placed (poured) into the forms. Forms are removed the next day. Concrete is kept moist, and kept from freezing for the first week. A plastic cover and straw works well to retain moisture and heat.

Foundation walls

Foundation walls are usually made of cast concrete or concrete blocks. Cast walls need forms. In many cases, forms can be built on the work site. Wall forms consist of plates, studs, walers, ties, braces, stakes, and sheathing. These parts are shown in Fig. 21-14. Manufactured forms come in pieces and are assembled on the site. Manufactured forms are used in Fig. 21-15.

The first step in setting wall forms is to lay them out. The lines on the batter boards should again be used to locate the corners of the building.

The outside wall forms are built first. Reinforcing rods are placed and tied with wire. Four tying methods are shown in Fig. 21-16.

Form ties are then attached to the outside walls. Form ties come in many lengths and designs. One of the many kinds is shown in Fig. 21-17. They are used as spacers between the inside and outside forms.

The inside wall forms are built after the steel rods and form ties are in place. They are set and held in place. Forms are made plumb and straight. A

Fig. 21-15. Concrete is being placed in manufactured forms. The bracing near the workers holds the forms straight. (Mary Robey)

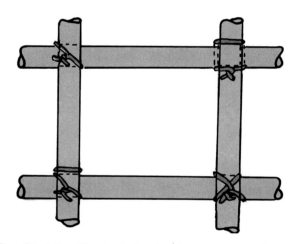

Fig. 21-16. Steel reinforcing bars must be held in place while other work is done. The method for tying them differs.

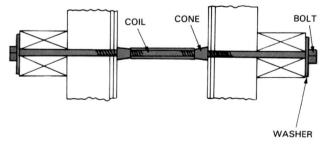

Fig. 21-17. Concrete forms are held apart with form ties. After the forms are removed, the ends are unscrewed to remove them. The holes in the concrete are then filled.

spirit level is used to plumb the forms, Fig. 21-18. A tight line is stretched along the wall to check straightness. The wall is aligned with the line. Braces and shoring hold the forms straight and

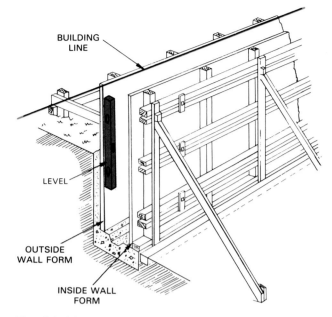

Fig. 21-18. A spirit level is used to plumb the forms. A tight line is used to straighten them.

plumb against the weight of the concrete.

Concrete is placed to the desired height and left to harden. In a few days the forms are removed. This is done by unscrewing or breaking off the form ties and removing the braces. The wall forms can then be removed and reused for another foundation project.

Concrete block walls use mortar to hold the block in place. *Mortar* is special concrete made with cement, sand, water, and lime. The mortar lets the bricklayer adjust the blocks. The blocks should be plumb and level. When the mortar hardens, the walls become solid. See Fig. 21-19.

Fig. 21-19. Concrete block foundation walls go up fast. (Caterpillar, Inc.)

Building Wood Foundations

Wood foundations are being used for small structures. They are made of pressure-treated lumber and plywood.

Details for a wood foundation were shown in Fig. 21-4B. Crushed rock is used under the foundation. It lets the water drain away. The footing is a wide board or concrete. The foundation wall is made of pressure-treated lumber and plywood. Framing techniques described in the next chapter are used to build these types of foundations.

WATERPROOFING FOUNDATION WALLS

Foundation walls must resist a third stress — water pressure. Water can soak through a solid concrete or wood wall. A foundation wall in contact with moist or water-laden soil can get damp inside.

Three methods are used to prevent damp walls — drainage systems, parging, and plastic sheets. *Drainage systems* remove the water from the soil around the building. Clay tile and plastic tubing are commonly used to remove it. Water runs out of the soil into the tile or tube and into drains. Clay tiles are placed end to end. Water gets into clay tiles through small spaces between them. Water enters the plastic tubes through small holes punched in the sides. A drainage system is shown in Figs. 21-4B and 21-20.

Parging is put on the outside of concrete block walls, Fig. 21-20. Parging is a layer of mortar. This layer is covered with a coat of asphalt. Asphalt is a sticky, black petroleum (oil) product. Asphalt is troweled or sprayed onto the wall. Sometimes fibers are mixed with the asphalt to keep it from cracking.

Sometimes, *plastic sheets* are used to waterproof foundations. Large sheets of plastic are hung on

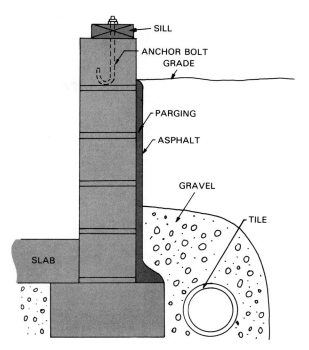

Fig. 21-20. Concrete block walls are waterproofed with parging and asphalt.

the outside wall. It keeps the soil from touching the wall. Fig. 21-21 shows a wood foundation. After it is erected, the outside wall is covered with plastic.

SUMMARY

The foundation supports and anchors the structure. The kind of foundation used depends on the bearing surface and the forces of the structure. A bearing surface, footings, and upright supports make up a foundation.

There are five kinds of footings. Concrete, steel, and wood are used in foundations. Drainage

SAFETY WHEN BUILDING FOUNDATIONS

1. Use care when working around heavy construction equipment such as backhoes and trucks. Since this equipment is large, it may not be able to stop quickly.
2. Be sure that excavations are properly sloped along the edges. Not enough slope may result in a cave-in.
3. Always wear the proper safety equipment on a work site. In most cases, a hardhat is required. For some tasks, eye and ear protection

may be required.
4. Always follow approved OSHA (Occupational Safety and Health Administration) guidelines when working on a building site.
5. Wear approved flotation devices (life jackets) when working on offshore job sites.
6. Be careful when working on scaffolding or ladders. In some cases, safety nets or lifelines may be required.

Fig. 21-21. Pressure-treated wood foundation walls are built much like other wood frame walls. Tough plastic film is used to waterproof them. (Hickson Corp.)

systems, parging, and plastic are used to waterproof basement walls.

KEY WORDS

All the following words have been used in this chapter. Do you know their meanings?

Bearing pile foundation	Friction piles
Bearing piles	Frost line
Bearing surface	Keyway
Cap	Mortar
Drainage system	Parging
Floating foundation	Pier foundation
Footings	Piers
Foundation	Plastic sheets
Friction pile foundation	Spread foundation
	Upright supports
	Waterproofing

TEST YOUR KNOWLEDGE

Place your answers on a separate sheet of paper. Please do not write in this text.

1. The best earth types for supporting heavy structures are _____ and hard clay.

Matching questions: Match the definition in the left column with the correct term in the right column.

2. Has flat footings wider than the walls.   A. Friction piles.
3. Transmits the weight of the foundation to bedrock.   B. Pier.
   C. Spread foundation.
4. Uses single concrete slab.   D. Bearing pile.
5. Uses either bedrock or bell-shaped footing in clay.   E. Floating foundation.
6. Uses pilings that never reach firm soil.
7. It is best if forms for concrete are put together using _____ nails.
8. What helps strengthen the joint between a footing and a poured foundation wall?
9. Use _____ under a wood foundation to allow water to drain away.
10. The concrete coating put on the outside of a concrete foundation wall to seal against water is called _____.

ACTIVITIES

1. Ask an architect what kind of foundations are used under large structures in your town.
2. Find out where the frost line is in your area.
3. Design a tower that extends 7 feet above ground. What kind of foundation will you use?
4. Design a foundation for a clubhouse. Will it be concrete or treated wood?

Chapter 22

BUILDING SUPERSTRUCTURES

After reading this chapter, you will be able to:
- ☐ Discuss highway projects, building walls, and wood and steel framing.
- ☐ Describe concrete paving machines, breakwaters, and types of asphalt.
- ☐ List and describe the parts of floor, wall, and roof framing.
- ☐ Define concrete and steel terms such as precast, tilt-up, standard rolled sections, and tag line.
- ☐ List and describe some types of roof coverings.
- ☐ Discuss the features of some roof types.
- ☐ Describe how doors and windows are installed.
- ☐ Discuss exterior wall coverings and their features.

The part of your school that is above ground is called the *superstructure.* It is secured in place and sits on the foundation. This chapter discusses four kinds of superstructures and how they are built.

KINDS OF SUPERSTRUCTURES

There are four kinds of superstructures:
- *Mass structures*—Mass structures are solid or nearly solid. They have little or no open space inside them. Dams are mass structures.
- *Bearing wall structures*—These structures have usable space in them. The solid or almost solid walls hold the floors and roof above them.
- *Framed structures*—Framed structures have a skeleton. They are made of wood, reinforced concrete, or steel. A skin encloses the frame.
- *Fabric structures*—This type of structure uses air and cables to support specially treated cloth.

The different types of structures can be used alone, or combined with other structures. The building in Fig. 22-1 shows three of the four kinds of structures. Can you identify them?

Fig. 22-1. This building has mass, bearing wall, and frame members. Can you find them? (Gang-Nail Systems, Inc.)

Building Mass Structures

Mass structures use large amounts of material. Most often materials are in their natural state. Soil, rock, reinforced concrete, and asphalt paving are used. Soil is dug, hauled, spread/mixed, and compacted. Processing is not costly. The cost seems high because huge amounts are used. The project in Fig. 22-2 used millions of tons of soil.

Rock is blasted or cut from a quarry. It is then placed on shorelines and breakwaters in ports to protect the harbor and shore from waves. Old concrete is recycled for the same purpose. Cut rock costs more. It is only found in certain places. It is purchased from a supplier.

Reinforced concrete is made of cement powder, aggregate, water, and steel. The retaining wall in Fig. 22-3 is made of concrete and steel.

When a concrete street is being placed, steel reinforcing rods are set. They are held off the subgrade (base material) with *chairs*. The paving machine spreads, screeds, compacts, and does some finish work on the concrete.

A *paving train* is shown in Fig. 22-4. All machines run on two tracks; one at the top and one at the bottom of the canal. *Asphalt paving* is made of aggregate and asphalt. Aggregate is a mixture of sand and gravel. The asphalt holds the aggregate together. Coarse aggregate is used in the first, thick layer, Fig. 22-5. The finish layer uses finer aggregate, Fig. 22-6. Rollers compact asphalt paving after it is spread to squeeze out the air.

Fig. 22-4. A paving train has two or more machines. This one places and finishes concrete. The third machine is a walkway. The concrete is troweled and curing compound is applied from the walkway. (CMI)

Fig. 22-2. Soil cement was used on this project. Soil, cement, and water are mixed together. Cement makes the soil harder. (Combustion Engineering, Inc.)

Fig. 22-3. This retaining wall is a mass structure. Concrete goes into the top of the form. (Miller Formless, Inc.)

Fig. 22-5. The first layer of an asphalt highway is thick. It is rolled with a compactor. (Ingersol-Rand Co.)

SAFETY WHEN BUILDING SUPERSTRUCTURES

1. Use care when working around heavy construction equipment such as backhoes and trucks. Since this equipment is large, it may not be able to stop quickly.
2. Be sure that excavations are properly sloped along the edges. Not enough slope may result in a cave-in.
3. Always wear the proper safety equipment on a work site. In most cases, a hardhat is required. For some tasks, eye and ear protection may be required.
4. Always follow approved OSHA (Occupational Safety and Health Administration) guidelines when working on a building site.
5. Wear approved flotation devices (life jackets) when working on offshore job sites.
6. Be careful when working on scaffolding or ladders. In some cases, safety nets or lifelines may be required.
7. When asphalt paving or roofing is applied, it is hot. Avoid coming into contact with the hot material. Make sure you wear gloves and long pants when applying asphalt.
8. Many times, materials suspended or being moved by a crane go unnoticed. Use care when working around cranes.
9. Nails and other fasteners have sharp points, and should be used carefully.

Fig. 22-6. The finish coat of asphalt is being placed on a parking lot. (Puckett Bros. Mfg. Co., Inc.)

Fig. 22-7. This old church has walls that are 3 feet thick. The structure has little space inside for the amount of materials used.

Building Bearing Walls

Bearing wall structures have strong walls, Fig. 22-7. Older structures used rocks and blocks held together with mortar. Walls were 3 to 4 feet thick and windows were small. Arches and lintels were used to bridge the openings.

Masonry walls are made of small units such as brick, block, and rock. The masonry units are held in place with mortar. See Fig. 22-8.

Tilt-up bearing walls are made of reinforced concrete. The concrete floor for a building is cast. Forms for the walls are built on the floor, Fig. 22-9. Steel is set in the forms. Concrete is placed, finished, and cured. The forms are then removed and the wall section is lifted into place. See Fig.

22-10. Steel rods that project out of the edges are welded together. Concrete columns are placed where the wall sections meet.

Building Frame Structures

Frame structures are made from wood, reinforced concrete, and steel. The structure in Fig. 22-11 is made of wood.

Frame structures are used in many ways, Fig. 22-12. Most of today's buildings are frame structures. The frame is made up of beams, rods, poles, or boards. The frame supports the roof and all floors, ceilings, and contents of the structure. Frame structures have many good features. They

Fig. 22-8. Bricks and blocks were used to build this bearing wall structure. (Pella/Rolscreen)

Fig. 22-9. Tilt-up bearing walls are made on the floor slab. Forms are built and steel mesh is set. Concrete is being placed on this site. (The Burke Co.)

Fig. 22-10. Cast walls are lifted and positioned with cranes. (The Burke Co.)

Fig. 22-11. A wood frame was used in this structure. Wood is strong and light in weight. (Mary Robey)

Fig. 22-12. Many frames are not enclosed. These were built to support something. A triangle shape is strong. (Bob Dale)

use less materials, are light in weight, and are easy to insulate.

One- to four-story buildings commonly use wood frames, Fig. 22-13. Taller buildings might use rein-

Fig. 22-13. Wood frames are easy to make with simple tools. Roof trusses do not need interior bearing walls. (Mary Robey)

forced concrete frames as shown in Fig. 22-14. The very tall structures generally use steel frames, Fig. 22-15.

Wood frames

Wood frames for buildings are built in four parts. These are the floor, wall, ceiling, and roof frames. Frame members are placed 12, 16, or 24 inches on center (O.C.). That way, 4 x 8 feet sheets of plywood will fit properly without extra cutting.

Fig. 22-14. Concrete and steel were used to make this office building's frame. Other materials were added during finishing. (The Manitowoc Company, Inc.)

Fig. 22-15. Steel frames are used for tall buildings. (HNTB Engineers)

Floor framing. Many small buildings are built on a concrete floor. Houses built over a crawl space or basement usually use *platform construction*. The platform is shown in Fig. 22-16. The first part of the platform frame to be installed is the sill. It is bolted to the top of a concrete or block foundation. Insulation is placed between the foundation and sill, Fig. 22-17. It prevents air and insects from getting into or out of the building.

Other frame members are used to provide strength. The members are set on edge so they have greater strength. *Joists* are fastened to the *joist headers* to keep them vertical. On long spans, joists are spliced over a supporting girder or beam. The names and placement of the other parts are shown in Fig. 22-16.

Wall framing. Wall frames consist of studs, plates, headers, and sheathing. See Fig. 22-18. *Studs* are the main members of a frame structure. *Plates* are used as a nailing surface for the studs at the top and bottom. Double top plates add strength, keep walls straight, and support the ceiling and roof. *Headers* provide support over an

A

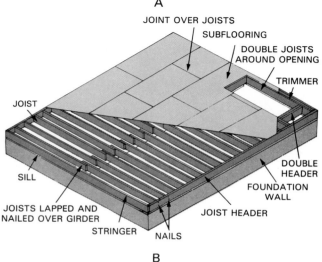

B

Fig. 22-16. Examples of platforms are shown. A—The worker is standing on the platform. B—Detailed drawing shows parts of a platform and construction materials. (Mary Robey)

Fig. 22-17. Insulation is being placed on top of the foundation wall. A plank called a sill is held in place with a bolt. (CertainTeed Corp.)

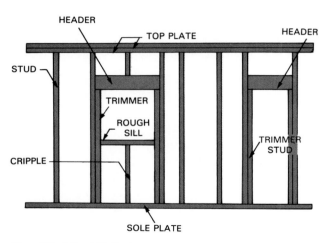

Fig. 22-18. Wall frames have top and bottom plates. Between them are studs, headers, cripples, trimmers, and rough sills.

opening such as a door or window. *Sheathing* is the covering for the structure.

New framing methods allow more space for insulation. Extra insulation saves on heating and cooling costs. Framing methods are shown in Fig. 22-19.

Rough openings are made in walls for doors and windows. They are about 1 inch larger than the door and window units. Doors or windows are placed in the rough openings, and are then framed in.

Sheathing is nailed to the outside of a wall. Plywood, fiberboard, and foam plastic are commonly used. See Fig. 22-20. Wood and metal *diagonal* (angled) *braces* are used to strengthen walls sheathed with foam plastic.

Framing ceilings. Ceiling framing ties the walls together. It supports the floor above and the ceiling below. One end of the *ceiling joists* rests on the outside walls. The other end rests on the inside bearing wall.

Framing roofs. Roofs cover the tops of buildings. Roofs are flat or pitched (angled), Fig. 22-21. Roofs are generally designed for the type of climate that you live in. Flat roofs, for example, are commonly used in the southern states. They are rarely used in the northern states because of snow buildup in the wintertime.

Flat roofs use *roof joists* covered with plywood. The plywood is called *decking.* Roofing methods are described in the next chapter.

Pitched roofs are designed in many ways. Parts of the roof framing are shown in Fig. 22-22. *Rafters* are the main part of a roof frame. They give the roof its shape. *Ceiling joists* provide a nailing surface for interior ceiling materials.

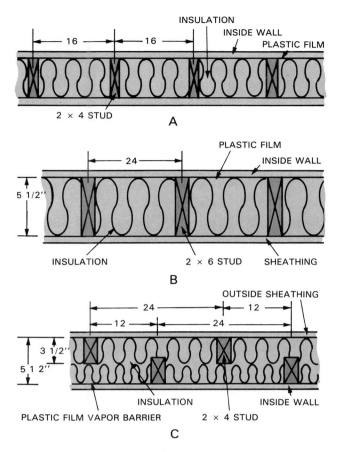

Fig. 22-19. The extra materials in a wall cost extra money. The savings in heating costs will pay for the materials in a few years. A—Standard wall. B—2 × 6 studs. C—Staggered 2 × 4 studs.

Fig. 22-20. The roof is sheathed with plywood. The walls are sheathed with foam plastic. The plywood is strong. The foam plastic insulates very well. (Sellick Equipment, Ltd.)

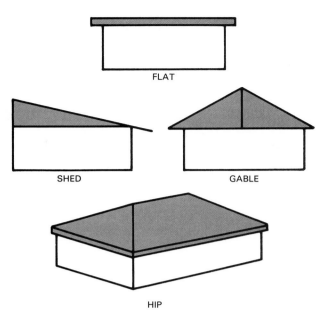

Fig. 22-21. There are many roof designs. Flat, shed, gable, and hip are the most common.

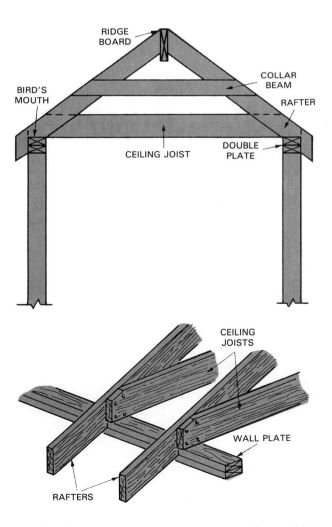

Fig. 22-22. Roof framing has joists, rafters, ridge board, and collar beams.

Roof trusses are commonly used for modern roof framing. A roof truss has both rafters and ceiling joists. Trusses are used in Figs. 22-1 and 22-13.

Reinforced Concrete Frames

Concrete is a good material for slabs and footings. It is also used for building frames. Concrete building frames can be cast-in-place or precast.

Cast-in-place concrete

Forms for the concrete can be built on the work site by carpenters. Other forms may be purchased or rented. All the concrete is placed and finished on the site. The parking structure in Fig. 22-23 has a cast-in-place frame.

Precast concrete

Precast concrete is cast in a plant in prefabricated (premade) forms. Some standard shapes are shown in Fig. 22-24. The panels or shapes are then hauled to the site and placed in a structure. The forms can be used many times. The process is closely controlled.

At the work site, precast parts are joined using cast-in-place methods. The building in Fig. 22-25 was built this way. Precast parts are used for the

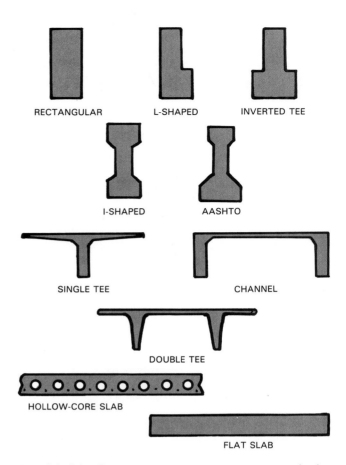

Fig. 22-24. Precast concrete parts are made in plants. There are some standard shapes for beams and slabs.

Fig. 22-23. This parking structure is being built in stages. Notice the progression from the bottom to the top of the structure.

Fig. 22-25. The use of precast parts speeds up construction. Floor panels and walls are precast. (The Manitowoc Company, Inc.)

floors and outside facing. The columns and support beams were cast-in-place.

Steel Frames

Steel frames make it possible to build skyscrapers and large bridges. The steel frame provides a high strength-to-weight ratio and does not burn. Steel framing was used for the structure shown in Fig. 22-26.

There are many types of common steel shapes. Standard rolled steel sections are in the form of letters. The letters I, U, H, and L are most common.

Steel is joined by welding and bolting. Both were used in Fig. 22-27. Girders and bracing are being joined to a column.

Fig. 22-26. Steel framing and a metal exterior make a building more fireproof. (Stran Buildings)

Fig. 22-27. The joints in steel structures have to be very good. They must hold for many years. (Mitchell/Giurgola Architects)

Cranes lift steel parts into place, Fig. 22-28. *Tag lines* are used to keep beams from swinging. Look again at Fig. 22-28 and notice the tag lines. Placing the highest or last piece of steel in a structure is called "topping out." See Fig. 22-29. A ceremony sometimes follows.

Fig. 22-28. Cranes lift steel in place. The operators are highly skilled. (The Manitowoc Company, Inc.)

A

B

Fig. 22-29. Putting up the final story of a building. A—Raising the final beam. B—Fastening it in place. (Frank Samargin)

Fabric Structures

Using fabric for a building material is not new. It has been used for thousands of years in tents. Buildings, in which fabric was a part, were first used as small temporary buildings. Now they are used for large sports arenas, zoos, and art centers.

Fabric is a building material in air-supported and tensile structures. Structures are made stable by inflating or removing air, or with masts and tightly stretched cables. *Air-supported structures* look like bubbles. An example is shown in Fig. 22-30. With a slight vacuum (air is removed), the structure looks more like a tent.

Tall, strong masts and heavy cables form the frame of *tensile structures.* Fabric is stretched and clamped to the cables. These methods were used in the convention center and exhibit hall shown in Fig. 22-31.

ENCLOSING STRUCTURES

Structures are enclosed to keep out the elements—wind, rain, cold, sun, heat, and dust. Enclosing the frame makes the contents safe from theft as well. Some frames are not enclosed. They are designed to withstand the weather. The materials used for these frames do not corrode, or those that do corrode have their surfaces coated. The frame in Fig. 22-32 is painted, although rust would not disturb its use.

Builders enclose structures as soon as they can. Then, rain will not stop work. Damage is avoided if wood frames are kept dry. Both roofs and sides of buildings must be enclosed. Roofs on low buildings are enclosed first. Windows and doors are installed next. Siding is applied last.

The lower floors of high-rise buildings are enclosed before the frame is complete, Fig. 22-33.

Fig. 22-30. Grain is stored in this air-supported fabric structure. They are easier to build and cost less than concrete, metal, and wood buildings.

Fig. 22-32. Frames are not always enclosed. Some frames are not for shelter; they only support something. (EXXON Corp.)

Fig. 22-31. Large spaces and a grand effect are created with this tensile structure. (BIRDAIR, Inc.)

Fig. 22-33. The steel frame for this structure is still being erected. Lower floors are enclosed. (Frank Samargin)

Steelworkers finish the frame one floor at a time. They are followed by concrete workers who cast the floor. Other trades install utilities and furnishings.

Enclosing Roofs

Roof types may be flat, pitched, or curved. Flat roofs are the least costly. There is less material and labor than for other roofs. Factories and commercial buildings often use flat roofs.

Pitched roofs are angled. Water and snow run off of them. The space under a pitched roof is hard to use. If roof trusses are used, most attic space is wasted.

Curved roofs are strong and decorate a structure. Some interesting roof lines are shown in Fig. 22-34. Sometimes a roof and wall are one unit. Can you tell the roof from the wall in Fig. 22-35?

A

B

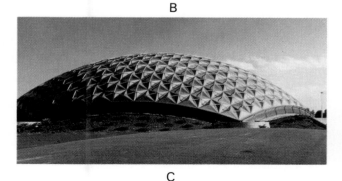

C

Fig. 22-34. These buildings have curved roofs. A—Arches form the roof. B—Hyperbolic curves are based on math. C—A geodesic dome. (Ball State University Photo Service; The Manitowoc Company, Inc.; TEMCOR)

Roof components

Most roofs have three parts:
- Deck.
- Roofing.
- Flashing.

A rugged roof is shown in Fig. 22-36.

Roof decks

Roof *decks* form a connecting bridge across the framing members. Decks support the roofing material.

Roof decks are made of many materials. Concrete, boards, plywood, fiberboard, flakeboard, and metal are the most common. Two roof decks are shown in Fig. 22-37. Some of the sheet metal roofing materials do not need decking. Sometimes decking is left visible from inside to decorate a room with a cathedral ceiling (a peaked, open attic area).

Insulation can be added to a roof deck. Rigid panels of foam and fiber are often used.

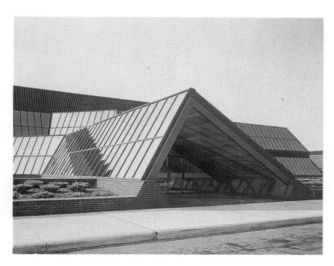

Fig. 22-35. Does this structure have walls? (Monsanto Polymer Products, Inc.)

Fig. 22-36. A roof consists of a deck, roofing, and flashing. Can you find the parts of a roof in this picture? (Owens-Corning Fiberglas Corp.)

A

B

Fig. 22-37. Common deck materials. A—Flake-board. B—Steel decking under ''cellular glass'' slabs. (SENCO Products, Inc.; Johns-Mansville Corp.)

Lightweight concrete and cast gypsum are used in concrete or steel structures. These materials are foamed or have foam plastic beads in them.

Roofing

Roofing protects the building from rain and snow. Built-up, one-ply, and liquid roofing systems are used for flat roofs. Shingles and sheet roofing are used on pitched roofs. Nails, clips, or glue fasten the roofing to the deck.

Built-up roof. Built-up roofing consists of building felt, bitumen, and gravel. *Building felt* is a sheet of fiber soaked with asphalt. *Bitumen* is a thick, black, and sticky material made from oil or coal.

Layers of hot bitumen are covered with building felt. Each layer is called a *ply*. The plies of built-up roofing are shown in Fig. 22-38A.

The last layer of hot bitumen is called a *flood coat*. While it is still hot, gravel is spread over it. The gravel protects the roofing from the sun and

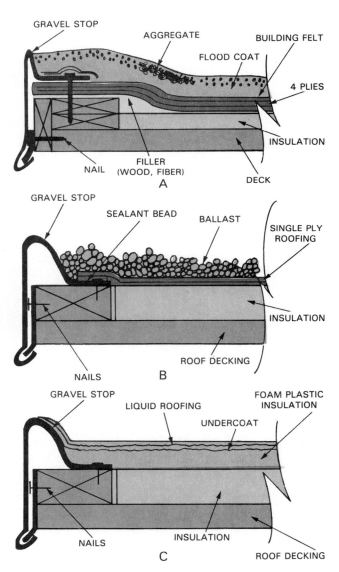

Fig. 22-38. Flat roofs are made in several ways. A—Built-up. B—One-ply. C—Liquid.

from people who walk on the roof.

One-ply roof. One-ply roofs are made of a sheet of special plastic or rubber that is put onto a smooth deck. See Fig. 22-38B. The sheets are overlapped and glued to each other and to the deck.

Liquid roofing materials. Liquid roofing materials are sprayed or rolled on and allowed to harden, Fig. 22-38C. The first coat is a foam plastic. It smooths the surface and insulates the structure. The final coat is made of silicone rubber. Liquid roofing works well on curved roofs.

Shingles. Shingles are small flat or curved pieces of material fastened to the deck. They are made of asphalt, wood, slate, metal, clay, plastic, or concrete. Five kinds of shingles have been used in Fig. 22-39. Most of them are measured and sold by the

Fig. 22-39. Roof coverings. A—Slate shingles. B—Asphalt shingles. C—Clear plastic roofing. D—Sawn red cedar shingles. E—Imitation clay tile. (Pella/Rolscreen; SENCO Products, Inc.; TEMCOR; Cedar Shake and Shingle Bureau)

square. A *square* covers 100 square feet of roof.

Asphalt shingles are laid on a solid deck (no gaps). Refer again to Fig. 22-37A. The roofer is putting on solid decking. Other shingles can be put on open decking, Fig. 22-40.

The white strip on the side and bottom edge of the roof in Fig. 22-41 is a drip edge. A *drip edge* protects the edge of the decking from water that could run under it.

Shingles are attached with nails and staples. The method varies with the kind of shingle. All nails should be hot-dipped galvanized steel, copper, aluminum, or stainless steel. Staples can be used to fasten asphalt and wood shingles. The worker in Fig. 22-42 is installing the cap using hot-dipped galvanized roofing nails.

Clay and slate shingles are laid in much the same way. The details differ some for each kind of shingle.

Fig. 22-42. The roofer is putting on the cap. Hot-dipped galvanized roofing nails are used. (Asphalt Roofing Manufacturers Assn.)

Sheet metal roofing. Sheet metal for roofing comes in many forms. Copper, lead, and aluminum do not need surface treatment. Steel must be plated or enameled. Copper is the longest lasting and the most costly. Metal is held to the deck with clips, screws, and nails, Fig. 22-43. Metal roofing is easy to install and lasts a long time. It provides adequate protection for the structure.

Flashing

Flashing is used to stop leaks. Leaks occur where a roof section joins another surface. Metal, asphalt roofing, and asphalt plastic cement are used for flashing. Places where flashing is used is shown in Fig. 22-44.

Enclosing Walls

Walls are also designed to keep building interiors comfortable and dry. At the same time, there must be openings that let in light and allow people to enter and leave. The openings are closed in by windows and doors. The permanently closed sections of the wall are made of wood, masonry, and other durable materials.

Installing doors and windows

Doors and windows are usually installed after the roof is complete. In this way, movement from roof framing work proceeds through clear door openings, and door and window frames stay dry.

Fig. 22-40. The deck for rigid roofing can be spaced.

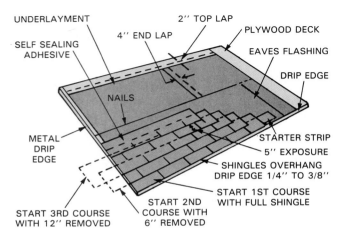

Fig. 22-41. The edges of the deck are protected with a drip edge. Shingles overlap so water cannot get in the structure.

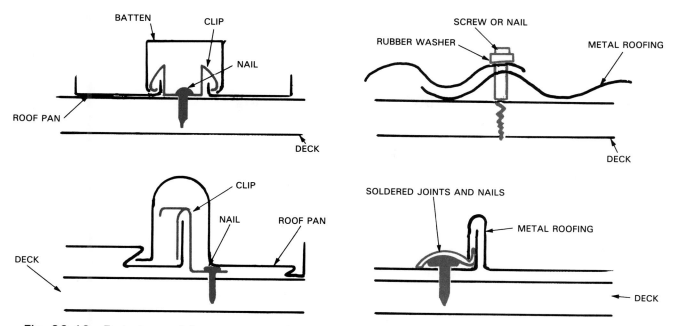

Fig. 22-43. End views of four ways metal roofing is attached to a deck. Many more ways are used.

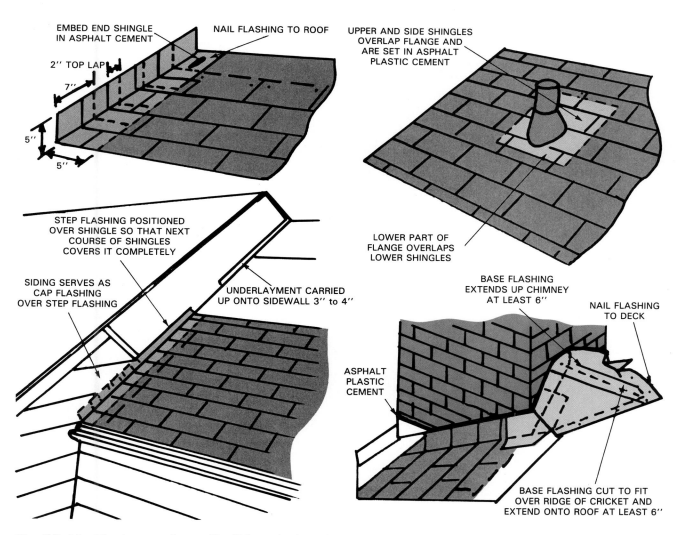

Fig. 22-44. The best roofers will still have leaks unless they install flashing. Here are four places where it is needed.   (Asphalt Roofing Manufacturers Assn.)

Doors. A door is installed in a rough opening in the wall frame. The rough opening for doors is usually 1 inch wider and higher than the frame. The opening is fitted with a door frame. Door frames are made of wood or metal. The frame holds the hardware and presents a finished appearance.

Parts of the frame are shown in Fig. 22-45. Wood shims (wedges) are used to hold the door plumb. Nails are driven through the jamb and shims into the framing. Trim boards cover the gap.

Windows. A window is another opening to close up in a wall. It lets in light and fresh air. Fig. 22-46 shows four types of windows. Double glazing and weatherstripping reduce heat loss. Screens keep out insects while letting in fresh air.

Window frames are made of wood and metal. The wood parts of some windows are clad (covered) with plastic and metal. Many types are made.

A special procedure is needed to properly install windows. This process is shown in Fig. 22-47.

COVERING OUTSIDE WALLS

Frames for buildings are designed to last. The materials that cover them must last, too. Outside walls are enclosed or protected with many kinds of materials. Wood, stone, glass, plastic, concrete, and metal are only a few. The materials come in many forms. They include blocks, strips, slabs, plates, and panels. Materials used to enclose a structure can provide strength as well as seal it from the elements. Others only cover the frame and seal it.

A

B

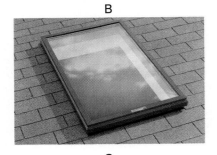

C

D

Fig. 22-46. There are many ways for windows to open. The four most common are shown. A—Double-hung windows slide up and down in a track. B—Casement units swing out on hinges. C—Ventilating skylights are placed on a roof on hinges. D—Awning units open from the bottom. (Pella/Rolscreen)

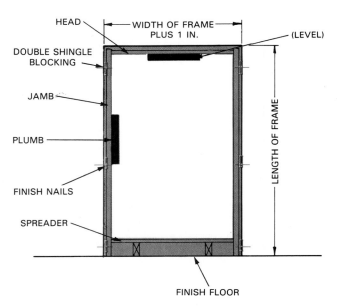

Fig. 22-45. Interior doors. Door frames are set level and plumb. Nails are driven through the jamb and shims into wall framing.

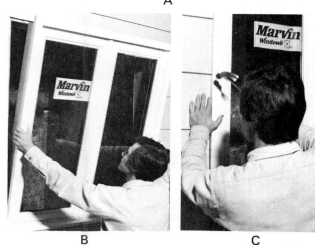

Fig. 22-47. Steps used to install a window. A— Make a rough opening. B—Set in window. Plumb and level. C—Nail in place. D—Caulk outside, and insulate and add trim inside.   (Marvin Windows)

Materials that Strengthen

The load-bearing and racking strength can be increased if spaces between framing members are filled. *Load-bearing strength* resists pressure from above. *Racking strength* resists pressure from the side.

Walls enclosed with wood and sandwich panels are stronger than those without it. Brick, concrete block, tile, or stone set in mortar also add greatly to the strength of a building.

Curtain Walls

Curtain walls are another way to enclose frames. Curtain walls are attached to the frame. They keep the forces of nature out and make the building look good. However, curtain walls add very little, if any, strength.

There are three basic kinds of curtain walls:
- Custom walls.
- Commercial walls.
- Industrial walls.

Custom walls are designed for one project. Fig. 22-48 shows this kind of curtain wall. The designer of this structure wanted the building to have a unique appearance.

Fig. 22-48. Custom curtain walls were specially made for these three buildings to cover their steel frames.   (Skidmore, Owings & Merrill)

Commercial walls are made up of standard parts. The office front in Fig. 22-49 is a commercial wall. In most cases, the standard parts do not need to be cut.

Industrial walls are built from pieces, strips, or panels of standard material. Bricks, siding, and plywood are industrial wall materials.

Fig. 22-50 shows the use of a special sheet that helps keep cold air out. It is put on before the outside materials are installed. Brick and stone pieces are then used to enclose the wall framing. Brick veneer construction is shown in Fig. 22-51.

Fig. 22-49. Standard stock metal and glass were used to enclose these walls. The fabricator cut them to size. The parts were assembled on site. (Elliott Corp.)

Fig. 22-50. An air, or vapor barrier is a way to make a building warmer in winter. It will reduce air infiltration, which inturn means fewer drafts will affect the building.

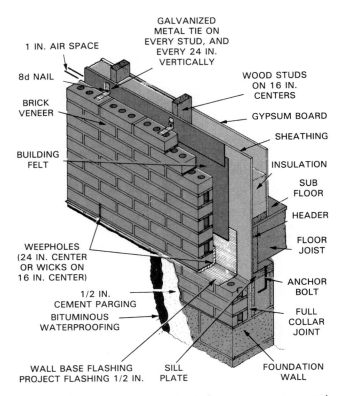

Fig. 22-51. Wood and steel frames are covered with brick and stone. Wall ties are used to hold the facing to the backing wall. (Brick Institute of America)

Metal and strips were used to enclose the buildings in Fig. 22-52. The materials come in many shapes and sizes. Fig. 22-53 shows vinyl (plastic) strips being used to cover the exterior of the structure.

Premade panels may also be used to cover a structure. These panels are made of stone, glass, concrete, metal, or wood. Panels may be single layers. Stone, glass, and hardboard panels were used for the structures shown in Fig. 22-54.

Panels can have more than one layer. They are referred to as *composite panels*. The layers of the panel provide special features such as looks, insulation, and strength. Thin metal, plywood, and rigid foam plastic may be joined. The metal resists weather and looks good. The plywood gives strength. The foam plastic keeps the building warm in the winter and cool in the summer.

Plaster stucco is also used as an exterior covering. *Plaster stucco* is like plaster with sand in it. Expanded metal lath is first attached to the outside wall. A scratch coat is then applied. The worker in Fig. 22-55 is putting on a scratch coat. The brown coat is put on next, and the finish coat is put on last. Stucco is strong and will last a long time.

A

B

Fig. 22-52. Metal and wood are used to enclose these buildings. A—Aluminum. B—Redwood. (California Redwood Assn.)

SUMMARY

Superstructures are usually above ground. Mass structures have little open space inside them. Bearing wall structures have thick walls. Cast concrete and masonry units are the materials used for bearing walls. Most structures today use frames. A frame is the skeleton made of wood, reinforced concrete, and steel. A skin is then applied.

Structures are enclosed to keep weather out. Roofs enclose the tops of buildings. They consist of decks, roofing, and flashing. Doors and windows provide openings in walls. Masonry walls can be load bearing. Most curtain walls are not load bearing.

A

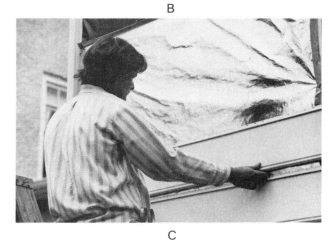

B

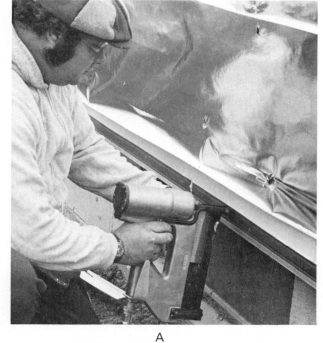

C

Fig. 22-53. Strip siding is attached from the bottom up. A—Starter strip is attached. B—The strips are kept level. C—Each piece hooks onto the last. (SENCO Products, Inc.; Masonite Corp.; Reynolds Metals Co.)

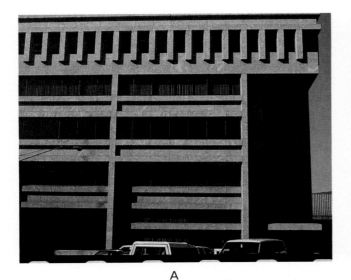

A

B

C

Fig. 22-54. These curtain walls are made from different types of panels. They are used to cover the frame. A—Indiana Limestone. B—Glass. C—Hardboard.

Fig. 22-55. Stucco is put on in three layers. This worker is applying the scratch coat. (Operative Plasterers and Cement Masons)

KEY WORDS

All the following words have been used in this chapter. Do you know their meaning?

Air-supported structures	Mass structure
Asphalt paving	One-ply roofing
Bearing wall structure	Paving train
Bitumen	Plaster stucco
Building felt	Plates
Built-up roof	Platform construction
Cast-in-place	Ply
Ceiling joists	Precast
Chairs	Racking strength
Composite panels	Rafters
Curtain walls	Reinforced concrete frames
Decking	Roof joists
Diagonal braces	Roof trusses
Doors	Roofing
Drip edge	Rough opening
Fabric structures	Sheathing
Flashing	Shingles
Flood coat	Square
Framed structure	Steel frames
Headers	Studs
Joist headers	Superstructure
Joists	Tag lines
Liquid roofing	Tensile structures
Load-bearing strength	Tilt-up bearing walls
Masonry	Windows
Masonry walls	Wood frames

TEST YOUR KNOWLEDGE

Place your answers on a separate sheet. Do not write in this text.

1. Masonry walls do not _____ very well.
2. When building a wood frame structure, insulation is put between the foundation and the _____.
3. Vertical wood members in a framed wall are called _____.
   A. studs
   B. joists
   C. headers
   D. plates
4. A ceiling joist is placed in the _____ position.
5. Roof sheathing is attached to the _____.
6. Steel is assembled by bolting or _____.
7. A _____ roof consists of several plies of building felt and bitumen with gravel on top.
8. A square of shingles will cover _____ square feet of roof.
9. Curtain walls support _____ weight.
10. Name one way to support fabric structures.

Matching questions: Match the definition in the left column with the correct term in the right column.

11. Top of a door frame.
12. Side of a door or window frame.
13. Surrounds the finish frame of a door or window.

   A. Jamb.
   B. Rough opening.
   C. Head.

Matching questions: Match the definition in the left column with the correct term in the right column.

14. Metal used to stop roof leaks.
15. Roof part to which roofing is attached.
16. Formed when two roof sections intersect.

   A. Decking.
   B. Flashing.
   C. Valley.

ACTIVITIES

1. Look in the basement or attic of your house. Find the parts of the frame. Name as many parts as you can.
2. Study your home. What kind of frame was used to build it?
3. What kind of structure was used in the stores you visit?
4. Make a model of a small section of a wall frame. Use balsa wood for studs.
5. Find out what kind of roofing your home has. If possible, look at it to see how it was installed.
6. Visit a building supply store. Find out what kind of roofing materials they sell. Get brochures on how to install them. Do the same with windows, doors, and siding.

Fig. 23-1. People and freight are moved with elevators.   (AMCO Elevators, Inc.)

Chapter 23

INSTALLING CONVEYANCE SYSTEMS

After reading this chapter, you will be able to:
☐ Discuss whether a stairway is put in before or after plumbing and climate control systems.
☐ State some rules for the design of safe stairways.
☐ Explain how two types of elevators work.
☐ Describe escalators, pneumatic tubes, dumbwaiters, and chutes.

Conveyance systems help to make structures useful. People and supplies are moved throughout buildings with conveyance equipment. See Fig. 23-1.

All structures over one-story high require upward and downward transportation. See Fig. 23-2. Stairways, elevators, escalators, and moving walkways carry people. Freight is moved with elevators, conveyors, and dumbwaiters. Papers and small items are moved through pneumatic tubes and chutes.

PEOPLE-MOVING EQUIPMENT

Many types of systems can be used to move people within or around a structure. In some cases, the system is used to move someone from one elevation (height) to another. Examples of this type of system include stairways and elevators. Other types of systems such as moving walkways allow a person to move from one point without changing elevations.

Stairways

The *stairway* is the basic way to move people around or into structures. Stairways always move people from one elevation to another. In some

structures, stairways take a direct route. In others, stairways either reverse direction or take a longer route. See Fig. 23-3.

A complete set of drawings includes stairway details. All stairway openings appear on floor plans. Fig. 23-4 is a drawing that shows the parts of a wood stairway. A carpenter or other tradesworker can figure out the unit rise and run

Fig. 23-2. These escalators carry an even flow of people. They do not have to wait.   (BIRDAIR, Inc.)

Fig. 23-3. Stairways are used in these projects. A—Spiral stairway mounted on a tank. B—Stairway has safety enclosure. C—Poles help support stairway and platform. D—Part of stairway using existing machinery housing as base. (Combustion Engineering; Texaco, Inc.; Universal Tank and Iron Works, Inc.; Stran Buildings)

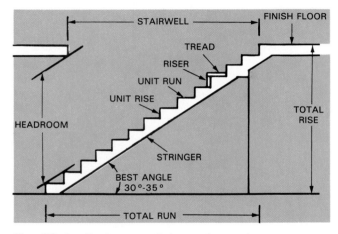

Fig. 23-4. Each part of the stairway has a name.

by knowing only the total run, total rise, and number of treads or risers.

Stairways are made in many shapes. Six shapes are shown in Fig. 23-5. The straight run stairway is the most common type. Handrails are required for all stairways.

Elevators

Elevators are machines that raise and lower people and freight in a structure. See Fig. 23-6. Elevators were invented when cities became crowded. Structures had to be built taller. Elevators were needed to build and occupy them. They bring material and workers to the workplace. After the

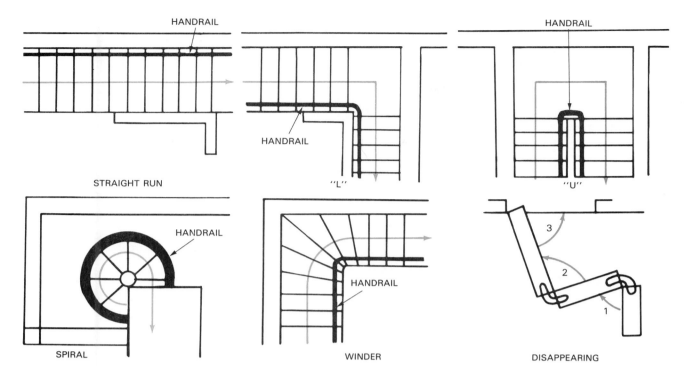

Fig. 23-5. These six stairway shapes are the most common.

STRAIGHT RUN "L" "U" SPIRAL WINDER DISAPPEARING

Fig. 23-6. Elevators move people and freight. Without them, tall buildings would be nearly worthless. (Dover Elevators)

structure is complete, elevators move people to the floors where they live and work. Today's elevators are both fast and safe.

Designing elevators

Architects/engineers (A/Es) decide on the number, size, speed, and kind of elevators that are needed for a structure. Building and safety codes state safety requirements. The A/Es have to design the system within those limitations.

Elevator service is planned to be convenient and save floor space. The number, speed, and size of elevators depends on how they are to be used. Four service plans are shown in Fig. 23-7. Plan A is for low buildings. All elevators stop at each floor. In Plan B, elevators stop only at certain floors. Plan C is for very tall buildings. Sky lobbies are used. The *sky lobby* is a transfer point where people change elevators. Shops are set up in the sky lobbies. Plan D uses double cars. The bottom car stops at odd-numbered floors. The top is for the even-numbered floors.

Uses and special-purpose elevators

Elevators in buildings move people and supplies. *Passenger elevators* get people to the floors with their homes or workplaces. Freight is hauled on *service elevators.* They are often larger than passenger elevators and move slower.

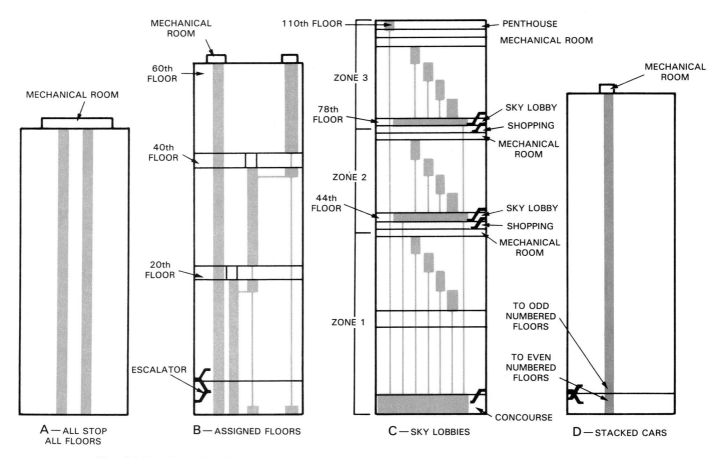

MECHANICAL ROOM

MECHANICAL ROOM

60th FLOOR

40th FLOOR

20th FLOOR

ESCALATOR

A—ALL STOP ALL FLOORS

B—ASSIGNED FLOORS

110th FLOOR

PENTHOUSE

MECHANICAL ROOM

ZONE 3

78th FLOOR

SKY LOBBY

SHOPPING

MECHANICAL ROOM

ZONE 2

44th FLOOR

SKY LOBBY

SHOPPING

MECHANICAL ROOM

ZONE 1

TO ODD NUMBERED FLOORS

TO EVEN NUMBERED FLOORS

CONCOURSE

C—SKY LOBBIES

MECHANICAL ROOM

D—STACKED CARS

Fig. 23-7. Plans for elevator service have been worked out to move people quickly.

Elevators are moved with mechanical and hydraulic power. See Fig. 23-8. *Mechanical elevators* use cables to move the car. They are used in high-rise buildings. *Hydraulic elevators* use high-pressure oil. They are quiet and smooth running.

Elevator operation

Until recent years, elevators were run by a person in the car. Modern elevators do not need operators. They are run by a *control system.* See Fig. 23-9. The control system "decides" who should be picked up first. The people are then taken to their floors. A *dispatcher* is on duty if anything goes wrong.

Installing elevators

Elevators and movable stairways are assembled and installed by persons or firms called *elevator constructors.* They also service and repair them. Careful testing is required. See Fig. 23-10.

Escalators

Escalators can move many people and keep them moving. People do not have to wait. Stoppage of

the traffic flow is reduced.

Escalators vary in width and in the speed they travel. They are set up in patterns. Fig. 23-11 shows two common patterns.

The escalator has a chain, steps, wheels, track, handrails, and drive unit. The *chain* has wheels that run in a *track. Steps* are attached to a wide chain that moves. *Handrails* move with the steps to make it safer to ride. The *drive unit* pulls the chain along.

Moving Walkways

Moving walkways are used in some airports. They move both people and luggage long distances. People step onto a moving belt and set their luggage beside them. A moving handrail helps people keep their balance.

MATERIAL-HANDLING EQUIPMENT

When constructing a building for a factory, an important part of the structure is a conveyance system. A *conveyance system* might include equip-

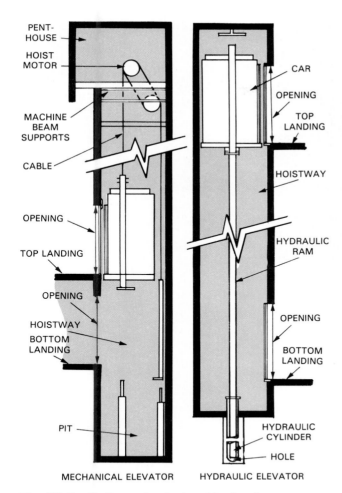

PENT-HOUSE
HOIST MOTOR
MACHINE BEAM SUPPORTS
CABLE
OPENING
TOP LANDING
OPENING
HOISTWAY
BOTTOM LANDING
PIT

CAR
OPENING
TOP LANDING
HOISTWAY
HYDRAULIC RAM
OPENING
BOTTOM LANDING
HYDRAULIC CYLINDER
HOLE

MECHANICAL ELEVATOR   HYDRAULIC ELEVATOR

Fig. 23-8. Both mechanical and hydraulic power are used for elevators. Left. Mechanical elevators have a penthouse. Right. A deep hole is dug for hydraulic elevators. (Westinghouse Elevator Co.)

ment for moving supplies or finished products. An assembly line is the most common arrangement for material handling. The line may or may not be manually monitored at multiple workstations. Fig. 23-12 shows material-handling systems that operate automatically. Parts for many conveying systems are standardized. The parts can be purchased from an equipment supplier.

Fig. 23-9. Elevator control systems can decide when to stop at a floor. Control panels use electronic circuits. (U.S. Elevator)

Fig. 23-10. Controls for elevators are installed by elevator installers. (U.S. Elevator)

SAFETY WITH CONVEYANCE SYSTEMS

1. Always wear the proper safety equipment on a work site. In most cases, a hardhat is required. For some tasks, eye and ear protection may be required.
2. Always follow approved OSHA (Occupational Safety and Health Administration) guidelines when working on a building site.
3. Be careful when working on scaffolding or ladders. In some cases, safety nets or lifelines may be required.
4. Use care when working with moving parts. Make sure the power to the equipment is turned off when working on systems such as moving walkways and escalators.

Fig. 23-11. Escalators are installed in several patterns. Separate, crisscross, or parallel patterns are most common. (Westinghouse Elevator Co.)

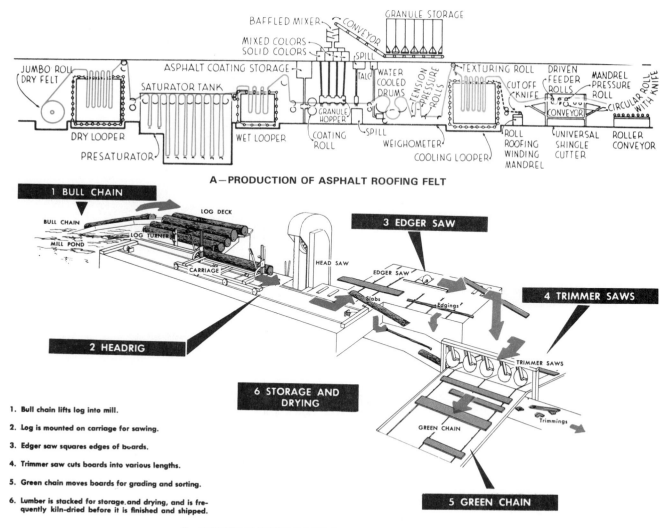

A—PRODUCTION OF ASPHALT ROOFING FELT

1. Bull chain lifts log into mill.

2. Log is mounted on carriage for sawing.

3. Edger saw squares edges of boards.

4. Trimmer saw cuts boards into various lengths.

5. Green chain moves boards for grading and sorting.

6. Lumber is stacked for storage and drying, and is frequently kiln-dried before it is finished and shipped.

B—LUMBER MANUFACTURE AT A TYPICAL SAWMILL

Fig. 23-12. Material-handling systems. A—System for making rolls of asphalt roofing felt. B—How lumber is produced at a saw mill. Very little help is needed from workers. (Asphalt Roofing Manufacturers Assn.; Forest Products Laboratory)

Conveyors

Conveyors carry paper, mail, and small items throughout a structure. See Fig. 23-13. They run horizontally and vertically. Conveyors reduce the work in delivering mail.

Most conveyors have chains running on sprocket wheels. Trays are fastened to the chains. Each tray has a sensing and controlling device on it. The device is set to push the tray off at the desired floor.

Dumbwaiter

A *dumbwaiter* is a small freight elevator. One is shown in Fig. 23-14. It is manually operated. A dumbwaiter can carry more weight than a conveyor, but it is not automatic.

Fig. 23-13. Conveyors save a lot of time and many trips. (Translogic Corp.)

Pneumatic Tubes

Pneumatic tubes are used to carry messages and lightweight pieces or parts. See Fig. 23-15. The message or part is placed in a bullet-shaped case. The case is put into the inlet of a tube. Moving air in the tube pushes the case to its destination.

Chutes

A *chute* is a round or square tube that runs between floors. When items are placed in the chute, gravity pulls them down. Chutes are used in apartment buildings to dispose of garbage. Some homes have clothes chutes for dropping dirty clothes from the upstairs to the basement.

Fig. 23-14. Dumbwaiters move freight in buildings. This one loads itself. Most can be manually operated from a panel. (Courion Industries, Inc.)

Fig. 23-15. Medicine is delivered quickly at this health care center. Air blows the cartridge through the tube. (Translogic Corp.)

SUMMARY

Efficient structures have conveyance systems that are easy to use. They move people and supplies. Stairways, elevators, conveyors, dumbwaiters, pneumatic tubes, and chutes are used. They are selected by architects and designed by engineers. The capacity, speed, and kind needed guide the engineer in designing the system. Elevator cars and hoist equipment are installed by elevator constructors.

KEY WORDS

All the following words have been used in this chapter. Do you know their meaning?

Chains	Mechanical elevators
Chutes	Moving walkways
Control system	Passenger elevator
Conveyance system	Pneumatic tubes
Conveyors	Riser
Dispatcher	Service elevator
Drive unit	Sky lobby
Dumbwaiters	Stairways
Elevators	Steps
Escalators	Stringer
Handrails	Track
Hydraulic elevators	Tread

TEST YOUR KNOWLEDGE

Place your answers on a separate sheet of paper. Please do not write in this text.

Matching questions: Match the definition in the left column with the correct term in the right column.

1. Describes the width and number of stairways to use in public buildings.
   A. Pneumatic tube.
   B. Tray.
2. Names of stairway types.
   C. Assembly line.
3. Can reach both the even- and odd-numbered floors.
   D. Stacked cars.
4. Common factory conveying arrangement.
   E. City code.
5. Holds small items for a chain drive conveyor.
   F. Winder, U, L, straight.
6. Message moves inside of this.
7. The most basic method used to move people in a structure is a _____.
8. List seven methods used to move people and things throughout a structure.
9. A system that uses moving trays and chains to move small items through a building is called a(n) _____.
10. A small, manually operated freight elevator is a(n) _____.

ACTIVITIES

1. Make a model of an elevator shaft out of balsa wood. Build the car and a pulley system. Make and adjust weights for the car and for a counterbalance.
2. What methods of conveyance are used in your school or your home? List and describe them.
3. Find out further details about escalators and moving walkways. How wide is the drive chain, and what metal is used for the chain, wheels, and steps? How much horsepower do most drive motors need?
4. As you enter places of business, look for ways people and things are moved.

Chapter 24

INSTALLING MECHANICAL/ELECTRICAL SYSTEMS

After reading this chapter, you will be able to:

☐ Discuss the climate control system in your home.

☐ Explain the purpose of thermostats and humidistats.

☐ Describe potable water systems, fire fighting systems, and waste water systems.

☐ Trace an electrical power circuit from the service transformer to a fixture.

☐ Describe three jobs when installing a mechanical/electrical system in a structure.

☐ Describe communication systems used in a structure.

☐ Discuss who installs mechanical and electrical systems.

The mechanical/electrical (M/E) systems make buildings livable. Climate control systems condition the air. Plumbing systems move liquids in, about, and out of a structure. Power to run other systems and to do work comes from the electrical power system. The communication system handles information.

Much of the M/E systems are placed in floors, walls, and ceilings. This work is called *roughing-in,* Fig. 24-1. Inside the structure, the bulky and rigid parts are roughed-in first. The most flexible materials are roughed-in last. Roughing-in starts with the ductwork for climate control systems and large plumbing pipes. The smaller water supply and

Fig. 24-1. Sewer lines and drains are placed before the concrete for the basement is placed. (Mary Robey)

drain lines are next. Finally, the electrical wire and communication cables are installed.

DESIGNING MECHANICAL/ ELECTRICAL SYSTEMS

M/E systems consist of appliances, fixtures, equipment, and service lines. *Appliances* consist of things such as dishwashers and computers. Appliances and fixtures are seen and used by the occupant, Fig. 24-2. Lights, registers, and toilets are considered to be *fixtures*. *Equipment* includes a water heater or furnace. Equipment is often hidden or placed in a mechanical room. Water and drain pipes, and electrical wires are *service lines.*

Architects choose the number, type, quality, and placement of fixtures and appliances. Engineers design the service lines and select equipment to serve the fixtures and appliances.

CLIMATE CONTROL SYSTEMS

Climate means the temperature, humidity, and purity of the air inside structures. Heating and cooling systems control the temperature. Other devices

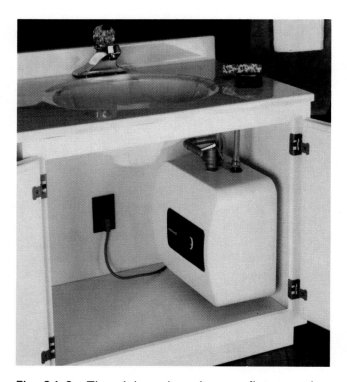

Fig. 24-2. The sink and vanity are fixtures; the tankless water heater in the vanity is equipment. The copper pipes are service lines. (Controlled Energy Corp.)

are used to control moisture in the air. Filters and electronic air cleaners remove dust from air.

Temperature Control

Many methods have been devised to maintain a comfortable temperature. All of them consist of the following parts:
- Energy source.
- Converter.
- Distribution system.
- Controls.

Energy sources
Fuels are materials that are burned to produce heat. In the past, wood and coal were used. Wood is still being used where it is easy to obtain. Coal is seldom used anymore to heat space.

Fuel oil is easy to burn and control. It requires a small storage space and is easy to move. Gas burns cleanly, requires no handling, and provides even heat. It is stored in tanks where it is used or is delivered to converters through buried pipes.

Electricity is easy to get and safe to use. It does not need to be moved or stored. Electricity needs to be generated (made) before it can be used. Hydroelectric (water) power is often used to generate electricity.

The sun gives off *solar energy.* It is free and will not run out. However, it is hard to collect, convert, and distribute.

Air and water have heat in them. Even when they are cold, heat can be removed and used.

Heating converters
Converters are used to change energy for use in heating or cooling. Fuel converters consist of a combustion chamber or burner and a heat exchanger. In the *combustion chamber,* air enters, the fuel burns, and fumes are exhausted (go out). See Fig. 24-3.

Coal and wood need a combustion chamber. Oil and gas need a *burner.* A burner is designed to mix the fuel and air.

A *heat exchanger* takes heat from the hot gases in the combustion chamber. Water or air is moved over the heat exchanger. Heat moves into the water or air.

New furnaces have efficient heat exchangers. See Fig. 24-4. They remove nearly twice as much heat as older furnaces remove.

Electric heaters use *heating elements* to convert energy. When electricity flows through an element, it gives off heat. Heat is removed by placing the

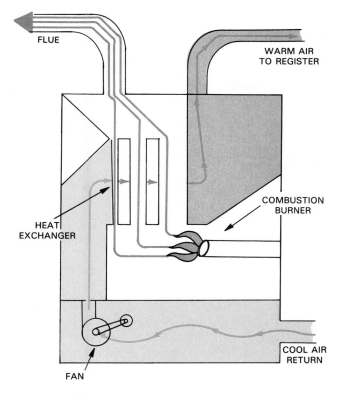

Fig. 24-3. Heat from combustion is transferred to the air that flows over the combustion chamber.

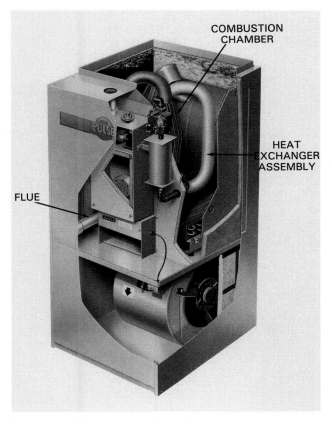

Fig. 24-4. A pulse furnace does not require a pilot light, burner, or chimney. The heat exchanger is very efficient. (Lennox Industries, Inc.)

elements in a liquid or by passing a liquid or air over them.

Solar collectors are used to convert sunlight into heat. See Fig. 24-5. A black surface is positioned toward the sun. The black surface is enclosed with glass. Most of the sunlight passes through the glass and hits the black surface. It is changed from light waves to heat waves. Heat waves do not pass through glass as easily as light waves. Therefore, the heat is trapped inside the collector. The heat can then be distributed to the structure.

Heat pumps can heat or cool a home. When it is hot inside, the heat pump works as an air conditioner. It removes heat from the inside. The machine works in reverse in cold weather. Heat from the outside air is removed and used to heat the inside.

Cooling converters

Air conditioners remove heat and water vapor from air. The heat is released outside the building. Water goes outside or into a drain.

Two separate currents of air move through an air conditioner. See Fig. 24-6. There is hot, humid air from the room. It passes across cold evaporator coils. Here it is cooled and dehumidified (water taken out). It is then blown back into the room. At the same time, air from the outside is blown over the hot condenser coils. The outside air cools the coils.

Coolers, Fig. 24-7, cool and moisten air in hot dry climates. A trickle of water keeps a loose material wet. A fan pulls outside air through the

Fig. 24-5. A solar collector converts sunlight into heat. The heat is used to warm water. (Reynolds Metals Co.)

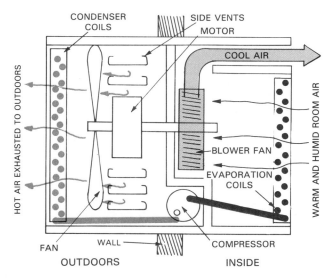

CONDENSER COILS — SIDE VENTS — MOTOR — COOL AIR — WARM AND HUMID ROOM AIR — HOT AIR EXHAUSTED TO OUTDOORS — BLOWER FAN — EVAPORATION COILS — FAN — WALL — COMPRESSOR — OUTDOORS — INSIDE

Fig. 24-6. Air conditioners cool air. A cool gas is warmed with inside air. A compressor puts it under pressure until it becomes a hot fluid. Outside air is blown over the pipes to cool the hot liquid. A valve lets it cool by evaporation again. Inside air is blown over the pipes that are cool. The cycle continues.

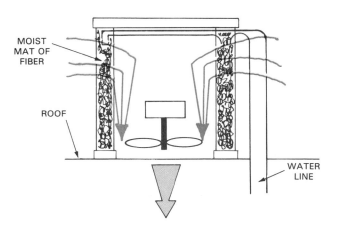

MOIST MAT OF FIBER — ROOF — WATER LINE

Fig. 24-7. Coolers cool and humidify air. Air is drawn through a moist mat.

wet mat. The air is cooled and moisture is added. The cool, moist air is distributed to the enclosed space.

Distribution systems

Distribution systems move heated or cooled air or water throughout a building. Heat can be moved in four ways. *Pipes* are used to move heated water. *Ducts* are used to convey heated air. Ducts are plastic or thin sheet metal tubes. Some electric heating systems use *wires.* Stoves and passive solar heating systems use *gravity.*

Pipe systems. Pipe systems consist of boilers and convectors or radiators. Converters that warm water or make steam have boilers. The *boiler* is used to store the hot water or steam. A pump is used to force the water through the pipes to a convector or radiator.

A convector or radiator is located in the room. A *convector* is warmed by the water or steam. Air begins to move past it. As the air moves by, it picks up heat. Some convectors have fans to help move the air. Chilled water can be pumped through convectors to cool a room.

A *radiator* gives direct radiation like the sun. Pipes placed in floors, walls, or ceilings also radiate heat.

After passing through the convector or radiator, the water is piped back to the boiler and is heated again. The pipes and boilers are covered with insulation to conserve heat. See Fig. 24-8.

Duct systems. Duct systems consist of a plenum, ducts, and registers. A *plenum* is a chamber that joins several ducts to an air inlet or outlet. See Fig. 24-9. The conditioned air enters the room through *registers.* The register spreads the air into the room.

Ducts are made of thin sheet metal, plastic, or fiber. They are round or rectangular in shape. Insulation keeps air cool or warm and lowers the noise of moving air. See Fig. 24-10.

Wire systems. *Electric radiant heat* is similar to radiant hot water heat. *Resistance wires* (instead of pipes) are embedded in walls, floors, or ceilings.

Fig. 24-8. Heat loss is reduced with insulation. Tape will hold the covering tight and in place. (CertainTeed Corp.)

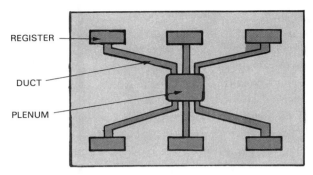

Fig. 24-9. A radial layout costs the least to install. Dampers are used to balance the system. Short lines are partly closed down. Long lines are left open.

Fig. 24-10. A fiberglass duct system is being installed. It reduces noise and heat loss. (CertainTeed Corp.)

Resistance wires get hot when electricity passes through them. They warm the surface, which radiates heat to people and objects in the room. Individual electric units can also be placed in each room.

This type of system does not require ducts or chimneys. There are no moving parts to wear out. Electric radiant heat is easy to install in new structures. However, it is somewhat costly to run. The structure should be well-insulated to conserve the heat.

Gravity. Heated air rises, cold air sinks. This is the rule that controls gravity systems. See Fig. 24-11. When wood is burned in a stove, the stove gets warm and heats the air around it. Warm air rises and cool air replaces it. Openings in the ceiling allow warm air to enter the upstairs rooms. Openings in the floor where air is the coolest will let the cold air drop. Gentle air currents start to flow.

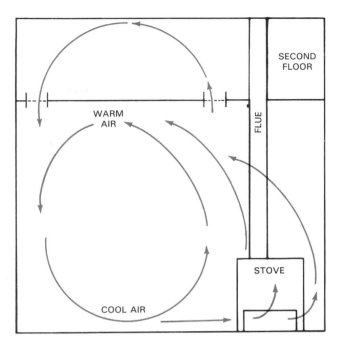

Fig. 24-11. Warm air rises; cool air sinks. The hot stove keeps the air moving.

Controlling temperature

Thermostats control temperatures. They can be designed to control the furnace, air conditioner, or a zone (part) of a building.

A timer-thermostat will automatically turn the heat up or down. New buildings have a system of *sensors* to detect small changes in temperature. When a temperature change is detected, a computer adjusts the temperature.

Changing humidity

Humidity is more correctly called relative humidity. *Relative humidity* is the amount of water vapor in the air. A relative humidity of 30-50 percent is preferred.

In the northern states, lower humidity is desired in the summer. This is called dehumidifying. Greater humidity may be wanted in the winter. The humidity can be raised by humidifying the air.

Dehumidifying. *Dehumidifiers* draw moist air over cool coils. See Fig. 24-12. Water condenses on the coils and runs off into a tray or into a drain. The drier air is returned to the room. In time, the relative humidity of the air is lowered. A *humidistat* can be used to control the system.

Humidifying air. When air gets too dry, we are uncomfortable. Sometimes our skin dries out and cracks. A *humidifier* adds moisture to the air.

Central humidifiers are a part of the furnace. Ductwork distributes the moist air throughout the

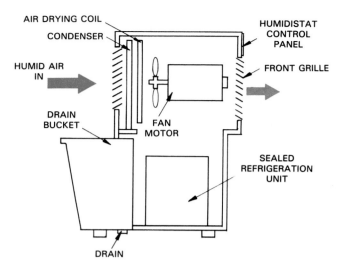

Fig. 24-12. Dehumidifiers remove moisture from the air. Cool coils condense the water in the air.

entire structure.

Ventilating. Air can become too moist, too warm, or polluted inside a structure. Fans are used to replace the moist hot or polluted air with drier, cooler, or cleaner air.

When air is exhausted in the winter, heat is lost. Cool air is lost from an air conditioned space if it is exhausted. This is wasteful. *Air exchangers* are used to save over 75 percent of the heat. Fig. 24-13 shows how they work.

Cleaning air

Dirt, pollen, and smoke pollute air. Machines can purify the air. Air filters and air cleaners can

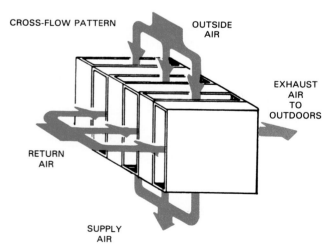

Fig. 24-13. An air exchanger saves heat when bringing in cold fresh air. The outside air runs in a cross-flow direction to the exhaust air. The outside air never mixes with the exhaust air. The cool air is heated by the warm air.
(Des Champs Laboratories, Inc.)

be used to remove the polluted air.

Air filters. *Air filters* remove a lot of dust in the air. Dirty air is pulled through a filter in the air distribution system. Some of the particles of dirt are trapped in the filter, which is replaced or cleaned when it is full.

Electronic air cleaners. *Electronic air cleaners* are used to remove pollen and smoke. Air is blown through the air cleaners. Electric charges throw the dirt against collection plates. The dirt sticks on the plates until it is washed off.

PLUMBING SYSTEMS

The pipes inside a structure are a part of the plumbing system. They transport liquids and gases into, throughout, and out of the structure. Plumbing is used to:
1. Provide fresh hot and cold water.
2. Remove waste water.
3. Transport water to fight fires.
4. Heat and cool buildings with steam and water.
5. Distribute gases to burn and to do work.
6. Provide fluids for industrial work.

Potable Water System

Potable (pronounced like "notable") *water* is pure enough to drink. In cities, water is made pure in a water treatment plant. Buried *water mains* transport the water throughout the city.

The water company taps into the water main and installs a *curb valve.* The curb valve diverts water from the main to the structure. A *water line* runs from the valve to the building. A *shutoff valve* and *water meter* are placed inside the building. There they will not freeze.

Cold water pipes are run directly to the fixtures. See Fig. 24-14. Hot water lines run parallel to cold water lines. They should be insulated for best results. Hot water lines are on the left of a fixture. Look again at Fig. 24-14. Water lines go to each fixture that uses hot or cold water. Not all fixtures use both hot and cold water. Can you find any in Fig. 24-14?

Waste Water System

There are two kinds of waste water in a community—runoff and sewage. *Runoff water* comes from rain and melting snow and goes into storm sewers. *Storm sewers* dump the runoff into disposal areas, such as streams.

Sewage water contains human and industrial waste. It goes into *sanitary sewers.* These sewers

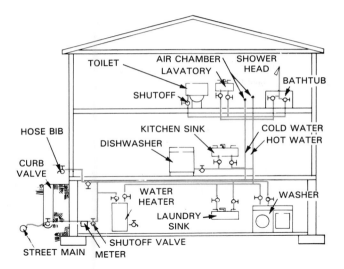

Fig. 24-14. The potable water system includes both cold and hot water lines. Trace each water line in this drawing.

take it to a waste water treatment plant or to private disposal systems (septic systems).

Drain systems in buildings have traps, lines, vents, and cleanouts. The assembly is called a *DWV (drain, waste, vent) system.* Its parts are shown in Fig. 24-15.

Toxic Waste System

Toxic wastes cannot be treated in water treatment plants. Toxic wastes cause health problems and perhaps death. Separate plumbing systems are used for toxic wastes. These systems move the wastes to a place where they are put into containers, permanently stored, burned, or processed so as to lose their toxicity.

Firefighting Systems

The firefighting systems are separate from the potable water system. The standpipe and sprinkler systems are the most common kinds. In Fig. 24-16, they are used together.

A *standpipe system* has a permanent source of water and hose connections. Each floor or section of the building is served. The permanent source of water may be a rooftop tank.

A *sprinkler system* is automatic. A sprinkler nozzle holds back the water. When the area gets hot enough, a plug in the nozzle melts and the water begins to flow. At the same time, a pump starts, providing water to the nozzle. The system sounds an alarm throughout the building and at the fire station.

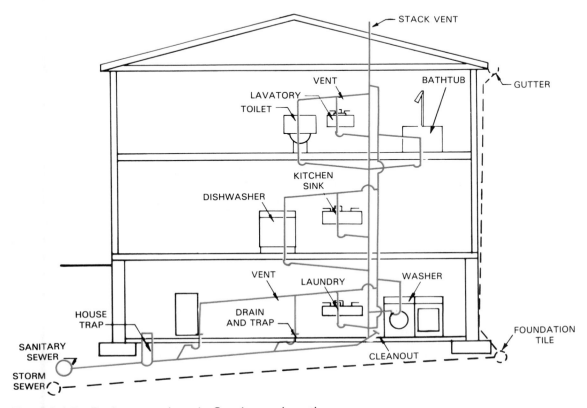

Fig. 24-15. Drains are sloped. Gravity makes the water flow. Parts include traps, vents, and cleanouts.

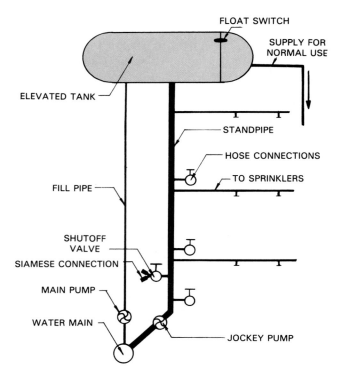

Fig. 24-16. A secure supply of water is needed in a firefighting system. Can you point out three ways that an extra supply of water is assured?

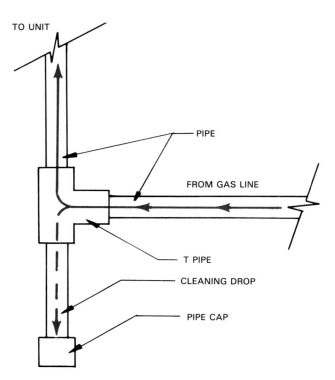

Fig. 24-17. Gravity causes dirt to fall into the cleaning drop. Dirt can clog burners if it is not removed.

Systems for Gases

Some plumbing systems transport gases. Natural gas is piped to furnaces, water heaters, clothes dryers, and kitchen stoves. Compressed air is used to run tools and inflate tires.

Gas lines have a cleaning drop, lines, and shutoffs. See Fig. 24-17. The lines are usually steel pipes.

Compressed air systems have more parts. See Fig. 24-18. There is a compressor, tank, lines, filter, regulator, gauges, and connectors. Air tools are attached to the connectors in the lines.

Systems for Process Fluids

Process fluids vary greatly. Cooling water, chemicals, and oils are process fluids. Special and separate systems are designed to move them. The system design is based on the liquid, volume, pressure, and temperature.

Installing Plumbing Systems

Plumbers cut pipe and tubing and join the pipe with fittings. The piping assemblies are attached to walls, floors, and ceilings. See Fig. 24-19. Most people do not see this work. It is covered when the inside wall coverings are installed.

Copper tubing systems

Copper tubing is used for water lines. Larger copper pipes are used for drain pipes. Copper does not corrode as badly as steel pipe.

Copper is easy to cut and join with *sweat joints*. See Fig. 24-20. The fittings slip over the ends of the pipe. Solder is used to seal the joint.

Copper tubing can also be joined by mechanical methods. The flare and compression joints are the most common methods. Look again at Fig. 24-20.

Plastic pipe systems

Plastic pipe is inexpensive (low cost). Some kinds of plastic pipe are stiff, while others you can bend. All plastic pipe can be used for cold water pipes. Only certain kinds are used with hot water. Larger sizes of plastic pipe work well for drains.

Each kind has its own fittings and method for joining. Some joints are similar to sweat joints. In plastic, they are called *cemented joints*. The pipe is cut to length and the burrs (rough edges) are removed. A cement is spread on the pipe to cover the outside end and the inside of the fitting. The pipe is then inserted into the fitting. In a short time the joint dries and becomes strong.

Mechanical joints are used with certain kinds of plastic pipe. Compression fittings are much like the copper fittings that were shown in Fig. 24-20.

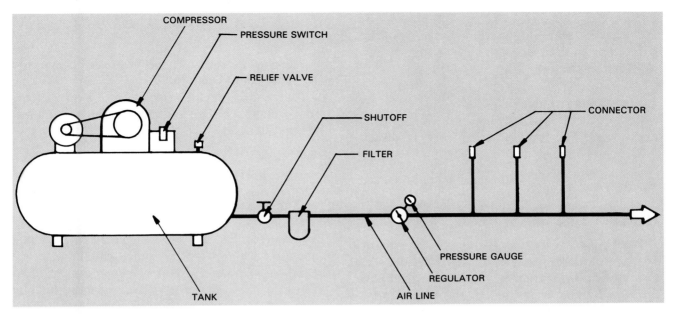

Fig. 24-18. Compressed air systems must be well sealed. High-pressure air can leak from a very small hole.

Fig. 24-19. Rough-in work will be covered after it is finished.

Steel pipe systems

Steel pipe is very strong. However, chemicals in water (and other fluids and gases) can corrode the pipes. Minerals in the fluids or gases often collect and make the inside of the pipe smaller.

Steel pipe less than 3 inches in diameter is joined with threaded fittings. They are bought as standard items already threaded.

Pipe threads are tapered. The more you tighten them the tighter they seal. Tiny gaps between the threads are sealed with a special plastic (Teflon®) tape and "pipe dope" (a thick liquid).

Large pipes are welded or held together with

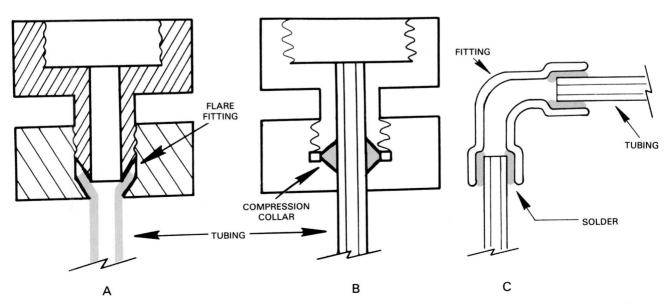

Fig. 24-20. Methods for joining copper tubing. A—Flare joint. B—Compression joint. C—Sweat joints.

flanges. See Fig. 24-21. Welded joints are hard to take apart. Gaskets are used to seal flange joints. A *gasket* is a soft, compressible material that is squeezed at the joint.

Cast iron pipe systems

Cast iron pipe is usually used for sanitary drains and sewers. The joint is sealed in three ways:
• Rubber gaskets.
• Oakum and lead.
• Sleeve and clamps.

Supporting Pipe Systems

Pipes must be securely fastened to a structure. *Hangers* support pipes that run horizontally. Metal and plastic *clamps* are used to secure vertical pipes. *Backing boards* are added to the framework to secure the ends of service lines.

Fig. 24-21. Flanges and welds are used to join these pipes. Flange joints can be taken apart. (AMOCO Corp.)

ELECTRICAL SYSTEMS

Electrical systems provide and distribute electricity throughout the structure. There are two kinds of electrical systems. One system is an electrical power supply system and the other is a communication system.

Electrical Power System

The *electrical power system* supplies the electrical energy that is required by a building. Electricity is used to run heating, cooling, and lighting equipment. It also powers the appliances and machines used by the people who live and work in buildings.

Electricity is made in a power-generating plant. Fig. 24-22 shows how electricity gets from a generating plant to a building. Outside the building is a service transformer. See Fig. 24-22. A *service transformer* lowers the voltage to that needed in the structure.

Power is carried from the service transformer to the structure through a *service cable.* The size of conductors (wires) in the service cable depends on the amount of power needed.

The service cable is wired to the meter base. This is where the meter is attached. A *meter* measures how much power is used. It is placed outside the structure where it is easy to read.

The power company installs the meter after the building's electrical wiring is installed. The work must pass inspection before the meter is installed.

A *service entrance* connects the meter with the *service panel.* Fig. 24-23 shows the service entrance. All wires are attached inside the service panel. This

SAFETY WHEN INSTALLING MECHANICAL SYSTEMS

1. Use care when working around heavy construction equipment such as backhoes. Since this equipment is large, it may not be able to stop or react quickly.
2. Always wear the proper safety equipment on a work site. In most cases, a hardhat is required. For some tasks, eye and ear protection may be required.
3. Always follow approved OSHA (Occupational Safety and Health Administration) guidelines when working on a building site.
4. Be careful when working on scaffolding or ladders. In some cases, safety nets or lifelines may be required.
5. Use care when working around fuels. Since these liquids and gases are explosive, they present a special hazard.
6. Many mechanical systems require electricity to work properly. Use only approved tools and methods when working with electricity to avoid the hazard of shock.
7. Some types of "pipe dope" have noxious fumes. Make sure that adequate ventilation is used when working with these supplies.

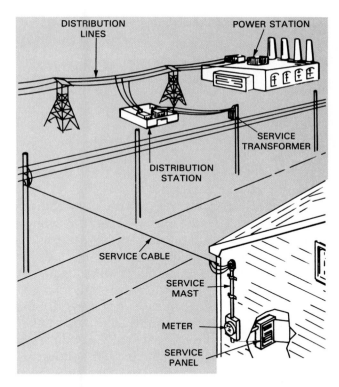

Fig. 24-22. Simple diagram of a total electric power system. Since electricity leaves a power plant at high voltage, the distribution station and small transformers reduce the voltage so it can be used in buildings.
(General Electric Co., Wiring Devices Dept.)

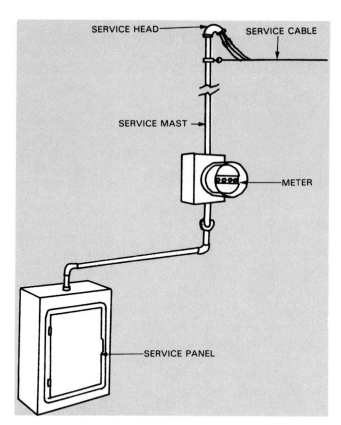

Fig. 24-23. The power company installs the service cable. They sometimes install the meter base. A subcontractor does the rest of the work.

box contains the **main breaker** that shuts off all power to the building.

A **branch circuit** is all of the wiring, electrical outlets, and lights controlled by one fuse or circuit breaker. If you look at Fig. 24-24, you can see three different branch circuits.

Some circuits, such as the one to the washing machine, supply electricity to only one appliance or outlet. Other circuits, such as the one going to the lights, have many things connected to them. This is done to balance the amount of electric current in each circuit.

A **circuit breaker** inside the service panel makes the final connection between the branch circuit and the electric power coming into the panel.

In industrial buildings, circuits used for lighting and machines are kept separate. Each large machine has its own circuit. Production lines often have very complex circuits. Fig. 24-25 shows a large control panel.

Installation Requirements

Many parts make up the power system inside a structure. They are circuit breakers and fuses, con-

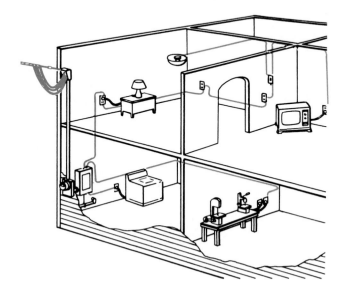

Fig. 24-24. How do you define a branch circuit? One branch circuit in the upper-left room supplies the table lamp, rear wall outlets, ceiling light, and ceiling light switch. A second branch circuit supplies the two workshop machines. Each branch circuit begins at a separate circuit breaker.
(General Electric Co., Wiring Devices Dept.)

Fig. 24-25. Complex controls play a big role in making glass. This console regulates the flow of special sand and other materials being put into a melting furnace. (Libbey-Owens-Ford Co.)

ductors, supports, junction boxes, receptacles, controls, and loads. Some knowledge of their operation is needed to make proper connections with the least amount of work.

Circuit breakers and fuses

Circuit breakers and fuses keep branch circuit conductors from overheating. Overheating can cause a fire. Circuit breakers work like switches. They allow a set amount of current to flow through them. When too much electricity flows, they turn the circuit off. Four circuit breakers are shown in Fig. 24-26. When enough load has been removed

from the circuit, the circuit breaker can be reset.

Fuses also turn a circuit off when too much electricity flows. In some fuses, a small strip of lead in the fuse melts to break the connection. Fuses generally need to be replaced rather than reset.

Conductors

Conductors carry electrical power. They come in the form of wires or cables. Copper conductors are used the most. A larger wire will carry more power than a thinner wire.

Wire and cable are covered with insulation. See Fig. 24-27. *Insulation* keeps wires and cables away from things they should not touch. Rubber and plastic are used to insulate wire.

A "live" wire has electricity flowing through it. If people touch live wires, they may get shocked. People get shocked when electricity flows through their bodies. Small shocks hurt; large ones can kill!

Many cables have more than one conductor in them. Most have two, three, or four conductors. The insulation is color coded to help an electrician keep track of the wires. Fig. 24-27 shows these cables.

Conductor supports

Conductors must be supported and protected. Cables in residential construction get support from framing members. Fig. 24-28 shows fastening hardware.

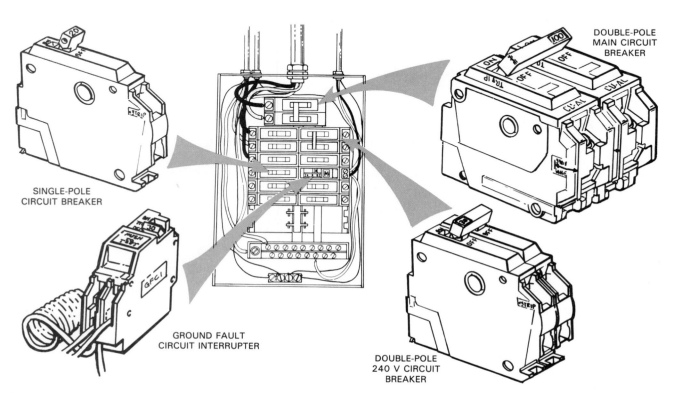

SINGLE-POLE CIRCUIT BREAKER

DOUBLE-POLE MAIN CIRCUIT BREAKER

GROUND FAULT CIRCUIT INTERRUPTER

DOUBLE-POLE 240 V CIRCUIT BREAKER

Fig. 24-26. The main circuit breaker and branch circuit breakers are in the service panel. The main breaker is at the top. Single-pole, double-pole, and ground fault circuit interrupter (GFCI) breakers are located at the center and below. (General Electric Co., Wiring Devices Dept.)

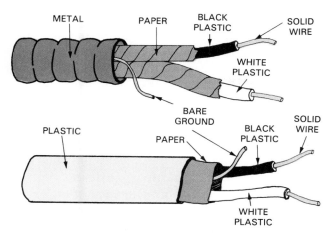

Fig. 24-27. Conductors are covered with insulation. The ground wire is left bare. Plastic and paper keep the conductors from touching, and hold them together in the cable.

Fig. 24-29. Conduit protects conductors. It also provides an organized construction path. (American Electric)

Fig. 24-28. Electrical conductors and conduit are secured to the structure's frame with these devices.

Fig. 24-30. Some floor decks have raceways placed in them. They save time. (American Electric)

Cables in public, commercial, and industrial structures require more protection and support. These circuits often use high voltage and receive a lot of vibration and wear. The wires are run through conduit and raceways. *Conduit* is metal or plastic tubes, Fig. 24-29.

Raceways are made of formed metal or plastic. They may be a part of the floor decking, and supply power to space above or below. See Fig. 24-30.

Junction boxes

Splices and connections between electrical conductors are made in *junction boxes.* A junction box

provides a safe place to make these connections. Fig. 24-31 shows common shapes and materials.

Receptacles

Receptacles are used to quickly disconnect and connect equipment to a circuit. Different kinds are used for different voltages, Fig. 24-32. The proper plug should be used with each type of receptacle.

Power controls

Switches are the simplest power controls. They open and close a circuit. *Dimmer switches* vary the

A

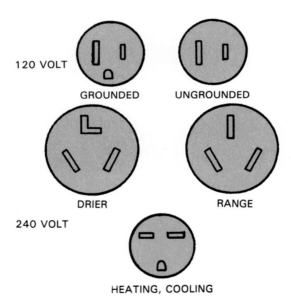

B

Fig. 24-31. Junction boxes vary in size, shape, materials, and design. Some can be ganged together. A—Metal units. B—Molded fiberglass units. (Allied Molded Products)

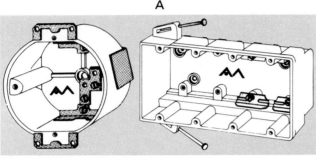

Fig. 24-32. The slot placements for five common receptacles are shown. The first two are used with 120 volts. The last three are 240 volt receptacles.

voltage in a circuit. They also have a switch built into them.

A timer switch can be used to turn lights and appliances on and off when you are not home. This will make it appear that someone is home.

Loads

Lights, motors, heaters, and electronic equipment are *loads.* The number and size of loads determines the size of the service entrance. The load is measured in amperes (amps). Most home circuits can provide 15-20 amperes of current.

COMMUNICATION SYSTEMS

Homes, schools, and office buildings must have a system for communicating. Different types of equipment are used to inform each other and to extend our senses and our control over events.

Kinds of Systems

The equipment may be simple or complex. Doorbells are an example of a simple communication system. Some apartments and houses have an intercom and electric door locks, Fig. 24-33. Signs are used to give directions and warnings. Telephone, television, and computer networks help us communicate with the world and process information. There are also monitoring and communication exchange systems.

Monitoring systems

Monitoring systems watch a place, a machine, or a process. Television monitoring systems are set up to watch places both inside and outside. One person can watch an entire plant with a television monitoring system, as shown in Fig. 24-34.

The performance of machines in some factories is communicated to control rooms. Sensors on the machine detect how the machine is working. The information is sent to a control room. A person

Fig. 24-33. An intercom system makes an apartment safer. This system uses one loudspeaker for both a microphone and a sound producer. (NuTone)

who gets the information decides what to do. Fig. 24-35 shows a control room at a power plant.

Sensors can also monitor a process. The quality of water is checked with instruments at a water treatment plant. Water quality is recorded on charts.

Exchange systems

Exchange systems involve people or equipment giving and getting information. Telephones, television, intercom, and computer systems are types of exchange systems.

Fig. 24-35. The operation of the entire power plant is monitored and controlled from this room. The men are using a computer. It retrieves (gathers) information and helps make decisions.
(Southern California Edison Co.)

Fig. 24-34. Television cameras are electronic eyes. They watch and transmit what they see to a monitor. One person can watch an entire factory from one place.

Telephone systems. *Telephone* equipment can transmit a person's voice. We can talk with people thousands of miles away. With a telephone system, it is easy to talk to almost anyone in the world. A large complex system serves mobile users. It consists of telephones, radio links, and exchanges. See Fig. 24-36.

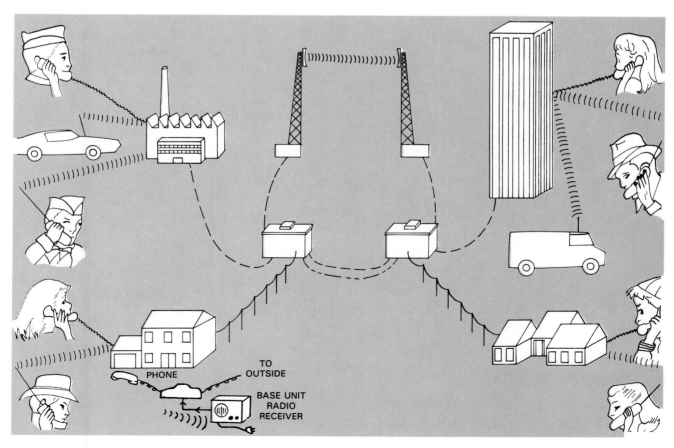

Fig. 24-36. Telephone service is provided by a company. They provide lines, process calls, and transmit messages. The users take care of everything in their own structures.

Television systems. Television systems transmit sound and pictures. Events can be watched from across the room or from the moon. Videotapes can be stored for later use. See Fig. 24-37.

A television system consists of a source for the message, a video recorder/player, cables and relay equipment, and a monitor, Fig. 24-38.

Computer systems. Information and records can be stored and retrieved with computers. We can learn, solve problems, and be entertained by information obtained with computers. Fig. 24-39 shows a person using a computer for drawing.

Computer systems are used to receive, process, and store information. They consist of a terminal, cables, central processing unit, and program.

A *terminal* is used to send and receive information. See Fig. 24-40. The information is changed into electrical impulses and sent to the central processing unit.

The *central processing unit (CPU)* processes the information. It may be located inside the terminal or be miles away. Several computers can be wired together. This is called a *computer network.*

Communication for distances less than 500 feet is carried on through a *cable.* The cable is installed between beams or studs or put in raceways. For longer distances, a telephone line can be used. A device called a *modulator/demodulator (MODEM)* is also needed to send and receive signals.

Fig. 24-37. People often have to teach themselves on the job. This man is using a computer to learn about a new company program. The computer program and booklet are sent to the dealership so that all salespeople can learn about the program. (General Motors)

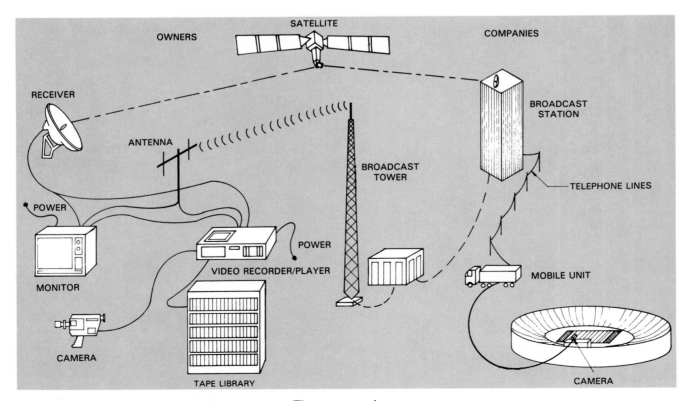

Fig. 24-38. The parts of a television system. They are nearly the same for all systems. They differ in size and quality.

Fig. 24-39. Computers can be used for making drawings. This person is learning to draw using a computer. The central processing unit (CPU) is a block away. It could be hundreds of miles away. (Dover Elevators)

Fig. 24-40. A terminal of a computer system is being used to design a piping layout. The layout is designed on the screen. A drawing is made by a plotter. (American Cast Iron Pipe Co.)

The fourth part of a computer is the *program.* The program provides instructions to the CPU; it tells the CPU what to do. Some programs are very simple to use. This is the type that you may use in your classroom. Others are complex, requiring the person who operates the computer to have special training.

Intercom system. Both the receiver and transmitter of an intercom system are owned and operated by the user. An intercom system is used for voice communications within a structure or complex. Large homes, apartment buildings, schools, and factories use intercoms. See Fig. 24-41.

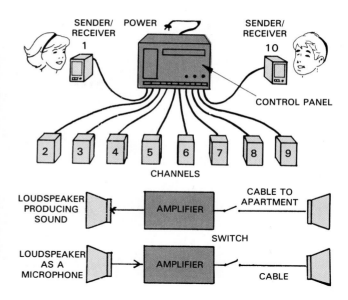

Fig. 24-41. An intercom system makes it easy to talk with people. It is used over a smaller area than telephones. Homes, schools, factories, and offices use the system.

An intercom system uses transmitters, cables, control units, and receivers. The transmitters and receivers are turned on and off manually. Many kinds of systems are available.

Signage system. Another way to give information is with signs. See Fig. 24-42. Signs can include printed or molded items or electrical and electronic displays. Large signs require braced wood posts or need metal channel trusses.

INSTALLING MECHANICAL/ ELECTRICAL SYSTEMS

M/E systems are installed by subcontractors. Workers are on the building site several times during the construction process. They run the service to the structure before the concrete for a basement floor is placed. They come again to rough-in ducts, pipes, or wires. They put them in the walls before the walls are finished. They return once more after the walls are enclosed to place and connect the fixtures, equipment, and appliances. See Fig. 24-43.

Communication systems are often installed by the firms that offer the service. Telephone service and television cable are two examples. Others are installed by the owner or contractors.

M/E systems are inspected by engineers and authorities. They make sure that the work was done right. See Fig. 24-44. The systems must be safe and work correctly.

A

B

C

Fig. 24-42. Signs are an easy way to provide information. A—Continually updated information. B—Traffic control. C—Give directions. (Electronics Display Systems; Richard Seymour)

SAFETY WHEN INSTALLING ELECTRICAL SYSTEMS

1. Use care when working around heavy construction equipment such as backhoes. Since this equipment is large, it may not be able to stop or react quickly.
2. Always wear the proper safety equipment on a work site. In most cases, a hardhat is required. For some tasks, eye and ear protection may be required.
3. Always follow approved OSHA (Occupational Safety and Health Administration) guidelines when working on a building site.
4. Be careful when working on scaffolding or ladders. In some cases, safety nets or lifelines may be required.
5. Use approved tools and methods when working with electricity.

Fig. 24-43. An electrician is connecting and installing the switches.
(Leviton Manufacturing Co., Inc.)

Fig. 24-44. Every system must be carefully checked. Complex piping systems have many places where leaks can occur.
(Standard Oil Co. of California)

SUMMARY

Engineers and architects design mechanical/electrical (M/E) systems. Subcontractors and suppliers install them. They run lines to the site, rough-in distribution lines, and install fixtures, equipment, and appliances.

Climate control systems provide clean air at the best temperature and relative humidity. Plumbing systems consist of pipes, equipment, appliances, and fixtures. Each plumbing system is kept separate.

Electricity is produced at a power-generating plant. A transmission system distributes the power. Subcontractors install the service entrance and rough-in branch circuits. Local electrical inspectors, engineers, and government people inspect electrical work.

Efficient structures have efficient communication systems. Communication systems move or process information. Signs, bells, intercoms, television, telephones, and computers are common methods of communicating messages.

KEY WORDS

All the following words have been used in this chapter. Do you know their meanings?

Air conditioners
Air exchangers
Air filters
Appliances
Backing boards
Boiler
Branch circuit
Burner
Cable
Cemented joints
Central processing
  unit (CPU)
Circuit breaker
Clamps
Climate
Combustion chamber
Computer network
Computer system
Conductors
Conduit
Controls
Convector
Converters
Coolers
Curb valve
Dehumidifiers
Dimmer switches
Distribution systems
Ducts
DWV system
Electric radiant heat
Electrical power
  systems
Electrical systems
Electronic air cleaners
Elements
Equipment
Exchange systems
Filters
Fixtures
Fuels
Fuses
Gasket
Gravity
Hangers
Heat exchanger
Heat pumps
Heating elements
Humidifier
Humidistat

Intercom
Insulation
Junction boxes
Loads
Main breaker
Meter
Modulator/demodula-
  tor (MODEM)
Monitoring systems
Pipes
Plenum
Potable water
Program
Raceways
Radiator
Receptacles
Registers
Relative humidity
Resistance wires
Roughing-in
Runoff water
Sanitary sewers
Sensors
Service cable
Service entrance
Service lines
Service panel
Service transformer
Sewage water
Shutoff valve
Solar collectors
Solar energy
Sprinkler system
Standpipe system
Storm sewers
Sweat joints
Switches
Telephone
Television monitor
Terminal
Thermostats
Toxic wastes
Traps
Water line
Water mains
Water meter
Wires

TEST YOUR KNOWLEDGE

Place your answers on a separate sheet of paper. Please do not write in this text.

1. List three ways you can change the climate inside a structure.
2. List five sources of energy. Give one advantage and one disadvantage of each.
3. A heat converter consists of a heat producer and a(n) _____.
4. Describe the four kinds of heating/cooling distribution systems.
5. Why would you ventilate a structure?
6. Circuits are made up of eight parts. List and describe the function of each.
7. List the kinds of communication systems. State the advantages of each.
8. A communication system set up to watch a place, machine, or process is referred to as a(n) _____ system.
9. Voice communications within a structure or complex are transmitted with a(n) _____ system.

ACTIVITIES

1. Talk with a custodian at school. Ask to see the mechanical room. Have him or her point out and explain the various pieces of plumbing equipment. How is the building heated, cooled, and ventilated? Is the air filtered? Ask about the energy source, converter, distribution system, and controls.
2. Do you or your neighbors have solar collectors on your house? Ask to look at the piping and control system. Make a sketch of the system showing each part and its locations.
3. Talk to installers of M/E systems and ask them about their work. Find out what the work is like, what tools are used, and what the working conditions are like.
4. Inspect the M/E systems in your house. Find the meters, shutoff valves, and equipment. Describe the pipes and wiring used.
5. Locate the circuit breakers or fuses. How many circuits does your home have? What is the ampere rating of each? Find out what is on each circuit.
6. Plan three branch circuits for lamps, portable kitchen appliances, and a clothes dryer (30 amp). Where will the wires go? Describe the kinds of cable to use. List all parts.
7. How are messages sent at school? Make a sketch of the system or systems used.

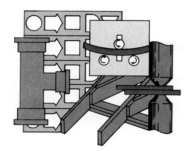

Chapter 25

ENCLOSING THE INTERIOR

After reading this chapter, you will be able to:
☐ List three ways heat is transferred.
☐ Describe how the R-value is affected by adding insulation.
☐ Explain how vapor barriers work.
☐ List four kinds of insulation.
☐ Explain the difference between bearing walls and partition walls.
☐ Describe the cross section of a joint on gypsum board.
☐ Discuss how to prepare masonry walls for coverings.
☐ Describe ceiling types.
☐ State the purpose of subflooring and underlayment.

Enclosing a structure involves insulating, and doing rough and finish work. Insulation and rough work is covered by the finish work. Insulating and rough work is described in this chapter. Finish work is discussed in Chapter 26.

The architect works very closely with the owner. They decide on the kind and amount of insulation and materials. General contractors see that the work is done. Much of the work is done by subcontractors. See Fig. 25-1.

INSULATING STRUCTURES

Well-insulated structures are quieter, cheaper to operate, and safer. They are quieter because they let in less noise from the outside. Inside noise is also controlled. They are cheaper to operate because heating and cooling bills are lower. Less heat is lost in the winter and less heat gets in during the summer. Filling the spaces in the walls makes them safer because they do not burn as well.

Fig. 25-1. There is a lot of finish work on most projects for carpenters. The contractor hires them.

How Sound Travels

Sound is energy waves. They travel in air and in all directions from the source. When the energy waves hit walls, floors, or ceilings, some of the energy is reflected. The rest is absorbed. Reflected sound can be heard as an echo. Absorbed sound goes through a barrier. It is heard on the other side. See Fig. 25-2.

Acoustical engineers are concerned with reverberation characteristics (echoes) and sound transmission. *Reverberation characteristics* relate to how long it takes for sound to be muffled in a room. Carpets, furniture, and people in a room

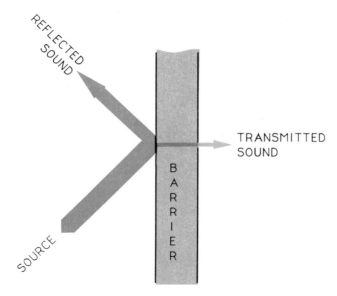

Fig. 25-2. Some sound is reflected back into the room and some is absorbed by the barrier.

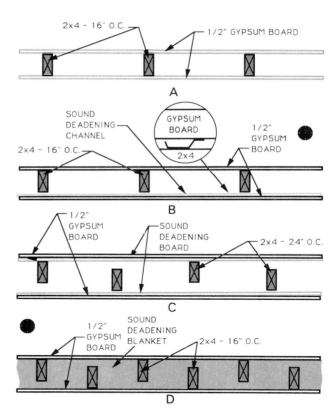

Fig. 25-3. Methods of decreasing sound transmission. A—Increasing the mass. B—Using a sound-deadening channel. C—Using staggered stud construction and sound-deadening board. D—Using staggered stud construction and sound-deadening blanket. Any combination of these techniques also reduces sound transmission.

reduce reverberation. However, muffling sound in a room does not reduce sound transmission.

Sound transmission occurs when sound moves through a barrier. Sound transmission is reduced by increasing the barrier's *mass*. Masonry walls and more than one layer of gypsum board increase mass. *Staggered stud construction* separates the moving surfaces. *Sound-deadening materials* cushion them. Fig. 25-3 shows four ways to reduce sound transmission.

How Heat Moves

Heat moves from warm matter to cool matter. It does it in three ways. See Fig. 25-4. They are:
• Conduction.
• Convection.
• Radiation.
When a fire burns in a stove, the outside gets hot. *Conduction* transfers the heat from the inside through the metal. Heat is conducted to your finger when you touch the stove.

Heat is conducted to the air around the stove. As it gets warmer, air begins to rise. Cooler air comes in to fill the space. The cooler air is warmed and rises, too. *Convection* currents have started. In this method, the heat is transferred by moving air.

Heat is also transferred through space by waves called *radiation.* That is how we get heat from the sun. Heat rays also radiate from the stove. When the waves hit our hands, they feel warm. Radiation only heats the objects it strikes.

Good heat transfer is desired at some times. At

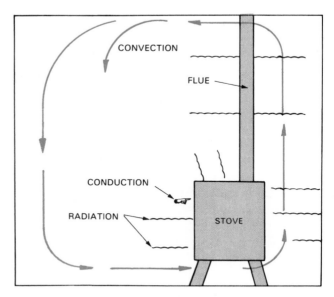

Fig. 25-4. Heat is transferred by conduction, convection, and radiation.

other times, we want to stop heat transfer. We want good heat transfer through the sides of the stove. We want poor heat transfer through outside walls of our house.

Some materials insulate better than others. This ability is called *resistivity*. Resistivity is measured as an R-value. It tells how well a material resists heat movement through it. The higher the R-value, the better it insulates. See Fig. 25-5.

What Insulation Is

Materials that trap air are used to reduce conduction. These materials are called *insulation*. See Fig. 25-6. Solid glass is a poor insulator. When glass is spun into fine fibers it becomes fiberglass. Fiberglass is mostly air, and is a good insulator. Wood fiber, cork, and foam plastic also have a lot of air in them. They are all good insulators against conducted heat.

Convected heat is lost through air currents. Either unwanted air gets into or heated air gets out of the structure. The first case is called *infiltration*.

Infiltration is slowed by sealing cracks. They can be found around doors, windows, and the foundation. *Weatherstripping* is used around doors and windows to stop air flow. *Caulking* is used to close other cracks in the structure. Storm windows and magnetic seals on doors seal buildings even tighter.

The entire outside of the structure may be wrapped, Fig. 25-7. An airtight plastic fiber sheet is used. This sheet lets moisture through while retaining the heat. The inside of a structure gets a

A

B

Fig. 25-6. Glass is spun into small fibers. The fluffy material traps and holds air. A—Heat will not pass through it easily. B— Acoustical batts and sound-deadening channels reduce sound transfer. (Owens-Corning Fiberglas Corp.)

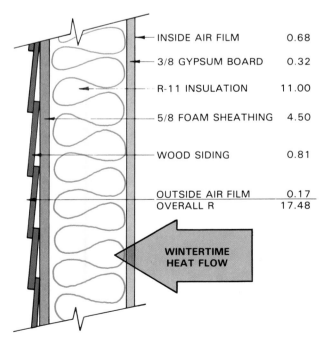

INSIDE AIR FILM	0.68
3/8 GYPSUM BOARD	0.32
R-11 INSULATION	11.00
5/8 FOAM SHEATHING	4.50
WOOD SIDING	0.81
OUTSIDE AIR FILM	0.17
OVERALL R	17.48

WINTERTIME HEAT FLOW

Fig. 25-5. The overall R-value is found by adding up the R-value of each layer in the wall.

Fig. 25-7. Air infiltration is reduced by wrapping the building with a plastic fiber sheet. Air cannot get through; moisture can.

similar covering. It does not let moisture into the insulation. In new construction, walls, ceilings, and floors are covered before gypsum board or plaster is installed.

Although sealing and wrapping makes a structure airtight, it can become *too* airtight. Fresh air cannot get into very tight structures. The air inside can become polluted. If tight seals are required everywhere, air exchangers are used. They bring in fresh air, get rid of stale air, and save energy.

Types of Insulation

There are four main types of insulating materials:
- Rigid boards.
- Batts and blankets.
- Loose fill.
- Reflective.

All except reflective insulation work in the same way. They prevent convection currents inside walls. Air in the tiny pockets slows conducted heat transfer.

Rigid boards are made of plant materials or foam plastic. They are commonly attached to the outside of the foundation wall. *Batts and blankets* fill the cavities between framing members, Fig. 25-8. In some cases, a paper backing is applied to the insulation. *Loose fill* is poured from bags or blown in place, Fig. 25-9. Loose fill insulation is commonly used in attics or in walls or structures that already have been constructed.

Reflective insulation works on a different principle than the other types. It has foil surfaces that stop radiant heat waves. The shiny surface works like a mirror. The heat wave hits it and bounces back.

Fig. 25-9. Old newspapers, melted rock, and glass can be made into a fluffy material. The material is used as loose insulation in walls and attics. (CertainTeed Corp.)

Vapor Barriers

Air has *water vapor* in it. Water vapor moves in the same direction as heat. See Fig. 25-10. It travels from the warm side of a wall to the cool side. In the winter, moisture moves from the inside to the outside. As moisture passes through a wall it gets cooler. Fig. 25-11 shows what happens. When the air cools, the water vapor condenses (turns to liquid). The water makes the insulation wet. The wet insulation lets out too much heat. The water can also cause the frame members to rot and cause the paint to peel.

A *vapor barrier* stops the water vapor. A plastic sheet placed under the inside wall covering works well, Fig. 25-12. The vapor barrier must always be placed toward the warm side of the wall. Wall

A

B

Fig. 25-8. How batts/blankets are held in place. A—Unfaced fiberglass batts are cut slightly large so friction holds them in place. B—Blankets have a kraft-paper facing. Staples hold them in the walls. (CertainTeed Corp.)

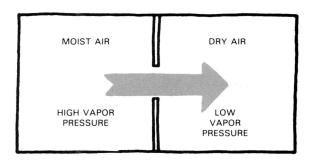

Fig. 25-10. Vapor pressure causes water to move to drier areas. (Manville Building Materials)

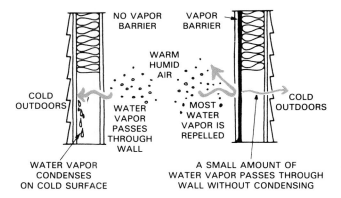

Fig. 25-11. A vapor barrier stops most of the moisture before it gets into the wall. (Manville Building Materials)

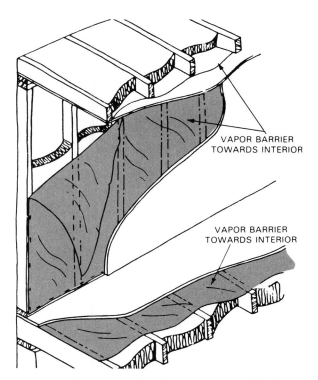

Fig. 25-12. Vapor barriers are placed facing the warm (inside) of the structure. (Manville Building Materials)

coverings or the insulation may be backed with foil. The foil will hold back the water vapor, too.

There are also vapor barriers that are applied as paint. It is applied with brushes, rollers, or sprayers. The paint is used when an old house is being insulated. After insulation is blown into an existing wall, the inside of the wall is painted. The plastic sheet vapor barrier is not used.

There are also paints that keep out standing water and block water vapor, Fig. 25-13. They are used on concrete block foundation walls.

What to Insulate

All exterior (outside) walls, ceilings, and floors should be insulated. See Fig. 25-14. Sometimes

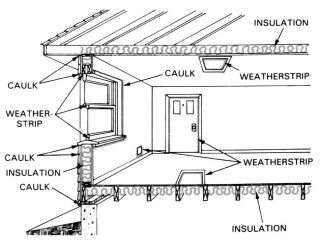

Fig. 25-13. This paint prevents water vapor from getting into the basement. Water vapor cannot get out either. (DRYLOK, Division of UGL)

Fig. 25-14. All outside walls, floors, and ceilings should be insulated.

pipes and junction boxes are located on outside walls. Insulation should be placed between the pipes or boxes and the sheathing as in Fig. 25-15. Pipes carrying hot or chilled liquids are insulated, Fig. 25-16.

Installing Insulation

Insulation must be installed properly, otherwise it may make you sick or cause itching. Proper work

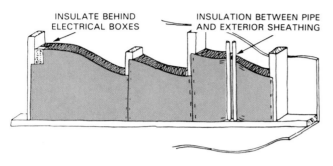

Fig. 25-15. Insulation behind junction boxes reduces drafts. Pipes will not freeze when insulation is between the pipes and the sheathing. (Manville Building Materials)

Fig. 25-16. Specially formed fiberglass tubes are used to cover straight and curved pipes. (CertainTeed Corp.)

clothes can prevent most problems. Fig. 25-17 includes clothing ideas when working with insulation. Wear a long-sleeve shirt and gloves. They keep the insulation off your skin. Goggles and a respirator keep it out of your nose and mouth. Loose-fitting clothes make it easier to work. Tight clothes will rub the insulation into your skin.

Shower with soap and water after working with insulation. Wash work clothes separately from other clothes. Then, rinse the washer before you use it again.

Placing loose insulation

Loose insulation is put in place by pouring and blowing. The material comes in tightly packed bags. See Fig. 25-18. It can be poured into spaces between walls and into attics. Some materials like loose plastic beads and vermiculite insulation are mixed with concrete. It is poured on roof decks to insulate ceilings.

Special blowers are used to fluff and place loose insulation in walls and attics. See Fig. 25-19. Always remember to wear proper clothing when working with insulation.

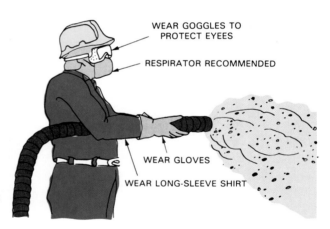

Fig. 25-17. Workers must be careful when they work with insulation.

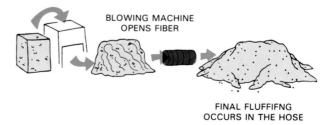

Fig. 25-18. Loose insulation is compressed into bags. A machine fluffs it up. (Manville Building Materials)

Fig. 25-19. Loose insulation is often used in attics. A blower on a truck moves the insulation through the hose to the attic. (CertainTeed Corp.)

Placing blanket and batt insulation

Blankets and batts are designed to fill the voids between framing members. You can buy standard widths for framing spaced on 16 and 24 inch centers. Blankets have a paper backing. Rolls are up to 24 feet long. The paper edge is stapled to the framing. Batts are 4-8 feet long, and are held in place by friction between the frame and batts.

Special methods are sometimes needed to hold insulation placed in ceilings or under floors. An example is a crawl space, where the vapor barrier must be up toward the heated space. The paper edges are not available for easy stapling. Many forms of wire fasteners can be used to hold the insulation in place. See Fig. 25-20.

A knife works well for cutting blanket or batt insulation, Fig. 25-21. A knife with a serrated (saw-like) edge is best. A hammer, stapler, measuring tape, straightedge, and ladder make the installation easy.

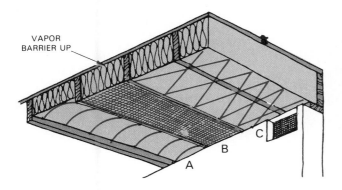

Fig. 25-20. Insulation in floors has to be held in place. A—Special fasteners. B—Wire mesh. C—Wire lacing.

VAPOR BARRIER UP

Fig. 25-21. Measure carefully when cutting blanket/batt insulation so they will fit tightly. (Owens-Corning Fiberglas Corp.)

Placing rigid insulation

Rigid insulation is nailed or glued in place. It is nailed to the outside of the framing as sheathing. See Fig. 25-22. An air space should be left between foil-faced boards and the siding. The air space will reduce conduction.

Foam plastic boards resist water. They are used to insulate foundations and concrete floors, Fig. 25-23. Glue or friction holds them in place.

Fig. 25-22. Foam plastic sheathing is a good insulator. This foam has foil faces. (SENCO Products, Inc.)

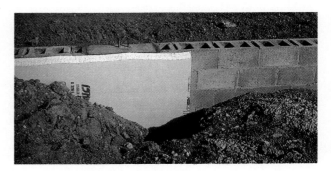

Fig. 25-23. Foam plastic board is used to insulate the foundation of buildings.

1. Use care when working around heavy construction equipment. Since this equipment is large, it may not be able to stop quickly.
2. Always wear the proper safety equipment on a work site. In most cases, a hardhat is required. For some tasks, eye and ear protection may be required.
3. Wear a respirator when installing insulation to avoid breathing fibers. Also be sure to wear gloves, goggles, and a long-sleeve shirt and long pants when installing insulation.
4. Always follow approved OSHA (Occupational Safety and Health Administration) guidelines when working on a building site.
5. Be careful when working on scaffolding or ladders.
6. Nails and other fasteners have sharp points, and should be used carefully.

FINISHING
INTERIOR SURFACES

Ceiling, wall, and floor coverings hide the framing, pipes, ducts, wires, and insulation. Gypsum board, plaster, tile, and paneling are commonly used for the coverings. Homes and schools need to be completely finished inside. See Fig. 25-24. The inside of some factories are left open, Fig. 25-25.

Enclosing Walls

Outside walls enclose the space within a structure. Inside walls divide the space. *Bearing walls* are inside walls that help support the structure. *Partition walls* only divide space. The inside of exterior walls and both sides of partition walls are usually covered. Exterior (outside) wall coverings were discussed in Chapter 22.

A

Fig. 25-24. The ceiling covers pipes, ducts, wires, and framing. The California redwood walls cover pipes and wires. The floor is soft, reduces noise, and improves the appearance.
(California Redwood Assn.)

B

Fig. 25-25. A—The framing, conduit, and pipes are left exposed in some factories. B—In refineries, little equipment is enclosed.
(Translogic Corp.; EXXON Corp.)

Plaster walls

Plaster walls are used to cover wall frames. *Plaster* is a mixture of sand, lime, and water. Walls to be plastered are first covered with metal or gypsum lath. Wood lath were once used, but have been replaced mainly by metal lath. *Metal lath* has many holes in it. When the first coat of plaster is applied, part of it is pushed through the holes. When it hardens it holds tightly. This coat is called the *scratch coat.* Gypsum lath replaces the scratch coat when it is used as a plaster base.

A second coat is called the *brown coat.* It builds up the thickness and levels out the first coat. The *finish coat,* Fig. 25-26, is applied last. This coat leaves a smooth, even surface.

Wallboard walls

Today, *gypsum board* (drywall) is used more than plastering. It comes in 4 foot wide sheets. They are strong and smooth, and can be installed fast. See Fig. 25-27. Gypsum board is fastened with nails, screws, or mastic. *Mastic* is a thick glue.

Fig. 25-26. These workers are putting on the finish coat that is smooth and even. Note that one worker is using stilts. (National Plastering Industry's Joint Apprenticeship Trust Fund)

Fig. 25-27. Gypsum board goes up fast and is low cost. Edges are tapered to allow for buildup of joint compound. (Owens-Corning Fiberglas Corp.)

When nails or screws are used, a small "dimple" (dent) should be left so that joint compound will stick to them.

Joints and screw or nail dimples are covered. *Joint compound* and *paper tape* are added to the joints, Fig. 25-28. This is called the *embedding coat.* Only joint compound is applied to the dimples. After the compound dries, the joints and nail dents are sanded or damp sponged. This smooths the joint compound. Another wider layer of compound is applied. This is called the *finishing coat.* In some cases, a *final coat* is applied. It is wider than the embedding coat. The wall is now ready to paint.

Concrete board resists water. This material is a sheet of concrete 1/2 inch thick. It is reinforced

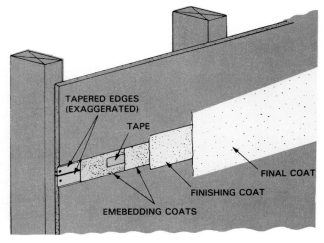

Fig. 25-28. Taping joints makes them stronger and look better. It keeps them from cracking. Allow the joint compound to dry and sand it after each step.

with a fiberglass mesh on both sides to make it strong. Concrete board or water-resistant gypsum board is used in damp places such as shower stalls and locker rooms. Ceramic tile or plastic coverings must be used.

Masonry walls

On masonry walls, furring strips are installed before applying gypsum board or other wall material. *Furring strips* are narrow pieces of wood. They are fastened with masonry nails, which are made of hardened steel. The nails can be driven into concrete. Insulation can be placed between the furring strips. See Fig. 25-29.

Enclosing Ceilings

Ceilings are the overhead surfaces in rooms. Some ceilings are the underside of the roof. Other ceilings have their own framing well below the roof structure.

Plaster and gypsum board ceilings

Plaster and gypsum board ceilings are installed before the walls are covered. The same skills, materials, and methods are used for ceilings as are used for walls.

Ceiling tiles

Ceiling tiles are small pieces of ceiling material. They are usually 12 inch squares or 24 inch squares. Their thickness varies. Ceiling tile can be fastened with staples. Mastic can be used to bond them to a flat surface.

Furring strips for ceiling tiles are narrow, 3/4 inch thick boards. The strips are nailed to joists that are overhead. See Fig. 25-30. Furring strips are spaced to support the tiles. Staples attach the tile to the strips.

Suspended ceilings

Suspended ceilings lower the ceiling height. They may be used to cover parts of the M/E systems like pipes, electrical wiring, or heating ducts. Wire hangers are attached to the framing above. See Fig. 25-31. The grid (frame) system is fastened to the wires. Ceiling panels and sometimes lights are set into the grid system. Commercial systems may also include heat ducts. Fig. 25-32 shows one type of commercial application.

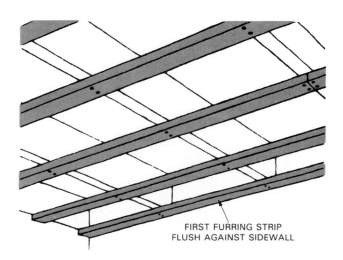

FIRST FURRING STRIP
FLUSH AGAINST SIDEWALL

Fig. 25-30. Furring strips are nailed to ceiling joists. Ceiling tiles are stapled to them. (Armstrong World Industries)

Fig. 25-29. Wood furring strips are fastened to concrete block walls. They provide space for insulation and a nailing surface for paneling or gypsum board. (CertainTeed Corp.)

Fig. 25-31. A laser beam is used to level this grid system. Ceiling panels and lights will be held up by the grid work. (Spectra-Physics)

314   Exploring Production

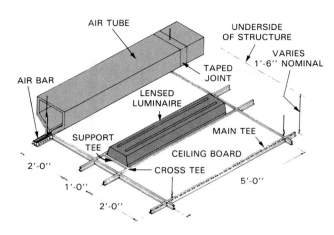

Fig. 25-32. Engineered ceiling systems have lights and air ducts in them.
(Owens-Corning Fiberglas Corp.)

Installing Floors

The floor is the last surface of a room to be finished. It receives two covers. One is called the subfloor. The other is the finish floor.

Subfloors

The subfloor frame structure is installed early in the construction of a building. A *subfloor* provides weight-bearing strength. It is used to store materials and as a work surface. In large structures and basements, the subfloor is made of concrete. In wood frame structures, it is plywood, lumber, or flakeboard. Fig. 25-33 shows a flakeboard subfloor.

Fig. 25-33. Flakeboard is a strong and smooth subfloor. Some products have tongue-and-grooved edges to hold the edges even.
(SENCO Products, Inc.)

A plywood subfloor is often covered with *underlayment.* See Fig. 25-34. Underlayment provides a smooth surface for floor coverings. Smoothed plywood, particleboard, and hardboard are common materials.

Concrete finish floors

Floor surfaces need to meet many demands. Factory floors must resist heavy traffic, oil, and other heavy use. Commercial floors must be good looking, easy to clean, and wear well.

Concrete floors are used in commercial and industrial buildings. Factory floors have heavy traffic. They may have a layer of special concrete placed over the concrete slab. Hard aggregate, short steel wires, or iron beads may be added to the concrete mix to provide extra strength.

Additional information regarding finish floors is discussed in Chapter 26.

Fig. 25-34. Underlayment is smoother than unsanded plywood. A thin flooring material will be laid over this underlayment. (MacMillan Bloedel Ltd.)

SUMMARY

Heat moves by conduction, convection, and radiation. Insulation is used to reduce heat loss, absorb sound, and retard burning. The types of insulation include rigid boards, loose fill, blankets/batts, and reflective. Vapor barriers keep moisture from condensing in the insulation.

Some walls and ceilings are not enclosed. Where people will see the work, skilled workers enclose the inside of structures. Ceilings are put up before walls are covered. The floors are done last. Plaster, gypsum board, and panels are used.

Floors consist of a subfloor and finished floor. Underlayment is often put over the subfloor. Floors with reinforced concrete surfaces are wear-resistant.

KEY WORDS

All the following words have been used in this chapter. Do you know their meaning?

Acoustical engineers
Batts/blankets
Bearing walls
Brown coat
Caulking
Ceiling tiles
Ceilings
Concrete board
Conduction
Convection
Embedding coat
Final coat
Finish coat
Finish floor
Finishing coat
Floor
Furring strips
Gypsum board
Infiltration
Insulation
Joint compound
Loose fill
Mass
Mastic

Metal lath
Paper tape
Partition wall
Plaster
Radiation
Reflective
Reflective insulation
Resistivity (R)
Reverberation
 characteristics
Rigid boards
Scratch coat
Sound
Sound transmission
Sound-deadening
 materials
Staggered stud
 construction
Subfloor
Suspended ceiling
Underlayment
Vapor barrier
Water vapor
Weatherstripping

TEST YOUR KNOWLEDGE

Place your answers on a separate sheet of paper. Please do not write in this text.

1. Which wall will let more heat pass through it — one with an R-value of R-19 or R-38?
2. How is heat being transferred when warmed air moves from a warm material to a cool material?
3. How do fluffy insulation materials reduce conduction?
4. How can you reduce infiltration?
5. Which one of the following is not a type of insulation?
   A. Loose fill.
   B. Thermoplastic.
   C. Blanket/batt.
   D. Reflective insulation.
   E. Rigid board.
6. Explain why you must have a vapor barrier in the outside wall of a heated structure.
7. How do you place loose insulation?
8. Where is blanket/batt insulation placed?
9. How is rigid insulation held in place?
10. Inside walls that help support the structure are called _____ walls.

11. When taping gypsum board joints, no fewer than _____ coats of joint compound are applied.
    A. two
    B. three
    C. four
    D. five
12. The three coatings of plaster are called the _____, _____, and _____ coats.
13. In many cases, plaster has been replaced with _____.
14. A moisture-resistant board called _____ is used to enclose walls of showers.
15. A wood subfloor is made smooth for thin floor coverings with _____.

ACTIVITIES

1. How can you insulate yourself from the heat in the following cases?
   A. Standing in the sun.
   B. Standing barefoot on asphalt in the sun.
   C. Being in the hot air stream of a hair drier.
   Try out some of your solutions.
2. Calculate the total R-value of the following layered structure:
   8 inches of fiberglass batt insulation
   1/2 inch gypsum board
   1/8 inch hardwood paneling
   The common R-values for these products are as follows:
   1 inch of fiberglass batt insulation — R = 3.13
   1 inch gypsum board — R = 1.00
   1 inch hardwood — R = 0.91
3. Test three concrete blocks for water leakage after using paints to seal two of the samples. First fill the core with mortar 1 inch thick to make a container out of the core hole. Then, use two types of paint on the outside of two blocks. Let them dry. Fill all three blocks with water to the top. Determine how long it takes for water to first bleed out and also to empty out. Make a chart of your results.
4. Find out how the floors in your home were made. Select a floor covering for a room of your choice. It can be a clubhouse, your bedroom, or another room in your house. What kind of subflooring do you need for the covering? How is it installed?
5. How would you enclose the walls in your garage or clubhouse? What tools would you need to buy to do it yourself?
6. List the steps to cover a wall in your garage with gypsum board. Describe ways to put up a ceiling in a room.

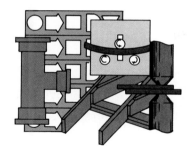

Chapter 26

FINISHING THE STRUCTURE

After reading this chapter, you will be able to:
☐ List the four finishing operations and state an example of each.
☐ State why trim is added to buildings and list some methods used.
☐ Describe paint types and painting methods.
☐ Discuss how walls and floors are decorated.
☐ Describe what is installed in a building and when the work is done.
☐ Compare rough-in work with finishing work on utilities.

Finish work in a house, on a highway, or at a plant is done last. Both the inside and the outside of a structure are finished. *Finish work* includes four jobs:
• Trimming.
• Painting.
• Decorating.
• Installing.
Trimming covers cracks and seals the structure from weather. *Painting* protects the structure from wear and weather. A surface may be covered with something other than paint. This is called *decorating. Installing* involves placing, connecting, and testing equipment, fixtures, and furniture.

WHY FINISH WORK IS DONE

Finish work is done for three reasons:
• Appearance.
• Protection.
• Usefulness.
Appearance is valuable in both an office building and factory. Finished projects are protected against

weather and use. They are not drafty, nor do they leak water. Finished structures last longer. Finish work is done to make the project more useful. Installed equipment makes the building easy to use. Fig. 26-1 shows examples of finish work.

WHO DOES FINISH WORK

Architects and interior designers select the materials, fixtures, equipment, and furniture. Architects design the outside. Interior designers select colors, materials, and finishes.
Interior designers have a background in art rather than construction. They use their skills to plan space. They combine colors, texture, and form within the space. They plan the insides of structures so they are more useful and attractive, Fig. 26-2. These professionals work closely with the owner. See Fig. 26-3. In some cases, homes are decorated by the owner.
Trimming may be done by the general contractor. Subcontractors often do the painting and decorating. They follow the working drawings. Equipment and furnishings may be installed by the suppliers.

METHODS USED IN FINISH WORK

Trimming closes up spaces in corners and around openings. Surfaces are covered and protected by painting. Coverings other than paint are used to decorate floors, walls, and ceilings. See Fig. 26-4. Installing equipment, fixtures, and furnishings occurs throughout construction.

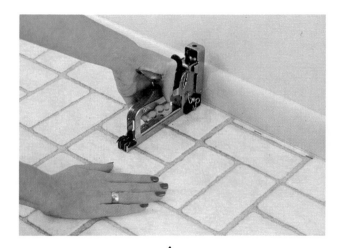

A

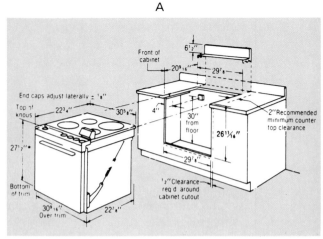

B

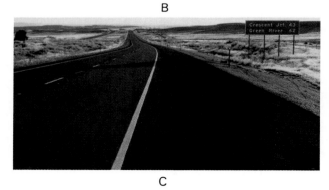

C

Fig. 26-1. Finish work takes place in all types of construction projects. A—Floor coverings beautify floors, are easy to clean, and protect the structure beneath. B—Installing may include building or placing the cabinets for appliances. C—Finishing shoulders, erecting signage and reflector posts, and painting strips are all finishing work done on highways. (Armstrong World Industries, Inc.; Frigidaire Corp.; Utah Department of Transportation)

Trimming a Structure

Spaces appear when wallcovering materials are not tight. Moldings and caulk are used to close up

Fig. 26-2. An interior decorator chose colors, textures, and forms. Painters, carpenters, carpet installers, and electricians finished the work. (Pella/Rolscreen)

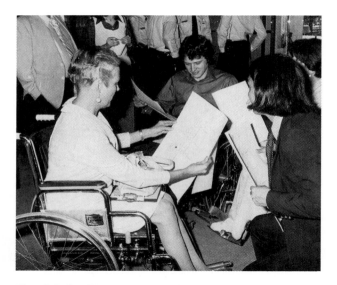

Fig. 26-3. The comfort of many people must be considered when designing the inside of a building. What conveniences might a person in a wheelchair require in a home? (President's Committee on Employment of the Handicapped)

spaces, Fig. 26-5. They add beauty to raw, unfinished edges. Moldings can "dress up" windows or doors and help attach them more solidly to framing. Trim work with moldings is done by skilled carpenters.

Moldings

Moldings and trim are used on the inside and outside. Outside spaces are covered to keep out weather, birds, and insects. See Fig. 26-6.

Moldings are made of wood, plastic, and metal.

Fig. 26-4. How many finishing processes were used to finish this office area? Can you list the jobs and put them in the order that they may have been done? (California Redwood Assn.)

Fig. 26-6. These trim boards conceal the rafters. The ventilator lets air circulate in attic but keeps out animals and insects.
(Owens-Corning Fiberglas Corp.)

Fig. 26-5. The wallcovering does not meet the carpet. The base molding is used to trim the joint. It also protects the wall covering. Cleaning machines will not scuff it.

Fig. 26-7. The dark molding was prefinished. That means it had the stain and coating on it when it was bought.
(Western Wood Moulding and Millwork Producers)

Moldings like the one shown in Fig. 26-7 are made of wood and plastic. You can buy them as raw wood or prefinished. Raw wood needs to be painted or finished. That job is done before it is cut and nailed in place.

Prefinished molding has a surface color or coating already on it. It only needs to be cut and nailed in place.

Special machines are used to cut exact angles on the ends. They make work easy and fast. See Fig. 26-8. Some types of molding, such as cove moldings, must be first cut to length with one machine and then trimmed by hand.

Metal, stone, and ceramic trim are also used. However, they are used more in commercial projects. Metal, stone, and ceramic trim do not require a finish. They are easier to clean and wear better than wood.

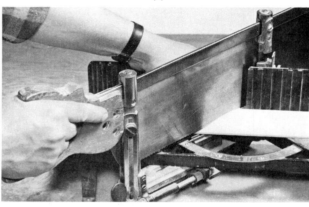

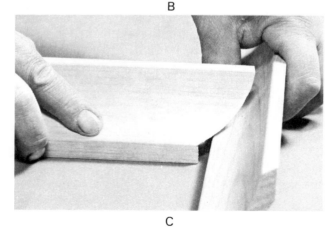

Fig. 26-8. Finish carpenters must be skilled. They use tools and machines to help them. A—Frame and trim saw. B—Miter saw used to make a 45 degree cut on a molding. C—Cove molding that has been cut with a coping saw, producing a coped joint. (Rockwell International Corp.; Western Wood Moulding and Millwork Producers)

Caulk

Caulk, (or caulking) is used inside and outside to keep water out. It helps to prevent rot, crumbling, and peeling paint. Caulk is used to seal cracks around doors, windows, and fixtures.

Caulk is clear or is available in several colors. Caulk comes in a tube with a nozzle. The end of the nozzle is clipped off and the tube is put into a device called a *gun,* Fig. 26-9. The worker uses the gun to squeeze out a bead of caulk. The nozzle forces it into the crack. Paintable silicone, latex, and oil-based caulk can be painted. The silicone and latex caulks cost more, but they last longer than oil-based caulk.

Silicone rubber is a good choice to seal cracks between tiles and fixtures. Some kinds are not used when it must be painted, because paint will not stick to them.

Painting a Structure

Inside, painting is often the first finish work to be done. It is faster to paint before the trim is attached and outlet covers are installed.

Paint is used for four reasons:
1. To make cleaning easier.
2. To protect the base material.
3. To add color.
4. To make space more pleasant.

Painted wood is easy to wash. A damp, soapy cloth can usually make the color bright again. Correctly painted steel is protected from rust.

The color of paint can add interest to a room. Paint also can create a mood. Light colors make a room seem happy and larger. Darker colors create a peaceful mood and make a room look smaller.

Fig. 26-9. Caulk is squeezed out of a tube with a gun. Both hand and air-powered guns are used.

Makeup of paint

All paint has three ingredients. They are the vehicle, pigment (color), and thinner. Special paints have more ingredients.

The *vehicle* is the coating material. Oil and latex are the most common. Usually, oil-base paint lasts longer. However, it costs more.

The color comes from the *pigment.* Paint comes in standard colors. There are also hundreds of colors that can be mixed at some stores.

Thinner controls the thickness of the vehicle and makes it easy to spread. When the thinner evaporates (leaves), paint is dry.

Paint has a *finish sheen*, or *luster.* It ranges from a flat (dull) finish to a gloss (shiny) finish. A semigloss is between these two types. *Flat paint* is used to reduce reflections. However, it is hard to clean. *Gloss paint* is easy to clean and wears better, but it has a glare. *Semigloss paint* has some of both qualities.

Stain, lacquer, and varnish

Stains add color to wood without covering the grain. *Lacquer* and *varnish* are applied over the stain. They preserve the stain and protect the wood. The surface is more durable and easier to clean.

Spreading paint

Paint is spread with brushes, rollers, and sprayers. *Brushes* are used on small areas. *Rollers* are used on larger ones. *Sprayers* are much faster than brushes or rollers. See Fig. 26-10.

When painters begin work, they prepare the surface. Dirt is removed. Cracks and holes are filled and rough spots are smoothed. A primer is used to seal gypsum board and other porous materials. See Fig. 26-11.

Masking tape, paper, and drop cloths are used to keep paint off floors, bushes, and windows. Preparation is the only way to get speed and quality in paint work.

Fig. 26-10. This machine makes sharp edges on the stripes. The worker does not need tape or template. (Kelly-Creswell Co., Inc.)

Decorating a Structure

Decoration can help make a house more beautiful. Walls can be decorated with wallcoverings, paneling, boards, and tile. Floors can also be decorated.

Wallcoverings

Wallcoverings come in rolls. Lengths of material are cut to fit the surface. A *paste* is used to hold

Fig. 26-11. The surface is sealed with primer. This saves paint during the final coat.   (UGL)

SAFETY WHEN FINISHING A STRUCTURE

1. Always wear the proper safety equipment on a work site. In most cases, a hardhat is required. For some tasks, eye and ear protection may be required.
2. Always follow approved OSHA (Occupational Safety and Health Administration) guidelines when working on a building site.
3. Be careful when working on scaffolding or ladders.
4. Paint or other liquid wallcovering materials may give off a noxious odor when being applied. Be sure that the area is ventilated.
5. Nails and other fasteners have sharp points, and should be used carefully.

it on the wall. Paste may already be applied to the wallcovering. If not, most paste can be brushed or rolled onto the backside of the covering. After putting paste onto the wallcovering, it is folded paste side-to-paste side, Fig. 26-12. This makes it easier to handle.

The covering is then placed on the wall. Care is taken to keep it straight up and down. Patterns are carefully matched at the edges.

Paneled walls cost more than gypsum board walls. Most *paneling* is made of thin sheets of hardboard or plywood. *Hardboard paneling* is made of processed wood fibers put into a mat and compressed under heat. Textured plates can put many patterns onto the panel. A vinyl (plastic) sheet with a pattern is put onto some paneling. The walls in Fig. 26-13 are covered with hardboard paneling.

Plywood is made up of thin layers of wood. The grain in each layer runs at right angles to the next layer. The layers are glued together to form a rigid panel. The panel is sanded and finished. Fig. 26-14 shows an example.

Paneling is easy to install with either nails or mastic. It is fastened directly to framing or furring strips. Thin paneling is sometimes applied over gypsum board.

Solid wood paneling is costly. The fewer defects the wood has, the more it costs. Nails and mastic are used to hold boards in place. See Fig. 26-15. A tongue-and-groove joint is used to keep the boards aligned.

Fig. 26-13. Hardboard paneling comes in many patterns. This one has a wood pattern.

Fig. 26-14. These plywood panels are called architectural plywood. The architect selected the veneer on the plywood. The panels were custom-made just for this room.
(Mutual Federal Savings Bank)

Fig. 26-12. Fold paper to touch paste side-to-paste side. Some papers must set at this stage for a few minutes before hanging.   (Glidden)

Ceramic and plastic *tile* is used in wet areas. See Fig. 26-16. Plastic tile costs less. Tile does not absorb water and will not rot. It is easy to clean. Tile can be set on moisture-resistant (MR) gypsum board or concrete board. The concrete board will last much longer.

Grout, a material like plaster, is used to fill cracks between the tiles. It can be made in colors to match or contrast with the tiles.

Fig. 26-15. Solid California redwood is a long-lasting wall covering. It adds warmth to a room. (California Redwood Assn.)

A

B

Fig. 26-17. Flooring materials. A—Carpeting. B—Ceramic tile for floors are made of clay. It is covered with powdered glass. When it is fired, the glass melts and bonds to the clay.
(Elliott Corp.; California Redwood Assn.)

Fig. 26-16. Ceramic tiles are used in showers and bathrooms. Tiles resist water, wear well, and are easy to clean. (Pella/Rolscreen)

Floor coverings

Floors are finished with ceramic or stone tile, resilient coverings, wood, carpet, or terrazo. See Fig. 26-17. Subcontractors do this type of work.

Ceramic tile floors wear well and look good. The tiles are set in a layer of mortar that holds them in place. Stone floors are laid in a similar way. Grout is used to fill the cracks between the pieces.

Resilient flooring is made of plastic and fibers. It comes in rolls or squares. Refer to Fig. 26-18. The material gives a little when you walk on it. It comes in many colors and patterns, is easy to clean, and wears well. See Fig. 26-19. It is held in place with an adhesive. Resilient flooring can be installed over concrete or wood, Fig. 26-20.

Wood flooring comes in strips, tiles, and blocks. Oak and maple are popular woods used for *strip flooring.* Note the strip type of wood flooring in

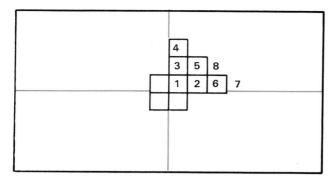

Fig. 26-18. Typical sequence for laying resilient floor tile. This is the pyramid pattern method.

A

B

Fig. 26-20. Resilient flooring can be put over wood, concrete, or existing smooth flooring. A—Mastic being used to fasten it down over wood. B—Adhesive is already on tiles. (MacMillan Bloedel, Ltd.; Armstrong World Industries, Inc.)

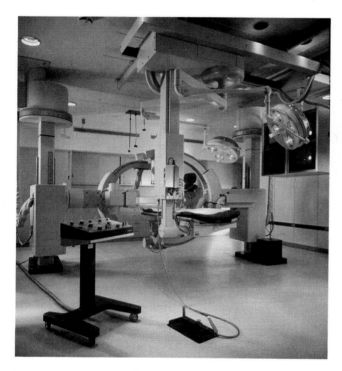

Fig. 26-19. A floor in a hospital must wear well and be easy to clean. This resilient floor is comfortable to stand on. It gives a little when you step on it. (Armstrong World Industries, Inc.)

Fig. 26-21. Wood tiles are made up of small pieces of wood. See Fig. 26-22. Wood blocks are short pieces of wood standing on end. The end grain is attractive and wears better than face or edge grains.

Wood flooring is installed over concrete and wood subfloors. Concrete must be waterproofed. Fig. 26-23 shows two methods.

Carpeting is placed over wood or concrete subfloors. Carpets often have pads under them. Pads are made of sponge rubber or plastic foam. A tack strip is placed around the edge of the room. See Fig. 26-24. The *tack strip* is made of a strip of plywood and short nails. Some tack strips are

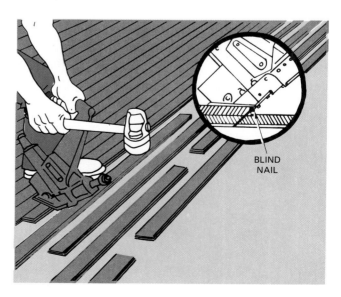

Fig. 26-21. Wood strip flooring is nailed down. A special tool makes it easy. The angled nail is called a blind nail, since it will not be seen. (National Oak Flooring Manufacturers Assn.)

Fig. 26-22. Wood tiles are laid one piece at a time. They are held in place with mastic. (Pease Flooring Co., Inc.)

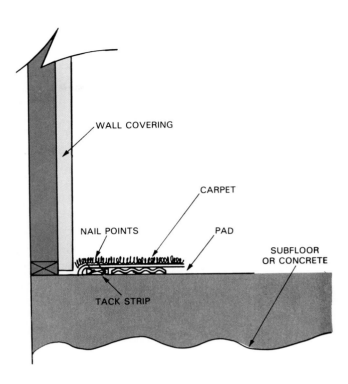

Fig. 26-24. Floors with carpets make the floor feel warmer. It is easier to hear in carpeted rooms.

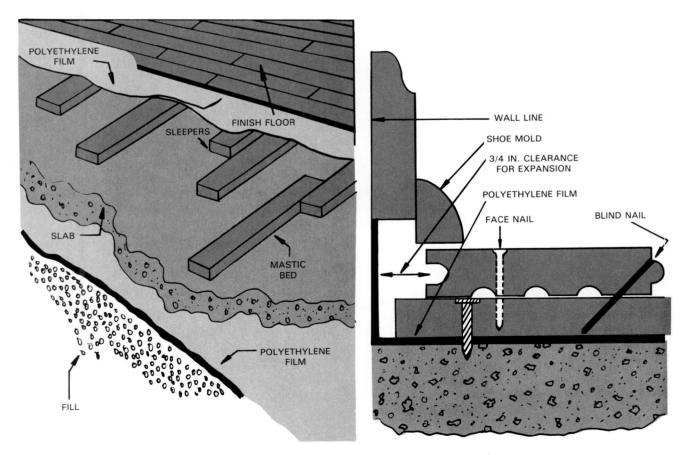

Fig. 26-23. Wood flooring must be kept dry. Plastic film keeps moisture away from wood. Two methods are shown. (National Oak Flooring Manufacturers Assn.)

metal with hooks to hold the carpet edge.

The pad is laid first. It is held in place with glue or staples. The carpet is cut to rough size. Next, it is rolled out in the room. Special tools are used to stretch it over the tack strip. Finally, the edges are trimmed and pushed below the level of the tack strip.

Terrazzo floors use a special concrete. Two layers of special concrete are placed on top of a concrete slab. See Fig. 26-25. The first layer is a sand/mortar mix. Metal strips are set on edge in the mortar. After the mortar hardens, a terrazzo mix is placed. *Terrazzo* consists of white Portland cement, coloring, sand, and marble chips. This mixture is placed, smoothed, and left to harden. It is then ground, polished, and sealed.

Installing Equipment, Fixtures, and Furniture

Equipment and fixtures become a part of the structure. Often, finish work must wait until equipment and fixture connections are ready. Finish work on the walls and placing cabinets must be done at about the same time. The furniture is not a part of the structure. It is installed after the ceiling, wall, and floor work is finished. See Fig. 26-26.

Equipment

Large generators in a power plant may be installed early. They would be too big to get into the building later. See Fig. 26-27. Other equipment is installed throughout construction.

Plumbers install dishwashers and water heater units such as the one shown in Fig. 26-28. The furnace, air conditioners, and other climate control units are installed by the heating, ventilating, and air conditioning (HVAC) subcontractors. Electricians make the electrical connections to all of the equipment.

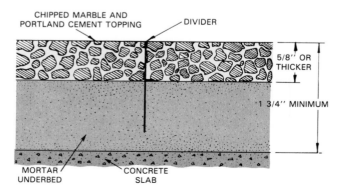

Fig. 26-25. Terrazzo is used on floors that must look good, last a long time, and are easy to clean.

Fig. 26-26. This sports arena has had sound and lighting equipment, seating fixtures, and furniture installed. The playing floor and close-by seating can be removed for other events.　(TEMCOR)

Fig. 26-27. Large pieces of equipment are installed before structures are enclosed.
(Southern California Edison Co.)

Fixtures

Subcontractors return to complete the work on the mechanical systems. The elevator constructors put in the pushbuttons and lights, and finish the cars. The controls are connected and tested.

HVAC people connect ducts and registers, and adjust the system. All parts of the system are then tested.

Carpenters put in doors, stairways, cabinets, handrails, and curtain rods. Doors may come in frames, Fig. 26-29. They are called *prehung doors*. The frames, doors, and hinges are separate for other doors, Fig. 26-30.

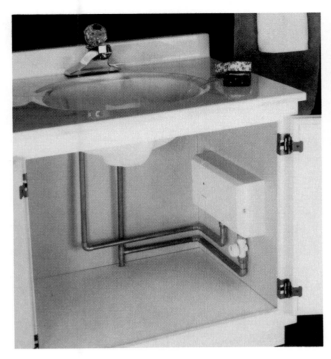

Fig. 26-28. Plumbers installed this tankless water heater. It is used to warm small amounts of water on demand. (Controlled Energy Corp.)

Fig. 26-29. A prehung door is complete. It has a frame, hinges, lock, and door. All are assembled at the factory. (Jordan Millwork)

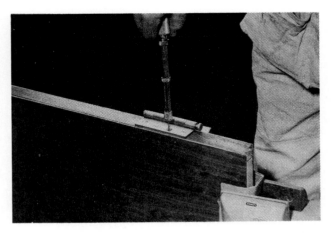

Fig. 26-30. This type of door is hung on the site. Note that a gain (a shallow recess for the hinge) is yet to be cut into the door stile (edge). Some carpenters prefer to check the screw alignment first. (The Stanley Works)

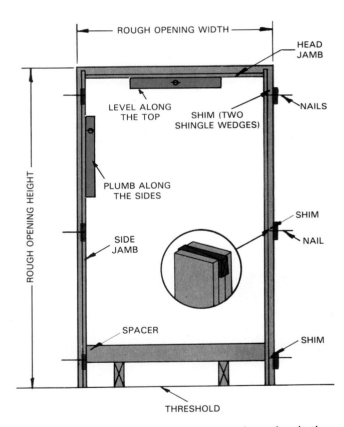

Fig. 26-31. Cedar shingles are used to plumb the door frame. The frame is held in place with nails or screws. Each pair of wedges is placed together. The excess is cut off flush with the door jamb.

Finish carpenters first set the frames. Fitting is done with shims. *Shims* are wedges of wood, usually sawn cedar shingles. The frames are made plumb and square. See Fig. 26-31. The doors are hung on hinges and the locks are then mounted.

Plumbers install plumbing fixtures such as sinks and toilets. They connect appliances and fixtures to the supply lines and drains. Piping systems are checked for leaks and flow rates.

Electricians install switches, outlets, and lights, Fig. 26-32. Electrical control systems in industrial

Fig. 26-32. Receptacles are wired and covers put in place after decorating is done. (Leviton Manufacturing Co., Inc.)

plants is precision work. The supervising electrician checks out all circuits.

Communications technicians install the telephones and other communication devices. Doorbells are simple, but some are very complex. In Fig. 26-33, a complex monitoring system for a new manufacturing process is being checked.

Furnishings

Furnishings include chairs, tables, and cabinets. Some structures have temporary wall systems. They are built in a factory. Parts are shipped to the site and then assembled. Wall surfaces and wiring are part of the system. See Fig. 26-34. Subcontractors often install these walls.

Fig. 26-33. Technicians are installing and checking this process monitoring system for a new manufacturing plant. (Honeywell)

Fig. 26-34. Engineered walls are easy to move. Room dividers are even easier. They do not reach the ceiling. Can you find two kinds in this picture? (Herman Miller, Inc.)

SUMMARY

Finishing of structures includes trimming, painting, decorating, and installing. Finish work is done on the inside and the outside of the structure. Finish workers take special care in their work because their work is seen. Equipment and fixtures are installed at a convenient time for blending with the wall, floor, and ceiling coverings. Plans may indicate furniture placement.

KEY WORDS

All the following words have been used in this chapter. Do you know their meaning?

Brush	Latex base
Carpeting	Luster
Caulk	Moldings
Caulk gun	Oil base
Ceramic tile floors	Painting
Decorating	Paneling
Finish sheen	Paste
Finish work	Pigment
Flat paint	Plywood
Gloss paint	Prefinished molding
Grout	Prehung door
Hardboard paneling	Resilient flooring
Installing	Roller
Interior designers	Semigloss paint
Lacquer	Shim

Sleepers
Solid wood paneling
Sprayer
Stain
Strip flooring
Tack strip
Terrazzo
Terrazzo floors

Thinner
Tile
Tongue-and-groove
Trimming
Varnish
Vehicle
Wallcovering
Wood flooring

TEST YOUR KNOWLEDGE

Place your answers on a separate sheet. Please do not write in this text.

1. State three reasons why structures are finished.
2. Surfaces are made to clean easily and look good by _____ and _____.
3. Paint is made up of three ingredients. They are the _____, _____, and _____.
4. An intermediate quality sheen on paint is called _____.
5. Three ways to apply paint are with _____, _____, and _____.
6. List three ways to decorate walls.
7. Describe terrazzo.
8. Describe resilient floor coverings.
9. In what three forms can you buy wood flooring?
10. What materials are used to close up cracks when trimming out a building?

ACTIVITIES

1. Compare your room with a classroom at school. List the materials, equipment, and furnishings for each. What different materials and methods were used to finish the two rooms?
2. Decide where you might add moldings to your room or an office. Make some samples showing joints for corners or where moldings overlap an existing board. Use saws such as the miter saw.
3. With your instructor's help, try common wood stains, varnishes, and lacquers to match or contrast two or more pieces.

Fig. 27-1. The site is cluttered during construction. (Mary Robey)

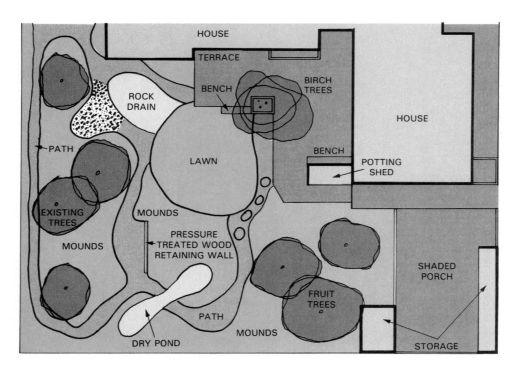

Fig. 27-2. The landscape plan is a drawing of the finished site.

Chapter 27

FINISHING THE SITE

After reading this chapter, you will be able to:
☐ Define the term "landscaping."
☐ Give examples of outdoor structures, equipment, and fixtures added to a building or road.
☐ Describe a landscape plan.
☐ List materials used for walkways and driveways.
☐ Tell what must be done to the soil before planting grass seed or laying sod.
☐ List plants and materials used as ground cover.

During construction, supplies and waste collect on the site. See Fig. 27-1. The ground is rough and torn up. Large equipment, fences, and temporary buildings break up direct traffic routes. This all changes when the structure is nearly complete.

Landscaping can begin when equipment and material storage needs allow for it. There are many jobs that are a part of landscaping work:
1. Holes are filled.
2. Piles of material are used or hauled away.
3. Debris is cleaned up.
4. Large machines are moved to another project.
5. Temporary fences are taken down.
6. Temporary buildings are removed.
7. The site is leveled or contoured (shaped).
8. Walkways are made.
9. Trees, shrubs, and grass are planted.
10. Fixtures (outdoor equipment) are placed.

This chapter discusses five site-finishing processes. They are: doing the final earthwork, building accesses, installing fixtures, planting the site, and cleaning the site.

WHO DOES SITE WORK?

The owner and landscape architect work with the lead architect. They produce the *landscape plan.*

See Fig. 27-2. The plan locates all structures and features. It describes the shape of the finished site. The location of each planting, walkway, or special piece of equipment is shown.

A high-rise building may need very little site work done, Fig. 27-3. On the other hand, a golf course, Fig. 27-4, is almost all site work.

Some landscaping plans are small and simple. See Fig. 27-5. Others are large and complex. See Fig. 27-6.

Earthwork is usually done by general contractors. They backfill around the foundation of structures. They then build the foundations for fixtures, and construct walkways and driveways.

The landscape subcontractors often provide the plants and fixtures. They finish the grading and cultivate the soil. Planting, watering, and cleanup are their jobs, too.

Fig. 27-3. The site work is a small fraction of the total cost for this structure.
(The Stubbins Associates, Inc.)

Fig. 27-4. Site work is the major construction cost for a golf course. (Robert Trent Jones II)

Fig. 27-5. This landscape project was simple. A little grading and a few plantings were all that was needed. (California Redwood Assn.)

Fig. 27-6. Much planning, work, and material went into this landscape project. (Pella/Rolscreen)

DOING THE FINAL EARTHWORK

As noted before, the ground is cluttered during construction. There are holes, trenches, scraps of material, and piles of dirt.

When clearing the site, earth was piled for later use during final earthwork. In contrast to early earthwork, final earthwork involves replacing and shaping the earth mainly for appearance rather than for support.

Replacing Earth

Holes may have been dug for basement foundations, pipelines, and underground tanks. The soil that was saved is used to backfill, Fig. 27-7. Backfilling fills in around structures above ground. It also covers those structures below ground like pipelines. During the backfilling process, the soil is compacted. Air is squeezed out, making the soil firm so it will not settle and crack foundations or ruin landscaping.

Topsoil is the best soil for growing plants. It is scraped from the top one or two feet of the site. Topsoil is piled out of the way during initial earthwork and saved. It is spread over the site after the site is leveled. Some sites do not have good topsoil. It has to be hauled from another site.

Shaping Earth

The site can be shaped to make it like a forest, meadow, valley, wild area, garden, clearing, or

Fig. 27-7. The fill dirt at the left will be used to cover a sewer line. This is called backfilling. The backhoe will be used to do the work.

even like a "business park." Fig. 27-8 shows one way the site can be shaped. Extra soil can be reshaped into mounds. The shape can provide drainage, add beauty, or make the changes in elevation gradual and easy for walking.

The *site plan* describes the shape of the site. It shows where mounds and flat areas are placed. The elevation (height) and shape of each is shown. Some machines used to shape sites are shown in Fig. 27-9. Bulldozers and graders move, level, and mix soil. Loaders and scrapers move soil to where it is needed, or remove excess soil. Small jobs are done with shovels, rakes, and wheelbarrows.

BUILDING ACCESSES

Buildings need driveways, loading docks, parking areas, and walkways. These are called *accesses.*

Driveways

Driveways are extensions of a street onto the site. See Fig. 27-10. Like streets, they are designed for a specific type of traffic. The strength of driveways or roadways depends on three things:

1. Volume of traffic. The more vehicles that travel the driveway or roadway, the stronger it must be.
2. Maximum weight of the vehicles. The larger the load, the stronger the road must be built.

A

B

Fig. 27-9. These machines move, level, mix, and compact soil. A—Large trucks can move soil quickly. B—A roadside is finished by grading and smoothing. (Caterpillar, Inc.; Puckett Bros. Mfg. Co., Inc.)

Fig. 27-10. A driveway leads to a parking lot for this sports arena. The walkway and entrance invite people to enter.   (TEMCOR)

3. Speed the vehicles travel. Stronger roads are needed for faster traffic.

Loading Docks

Plans will usually include loading docks at industrial sites. Most factories need *loading docks* for semitrailers. Other factories need rail car accesses. Some need ship docks for access.

Fig. 27-8. This site was shaped. Notice how walls allow the steps to be on gentle slopes. (California Redwood Assn.)

Walkways

Walkways are made in many shapes and with many materials. Concrete walkways are the most common, Fig. 27-11. They last the longest and are easy to build. Concrete can be cast in any shape and finished in many ways.

The bearing surface for concrete walkways and roadways is compacted soil. Porous (lets water through) gravel fill is the foundation. Steel rods and wire are used to reinforce concrete. The surface is finished with brooms, trowels, or texturing tools.

Pressure-treated wood, stone, brick, and asphalt are also used for walkways. More patterns can be made with some of these than with concrete.

Pressure-treated wood lasts long and does not rot quickly. It makes a walkway with good drainage, Fig. 27-12. Wood walkways are nailed to stringers. *Stringers* hold the top boards together and off the ground. They run the length of the walkway. One is placed on each side. They are laid in a bed of gravel or attached to posts or concrete footings. The boards on the walkway surface are fastened to each stringer with nails or screws, Fig. 27-13.

Brick and stone are set in a bed of sand or on a concrete slab. Sand or mortar is used to fill in the spaces between units. An example of a brick walkway is shown in Fig. 27-14.

INSTALLING OR BUILDING FIXTURES

Fixtures are then added to the site. *Fixtures* are small structures. They include signs, lights, shelters, and other items not considered part of the main structure. Railings, seats, and shelters are also types of fixtures. They have substructures and superstructures.

Some fixtures require electric or gas lines. The size of foundation varies. It depends on the bearing surface, frost line, and forces on the superstructure.

Fig. 27-11. These walkways are made of concrete. Notice how walks keep soil types separate for easy filling. (DYK Prestressed Tanks, Inc.)

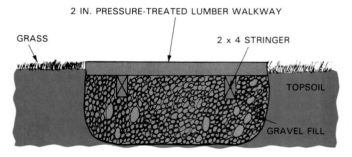

Fig. 27-13. Pressure-treated wood walkways are easy to build.

Fig. 27-12. Wood walkways are attractive. The lines show where stringers are placed.
(Product of Wolmanized® Pressure-Treated Wood)

Fig. 27-14. Brick and stone make good walkways and driveways. They are made in many colors, styles, and textures.

The superstructures are often manufactured. See Fig. 27-15. They are installed by the general contractor or the landscape subcontractor. Other superstructures are built on the site, Fig. 27-16.

A *sprinkler system* is a fixture used to water grass and flowers. Water pipes are run underground. Sprinkler heads are placed so that the entire site can be watered. The system can be turned on manually or with timers. The heads of some types of sprinkler systems drop below the grass when the water is turned off.

Fixtures on highway projects include railings, lights, signs, and reflectors. Most of them are built to increase safety.

PLANTING THE SITE

Planting makes the site and structure look natural. The land around some projects is already

beautiful. The architect may design the building to fit the natural setting. See Fig. 27-17. If the land is plain, it may be changed with ponds or stone walls, Fig. 27-18. Note in Figs. 27-17 and 27-18 that more landscape work was done around the building in Fig. 27-18. Existing plants can be left in or new plants and grass are planted.

Fig. 27-17. The plants and shape of the site were left natural in this landscape plan.   (Pella/Rolscreen)

Fig. 27-15. Note the fixture that was manufactured on this site.
(Scyma Div., Michigan Industrial Co., Inc.)

Fig. 27-16. Common materials were used to build these fixtures on the site.

Fig. 27-18. This building has simple lines. The landscape is free of clutter, too.

Preparing the Soil

The soil must be prepared for planting. It is first *cultivated*. Rototillers or harrows are used. They have fingers that dig into the soil. The dirt clods are broken and rocks are brought to the surface for removal.

Fertilizer is spread and mixed with the soil to make the plants grow better. Other chemicals are used to destroy harmful insects and weeds.

Planting Trees, Shrubs, and Flowers

The landscape plan describes the kind and placement of each tree, shrub, or flower area. See Fig. 27-19. When timing is important, a *planting schedule* is used. Digging the proper sized hole for a tree is done before putting in a lawn.

The bottom third of a planting hole is filled with water to keep air from the roots and to soften the soil. The tree, shrub, or flower is placed in the hole, Fig. 27-20. Soil is replaced and packed around the

Fig. 27-20. Trees can be transplanted (moved) from one place to another. (Vermeer Manufacturing Co.)

roots. No air pockets should remain around roots. More water is added after the tree, shrub, or flower is in place.

Trees need extra support until the roots grow. Three or more ropes or wires and some padding are used. These lines, sometimes called *guy wires,* are tied to the tree trunk, Fig. 27-21. Stakes hold the other end of the support line. Each support line goes in a different direction. Trees and plants are watered until their roots are established.

Using Ground Cover

Ground cover is used to keep the soil from washing away. It can also cover unattractive soil. Ground cover usually means some kind of low plant, but the term can refer to wood and mineral products used for mulch. *Mulch* is a covering of small wood chunks or other material spread over the soil or mixed with the soil. Bark and chipped branches are common mulches. See Fig. 27-22.

Fig. 27-19. The landscape subcontractor follows a plan to determine the placement of trees, shrubs, rocks, and flowers.

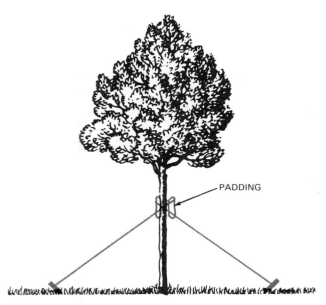

Fig. 27-21. Padding protects the tree trunk from damage.

Fig. 27-22. Grass and coarse bark mulch are used for ground cover at this home. Bark discourages weeds. The driveway has good drainage with gravel. (Pella/Rolscreen)

Fig. 27-23. A hydro-seeding method was used. Seed, fertilizer, and straw were blown onto the site. The straw protects the seeds and holds the moisture.

Fig. 27-24. A seeded patch. Cover freshly seeded areas with straw or burlap to hold in moisture and to discourage birds. (California Redwood Assn.)

Fig. 27-25. What method was used to start this grass? (Manville Building Materials)

Rock, chipped marble, and crushed brick last longer.

The most common ground cover is grass. Lawns are started by planting seed or placing sod. *Seeding* costs the least, but takes more time to grow. *Sodding* is faster, but more costly.

Seed is spread by hand or machine, Fig. 27-23. Rakes are used to mix the soil and seed. The seedbed is rolled. Seeds grow better if they are tight against the soil. The soil is covered to help it hold moisture. Straw or burlap is used. See Fig. 27-24. It also keeps the soil from washing and blowing away. The soil is kept moist until the lawn gets a good start.

Sod is laid over the bare soil. See Fig. 27-25. It is tamped in place and watered. The sod is watered until the roots are well established. In some areas where it is dry, even mature lawns are watered during the entire growing season.

CLEANING THE SITE

Cleaning involves picking up and disposing of all debris. Debris includes empty bottles, cans, boxes, and scrap of all kinds. Fixtures must be cleaned and walkways swept. Cleaning includes removing any straw or burlap from a lawn project once the lawn is established. Cleaning can also involve removing stains on building materials.

SUMMARY

Landscaping improves drainage and makes the site look better. Architects work with the owners and landscape architects to draw up landscape plans. General and subcontractors carry out the plan.

Landscaping involves earthwork, and building accesses and fixtures. In addition, landscaping includes planting and cleaning.

KEY WORDS

All the following words have been used in this chapter. Do you know their meaning?

Accesses	Mulch
Cleaning	Planting schedule
Cultivating	Pressure-treated wood
Driveways	Seeding
Fertilizing	Site plan
Fixtures	Sodding
Ground cover	Sprinkler systems
Guy wires	Stringer
Landscape plan	Topsoil
Landscaping	Walkways
Loading docks	

TEST YOUR KNOWLEDGE

Place your answers on a separate sheet of paper. Please do not write in this text.

1. Name three things that are described on the landscape plan.
2. Who usually does most of the final earthwork?
3. Who provides the plants and does the final grading, planting, and the cleanup?
4. Final earthwork is done mainly for _____ rather than for _____.
5. The strength needed for an access roadway depends upon traffic _____, _____, and _____.
6. Name two building accesses needed by a home.
7. Name four materials used to build walkways.
8. The boards on a walkway surface are nailed down to _____.
   A. struts
   B. joists
   C. pilasters
   D. stringers
   E. wales
9. The steps for putting plants on a site include _____, _____, _____, _____, and _____.
10. Grass seeds are worked into the earth with a _____ or _____.

ACTIVITIES

1. Ask a landscape architect to visit your class. Have him or her describe how to plan landscape projects.
2. Make a sketch of your backyard. Imagine improvements you could make. Develop a landscape plan. Call a nursery to find out what it would cost to carry out the plan.
3. Visit a construction site that is being landscaped. Make a list of machines and tools being used. What are workers doing? What work would you choose to do?

Landscaping involves planting trees and shrubs to beautify the area.   (Davey Tree Expert Company)

Section VI
PRODUCTION AND SOCIETY

Chapter 28
PRODUCTION AND SOCIETY

After reading this chapter, you will be able to:
☐ List and describe the five major economic stages a society goes through as it matures.
☐ Name the four basic requirements for industrialization.
☐ Discuss the new role of workers in production.
☐ Describe what is meant by an information society.
☐ List and describe four important uses of high technology in production.
☐ Explain just-in-time inventory scheduling.
☐ Demonstrate an understanding of computer process control and give examples.
☐ Describe the production facility of the future.

Humans have always produced tools and goods to meet their needs. They also made shelters to protect themselves from the weather and enemies. The production systems they developed to produce these goods and shelters have changed over time. This change can be viewed in five major periods:
• Hunting and fishing period.
• Agricultural period.
• Handicraft period.
• Industrial period.
• Information period.

HUNTING AND FISHING PERIOD

Earliest humans survived off the land. They hunted the animals that roamed the earth. They harvested wild berries, fruits, herbs, and roots. They fished the lakes and streams. These people were at the mercy of nature.

Very little production took place during this period, Fig. 28-1. They fashioned crude weapons and clothing and shaped tree limbs into clubs. Sharp stones became spears and knives. Hides were sewn into clothing and shelters. Logs and other natural materials were used to provide housing.

Life was hard and primitive. The family was the basic unit. Simple housing and products were produced to meet the family's needs.

AGRICULTURAL PERIOD

Over time, the population of the earth grew. People could no longer depend on nature for food. Droughts led to famine. People starved to death. The survivors moved to the river valleys to farm.

Fig. 28-1. Early hunters and fishers used crude tools to make simple products. This one is using a bow drill for drilling a hole.

Construction played a large part in this change. Irrigation systems had to be built so crops could be watered. Food was stored in buildings for later use. A dependable source of food was available. Larger numbers of people could live on smaller parcels of land.

Most early civilizations went through an agricultural period. The people were farmers and were ruled by kings. Early civilizations sprang up along the Nile River in Egypt. This is a good example of an economy based on agriculture.

HANDICRAFT PERIOD

As people became better at growing food, they produced more than they needed. This allowed a *division of labor.* Not all people were needed as farmers and rulers. Some could develop a *handicraft* (skill at making one type of product). This is how the skilled trades were born. People became carpenters, cobblers (shoemakers), spinners, weavers, and blacksmiths, Fig. 28-2. They worked at what they did best. People traded the output of their labor for things they wanted. The carpenter traded work for food. The cobbler exchanged shoes for fish. A local economy developed. The members of a community produced goods for each other.

People could increase their wealth by trading. They built better homes and shops. Buildings of stone and wood formed villages. As this system grew, certain areas became known for a special handicraft, Fig. 28-3. One community became known for its furniture making. Another community became famous for making clocks.

Trade expanded so that communities could exchange goods. A wholesale trade started. Traders bought goods in one area. They hauled them to another community. There the goods were traded. Expanded trade required better roads. Certain workers constructed the roads using the technology of the time.

Money was introduced to help people trade. The trader did not have to exchange one product for another. Products were bought and sold for money.

INDUSTRIAL PERIOD

The output of the handicraft system was limited. A single person often built an entire house. She or he would complete all the tasks with little help. In small shops, skilled craftspersons designed, built, and sold products, Fig. 28-4. The shop served as both a workshop and a store. Their output was controlled by their physical skill and speed. This fact limited the number of products and buildings available. Often the demand was greater than the supply. This became a major problem. The population was growing. People needed more and better

Fig. 28-2. These young people are practicing trades of the handicraft era.

products. This demand led to the factory system.

Humans began to move manufacturing from small shops into a central location. Factories were built and towns grew into cities. Better roads and highways were needed. Canals and railroads were built. Utility (electric and gas) and sewage systems were constructed. The entire nature of the society changed by production technology.

Specialized tools and machines were developed. Factories used water and steam for power. Later, electric power replaced these early sources. Work was separated into jobs. Labor was divided. Less skill was required to do each job, Fig. 28-5. Fixed hours and wages were set. The worklife of people changed. The individual craftsperson gave way to the factory worker.

Special people, called *managers,* helped run the factory. This new system was called *industry.* It soon became the major employer of people. In the United States, industrial employment passed agricultural employment by 1890.

At first, men, women, and children worked under poor conditions. The hours were long, the pay was poor, the work was hard. Lighting was bad. Later, the union movement forced companies to improve the workplace. Moving from an agricultural to an industrial economy is called *industrialization.* It generally requires:

- Products designed with interchangeable parts. Used by Eli Whitney as early as 1788.
- Continuous processing of materials. Used by Oliver Evans.
- Material-handling systems to move product from

Fig. 28-3. As the handicraft era progressed, certain communities became known for special handicrafts.

Fig. 28-4. Turning machines evolved from the potter's wheel.

Fig. 28-5. This worker completes only part of the total job of making a microchip.

operation to operation. The movable conveyor used by Henry Ford, Fig. 28-6.

- Division of labor so that each worker builds only a part of the product. Used by almost all factories and on most construction projects.

In addition, industrialization requires complex constructed structures. Modern power lines must deliver power. Pipelines bring water, natural gas, and other utilities to the plant and take sewage and waste away. Industrialization also required good transportation and communications systems that had to be constructed.

INFORMATION AGE

We are now moving into the information age. It started to arrive with the invention of the computer and, later, the microchip. During the industrial period, companies that could process the most materials in an efficient manner usually succeeded. This took large, continuous manufacturing plants, like the automobile factories of the day. They employed thousands of people and used millions of tons of materials.

The computer allows a new type of production to be developed. This is highly flexible and can quickly and inexpensively respond to change. In factories, people with low or narrow skills are replaced with computer-controlled machines, Fig. 28-7. The workers that remain are more highly trained and motivated to work.

Construction projects and structures are also changing. New techniques allow buildings to be

Fig. 28-7. These machining centers are loaded and unloaded by robots. Parts are carried from machine to machine by automatic guided vehicles. (Kearney and Trecker)

designed and constructed more inexpensively. Special-purpose, low-cost structures are now fairly common, Fig. 28-8.

Also, management is less distant from the worker. The entire workforce is seen as a team with each person having an area of responsibility. Managers may be responsible for setting goals and controlling money. Workers are responsible for producing products or building structures. Everyone is responsible for work procedures and product quality.

Information Age Production

The information age has given us challenges and opportunities. It causes people to interact (share

Fig. 28-6. These household appliances are moved through the factory by overhead conveyors. (General Electric)

Fig. 28-8. These inflatable structures are used to store overflow grain from the elevators behind them.

information) with people. We can now receive new information almost immediately. The telephone directly connects people. Computers send information over long distances. Communication satellites interconnect every part of the world. More than ever, we are dependent on information.

The movement to an information society does not mean production is less important. It is, however, different. The number of people actually producing structures and products is becoming smaller. Reports suggest that 10 to 15 percent of the workforce is engaged in manufacturing operations. Similar reductions are expected in the construction industry.

We can divide the people working in production into two groups:
- Production (manufacturing and construction) workers.
- Professional workers.

Both groups must be skilled. The production workers use information, but their main skill is working with machines and materials, Fig. 28-9. They build products and structures that are designed by other people.

Professional workers are information workers, Fig. 28-10. They use information to manage others, design structures and products, supervise production activities, and control outputs.

PRODUCTION AND TECHNOLOGY

Managers and production workers have always used technology. They have used tools and systems to improve their work. Today, a new term, *high technology,* is being used. It indicates the use of complex machines to replace human labor. "High

Fig. 28-10. This professional worker is an information processor. (AC-Rochester)

tech" is found in many areas of production. Four important areas, shown in Fig. 28-11, are:
- Design and engineering.
- Planning and scheduling.
- Manufacturing and construction.
- Quality control.

Design and Engineering

Some of the earliest uses of high technology were in design and engineering. These activities are closely related to mathematics. They could, therefore, be adapted to computer processing. Lines could be described as "starting at point A and

Fig. 28-9. These construction workers are using machines and materials to build a new home.

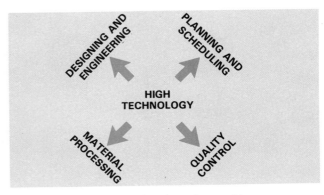

Fig. 28-11. High technology is used in many areas of manufacturing.

ending at point B." The computer could follow these instructions.

The result was *computer-aided design (CAD).* Early CAD programs could only draw in two dimensions. They could show width and length. Newer programs let the designer show objects in three dimensions, Fig. 28-12.

CAD systems are also being introduced to the construction industry. Buildings and other projects are being designed on a computer. Community planning activities are aided by CAD systems.

Planning and Scheduling

Another use of computer technology is in scheduling. Efficient use of human, material, and equipment resources is necessary. Also, efficient inventory control is important.

A new inventory technique has been developed. It is called *just-in-time.* This means materials should arrive at the construction site or manufacturing plant "just in time" for processing.

In manufacturing, purchased parts should arrive "just in time" for assembling. Final products should be completed "just in time" to meet orders. All these actions reduce costs. Money is not used to buy extra materials or parts. Finished products are not held in warehouses awaiting orders.

The use of equipment and people is likewise scheduled. Machines are scheduled for maximum use and workers are kept busy. Proper scheduling increases productivity without causing people to work harder.

Manufacturing and Construction

Great advances are also being made to improve the way material is processed. Primary processing

activities are using computers for control. The computer:

- Improves product quality.
- Saves raw material.
- Reduces energy use.
- Increases productivity.

Sensors (electronic eyes, heat probes, etc.) gather information. The data they collect is fed into computers. They analyze the information and adjust the process.

Process control increases the amount of lumber obtained from logs in sawmills. It also causes steel to be rolled to a more uniform thickness. It produces paper to more exact standards, Fig. 28-13.

Secondary manufacturing processes also are using high technology. Computer-controlled equipment is used to machine materials, spray finishes, and weld metals.

More complex machines have been designed for manufacturing. They complete a number of operations without an operator. The machine positions the work and then performs the required operations. Such machines can also change tools between each operation. Such machines are called *machining centers.*

The construction industry has more difficulty using computer-controlled processing. Structures are usually built where they are used. It is not possible to put computer-controlled equipment on sites where weather would damage or destroy them. Further, the size of the equipment would make

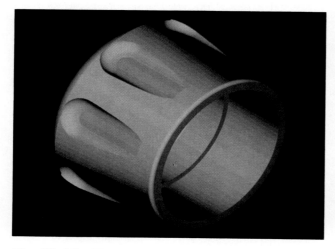

Fig. 28-12. This 3-D view of a part was developed on a CAD system. (Schlumberger CAD/CAM)

Fig. 28-13. These workers control complex steel rolling machines from this control room. (Inland Steel Co.)

transporting them difficult. Also, many structures are one-of-a-kind projects. This fact makes computer applications very difficult.

Quality Control

High technology has also been useful in quality control. Various automatic devices measure product features. This information is used to adjust machines. Also, defective products are automatically removed from production.

PRODUCTION IN THE FUTURE

New technologies and techniques are being developed as you read this book. Many of these technologies include computers, automated machines, and robots, Fig. 28-14. "Thinking" computers will be used in production systems in the near future. These systems will be able to perform human-like activities. They will have the capabilities to see, hear, feel, and even make reasonable choices.

Fig. 28-14. Robots have become very important in manufacturing activities.   (Adept Technology, Inc.)

Manufacturing in Space

Manufacturing will move beyond its traditional boundaries. Experiments of manufacturing in space are now being performed. A leading producer of agricultural machines is a major partner in space research. This company is using the low gravity setting of space to conduct research on the structure of iron. The surroundings of space allow for a better study of what happens when molten iron solidifies.

As a result of this experiment and others like it, some manufacturing processes will move into space. This setting allows for better process control. These *space factories* are designed to produce items in space that cannot be produced on the earth. Weightless and pollution-free environments will improve many processes. These conditions are ideal for producing things such as blended alloys, perfectly round beads, ultrapure materials, and precisely formed crystals.

Manufacturing in space will be successful. Many people think that several billion dollars worth of electronics materials and equipment will be manufactured in space by the 21st century. Even though manufacturing will thrive in space, earth-bound manufacturing will still prosper.

Construction in Space

Currently, most structures are built on existing land sites. However, people's needs for constructed structures are increasing. At the same time, desirable land sites are becoming more scarce. In the future, more structures will be built underground, underwater, and in the air over other structures such as highways. In Japan, rock from the tops of three mountains is crushed and used to build an island for an airport. The island measures about 3/4 mile wide and 2 1/2 miles long with 1263 acres of land. These are interesting solutions to problems of the future, but the real challenge is building structures in space.

Features of space construction. Constructed structures in space are not build *on* a site and anchored *to* the earth. They are built *at* a site and held *in* space. Footings and anchors hold structures to the earth. A balance of centrifugal and centripetal forces hold structures in space, Fig. 28-15. *Centrifugal forces* act in a direction away from the center of a spinning or rotating object. *Centripetal forces* act in a direction toward the center of a spinning object. These forces work like this. Tie a five-pound bag of sand to the end of a five-foot rope. While holding onto the other end of the rope

Centrifugal Force

Centripetal Force

Fig. 28-15. Centrifugal force is the outward pull caused by the spinning weight that wants to travel in a straight line. The centripetal force resists the outward pull. When the two forces are equal, the rotating object will stay in orbit.

tightly, swing the bag of sand fast enough to keep it in the air. The force pulling the bag out is called the centrifugal force. The force you are exerting to the end of the rope is centripetal force. If centrifugal and centripetal forces are equal, the bag will remain in air and in the same orbit. What happens if you let go of the rope? What happens if you increase the speed of the bag by spinning it faster? What happens if you decrease its speed?

Rockets are used to launch structures into space and make them travel around the earth at a high rate of speed. This results in centrifugal force that pulls the structure out into space. *Gravity* (not the rope) is the centripetal force used to keep space structures from flying out into space. Gravity is an unseen centripetal force that pulls objects toward the center of the earth. These forces cause the structure and their contents to be weightless and float in space.

Purposes of space structures. Structures in space may serve a single purpose or have multiple purposes. Communications satellites are examples of unmanned *single-purpose* structures designed to relay messages, Fig. 28-16. "Space Station Freedom" is the name given to the first *multiple-purpose* space station planned for the year 2000.

Many multiple-purpose structures in space have an aluminum frame. See Fig. 28-17. A variety of *modules* are attached to the frame to serve different purposes. When people have to work in space, they need to have living quarters. People need places to eat, exercise, work, and sleep.

Research laboratories are used to study the earth and space. The effects of weightlessness on people, plants, animals, bacteria, and virus are also studied. It is possible to study the weather, oceans, and climates that affect the entire earth. The sun and stars are easier to study. Space stations are above the earth's atmosphere. Therefore, the effects from the atmosphere are eliminated.

Communications modules are designed to receive, process, and transmit information to and from earth and other satellites. Many of our television and telephone messages are brought and sent to us by satellites.

Storage is needed for supplies and materials. Astronauts store the things they use to carry out missions. They have to bring everything with them.

Fig. 28-16. A single-purpose satellite is being unloaded from the cargo bay of a space shuttle. (Honeywell)

Fig. 28-17. This design of a space station has several modules. How many modules can you find? (Honeywell)

A lot of storage will be needed when the space station is used as a "jumping-off point" for further exploration into space. These storage facilities will serve as the "grocery stores" and "filling stations" of the future. Enough supplies, materials, and fuels could be stored for an entire mission.

Modules called *power stations* are used to produce the fuels needed to run life-support systems and perform work in the other modules. Solar cells are used to convert sunlight into electrical energy. Power stations may also be used to convert water into liquid hydrogen and oxygen. This energy can be used to power space ships used to explore deeper into space.

Sometimes structures in space break down, do not function correctly, or need to be maintained. Specially made *service modules* are built to perform these tasks. Plans are being made to correct the fuzzy vision of the Hubble Space Telescope. The problem is in a 94-inch diameter mirror. The scientists are planning to put corrective mirrors on new instruments, and then replace the existing instruments with the new ones.

The Shimizu Corporation from Japan is thinking about building a *space hotel*. They feel it would make a nice vacation for wealthy, adventure-loving people. Visitors would travel to the resort in a space airplane and engage in zero-gravity sports and activities.

Building space structures. The size and design of the structure determines how it will be built. Small single-purpose structures may be entirely built in a factory, launched into orbit, and put into service.

Larger structures with more than one module may be manufactured in factories and tested on earth. They are made so they can be folded into a small package. The package is loaded onto a *Heavy-Lift-Vehicle (HLV)* and launched into space. When the HLV is at the correct orbit, the structure is unloaded and unfolded. Other structures are like bags. They are inflated when they reach their correct orbit. Two or more of the structures are then joined before they are put into service.

Very large structures have the pieces and assemblies made on earth. They are then launched into space. Specially trained people wear *manned maneuvering units (MMU)* while they assemble the pieces of the structure.

CHALLENGES FACING PRODUCTION

The challenge facing our society is easy to pinpoint. We want to improve the quality of life for people. This goal is complex. There are no easy answers. Construction and manufacturing industries have their part to play.

Production activities must create products and structures that meet human needs. They must also make good use of our valuable resources. Every effort must be made to conserve materials and energy. People must be provided jobs that are important to them. Everyone must believe that she or he is important.

We must do certain things because of these challenges. Workers and management must work together. People must become production teams. Individuals must contribute their part to the total task.

We must conserve the available materials and energy. Energy-efficient structures must be built. Products that use energy effectively must be designed. Used products and structures must be recycled. Materials can be reclaimed. Older buildings need to be remodeled for new uses. The "use it—discard it" way of thinking must be changed.

Protection of the environment must continue to be a prime concern. Disposal of hazardous waste is important. Clean air and water must be protected for future generations.

These and other issues are the challenges to production. The degree to which we meet them is important. Only through solving society's problems can we have a better life.

SUMMARY

Production is very important to all societies. Each group of people must produce products and structures to meet its needs. However, nothing remains unchanged. For example, in 1900 one-third of all working Americans were farmers. Today, only about three percent of the labor force is needed to grow our crops. In fact, more people have full-time employment in universities than on farms. This does not mean farming is less important. It is more efficient. Our farmers are the most productive in the world.

Likewise, production is changing. We are becoming more productive. Automatic machines are taking over the manufacture of products. More houses are being built in factories. Fewer workers are needed to meet our need for goods.

Production jobs are becoming information-based. The employees use information to guide machines and people. The production jobs of the future will be different. They will require fewer manual skills. Skills of the mind will be needed. Each of us needs to be ready for this change.

KEY WORDS

All the following words have been used in this chapter. Do you know their meaning?

Agriculture
Communicators
Division of labor
Handicraft
High technology
Industrialization
Process control
Production workers
Professional workers

TEST YOUR KNOWLEDGE

Place your answers on a separate sheet of paper.

Do not write in this text.
1. All societies move through five stages of development. List these stages.
2. As more food became available, not as many people needed to work at gathering or growing food. This allowed for _____ of labor.
3. Industrialization generally requires:
   A. Products with _____ parts.
   B. _____ processing of materials.
   C. _____ _____ systems to move products from operation to operation.
   D. Division of labor so that each _____ builds only a _____ of the product.
4. With computers and robots taking over many of the tasks formerly performed by factory workers, explain the new role of people in modern production.
5. People in manufacturing can be classified in two groups: _____ workers and _____ workers.
6. List the four important areas of manufacturing where high technology is being used.
7. Using computers to make drawings of a new product is called _____.
8. Just-in-time inventory control means (select all correct answers):
   A. Materials should arrive in the plant as they are needed for processing, not before.
   B. Purchased parts should arrive as they are needed for final assembly of the product.
   C. Product should be completed just as storage space is available.
   D. Product should be completed as needed to fill customer's or distributor's order.
9. List four advantages of having a computer control primary processing of materials.
10. Explain why it has been difficult for construction industries to use computer-controlled processing.

ACTIVITIES

1. Select one of the periods of society's growth. Prepare a report describing the production activities in that period.
2. Invite a historian to class to discuss the development of production activities through history.
3. Invite a manufacturing or construction manager to discuss high technology with your class.
4. Collect several articles from newspapers and magazines which describe the use of high technology in construction and manufacturing.

INDEX